BUILDING LEGITIMACY

THE
MEDIEVAL MEDITERRANEAN

PEOPLES, ECONOMIES AND CULTURES, 400-1500

EDITORS

Hugh Kennedy (St. Andrews)
Paul Magdalino (St. Andrews)
David Abulafia (Cambridge)
Benjamin Arbel (Tel Aviv)
Mark Meyerson (Toronto)
Larry J. Simon (Western Michigan University)

VOLUME 53

TUTA SUB AEGIDE PALLAS

· 1 6 8 3 ·

BUILDING LEGITIMACY

*Political Discourses and Forms
of Legitimacy in Medieval Societies*

EDITED BY

ISABEL ALFONSO, HUGH KENNEDY
AND JULIO ESCALONA

BRILL
LEIDEN · BOSTON
2004

This book is printed on acid-free paper.

Library of Congress Cataloging-in-Publication Data

Building legitimacy / edited by Isabel Alfonso, Hugh Kennedy, and Julio Escalona.
    p. cm. — (Medieval Mediterranean ; v. 53)
    Includes bibliographical references and index.
    ISBN 90-04-13305-4
    1. Legitimacy of governments—Europe—History—To 1500. 2. Europe—Kings and
rulers—Succession. 3. Law, Medieval. I. Alfonso, Isabel. II. Kennedy, Hugh (Hugh N.)
III. Escalona, Julio. IV. Series.

KJ755.B85 2003
320.94'01'1—dc22

2003052249

ISSN   0928–5520
ISBN   90 04 13305 4

PRINTED IN THE NETHERLANDS

CONTENTS

PART TWO

DISCOURSES OF POLITICAL LEGITIMATION

LIST OF CONTRIBUTORS

ISABEL ALFONSO ANTÓN, Ph.D. (1980) in Political Science, Universidad Complutense (Madrid), is Investigadora Científica at Instituto de Historia (CSIC), Madrid. Her research covers medieval rural history, the Cistercians, and legal and political culture, including the co-editing of *Lucha política. Condena y legitimatión en la España Medieval* (Lyon, 2003).

FRANCES ANDREWS is Lecturer in Mediaeval History at the University of St. Andrews, Scotland. She specialises in Italian ecclesiastical and social history and her recent publications include *The Early Humiliati* (1999).

JULIO ESCALONA MONGE, Ph.D. (1996) in Medieval History, Universidad Complutense (Madrid), is Investigador Contratado at Instituto de Historia (CSIC), Madrid. He has published on medieval territoriality, and on document forgeries and the invention of the past, and co-edited *Lucha política. Condena y legitimatión en la España Medieval* (Lyon, 2003).

CARLOS ESTEPA is Research Professor at the Instituto de Historia (CSIC), Madrid. He specialises in history of Castilian countries in the Middle Ages. His recent publications are *Los señoríos de behetría* (coord. with Cristina Jular) (2001) and *Las behetrías castellanas* (2003).

PAUL FOURACRE is Professor of Medieval History at the University of Manchester, England. He specialises in early medieval history and his recent publications include *The Age of Charles Martel* (2000).

CHRIS GIVEN-WILSON is Professor of Late Mediaeval History at the University of St. Andrews, Scotland. He specialises in the political and social history of late mediaeval England, and in historical writing. His recent publications include *Chronicles of the Revolution 1397–1400* (1993) and *The Chronicle of Adam Usk*.

PIOTR GÓRECKI is Associate Professor of History at the University of California, Riverside. He specializes in the social history of law, with emphasis on thirteenth-century Poland. His recent publications include numerous articles, and, as co-editor, *Conflict in Medieval Europe: Changing Perspectives on Society and Culture* (2003).

PATRICK HENRIET is "Maître de conférences" at the university of Paris IV-Sorbonne. He specialises in hagiography. His recent publications include *La parole et la prière au Moyen Âge.* (2000), and *A la recherche de légitimités chrétiennes? Représentations de l'espace et du temps dans l'Espagne des IXe–XIIIe siècle* (éd.) (2003).

JOSÉ ANTONIO JARA FUENTE is a Research Fellow at the Instituto de Historia (CSIC), Madrid. He specialises in Urban History in the Late Middle Ages and his recent publications include *Concejo, poder y élites. La clase dominante de Cuenca en el siglo XV* (2000).

CRISTINA JULAR PÉREZ-ALFARO is a Research Fellow at the Instituto de Historia (CSIC), Madrid. She specialises in clientship and patronage amongst the Castilian medieval noblemen and royal delegates. Her recent publications include (coord. with Carlos Estepa) *Los señoríos de behetría* (2001).

HUGH KENNEDY is Professor of Middle Eastern History at the University of St. Andrews, Scotland, and has published extensively on the Islamic World in the Middle Ages, including *The Prophet and the Age of the Caliphates* (London, 1986) and *Muslim Spain and Portugal: a political history of al-Andalus* (London, 1996).

STEPHEN D. WHITE is Professor of Medieval History at Emory University. He specialises in the history of eleventh- and twelfth century France and England and his recent publications include "Fiefs for Service or Service for Fiefs," in Gadi Al-Gazi et al. eds., *Négocier le don* (2003).

INTRODUCTION

Isabel Alfonso and Julio Escalona
Instituto de Historia (CSIC)

This book presents a selection of papers exploring the many ways by which medieval political powers sought to legitimize themselves, the political discourses through which this was effected, and a wide range of related problems. All of the papers were produced in the course of a series of collaborative projects running from 1999, and still going on today. With the precedent of a meeting on *Legal development, judicial practice and political action*,[1] the main core of this research group gathered around a project at the Instituto de Historia (CSIC, Madrid)[2] which was expanded with a bilateral project with the Department of Mediaeval History of the University of St. Andrews (UK).[3] Gathering a large group of scholars from different academic backgrounds and fields of expertise is always a complicated task, but also the best way to establish comparative perspectives, and to foster discussions on concepts, methods and approaches. Over two years communication was intense, members of both institutes exchanging visits, seminars and discussions. After a plenary meeting in Madrid, a Symposium was held in March 2001 in St. Andrews, in which occasion other invited scholars joined the group.

Nine out of eleven essays in this volume have been selected from the much larger material resulting from those activities up to the St. Andrews symposium. Two—Henriet, Jular—are contributions by members of the French CNRS-sponsored SIREM project,[4] to which

---

[1] Meeting convened by Isabel Alfonso in Madrid, 1997, published in Alfonso, I., coord. (1997): "Desarrollo legal, prácticas judiciales y acción política en la Europa medieval", *Hispania*, 197: 879–1077, with contributions by I. Alfonso, John Hudson, Josep María Salrach, Daniel L. Smail, Stephen White and Chris Wickham.

[2] Research Project *Lucha y legitimación política en León y Castilla (siglos X–XV)*, led by Isabel Alfonso and funded by the Spanish Ministerio de Ciencia y Tecnología [PB98–0655].

[3] *Political discourses and forms of legitimation in the Middle Ages* (project jointly sponsored by the Spanish Ministry of Education and the British Council between 1999 and 2001, and led by I. Alfonso and J. Hudson).

[4] *Séminaire Interdisciplinaire de Recherches sur l'Espagne Médiévale* (SIREM), GDR 2378, CNRS, led by Georges Martin (ENS Lyon, France). Exchange between the Instituto

several members of the Madrid group also belong. Because of the scope of Brill's Mediaeval Mediterranean Series, the focus is set on southern Europe: Castile, Italy, and France. Yet, the editors have tried to avoid the impression that the issues discussed here are specifically Mediterranean—let alone Iberian—and have enhanced the comparative dimension by including contributions on Carolingian Francia, Poland and England. Even if the Mediterranean focus remains evident, this must make clear that the subjects addressed by every individual author belong to a broad field of inquiry, especially adequate for comparative perspectives and exchange.

By the same reason, no particular consistency should be expected in terms of geography or chronology. Chapters range from Poland to England, to Italy, to Castile, and from the seventh to the fifteenth centuries, and—it goes without saying—no attempt has been made at filling the huge gaps in between. Conversely, there is a remarkable consistency and interrelation with regard to the subjects addressed and the exploratory strategies deployed. Even if every author keeps to his or her individual perspective, after several years of joint efforts, a range of common questions and interests has grown. The subject is enormous and, in many respects, unnervingly elusive, but detecting it as a field in need of research and developing an awareness of its bearing on a wide range of related subjects must be the essential starting point. In this respect, we think that the greatest value of the essays presented here is precisely to point out the importance of investigating medieval processes of legitimation, and, in doing so, to suggest new perspectives in our understanding of political power in history.

Rather than by time, or place, the book's twofold arrangement is defined by the authors' chosen perspective. The first block is context-centered; it comprises papers dealing with specific contexts in which legitimation processes operate, normally building on a wide range of resources, and amidst political competition and/or conflict. The second block is source-centered. Authors analyse a text or group of texts, trying to show the political discourses they contain and to relate them to their particular historical context. This does not mean, obviously, separate worlds; most papers contain elements of both

de Historia and the SIREM led to a Colloque with a stronger Iberian focus (Madrid, Casa de Velázquez, Dec. 2001) to be published soon as Alfonso, I.; Escalona, J.; Martin, G. (eds.): *Lucha política: condena y legitimación en la España medieval*, Annexes de Cahiers de Linguistique et de Civilisation Hispaniques Médiévales (Lyon: forthcoming).

approaches, and they are no less relevant to the same conceptual problems and questions we all have been working on. But to the editors' minds the distinction seems relevant inasmuch as it reveals two major positions from which basically the same problems can be faced, and because of the methodological issues this raises.

Comparative research needs negotiating a common language and an agreed set of meanings. Repeatedly throughout the working sessions this proved to be a sensitive matter, especially regarding the two concepts that lay in the core of our interest: *legitimacy* and *legitimation*. Both terms—and a wide range of related notions—belong to our common vocabulary and experience, a sort of shared cultural background that can be easily detected in many studies on power and ideology, even if they make no explicit claim to analyse legitimacy or legitimation. However, when handling both concepts as the main axes of a more focused inquiry, they promptly become problematic categories, a fact that needs to be recognized and admitted before we can make explicit our own assumptions on the subject and envisage new ways of re-thinking it.

This is especially the case of *legitimacy*, whose most immediate meaning seems to refer to a—established, recognized, official, ultimately 'true'—legal framework, as the paramount attribute of every political authority. A distinct 'Webberian scent' can be spotted in this univocal, moralizing concept, that seems to stem from a widely shared, consistent set of values and yet remains external to it. However, neither legitimacy nor social values are unique, but diverse,[5] heterogenous and contradictory, as increasing criticism from Sociology and Anthropology is making ever more evident. From both disciplines it has been stressed that the hierarchical, arbitrary character of relations of power can be obscured, even denied, by presenting them as legitimate. It is now widely recognised that the operations of 'social alchemy'—in Bourdieu's words—by which economic power becomes social, play a crucial role in making acceptable the violence and unequality inherent to every exercise of power.

Legitimation is a key conceptual development. Far from being a static attribute of power, legitimacy has to be dynamically maintained, competed for, and denied to rivals, and this is valid not only in cases of open conflict, or when rulership is at stake, but also as a continuous

---

[5] See the remarks by Gabriella Grivaudi in her introduction to the monographic issue on 'Conflitti, Linguaggi e Legitimazione', *Quaderni Storici*, 94, 1997, pp. 3–20.

process of competition for social power. It is the processual character of those phenomena that the term *legitimation* highlights, and, in
doing so, it paves the path for exploring how legitimacy is constructed in specific contexts, and how its contents and parameters
are debated, agreed upon or rejected within processes of social competition and/or conflict.

On the other hand, legitimacy is rarely homogeneous in any given
society, which calls for exploring the different degrees of social acceptance or rejection of it, depending on the many forms in which legitimation can be pursued. Because alternative forms and strategies of
legitimation may compete within the same social framework, *de-legitimation* becomes another crucial concept affecting, among others, our
capacity to recognize rivalling, unequally visible processes of legitimation.

Finally, the multilayered character of political legitimation and the
importance of exploring how different social strata or groupings participate in the creation, difussion or rejection of political legitimacy
must also be taken into account. There is a widespread assumption
that the term *political* must be employed in its restricted aception,
meaning the specific exercise of governance and administration. This
approach is largely based upon hindsight, building on the historical
development of state apparatus. It tends to present modern political
powers as quintessentially 'public', by contrast to other spheres of
power, such as religious power, and to other activities and practices
that are seen as 'private'. It even tends to formulate the exercise of
power as detached from the actors of political processes themselves.
Narrow as this concept of 'political' is, its bearing on the work of
many scholars remains heavy.

The papers in this book may be a good pointer to this problem,
for whereas those dealing with spheres of power that can be promptly
recognized as political—kingship, rulership, urban governance—felt
no need to make explicit statements on this point, the two chapters
that study legitimation in ecclesiastical contexts certainly did. Therefore,
Piotr Gorécki describes as a 'political lesson' the reconstruction of
social memory in the key of law and power performed by Abbot
Peter in favour of his Henrykow monastery. Even more strongly,
Patrick Henriett shows the connection between lay and ecclesiastical political developments: if an attempt to dominate space and people can be seen as 'political', then episcopal struggles for primacy
must be considered so, even if no kings or aristocrats are explicitly
involved. Likewise, relations of power in the aristocratic sphere come

wrapped in a vocabulary in which personal, face-to-face relationships seem to predominate. Stephen White's detailed analysis of *fidelitas* in eleventh-century southern France eloquently shows the strong political dimension of a vocabulary notionally belonging to the 'private' realm of the affective, emotional, contractual.

By the same reasons, a narrow conception of *political* blurs the role of the lower social strata. True, these groupings are often—but not always—excluded from the high, learned spheres where the great political decisions are taken; but they must not be denied actual political agency in defence of their rights and interests, either in local communities, urban contexts, or even by direct appeal to central power. Moreover, it is precisely because local societies do have a strong political dimension that the local milieux are essential in the social spread of political legitimation. The legitimation of central power is enacted locally, often by mechanisms which simultaneously legitimate local order and power, as well as notions of membership and political identity. This is addressed—in remarkably different contexts—by Paul Fouracre, Cristina Jular, Frances Andrews and José Antonio Jara. All four make clear that a wide conception of 'political' helps recognize the complex mechanisms operating locally, which are essential in maintaining and reproducing power in its many phacets.

Legitimation in Context

The six papers in Part I, while discussing very different areas and periods—from seventh-century Francia to fifteenth-century Cuenca—have in common a context-centered approach: they all focus on specific contexts in which processes of legitimation can be seen in action. Being kingship the usual form of government in medieval Europe, it is hardly surprising that royal power is discussed in four out of six papers. Two of them deal with contexts of intense change in which legitimation becomes exceptionally important. Paul Fouracre analyses the forms of legitimation developed by the long-established Merovingian dynasty by contrast to those used by the Carolingians to undermine them and support their own claims to rulership, as well as how important innovations come interwoven with elements of continuity between both periods. The Merovingian notion of time-less order and legitimacy, ultimately derived from the assumption of

Late Roman state resources and personality will be replaced by a new one, based upon intense political agency, which constitutes a consciously programmed assault on Merovingian legitimacy: effective exercise of power, improvement of justice, restoration of the Church, fight against the enemies of Christendom. Yet, the Caroligian need to support the longest-sustained legitimating process in the early medieval West—in Fouracre's words—is in itself witness to the difficulties of totally eroding the long-established Merovingian legitimacy, particularly the one derived from blood-links. This is especially important, since Fouracre's analysis succeeds in overcoming the straightforward picture of the defeat of Merovingian legitimacy by the Carolingian's and exposes how legitimating resources are deeply rooted in medieval political cultures. Once a given element— say, dynasty—is wrapped with prestige and respectability, it becomes a durable legitimating device that must be controlled. This also affects the ways in which legitimating strategies can be 'exported', that is, taken to a different context to perform different functions, as shown below by Escalona's discussion of the uses of Carolingian discourse strategies by the Asturian kings.

Continuity and change also play a crucial role in the fourteenth-century English case studied by Chris Given-Wilson. Situations in which royal succession is uncertain can be seen as moments of crisis, even if dynasty itself is not formally at stake. In this context, a wide range of arguments are deployed to legitimate each candidate's claims, ranging from royal power (the king's capability to designate his successor) to personal qualities, or lack of them (the 'Crouchback legend'), to institutional expressions of social consensus (ratification by the Parliament). Given-Wilson explores how informal mechanisms—namely the king's personal choice—intervene in systems of succession that appear to be highly institutionalised, as well as the wave of conflicting interests and arguments that this triggers. Conflict and competition on royal succession are recurrent situations in medieval monarchies, and a previleged ground for exploring the subtle relations between norms and processes, as well as between political institutionalisation and the pursuit of legitimation. The analogies are many with the case studied below by Carlos Estepa.

By contrast, the topics adressed by Isabel Alfonso and Cristina Jular belong to situations dominated by continuity and smooth evolution, rather than abrupt change or disruption. In those contexts, law, institutions and institutionalised space play a pivotal role in the reproduction and maintenance of social order and authority. To start with the latter, royal assemblies—judicial as well as political—where important scenarios of legitimation throughout medieval Europe. Castilian royal judicial meetings are analysed here by Alfonso as the spaces where 'truth' was constructed and acknowledged, in a circular movement that vested legitimacy in the decisions taken, whilst the actors also legitimated their own position by taking part in the meeting. The same circularity can be noticed in both the king's role at such assemblies and in the distinctly ecclesiastical discourses—often our only extant written record—that embody the Church's claims to property and jurisdiction which are acknowledged in court rulings. Moreover, her analysis of the 'rhetoric of restoration' exposes how enhancing a particular attribute of the king's—which helps to reinforce the ruler's overall legitimacy—may be a way of calling to action in favour of specific ecclesiastical earthly interests, when they are put to doubt on a judicial arena.

In a similar way, Cristina Jular points out that the existence of a legally defined model of administration—the one enunciated in Alfonso X of Castile's legal works—provides a particularly solid framework for the legitimate exercise of delegate power. In the royal legal texts, the territorial officials indispensable for the local effectiveness of central power are portrayed as the king's *alter ego*, responsible for carrying out locally the king's function of creating 'good order'. Thus the royal official loses his individuality and becomes another piece in the state machinery that makes the distant king locally tangible. This ideal impersonalization purports to make royal power omnipresent, but—again in a circular movement—it also covers with the king's own legitimacy those who hold office from, and formally represent the ruler.

However, legal discourses are only one side of the coin. Jular's analysis of the non-legal aspects of territorial office shows that, beyond the ideal of representation/delegation, royal office also entails the local redistribution of central power, a crucial element in the continuous competition among local elites—an idea that Fouracre also discusses for the merovingian period. Royal office comes hand in hand with interaction and involvement in local webs of patronage and property. This issue is all the more relevant, since there is a whole historiographical tradition considering that it is the very acceptance of such webs of 'private' dependence as legitimate exercise of power that marks the transition to feudalism. Yet, after all the debates on this subject, it seems healthy to remember that the relationship between 'official' and 'unofficial' political forms and practice is still in need of much research.[6] Neither Fouracre, nor Jular, though, rehearse the traditional approaches 'from top down', but they both pay much attention to the role of communities and, in general, the local societies where delegate power is exercised, by pointing out how acting against law and custom results in de-legitimation. The cases analysed by Jular show how the king's authority behind royal delegates may in turn legitimate local communities in their claims against wrongful officials. Royal power, again in a circular movement, may find itself locally legitimated by acting accordingly in favour of law and custom, and correcting the evildoers.

Moving away from kingship, the papers by Stephen White and José Antonio Jara show how processes of political legitimation are not restricted to the highest spheres of power, but permeate the whole social body, shaping the way in which people interact with one another and with the overall political system. From very different positions, both White and Jara remark the continuous use of similar legitimating resources and discourses throughout society. Fouracre's point that the argument employed by the Carolingians to undermine their predecessors were turned against them in the dynasty's period of decline, finds a continuation in White's analysis of the body of norms and notions behind the relations between lords and vassals. Building on the idea that there is no single 'objective' reading of the documents, White moves the focus to the ways in which historians construct their analytical models of political practices. By reassessing texts of the kind used by other authors in support of the notion of a 'feudal revolution', he describes in detail the constituent elements of a model of legitimacy in political practice based upon oaths of fidelity. This predates the crisis of the Carolingian regime, which appears as the main referent from which conflicting claims and accusations are formulated, justified, and eventually officialized.

Jara's paper raises issues of political membership and legitimation through effective political agency. His analysis of local government in late medieval Cuenca suggests that the system's legitimacy was continually renewed by permitting a wide range of social groupings

---

[6] See Briquet, J.-L., 'Potere di notabili e legittimazione. Clientelismo e politica in Corsica durante la Terza Repubblica (1870–1940)', *Quaderni Storici*, 94, 1997, pp. 121–154.

to have a share in the exercise of power. Although an urban elite ultimately held the main keys to local power, members of lower social strata formed an 'elite of participation' by taking part in local government through informal mechanisms of pact and agreement which were never codified as 'law'. The legitimacy that the whole political model gained by partly sharing the exercise of power, generated social order and peace. Jara's suggestion that socially widespread legitimacy downplayed conflict would be worth checking in other contexts, particularly when exploring how conflict and disorder relates to a lack of legitimacy—or succesful de-legitimation.

Discourses of Political Legitimation

The five chapters in Part II are likewise various. Again, contexts range from royal entourages to ecclesiastical discourse, to urban power and government, and, therefore, the analogies with papers in Part I are evident. To cite only two examples, the reader will immediately notice the obvious connections between the cases analysed by Given-Wilson and Estepa, on the one hand, and by Jara and Andrews, on the other. The group's distinctiveness lies in that all five set the focus on sources and approach their subjects through the analysis of textual discourse strategies. Three papers—Piotr Górecki, Carlos Estepa, Patrick Henriet—focus on one single text each, while Frances Andrews analyses two Italian political thinkers and Escalona explores the image of a king in three interrelated narratives. This brings to the foreground the complex discourse strategies contained in medieval sources and the ways in which those discourses—whether written or not—constitute a major form of political agency within long-running processes of competition.

Legitimation and de-legitimation are often two sides of a coin, reflecting the processual character of political struggles. Medieval political competition was often accompanied by conflicting discourses, some of which never made their way into written, as pointed out by I. Alfonso, whose paper in Part I provides good examples of the difficulties of exploring the oral discourses actually deployed in judicial assemblies through the written records created by the winning party. Those were societies—especially in the earlier periods—in which written material was created through very specific mechanisms controlled by a restricted minority whose connections with political powers need not be rehearsed here. When modern historians face such monochromatic discourses, they must consider whether there were alternative ones that needed to be *deactivated*. This could be effected in several degrees. In extreme cases, the other's discourse could be either totally contradicted and falsed, in order to show its lack of legitimacy, or, in the opposite case, it could be completely silenced, in which case, few traces will be left of it for the historian to detect its presence. But, between both extremes, there is a wide range of possibilities, including to totally rewrite the other's discourse in one's favour. In this cases, privileged access to the written is essential in minimizing the other and imposing one's version. This is especially evident when discussing historical material, or, in general, those texts which present an argument for the claims of the present by reviewing and rewriting the past, even when it is a very recent past, approached from hindsight, as it is the case of the fourteenth-century chronicle studied by Carlos Estepa.

Political centralization and the strengthening of royal power is a typical ground for the development of legitimating discourses in medieval times. While careful analysis of specific political developments constantly shows the complexities of medieval politics and the many ways in which rulers had to negotiate their decissions through a thightly knit web of shared/delegated power and authority, the royal chronicle analysed by Carlos Estepa insists in reshaping political process in the key of strong personal rulership by King Alfonso XI. This case is particularly relevant, since it presents the evolution from the king's minority to his coming of age as a painful transition from chaos to order. Estepa highlights the many elements of real, effective conflict that were present in Alfonso's early years and exposes the chronicler's strategy of translating every episode into a linear narrative that leads from chaos while the king is underage—so inactive—to order when the king is able to take hold of his kingdom. Internal order is not the final point; it is the indispensable condition for engaging in war against the Muslims, the ultimate source of legitimacy for a Castilian king. So 'justice'—that is, inner stability—is a requirement for being a good Christian king and leading his people against their foes. Royal action is so prominent in this narrative that it tends to divide other political agencies in two groups: those who do wrong and oppose the king, and those who do right and become a tool of the king's policies. Most elements of political negotiation and exchange are therefore obscured in pursuit of the image of a strong, God-favoured king who moulds up society according to an undebated, pre-established royal model that has much to do with the ideal picture delivered in the legal texts discussed above by Jular. Just as Jular's paper invites to question the actual validity of a legal model based in extreme institutionalisation, and denial of other, more informal political resources, the ones by Estepa and Given-Wilson underpin the high relevance assigned in medieval narratives to individual agency, an element which, in Alfonso XI's chronicle, becomes—perhaps paradoxically—a clear metaphor of formal royal government.

The case analysed by Estepa is one of 'positive discourse', in which reality is straightforwardly coloured as desired, with little attention paid to other, alternative visions of the same processes. Apparently, the same could be said of the early Asturian texts analysed by Julio Escalona. The new political situation—territorial expansion, political development—which emerged in the second half of the ninth century triggered, under Alfonso III, a whole revision of the Asturian origins by means of three succesive royal chronicles. A carefully woven, solid picture of the Asturian kings as the heirs—biological as well as political and historical—to the Visigothic royalty was created, which proved extremely succesful in becoming the undebated orthodoxy for most history writers thereafter up to the twentieth century. Yet, a reading of the Asturian royal chronicles as 'response' to opposing arguments, together with careful inspection of other—even if thin—evidence, rather suggest that the royal chronicles were not only an essay in 'positive' discourse, but also, at the same time, a 'negative' argumentation, purporting to de-activate the other's discourse by both silencing its existence and reverting its arguments, offering a totally different version of the Asturian eighth century. A whole vision of the Asturian origins, created in the late-eighth century under heavy Carolingian influence—and one which strongly rejected all links with the Visigothic past—was thus replaced with a new one, which denied all Carolingian links and reinterpreted all political developments as steps towards the recover of the Visigothic grandeur, lost to the Arabs in 711. Escalona shows the figure of mid eight-century Asturian king Alfonso I to be an essential 'discourse node' in this reconstruction of the Asturian history, either by inventing some of his deeds or by assigning to him those of other, denigrated monarchs, such as Fruela I. Traces of silenced, alternative discourses are thus recovered which failed to enter later Leonese and Castilian historiography.

The need to state one's claims by fighting the opponent's discourse is taken one step further in the thirteenth-century Polish case studied by Piotr Górecki. Górecki exposes the subtle means by which Abbot Peter of Henryków' purported to support his monastery's position within a complex web of regional relations of power. The narrative includes detailed descriptions of the political initiatives taken by the monks in order to secure favour from the duchal authority, in fighting the claims of regional knights to patronage over the abbey and in leading judicial action against their oponents. Just like the more abstract notions of law and property, the higher political power appears again here as the ultimate legitimating referent for conflicting actors, and one that increases its own legitimacy by playing this referential role. But discourse—especially the mere fact of committing all this material to script—is here evidently another form of agency, and one that explicitly intends to operate in the long term, as an argumentative weapon for the future. By creating his own version of the past and his own account of the monastery's history, Abbot Peter provided his house with a powerful discursive weapon to wield in front of their foes' arguments, something that was actually taking place, whether in formal assemblies or more casually within the aristocratic milieu, and something that could be indeed expected to go on happening in future years.

The fact that the monastery's points of view have reached us in written form should not mislead us. Abbot Peter was not arguing from the privileged position that would enable him to simply write out the opponents' stories. Those were surely spread widely enough to make him adopt a different strategy. Therefore, the other's discourse is not hidden or silenced, but presented and contested, sometimes piecemeal and, in doing so, Abbot Peter provides most valuable evidence of otherwise unrecorded political action in the form of discourses which never made it into script, and can only be studied through the 'negative' print they left in the writings of their enemies.

The Castilian thirteenth-century case studied by Patrick Henriet poses similar questions in even cruder terms. Just like I. Alfonso's written accounts of judicial assemblies, the *Pars Concilii Laterani* is the written presentation of an oral debate, and one in which the discourse line favoured by the author takes issue at length with those of his opponents. If medieval ecclesiasts were the quintessential masters of the script within basically oral societies, the text analysed by

Henriet shows—amidst a strongly scholastic setting which is reminiscent of both scholarly exercises and the burgeoning genre of religious polemy—their phacet as masters of rhetoric. Here the other's discourses are presented, deconstructed, falsed piece by piece, and argument by argument, to a point in which the reader comes close to forgetting that this is not the record of an oral debate, but a carefully designed narration that only lets the other speak in order to bring the argument one step closer to the expected final defeat. Yet, Henriet's analysis is able to show how the clashing discourses keep to different ideological referents and discourse strategies: the relative importance assigned to relics, or to the historical tradition; the role of 'law' and pontifical authority; the links with the secular politics that cast their shadow on the whole debate; most importantly, the antagonistic points of view regarding the historical basis of the single most important religious phenomenon in central medieval Iberia: the cult of St. James at Compostela! Even different conceptions of historical time—undefined, timeless tradition for Braga, firm roots in the Visigothic period for Toledo—can be recognized in the text, indicating that, in spite of being written in favour of Toledo's claims to Iberian primacy, the source probably reflects with some accuracy the arguments and discourses deployed by its competitors in actuality.

The use of discoursive techniques for vesting legitimacy in the exercise of, and competition for, power is also the core of the Italian material discussed by Frances Andrews. Her study of the works of Albertanus of Brescia and Rolandinus of Padua brings in the paramount role played in the evolution of communal government in the Italian towns by a class of literate legal specialists. Making use of a wide range of resources which are typical of ecclesiastical scholastic education, the struggle for legitimate authority within the town is pursued through a colourful palette of legal notions, moral arguments, persuasive rhetorics, even typically ecclesiastical discourses which are subtly devoided of their clerical character, but stay nonetheless powerful. In the discourses constructed by the literate professionals, a painful political past is recycled, either by the *damnatio memoriae* or the demonisation of earlier government. This undoubtedly goes to legitimate recent changes and the exercise of power in the present, but it also covers with prestige and wide acceptance the role played by those who claim for themselves the function of giving good counsel and mediating in future conflicts. Thus, a whole professional group finds its place in the political arena by exercising action through the creation of discourse. This is, though, a case in which audience becomes a fundamental element, less prominent in other chapters, although it must be taken in consideration for all. The 'interface between the written and the oral'—to use Goody's wording[7]—gets thus blurred when written discourses are publicly read for all citizens. The same notion of community membership and identity through agency and participation pointed out by both Alfonso and Jara can be recognized here. By listening to the public performance of the text, its potentially restricted, literate audience expands to a vague, comprehensive notion of 'whole', triggering the circular process of gaining legitimation by acknowledging and accepting, but also by being acknowledged and accepted.

In these brief comments the editors have chosen to highlight a number of issues raised by the individual authors which are seen as especially adequate for general, comparative discussion regardless of time and space. Yet, the material gathered here contains plenty of interesting suggestions that will appeal as much to those with a specific interest in the contexts addressed. We think nevertheless that, when put side by side, the papers in this volume make a lot more sense than just individually, not only because they cover a wide range of subjects, but mainly because they pose a good number of questions which—whether they are answered or remain open—should become a part of a future agenda for large-scale comparative research of political power in medieval societies. Now it is time for the authors to speak for themselves.

Acknowledgements

The editors are indebted to a great number of people whose enthusiastic cooperation has made this book possible. First of all, of course, the individual authors, and all the members of our research group, and invited participants, who took part in the seminars, meetings and discussions. We would also like to thank the British Council and

---

[7] Goody, J. (1987) *The interface between the written and the oral*, Cambridge University Press (Cambridge: 1987).

the Spanish Ministerio de Ciencia y Tecnología for their support and sponsoring. Brill Publishers, and especially Marcella Mulder, have been indispensably encouraging, both in welcoming the project of this book and in coping with some undesirable delays. Last, but not least, the translators, Carolina Carl, Simon Doubleday and Chantell Arcand did a great job in a very short time.

Needless to say that, for all the many ways in which all the aforesaid have contributed to improve this book, whichever possible shortcomings remain are the editors' indisputable responsibility.

PART ONE

LEGITIMATION IN CONTEXT

CONFLICT, POWER AND LEGITIMATION IN FRANCIA IN THE LATE SEVENTH AND EIGHTH CENTURIES

PAUL FOURACRE
The University of Manchester

The following essay will draw attention to the different ways in which power was legitimated in seventh century Francia. It will then discuss conflict in Francia in the late seventh century, arguing that at this time conflict was the effective means through which power was redistributed. It was not, therefore, a contested legitimation which was the cause of conflict, but, rather, a struggle for power already defined as legitimate. In the eighth century this situation appears to change with the violent rise to power of the Carolingian family, which then sought different sources of legitimation in order to justify the formation of a new political order. I shall, however, suggest that this appearance is misleading. For although the new regime may have emphasised ways in which its power was morally superior to, and practically more effective, than that of its predecessor, the ways in which effective power was constituted in the locality remained basically the same.

We can identify three interlinked areas in which legitimation was grounded in later Merovingian Francia: first, in the delegation and execution of royal authority, second in the operation of law and custom, and, third, in the rules and moral discourse of the church.[1] In all three areas the advent of a new dynasty did not lead to structural change. Nevertheless, because there were several strands to the legitimation of power, particular sources of legitimation might be stressed at different times, and by different power elites, in line with the needs of the political situation. At a simple narrative level, the incoming Carolingians justified their power by stressing that their victories were God-given. In a progressively more sophisticated manner, they then privileged the moral aspect of power in order to further justify their seizure of the throne in 751, thus associating royalty with morality and justice.[2] But by the end of the Carolingian period,

---

[1] On the nature of political institutions in this regime, Fouracre (1998).
[2] On the Carolingian emphasis on justice, Fouracre (1995).

this association was becoming weaker, and magnates were beginning to appropriate for themselves a degree of moral legitimation. This they did by positioning themselves as protectors of the church and also by stressing rights of power enshrined in law and custom. By the time of the later ninth century, church leaders themselves were arguing that since royal authority depended upon moral legitmacy, kings should follow the guidance of bishops, the arbiters of morality.[3] The essay will close by asking what the patterns of legitimation can tell us about the nature and distribution of power over the Frankish period in general. Let us begin with the seventh century.

Almost every genre of writing in the later Merovingian period carries a strong sense that royal authority was a primary source of legitimate power. Charters were authenticated by regnal dating and transactions guaranteed by calls upon the royal fisc to punish non-compliance by heavy fines. Royal charters were highly prized as a records of judgements and privileges that had complete dispositive force. Already in seventh century we meet the phenomenon of transactions disguised as judgements (*placita*), a fiction which led to the production of charters backed with the full authority of the king and the royal court. Laws written down in the seventh and eighth centuries have the king as the central figure of authority. Saints Lives of this period invariably show the career of the saint affected at some point by royal authority, and the two seventh and early eighth century chronicles portray a political world in which royal authority was at the centre.[4] The different sources also all agree that legitimate kingship could lie only in the hands of the descendants of Clovis, the Merovingians. In the works of Gregory of Tours, later sixth-century Gaul/Francia is portrayed as a land torn apart by frequent and futile civil wars, and over a century later the early eighth-century chronicle, the *Liber Historiae Francorum* still lamented the tendency of Franks to cut down Franks.[5] But there are good reasons for thinking that Gregory was overly pessimisitc,[6] and what strife there was, was con-

---

[3] Nelson (1977) for the development of this line of thought in the writings of Hincmar, archbishop of Rheims 845–882.

[4] The chronicles are the *Chronicle of Fredegar* book IV, which goes up to the mid seventh century, with continuations up to 768, and the *Liber historiae Francorum*, completed by the year 727.

[5] *Liber historiae Francorum* c. 51.

[6] On the nature, structure and purpose of Gregory's writing of history, Goffart (1988), Heinzelmann (1994), Breukelaar (1994).

ducted through and in the name of the Merovingians. Factions grouped themselves around particular Merovingians, whose cause they sought to advance at the expense of other members of the same family. Only on one occasion before 751 was a non-Merovingian made king, but even though this person was called by a Merovingian name, Childebert, and had been adopted as the son of a king, the Frankish magnates nevertheless rose up and attacked his family, the ancestors of the Carolingians.[7]

Why the Franks were, to a greater extent than any other European people, so attached to a single bloodline of kings has never been completely explained. Explanations in terms of the Merovingians' mythical ancestry and their magical powers lie in the realm of the imagination, not in that of history.[8] A more mundane suggestion, but one which better fits the available evidence, is that the Merovingians established an exclusive right to royal power by destroying all potential rivals at that moment at which the Franks established their hegemony over Gaul and Western Germany. As rulers over this massive portion of what had been the Roman Empire, the kings appropriated the legal powers and bureaucratic machinery surviving from the later Roman provincial government, to which they added their role as Frankish war leaders, and as protectors of the church. They thus became the mediators between the various groups which made up this ethnically and regionally diverse kingdom. In these circumstances, choosing kings from a single bloodline had the effect maintaining a balance between the different groups—regional, family and ecclesiastical— who exercised power in Francia. Tension, faction and even conflict between groups there certainly was, but it was ultimately limited by a common acceptance of Merovingian authority. In this way, attachment to the dynasty was not merely symbolic, but became the focus of a consensus which gave some measure of cohesion to a Frankish polity that was otherwise massive, unwieldy, and essentially weakly governed. It was a consensus which understood royal authority as a source of legitimation, but within which the different interest groups preserved their own rights and sense of legitimate privilege Historically, this arrangement was fortunate never to suffer the great shocks which

---

[7] This is the so-called 'Grimoald coup', on which the literature is voluminous. For works up to 1987 see the bibliography in Gerberding (1987), and up to 1994, the notes in Becher (1994), and the bibliography in Wood (1994).

[8] Murray (1998).

upset the balance of power in neighbouring kingdoms. Unlike Spain
or Italy, Francia did not experience large-scale invasion, nor was it
subject to serious destabilisation.at the hands of the Byzantines.

One can identify two main considerations which encouraged magnates to gravitate towards the kings and accept their authority as a
prime source of legitimate power. First was the access to the power
and wealth which came from exercising command in the king's name,
and second was the protection of property and privilege to which
the kings were committed. At least in theory, the king's command was,
like that of the Roman Emperor, law, and sometimes it was expressed
in very Roman terms. This claim to command with irresistible authority is clearly evident from late sixth- and early seventh-century legislation.[9] Of particular interest to us here as a visible means of
conferring legitimation is the institution of *trustis*, that is, a posse, the
members of which enjoyed special status as royal agents. Placing
someone *in truste* was, literally, empowerment, in that it enabled individuals to cross physical boundaries and take actions which would
otherwise have been forbidden to them. Here legitimation came
directly from the mouth of the king. The conferring of *trustis* membership seems to have been directed at people of relatively humble
status, such as *centenarii*, that is, at agents rather than at lords. A.C.
Murray has termed such people 'the regional constabulary', although
the *antrustiones* who served the king were no doubt more like bodyguards.[10] But lords too were empowered by office, as dukes, counts,
domestici and bishops, for in their official capacity, they too acted in
the name of the king. The idea of acting in the name of the king,
meaning the exercise of power derived from royal authority, was one
upon which contemporaries reflected, because they were aware that
the exercise of legitimate power might bring about in justice and
corruption if kings were unable to keep unscrupulous or greedy
officers in check. What must have concentrated minds on this issue
in the seventh century was the advent of child kings, for rule by

---

[9] See, for example, the splendidly Roman-sounding dictat King Childebert II
demanding the death penalty for murder (ca. 596). Childebert forbade compensation and decreed the death penalty for murder *quia iustem est ut qui novit occidere, dis-
cat morire. (Childeberti Decretio* c. 5).

[10] Murray (1988) 87. *Pactus Childeberti I et Clotharii I* c. 15: *Pro tenore pacis iubemus ut
in trusti electi centenarii ponantur* The *centenarii* should *inter communes provincias licentia
habeant latrones persequere*. This legislation is pre 558. For the ceremony through which
people became *antrustiones, Marculfi Formularum libri duo* I, no. 18. Note that this ritual swearing of fidelity *in manu* is essentially similar to later so-called 'feudal' ritual.

children was the inevitable biological consequence of strict adherence to a single bloodline. It must also be said that only in Francia was child kinship feasible, because here, unlike, say, in Visigothic Spain, it was possible to divide kingship, the 'name of king', off from the personal leadership of particular kings.

It was above all the fact that children ruled Francia in the 640s and again in the late 650s and early 660s that led to the rise in importance of the mayors of the palace, in conjunction with three dowager queens regent. The mayors of the palace have not been treated sympathetically by modern historians, who have tended to see them as usurpers of royal power, and have made them largely responsible for the decline and demise of the Merovingian dynasty. The mayor of the palace was the chief non royal officer in the land. He was important because he ran the palace and transmitted the king's commands. He controlled access to the king, and this gave him immense political power. If he could influence the king to the extent that the king commanded what he wished, then in effect he could wield royal authority. This capacity to rule with the authority of a king is what has persuaded historians that the mayor's power was detrimental to that of the king, and it is indeed the case that other Frankish leaders were alarmed at the prospect that the mayor might use the king's authority against them. Nevertheless, it was the mayors and the queens who made it possible for children to reign by ruling in their name. And this was in turn possible because the Frankish magnates generally tolerated rule by mayors and regents in order to maintain a status quo in which the exercise of royal authority continued to legitimate their own power. The magnates did, however, jealously guard the right to attend annual assemblies, the so-called 'Marchfield' (*campus martius*) which were held each Spring. These assemblies were important occasions on which obeisance to the kings was ritually affirmed and at which kings and magnates met together to discuss the 'well being of the kindgom' (*tractare de utilitate regni*).[11] We have legislation and charters which make it clear that formal

---

[11] The *Childeberti Decretio* opens: *cum in Dei nomine nos omnes kalendas martias de quascumque condiciones cum nostris optimatibus pertractavimus, ad unumquemque noticia volumus pervenire.* What follows are the agreements made at the last three meetings. Two *placita* charters from 693 and 697 both dated to the kalends of march have lists of the magnates who were sitting in tribunal, which suggests that the tribunal was drawn from those who were gathered for the Marchfield assembly: *MGH Diplomata Merovingicarum Regum Francorum e stirpe Merovingica* nos. 141, 149.

decision making and judgements were part of this annual meeting. Apart from being very practical meetings which served to communicate orders to a gathering of magnates drawn from every region, the assemblies were also an organ of legitimation, both for the power of the king, and for the power of the magnates. Each was committed to upholding the authority of the other.

In the locality the legitimation of the count's power was, as we have seen, derived from his exercise of royal authority. Like the mayor, the count acted in the king's name. But, interestingly, legitimation in the count's case depended on his obeying laws as well as enforcing them. At stake here was the protection of rights and property. The count had the power to distrain property, but this was viewed as legitimate only if proper procedures of collective local judgement had been followed. The local community wished the count to have the power to protect their property, but not the power to take it away from them arbitrarily. Late sixth-century legislation strongly supported the local community here in stating that where counts deliberately flouted procedure and took property without due leave, they should be put to death.[12] On the other hand, counts and locals seem to have been in complete agreement about how the unfree should be treated. The unfree were on the receiving end of a series of harsh penalties for all manner of crimes.[13] The nature and severity of their treatment marked them out from the free peasant population. Unlike the free, the unfree had virtually no means of redress against power used arbitrarily against them. In the locality, therefore, the legitimation of social power drew upon royal authority through the agency of the count. But legitimation in the local context also drew upon a body of customary law and procedure which actually served to limit the exercise of royal authority, and which at the same time legitimated the divide between free and unfree. The observations of the legal anthropologist S. Roberts are most useful here in pointing out that in pre-modern societies which had essentially weak government, central authority tended to have a presence in the locality only when and where it was invited in to help local people settle disputes and to maintain their privileges.[14] Merovingian legislation

---

[12] *Edictus Chilperici* c. 8. There is no record of a count actually losing his life in this way.

[13] Compare the penalties for theft by freemen, *Pactus legis Salicae* cc. 2–11 with those for theft by slaves, *Pactus legis Salicae* c. 40.

[14] Roberts (1979), (1983).

actually uses the term 'invite' for the count's intervention in disputes at the behest of locals.

What the social status of these locals was we cannot exactly tell. Frankish laws did not differentiate the free, and the dividing line between free and noble is notoriously difficult to find.[15] On the basis that the number of high offices was exceeded by the number of nobles, we may assume that there was a class of nobles who did not exercise power in an official capacity but who could nevertheless be described as powerful. The *senatores* who appear in the late seventh-century *Passio Praejecti* might be such people. Their power in the Auvergne seems to have been unchallenged until Praejectus the local bishop stood out against them, with the result that they killed him. The terms used to refer to the powerful (*potentes/potentiores, proceres, optimates, viri inlustri, praestantiores* etc.) are unhelpful: by the seventh century they had lost their precise Roman connotations, and now they marked people out as pre-eminent, but tell us nothing about the nature of their power. Collectively, therefore, *potentes* must have included both those who held offices, and those whose power was derived from birth and wealth without office It is of course also true that by the later seventh century, wealth and high birth were essential qualifications for the holding of high office, so it would be pointless to try and divide off 'private' from 'public' power. It is nevertheless interesting to note that both Merovingian, and even more, Carolingian legislation, refers to the *potentes* in invariably negative terms. Their power, which allows them to pursue their interests at the expense of others (including the kings), is seen as a threat to the social order and machinery of government. Legislation thus refers to what these *potentes* were doing wrong, rather than to what their rights were. They unjustly oppressed the poor. They formed armed followings when they should not have done. They tried to bribe and bully courts into deciding cases in their favour. They killed in revenge rather than sought remedy through the courts. Where they held immunities they failed to deliver up criminals to the counts.[16] These, it seems, were people who did not often 'invite the count in', or if they were counts, they

---

[15] Fouracre (2000a).

[16] See for instance *Edict of Paris* (614) c. 15, and the *Capitulary of Herstal* (778) cc. 9, 14. Complaints against the harmful power of *potentes* go back to late Roman legislation, and the opposition between 'powerful' and 'weak' is in part rhetorical. Morris (1976) on the rhetoric of 'powerful' and 'weak' in tenth century Byzantine legislation.

were no doubt the sort of counts who took the property of others without being invited. As lords, *potentes* had rights over tenants, both free and unfree. Where they did not hold office, their power was based on wealth and privilege. Their wealth was protected by law in the same way that every free person enjoyed protection, and we may imagine that social custom protected their honour and privilege. Even if they had wished to do so, the weak governments of the early middle ages were unable to cut down the power and privilege of these people, for they depended upon the *potentes* for both political and military support. We can also see from charter witness lists that magnates had lesser nobles as clients, and that therefore patronage must have been another factor in the legitimation of the latter's power. But in as much as the power of this amorphous group ultimately depended upon their wealth, so did their wealth legitimate their power.

Let us now consider to the church, the third element in the legitimation of power. The church, of course, had long articulated a defence of its own power. It had developed a justification for its massive property holding. Property, it argued, was held on behalf of the whole Christian community, and it was necessary to have wealth to fund liturgical functions, to support pastoral care and to care for the weak in society.[17] The Catholic Church had the only formally constituted hierarchy in Francia and it was in theory a self-legitimating, rule based organisation, although Merovingian church councils, the body which made or monitored the keeping of the rules, were held under the aegis of royal authority. The power of every grade in the ecclesiastical hierarchy was defined by its own law, Canon Law. The church was, however, also vigorously active in the secular law courts in which individual churches and monasteries defended their interests against lay persons, and also against other ecclesiastical institutions. When churches had been granted privileges of immunity on their lands, they ran the local courts and exercised some of the rights enjoyed by counts elsewhere. So in terms of property-based power, churches were not unlike the other powerful in drawing upon law and custom and royal authority to legitimise their operations. In addition, bishops and more powerful abbots were essentially magnates who took part in assemblies, joined in the making of judgements and legislation, and exercised authority in the name of the king. In short, they shared in that legitimation which came from being in the penumbra of royal

---

[17] Ganz (1995).

authority. But the church also claimed to be arbiters of what was right for all people, and as the guardians of morality, they sanctioned (or challenged) the moral legitimation of power.

Religious values were influential not just because they were in theory universal in application, but also because churchmen exercised power in the secular as well as in the ecclesiastical world. Royal legislation was drafted by churchmen. It became increasingly coloured by the language of moral legitimation, and increasingly focused on matters of ecclesiastical concern.[18] We must also consider supernatural affirmation as another element in the legitimation of power. In an age in which many new saints were created, it became relatively common for the leading families, including the Merovingian family itself, to have a family member declared a saint. In fact the cult of family members became so common that historians have spoken of a general process of 'aristocratic self-sanctification', through which a pre-Christian charisma of power became christianised.[19] The process was not quite as common nor as self-conscious as has been suggested, nor is there evidence of any pre-Christian charisma. It is nevertheless true that the social power of many leading families was reinforced through the acquisition of religious prestige which came from the growth of a cult around a family member, and through the patronage of other leading cult centres.[20] In legislation and in royal charters, supernatural power is seen an essential counterpart to earthly power. Through gifts to the church it was hoped to merit the prayers of the clergy for the well being of the king and kingdom. This was, in effect, a spiritual affirmation of the king's right to exercise power. Private charters also hoped that gifts would earn spiritual merit, in the form of present well-being and future salvation, but in private charters it was only the immediate family of the donor which hoped to benefit. Let us now bring conflict into the picture.

I shall focus first of all on political conflict in the 670s, because this is unusually well documented. One of the protagonists was a bishop, Leudegar of Autun. He was executed and held to be a martyr. It is his *Passio*, or record of his sufferings, composed within few years of

---

[18] Note, for instance, the overlapping of the secular *Edict of Paris*, and the ecclesiastical *Council of Paris*, both coming from the year 614. See Fouracre (2000b) 12.

[19] The term (*Adelsselbstheiligung*) was first coined by Friedrich Prinz (1965) 489–93, for problems in using the term Fouracre and Gerberding (1996) 49.

[20] Fouracre (1999) on how patterns of sanctification changed under the early Carolingians.

his death, which is the main source for these events.[21] It is important
for our purposes because its author reflected on the nature of power.
Leudegar's suffering would also later figure in the Carolingian argument that it was necessary for this family to establish a new regime.

In 664 Francia consisted of two kingdoms, Austrasia, and Neustria-
Burgundy. Austrasia was ruled by a child, Childeric II, along with
a dowager queen, Himnechild, and a mayor of the palace named
Wulfoald. Neustria-Burgundy was ruled by Childeric's elder brother,
Clothar, another dowager queen, Balthild, and the mayor of the
palace Ebroin. When Clothar reached his majority in about 664,
Balthild was forcibly retired, but Ebroin remained in power. His
power, however, was, according to the *Passio Leudegarii*, unjust, because
he made people pay in order to secure justice, but at this stage
Ebroin's power was also legitimate, and the author feels the need to
explain why Leudegar was accused of disobeying the mayor's orders.
Ebroin then issued an *edictum tyrannicum*, namely that no-one from
the region of Burgundy (Leudegar's region) was to come to the palace
without his permission. This author, and several others, used the
term *tyrannicus* very carefully to describe power which was exercised
illegally. What Ebroin's edict did was to restrict the right of access
to the king, and no-one, not even the mayor of the palace, could
legally do this. Ebroin got his come-uppance when the king, Clothar,
died in 673, and he tried to prevent the magnates assembling to
raise another Merovingian to the throne. This move challenged the
whole basis of legitimate power, for

> as long as he kept the king, whom he ought to have raised up before
> the people to the glory of the fatherland, in the background and just
> used his name, Ebroin would be able to do harm to whosoever he
> wished, with impunity.[22]

This extraordinary, and rightly well-known passage, shows an acute
awareness of how power might be misused when royal authority was
wielded against, rather than in conjunction, with the magnates. It
makes it clear that legitimation depended upon agreement about
how power should be used. In the event, the magnates turned upon
Ebroin, and chose another king, Childeric of Austrasia. Leudegar

---

[21] *Passio Leudegarii* I, trans. with commentary Fouracre and Gerberding (1996)
193–253.
[22] *Passio Leudegarii* c. 5.

became the chief advisor to Childeric, and Ebroin was exiled to the monastery of Luxeuil. Childeric was then persuaded to issue legislation which safeguarded the rights of the magnates by preserving regional laws and customs and by forbidding officials to enter provinces other than those in which they held office. In order to prevent the mayor exercising tryannical power, that is, usurping royal authority as Ebroin had done, the position of mayor was to be made more open. But then Childeric fell out with the nobles of his new kingdom. Leudegar was exiled, in fact he was made to join his old enemy Ebroin in Luxeuil. In 675 Childeric was assassinated by the magnates, because, says the *Liber Historiae Francorum*, he had enraged them by tying one of them to a stake and beating him. This was *sine lege*, illegal: freemen could not be bound and humiliated in this way.[23] Childeric, it seems from charter evidence, had intruded his own Austrasian supporters into positions of power in Neustria- Burgundy, and he had broken with the political consensus which was the mainstay of royal authority. Treating a noble like an unfree person was the last straw.

In the aftermath of Childeric's death there was, literally, a race for power between Ebroin and Leudegar. Ebroin eventually won, and then had Leudegar arrested, mutilated, tried, and, finally, executed. Drawing on Isidore of Seville, the author of the *Passio Leudegarii* describes a chaotic interregnum before a new king was raised to the throne and the royal palace reconstituted. When no king was there to impose order:

> Those who should have been the rulers of the provinces rose up against each other—those who should have banded together to keep the peace began to challenge each other in hatred, and since no king sat firmly on the throne, each saw as right whatever he wished to do, and that is how they began to act, without any fear of discipline.[24]

Interestingly, the author who is virulently anti-Ebroin, admitted that things calmed down when Ebroin had once again become mayor. He was unjust, and wicked, full of *malitia*, but by becoming mayor again he had acquired the *ius potestatis*, the right of power, and he used this right to re-establish order. Our author here refers to the issue of an edict which seems to draw on a law from the Theodosian code which concerned the settling of property claims in the aftermath

---

[23] *Pactus legis Salicae* c. 32.
[24] *Passio Leudegarii* c. 15.

of barbarian invasion.[25] Ebroin then ruled vigorously for several more years until he was in his turn murdered in 680.

Although the conflict in these years raged across the different regions of Francia, it was clearly about control of the centre, which meant domination of king and palace, as the source of the power to issue binding commands throughout the kingdom. It was thus vital for a faction to have a king in order to legitimate their claim to power, and it was also necessary to have king in order to raise a large army. In 675 when Ebroin had been had been excluded from the palace, the *Passio Leudegarii* tells us, he raised his own king (supposedly a pretender) to the throne. This allowed him both to raise an army, and to demand support on the basis of loyalty owed to this new found king. 'They [Ebroin and his supporters] gave orders to the judges in the name of their king', said the *Passio* author, and they 'commanded that whoever wished to refuse obedience to them should give up his right to hold power.'[26]

Because legitimate power was so sharply defined in relation to 'royal orders', changing control of the palace was the effective means of re-distributing power amongst the different factions of magnates. In the next decade, we see the same process again, as the Austrasians fought the Neustro-Burgundians for control of the palace, and forced them to share power. As in the 670s, once the power struggle was resolved, notably at the Battle of Tertry in 687, order was re-established and the magnates came back together again in assemblies around the king. There followed a generation of peace in which the Merovingian regime seems to have been working as well as it had ever done, with a king, Childebert III, who was lauded in the *Liber Historiae Francorum* as a *rex justus*. It is from this time, too, that we have the bulk of surviving original *placita* documents, which record the settle-ment of disputes between magnates and ecclesiastical institutions in the royal court. We should note that in some of these cases judge-ments were made against the Pippinid family (the ancestors of the Carolingians, who had taken control of the palace after the Battle of Tertry). A legitimation of power which depended on the willing participation of the wider magnate group, naturally required non-royal leaders on occasion to accept the judgement of their peers. It

---

[25] *The Theodosian Code* XV, 14. See also Fouracre and Gerberding (1996) 243–4.
[26] *Passio Leudegarii* c. 19. Note that Charles Martel did exactly the same by rais-ing Clothar IV to the throne in 717–718, see Fouracre (2000b) 69.

was when they refused to do this that conflict was likely to break out. In this sense, by enabling a balance of power to be re-established, conflict helped to reinforce that legitimation which derived from an acceptance of royal authority that was mediated through the palace, and upheld by magnates in the provinces. On the other hand, it was conflict which had given legitimate power to the victors, and prolonged conflict in the next generation would make victory itself the main justification for the holding of power. It would be at this point that the Merovingian kings really would be pushed into the background, and used simply for their name.

We see a sign of this development in the *Passio Leudegarii*. Although the author saw power in terms of a 'right' which was legally constituted, he also saw God as the ultimate judge of who should hold power. And God judged according to how power was exercised. Both King Childeric and the mayor Ebroin exercised power without justice, and God sanctioned their assassinations. Childeric's murder was described as 'a divine sentence', Ebroin's as fitting punishment for his many sins. This idea would be further developed by the Carolingians as they reflected upon the justification for their power. The victories they won over those who resisted them were seen as God's judgement. The context for this shift in emphasis was all out military conflict.

The Carolingians had to fight every inch of their way to power. The political consensus re-established after the battle of Tertry collapsed on the death of the leader of the family, Pippin, at the end of 714. There followed a whole generation of warfare as Pippin's son Charles Martel fought, first to gain control of the Neustrian palace, and then to have his power and authority recognised throughout Francia. Whereas Pippin as mayor of the palace had been prepared to share power with the leading magnates in Neustria-Burgundy (as the judgements against the family suggest), his son Charles Martel was unable and unwilling to share power when he became mayor. One reason for this is that the struggle over the mayoralty in the years 715–24 had been so fierce and prolonged that the kings had disappeared as figures of mediation. By 725 Charles Martel had become dominant in the palace to the extent that he now seems to have been in a position 'to keep the king in the background and just use his name' in the way that the *Passio Leudegarii* tells us, Ebroin had threatened to do in 673. But Charles Martel went even further than that when in 737 the king, Theuderic IV, died. Charles did

not allow another Merovingian to be raised to the throne, but he
did continue to exercise authority in the king's name. Although the
magnates in the Frankish heartlands do not seem to have had sufficient
power after 725 to stop Charles Martel behaving in this way, the
leaders in Aquitaine, Provence, Alemannia and Bavaria fought him
until they were exhausted. And when Charles Martel died in 741
there was a concerted effort to drive out his sons Pippin and Carloman.
They in their turn did raise another Merovingian to the throne as
a way trying to legitimise their power and disarm opponents who
no doubt regarded them as *tyrannii*, usurpers of legitmate power.[27]

Alas, we have no source like the *Passio Leudegarii* to comment on
these events. What we do have is a near contemporary narrative,
commissioned by a member of the Carolingian family, the *Continuations
of the Chronicle of Fredegar* which portray Charles Martel and his sons
as the rightful leaders of Francia. Their opponents were simply wrong.
Right was demonstrated through a string of military victories in terms
which invited analogy with the Old Testament leader Joshua, to
whom God granted victory over the enemies of Israel. Invasion by
Arab forces from Spain and war with pagan Saxons and Frisians
helped construct an image of the Franks as a chosen people fighting,
like the Israelites, against unbelievers, and this image would play an
important part in the legitimation of Carolingian power. The sons
of Charles Martel also convened church councils which castigated
the Frankish church as being in urgent need of reform. Calling councils was a practical way of gaining control of the church, but it was
also a statement of legitimation, which presented these warlords as
having moral responsibility for the spiritual well being of the Franks.
Again, the regime represented itself as being surrounded and threatened by hostile gentile forces, the urgency of the situation being the
regime's justification for commandeering church resources.[28]

Pippin and Carloman also built upon links with the papacy. The
popes had since the time of Charles Martel been keen to secure the
support of the Franks against a resurgent Lombard regime. Links with
Rome were not confined to these two leaders, nor were they at all
new in the mid eighth century, but the Carolingians represented them
as special, and found in them further legitmation. Famously, it would
be through a supposed dialogue with the pope that they received

---

[27] Fouracre (2000b) for interpretation of the career of Charles Martel.
[28] *Council of Estinnes* c. 2.

permission, as it were, to take the throne from the Merovingians. According to the *Royal Frankish Annals*, which were produced at Charlemagne's court, Pippin sent emissaries to Rome to ask

> whether it was good or not that the kings of the Franks should wield no power, as was the case at the time. Pope Zacharias instructed Pippin that it was better to call him king who had the royal power than the one who did not. To avoid turning the country upside down, he commanded by virtue of his apostolic authority that Pippin should be made king.[29]

In other words, the name of king had to be joined with real power, and the one was the justification for the other. The notions that the legitimation of Carolingian kingship lay in the need to unite power and royalty, and that there was a spiritual mandate for the holding of royal authority, would be the key to Carolingian thinking about the nature of power. In 753 pope Stephen II travelled to Francia and anointed the whole immediate family, conferring royalty upon them. The Merovingian kings had never been anointed, for their royalty lay in their blood. A different dynasty required a different inauguration ritual. Then in a letter to the family, Stephen stated that in future only their descendants should be kings of the Franks. Charlemagne had all surviving papal correspondence from the time of Charles Martel onwards copied into a codex. This was, said the preface to the codex, because the original papyrus documents were decaying. But copying the letters had the effect of re-documenting the steps by which the family had moved from being mayors of the palace to becoming rightful kings, and gathering the correspondence together in a solemn codex further enhanced its status. In other words, this volume told of how a new exclusive bloodline had been established, and of how the new kings had become the saviours of Rome.

Although the Carolingians in part derived legitmacy from their role as protectors of St Peter, and despite the fact that there was a Romanising tendency in Frankish culture at this time, with Charlemagne, of course, eventually being crowned 'Roman Emperor', the rulers also distanced themselves from the memory of the Roman Empire. This was on the basis that in former times the Empire had been pagan, and in present times, its successor, the Byzantine Empire,

---

[29] *Royal Frankish Annals* s.a. 749. McKitterick (2000) on how royalty for the Carolingians was constructed in the *Royal Frankish Annals*.

was hostile, doctrinally impure, and ruled by a woman.[30] The earliest explicit Carolingian statement on the justification of their power comes in the Prologue to a revision of *Lex Salica*, from the time of King Pippin (751–768). It states that the Franks beat the Romans in battle and then having been baptised, honoured those martyrs whom the Romans had persecuted. Victory and faith gave them legitimate power, and the right to issue laws. From the narrative of the *Continuations of Fredegar* and from the early sets of annals, however, we can be certain that at this stage the Carolingians were barely acceptable as leaders of the Franks. What followed in the next generations was the most sustained attempt at political legitimation that the early-medieval West ever saw.

The nub of the Carolingian argument that they were the rightful kings of the Franks lay in the words that the *Royal Frankish Annals* had put into the mouth of Pope Zacharias, namely, that those who had the power should have the name of king. This statement became the basis for a sustained assault upon the reputation of the Merovingian dynasty. The most famous example of such an attack is the opening to Einhard's biography of Charlemagne. Einhard went into graphic detail to illustrate the powerless of the last Merovingians, and to show how real power lay in the hands of the mayor of the palace, Pippin, which explained why the Pope had issued the order to depose the Merovingians. Einhard was writing probably in the 820s and here he was elaborating a view first stated in the 760s and widely circulated thereafter. It appears in garbled form, for instance, in the Chronicle of Theophanes in Constantinople.[31] The relentless nature of the assault upon the reputation of the Merovingians suggests that it was in fact very difficult to break with traditional loyalties to the old dynasty, not simply in political terms, but also because it had been through the Merovingians that power had been more widely legitimated.[32] Not surprisingly, the most sensitive point of all was the tradition of annual assemblies around the king, for not only were these the moments at which legitimation was expressed through ritual obeisance, the assemblies were also indispensable for the running of

---

[30] Alcuin's letter to Charlemagne of June 799, seemingly written in the context of discussion about Charlemagne's imminent imperial coronation, expresses Frankish superiority in the face of the deterioration of 'Old' and 'New Rome': *Alcuini Epistolae* no. 174.

[31] *The Chronicle of Theophanes* pp. 556–7.

[32] Fouracre (forthcoming) on the Carolingian denigration of their predecessors.

the kingdom in a very practical sense. The Carolingian answer to tradition was to represent the new dynasty as dynamic where the old had been sluggish, thus yet again making the point that the name of kings should reside where the power was. This theme works its way even into the simplest of narratives. For the year 790, for instance, the *Royal Frankish Annals* had virtually nothing to report: Charlemagne did nothing of note that year. But a generation later, the Revised version of the Annals expanded the 790 entry with the remark that 'the king, lest he should be thought of as becoming sluggish through inactivity', travelled up and down the River Main. It was not just military necessity which kept Carolingian kings on the move, their right to hold power was justified by incessant movement.

Right was also determined by how power was exercised, and here the Carolingians picked up on the themes of justice and divine sanction that we saw expressed in the *Passio Leudegarii*. In fact use was made of the *Passio* text in the *Annales Mettenses Priores*, composed in 805. This is a work which chronicled and justified the family's rise to power.[33] Leudegar's treatment by Ebroin was made a paradigm of Neustrian injustice. Neustrian exiles begged Pippin to intervene to re-establish justice. When he reluctantly did so and confronted the king and the Neustrians at the battle of Tertry, God signalled approval by giving him victory. Bright sunlight blinded the Neustrians, but illuminated the justice of Pippin's cause. Thereafter he dutifully respected the kings, but he had the real power, which he used to protect the weak and to defend the church. Justice and victory are twin themes throughout Carolingian narratives. Perhaps the most striking examples of this come from the those narratives which were concerned with Bavaria, where God delivered victory to the Franks in 743 in recognition of the justice of their cause. The *Royal Frankish Annals* for 787–8 tell of Charlemagne's final suppression of the duchy of Bavaria, and again, the justice of his cause is very carefully outlined. Justice was particularly stressed in relation to Bavaria because not only was this an area in which the Carolingian right to rule had been most strongly challenged, but also the ruler of Bavaria, Tassilo, was a descendant of Charles Martel The annexation of Bavaria required very careful justification indeed.[34] Tassilo had to be ritually humiliated

[33] On the *Annales* and the rise of the Pippinid family, Haselbach (1970), also Fouracre and Gerberding (1996) 350–70.
[34] Airlie (1999).

in order to place him symbolically outside the Carolingian family, for by the time of Charlemagne, being a member of the family was one justification for holding power.

One could argue that the stress on justice in Carolingian legislation points to another area in which their authority was not clear cut, if not actually contested. As we noted earlier, the legitimation of power in the locality was in part derived from royal authority, but it also rested upon self-standing legal procedures and local customs, besides being influenced by the situation on the ground in terms of those who had social power. Charlemagne's legislation attempted to strengthen the ruler's part in this configuration by making statements about the quality of justice which sought to privilege divinely, or scripturally, inspired norms over local arrangements. The agents and arbiters of this high quality justice were the *missi* whose judgements supposedly superseded those of the counts. In the *Capitulary of Herstal* (779) it was said that if a count failed to administer justice properly in his area, a *missus* was to go and stay with him in his household until justice was done. To go back to Roberts' observations, do we have in these no doubt burdensome guests, the evidence of a state which had sufficient strength to ensure that its agents could intervene in matters of local justice without being 'invited in'? The answer must be a qualified 'no', because for all its talk of intervention, there is little evidence that the Carolingian regime did intervene much in local affairs, and when it did, this seems to have been at local invitation, or in particularly politically sensitive areas like Bavaria. But the qualifications to this question are worth examining, for the Carolingians worked so hard to justify their power that their arguments and rhetoric were not without some effect on wider perceptions of how power was legitimated.

At the same time as the Carolingians sought to justify their rule, they also increased their power, largely by military conquest, for the campaigns against opponents on the Frankish periphery which characterised the age of Charles Martel and his sons, turned into campaigns against non-Frankish neighbours once all internal opposition had been crushed. As we have seen, victor y was regarded as proof of their right to hold power, and up to the death of Charlemagne in 814, the Carolingians won an impressive range of victories. But the justification for holding power was bound up with the struggle to impose control over their own people as well as over those unfortunate enough to be neighbours to the Franks. In the sphere of justice, the concept of improving quality went hand in hand with an extension of royal rights, for the term *iustitia* of course has a double meaning: of justice in an abstract sense and of rights in a concrete sense. It was in the latter sense, for instance, that the papacy sought to defend the *iustitia* of St Peter.[35] Likewise a rhetoric of spiritual improvement and a commitment to defend the church not only strengthened the moral legitimation of the regime, it also gave it wider scope for intervention in the lives of its subjects, and reform of the church meant establishing a stronger control over it. Charlemagne even decreed that no new saints be declared without his permission, again a double edged demand meant both to stop the veneration of false saints, and to remove supernatural affirmation from potential rivals.[36] Similarly, defending the rights of St Peter was bound up with the acquisition of power in Italy. All in all, the Carolingian regime, especially under Charlemagne, was relatively effective in corralling what power was available to it, and in focussing legitimation upon itself.

As Regine le Jan has recently argued, it is sensible to imagine that the Carolingians did make an impact on the behaviour of the nobility, especially the higher nobility.[37] In brief, the elite did react to the messages the regime sent out. The mid ninth century hand book of the lady Dhuoda is witness to how much aristocratic culture had come to focus upon the Carolingians. The lesser nobility were also affected by the demands of the regime. Carl Hammer, for instance, has shown how nobles in Bavaria in the later eighth century were forced to sell land to pay for the horses and weapons needed to meet the military obligations place upon them.[38] And for the Rhineland, Matthew Innes has described how in the eighth century the nobility shifted the focus of their activities from the cities on the Rhine to rural monasteries. Here they were following the lead of the rulers in forming close associations with newly founded monasteries.[39] Everywhere there was a massive rise in the number of charters which survive, and it seems clear that many more charters were produced under the Carolingians than had been under the Merovingians. All this the regime encouraged. It was very keen on making records. It was interested in how the nobility behaved, how estates were run, in what

---

[35] Fouracre (1995).
[36] *Council of Frankfurt* c. 42; see also Fouracre (1999).
[37] Le Jan (1995) 126–53.
[38] Hammer (1997).
[39] Innes (2000).

happened in immunities, in how disputes were settled, how armed followings were made up, how marriages were made, and so on. And of course it was interested in how its officials behaved, especially in a judicial and fiscal capacity, and above all, in the conduct of those who served the church. It is in this context not surprising that the Frankish nobility appears a rather more homogenous group in 800 than it had in 600. Partly, this was a result of the demands placed upon it from the centre, but perhaps even more, it reflects a process of acculturation as regional nobilities absorbed the core culture of the Franks. It was their willingness to do so, at a time when co-operation with a highly successful regime brought rewards, that made them so tractable.

We have seen that in the later seventh century conflict was the means through which power was redistributed between the different factions of the nobility at times when mediation had failed. The eventually complete victory of the Carolingians meant that such conflict ceased, and references to different factions of magnates are no longer found after the mid eighth century. The office of mayor of the palace came to end as soon as Pippin became king in 751. There would now be no senior non-royal leader to stand between the king and the magnates. It is logical to suppose that power now came to rest, relatively undisturbed, in the hands of a few favoured families closely linked to the Carolingian family itself. This group is often referred to as the 'Imperial Aristocracy'. Regine Le Jan has argued that the effect of this more stable situation was to strengthen the hierarchy within the nobility. Following the message of Carolingian legislation we can imagine that at the same time, counts and other officials were made more clearly aware of the rights and duties in their care. We are therefore faced with a paradoxical situation in which more active intervention from the centre had the effect of strengthening the power of officials in the locality. But given that that intervention had not really eaten away at the social power of those who held land and had many clients, and who drew upon law and custom to protect their property and privilege, the overall effect of Carolingian rule was to strengthen the legitimation of the power of those who held both land and office. To this was added the moral legitimation which came from association with the regime. We may see here the basis for that devolution into units of comital power which characterises the post-Carolingian world of the later tenth and eleventh centuries. It is significant that the term 'district' was later used for such units, for the term is the past participle of *distringere*, and the very root of the count's power was the right to distrain, a right which had actually been sharpened by the Carolingian regime. From the tenth century onwards we see within the *districtus* a greater emphasis on custom, *consuetudines*, but these were changing from that custom which protected the rights of free people against the arbitrary use of power by the count, into rights which the count exploited to his own advantage. Again, we can argue that this change reflected a reinforcement of the counts authority which had come with the regimes blessing in the late eighth and early ninth centuries. The dislocation of the Carolingian state has often been explained by the politics of succession, which released forces opposed to the centre, but one could equally argue that the strengthening of the legitimation of power at first regional and then local levels was the consequence of the regime's activity, rather than of its inactivity and failure. It nevertheless remains true that a regime which sought legitimation through morality and victory would always remains a hostage to fortune. Military failure begged questions about fitness to rule, and we see a return to the old question about whether the person who had the 'name of king' had an unquestioned right to power. Addressing the young king Louis III in 881, Hincmar of Rheims reminded him that though he might be called 'king', this did not necessarily mean that he was capable of ruling.[40]

I would like to conclude with an important *caveat* to this dominant model of Carolingian rise and decline. We can never be sure that what we identify as change and development in the configuration of power at local level is not simply the result of an increase in the amount of evidence at our disposal. In other words, it may be the case that the increase in charter evidence from the mid eighth century onwards allows us to see for the first time patterns of local power which were in fact very much older. This is a possibility which Le Jan, or Innes, for instance, have never really taken on board. But a stress on what we might term sub-Roman continuities actually helps put the issue of legitimation into a clearer perspective. For we have seen that under the Merovingians royal authority which was in part derived from late Roman office conferred legitimacy. In this sense, power exercised through office was a primary source of legitimation, but this sat somewhat uneasily alongside local rights and

---

[40] Hincmar, address to Louis from the synod of Fismes, c. 8. He warns the young king: *ut nomine potius quam virtute regnetis.*

customs which legitimated social power in the locality. Locals, remember, could in theory bring about the death of the count if he infringed these rights. Conflict, however, ultimately had the effect of making power, or victory, the primary source of legitimation, and what followed was a discourse of justification, through which the first properly post-Roman ideas of legitimation were articulated. The Carolingians, we have seen, represented the Franks, that is, themselves, as better than and different from the Romans. Stress on moral legitimation, and upon the exercise of justice, in a rather abstract way gave a unifying legitimation to what remained a plurality of laws and customs. Because this arrangement could justify the exercise of power at all levels, it was both durable and eminently exportable. It could accommodate those shifts in relations of power which had their roots in economic growth, and those shifts in the balance of power which came from the vicissitudes of dynastic politics. Disparities of information from the localities, and across time, mean that ultimately we cannot say whether the Carolingians were the authors of, or simply the witnesses to, the stabilisation of power in the hands of local elites. But what we can say, is that it was through conflict that the Carolingians rose to power, and that it was the need to justify power gained in this way which led to the setting up of models of legitimation which others could interpret according to their needs.

Bibliography

Primary Sources

Alcuini Epistolae, ed. E. Dümmler, *MGH Epistolae* IV (Berlin: 1895) 18–481.
Annales Mettenses Priores, ed. B. von Simson, *MGH SRG* (Hanover and Leipzig: 1905), years 687–725 trans. with commentary Fouracre and Gerberding (1996) 350–70.
Capitulare Haristallense ('Capitulary of Herstal'), ed. A. Boretius, *MGH Capitularia Regum Francorum* I (Hanover 1883) 46–51.
Childeberti II Decretio, ed. A Boretius, *MGH Capitularia Regum Francorum* I (Hanover: 1883) 15–18.
Clotharii Edictum ('Edict of Paris'), ed. A. Boretius, *MGH Capitularia Regum Francorum* I (Hanover: 1883) 20–3.
Codex Carolinus ed. W. Grundlach, *MGH Epistolae* III (Berlin: 1892).
Concilium Liftinense ('Council of Estinnes'), ed. A. Werminghoff, *MGH Concilia* II, I (Hanover and Leipzig: 1906) 6–7.
Concilium Parisiense ('Council of Paris'), ed. C. de Clercq, *Conciliae Galliae a 511–695*, *Corpus Christianorum*, series latina 148A (Turnhout: 1963) 272–82.
Dhuoda, *LiberManualis. Dhuodane quem ad filium suam transmisit Whilhelmum*, ed. and trans. P. Riché, *Dhuoda, Manuel pour mon fils* (2nd edtn. Paris: 1991).

Die Urkunden der Merowinger, ed. T. Kölzer, *MGH Diplomata Regum Francorum e stirpe Merovingica* (Hanover: 2001).

Edictus Chilperici, ed. A. Boretius, *MGH Capitularia Regum Francorum* I (Hanover: 1883) 8–10.

Einhard, *The Life of Charlemagne*, ed. and trans. P. Dutton, *Charlemagne's Courtier. The Complete Einhard* (Ontario: 1998).

Hincmar, *Capitula in synodo apud S. Macram ('Synod of Fismes') c. 8 'ad regem'*, *PL* 121 i, cols. 1084–6.

Liber Historiae Francorum, ed. B. Krusch, *MGH SRM* II (Hanover: 1888), cc. 43–53 trans. with commentary Fouracre and Gerberding (1996) 87–96.

Marculfi Formularum Libri Duo, ed. and trans. A. Uddholm (Uppsala 1962).

Pactus Childeberti I et Clotharii I, ed. A. Boretius, *MGH Capitularia Regum Francorum* I (Hanover: 1883) 4–7.

Pactus Legis Salicae, ed. K. Eckhardt, *MGH Legum sectio* I, vol. 4, pt. 1, trans. K. Fischer Drew, *The Laws of the Salian Franks* (Pennsylavania: 1991).

Passiones Leudegarii Episcopi et Martyris Augustodunensis, ed. B. Krusch, *MGH SRM* 5 (Hanover: 1910) 249–363, *Passio Leudegarii* I, trans. with commentary Fouracre and Gerberding (1996) 193–253.

Passio Praejecti Episcopi et Martyris Arverni, ed. B. Krusch, *MGH SRM* 5 (Hanover: 1910) 225–48, trans. with commentary Fouracre and Gerberding (1996) 254–300.

Royal Frankish Annals, trans. B. Sholz, *Carolingian Chronicles* (Ann Arbor: 1972).

Synodus Frankofurtensis, ed. A. Boretius, *MGH Capitularia Regum Francorum I* (Hanover: 1883) 73–8.

The Chronicle of Theophanes, trans. C. Mango and R. Scott (Oxford: 1997).

The Theodosian Code, trans, C. Pharr (Princeton: 1952).

The Fourth Book of the Chronicle of Fredegar with its Continuations, ed. and trans. J.M. Wallace-Hadrill (London: 1960).

Secondary works

Airlie S. (1999) "Narratives of Triumph and Rituals of Submission: Charlemagne's Mastering of Bavaria", *Transactions of the Royal Historical Society*, 6th series, 9 (1999) 93–119.

Becher M. (1994) "Der sogenannte Staatsstreich Grimoalds. Versuch einer Neubewertung", in *Karl Martel in seiner Zeit*, ed. J. Jarnut, U. Nonn, M. Richter, Beihefte der *Francia* 37 (Sigmaringen: 1994) 119–47.

Breukelaar A. (1994) *Historiography and Episcopal Authority in sixth-century Gaul: The Histories of Gregory of Tours interpreted in their historical context* (Göttingen: 1994).

Fouracre P. (1995) "Carolingian justice: the rhetoric of improvement and contexts of abuse", in *La Giustizia nell 'alto Medieovo (secole V–VII)*, Settimane di Studio del Centro Italiano di Studi sull'alto Medieovo 42 (Spoleto: 1995) 771–803.

—— (1998) "The nature of Frankish political institutions in the seventh century", in *Franks and Alamanni in the Merovingian period. An ethnogrqphic perspective*, ed. I. Wood (Woodbridge) 285–301.

—— (1999) "The origins of the Carolingian attempt to regulate the cult of saints", in J. Howard-Johnston and P. Hayward (eds.), *The Cult of Saints in Late Antiquity and the Early Middle Ages* (Oxford: 1999) 143–66.

—— (2000a) "The Origins of the Nobility in Francia", in J. Duggan (ed.), *Nobles and Nobility in Medieval Europe* (Woodbridge: 2000) 17–24.

—— (2000b) *The Age of Charles Martel* (London: 2000).

—— (forthcoming) "The Long Shadow of the Merovingians", in J. Story (ed.), *Charlemagne* (Manchester forthcoming).

—— and Gerberding R. (1996) *Late Merovingian France. History and Hagiography 640–720* (Manchester: 1996).

Ganz D. (1995) "The ideology of sharing: apostolic community and ecclesiastical property in the early middle ages", in W. Davies and P. Fouracre (eds.), *Property and Power in the Early Middle Ages* (Cambridge: 1995) 17–30.

Gerberding R. (1987) *The Rise of the Carolingians and the Liber Historiae Francorum* (Oxford 1987).

Goffart W. (1988) *The Narrators of Barbarian History* (Princeton: 1988).

Hammer C. (1997) "Land sales in eighth and ninth century Bavaria: legal, social and economic aspects", *Early Medieval Europe* 6 (1997) 47–76.

Haselbach I. (1970) "Aufstieg und Herrschaft der Karolinger in der Darstellung der sogenannten *Annales Mettenses Piores*" *Historisches Studien* 412 (1970) 1–208.

Heinzelmann M. (1994) *Gregor von Tours (538–594) 'Zehn Bücher Geschichte': Historiographie und Gesellschaftskonzept im 6 Jahrhundert* (Darmstadt: 1994).

Innes M. (2000) *State and Society in the Early Middle Ages. The Middle Rhine Valley 400–1000* (Cambridge: 2000).

Le Jan R. (1995), *Famille et Pouvoir dans le Monde Franc (viie–xe siècle). Essai d'anthropologie sociale* (Paris: 1995).

McKitterick R. (1997) "Constructing the Past in the Early Middle Ages 2, *Transactions of the Royal Historical Society*, 6th series, 7 (1997) 101–29.

—— (2000) "The Illusion of Royal Power in the Carolingian Annals", *English Historical Review* 115 (2000) 1–20.

Morris R. "The powerful and the poor in tenth century Byzantium", *Past and Present* 73 (1976) 3–27.

Murray A.C. (1988) "From Roman to Frankish Gaul: 'Centenarii' and 'centenae' in the administration of the Merovingian kingdom", *Traditio* 44 (1988) 59–100.

—— (1998) "*Post vocantur Merohingii*: Fredegar, Merovech and 'Sacral Kingship'", in A.C. Murray (ed.), *After Rome's Fall. Narrators and Sources of Early Medieval History. Essays presented to Walter Goffart* (Toronto: 1998) 121–52.

Nelson J. (1977) "Kingship, Law and Liturgy in the Political Thought of Hincmar of Rheims", *English Historical Review* 92 (1977) 241–79, reprinted in Nelson J., *Politics and Ritual in Early Medieval Europe* (London: 1986) 133–72.

Prinz F. (1965) *Frühes Mönchtum im Frankenreich* (Munich: 1965).

Roberts S. (1979) *Order and Dispute. An Introduction to Legal Anthropology* (London: 1979).

—— (1983) "The study of disputes: anthropological perspectives, in J. Bossy (ed.), *Disputes and Settlements. Law and Human Relations in the West* (Cambridge: 1983) 1–24.

Wood I. (1994) *The Merovingian Kingdoms* (London: 1994).

A CRISIS OF FIDELITY IN C. 1000?

STEPHEN WHITE
Emory University

> "FÉODALITÉ. N'en avoir aucune idée précise, mais tonner contre."
>
> Gustave Flaubert, *Dictionnaire des idées reçues*

When in 1953 the late Georges Duby traced the abrupt transformation of a Carolingian society into a feudal society in the county of Mâcon between 980 and 1030, he broke this epoch-making change down into a sequence of three main developments: first, the collapse of Carolingian public institutions, notably the court of the count of Mâcon (*mallus publicus*), which the great lords of the county abandoned while simultaneously establishing themselves as independent lords of castles, that is, castellans; second, the usurpation and privatization by these newly independent castellans of the Carolingian *ban* (i.e. the power of command) that Carolingian public officials such as counts had previously monopolized; and, finally, the use of the *ban* by castellans to establish private lordships (*seigneuries banales*) over both slaves and free allodialists, who, in the new feudal society, merged together to form a newly constituted class of serfs in what had become, in Marxist terminology, a feudal, as opposed to a slave, mode of production.[1] Paradoxically, however, Duby firmly denied that the establishment of what F.L. Ganshof had called "feudalism . . . in the legal sense of word", that is, "the system of feudal and vassal institutions", had played a part in the transformation of the Mâconnais into a feudal society in the years around 1000.[2]

Duby had both empirical and theoretical grounds for taking this position on feudalism. In the eleventh-century Mâconnais, he found that fiefs, as compared with allods, were relatively unimportant; that "the relationship of vassalage [was] a tie of mutual friendship similar

---

[1] Duby (1953).
[2] Ganshof (1964) xvi.

to that which bound the family together", just as it had been in the
tenth century; and that "personal relationships" among nobles were
complicated by the "inheritance and exchange of [feudal] tenures",
and by "plurality of homage".[3] Moreover, instead of following historians
of feudal institutions in treating feudal lordship as the only existing
form of political power over nobles in the eleventh-century Mâconnais,
Duby argued that nobles were constrained by political pressures exercised through social networks constituted by several different kinds
of ties, including fidelity, associations with religious communities, and,
above all, kinship, which together constituted a more important force
for political cohesion than did lordship, though conflicts chronically
arose out of all such ties, including ties between lords and men.[4] It
was these changing social networks and not a feudal system, Duby
implied, that constituted the political arena in which aristocratic politics were played out in the eleventh-century Mâconnais. Finally,
instead of regarding the fief and vassalage as legal institutions that
regulated, determined and legitimated aristocratic politics in early
feudal society in the Mâconnais, Duby maintained that

> in the final analysis, feudal institutions were adapted to the previous
> structure of the upper class, without significantly modifying it. . . .
> Vassalage and fief, customary practices born of private usage, organized
> the relationships already imposed by an unequal division of wealth
> and power. They did not create new ones. In [the] eleventh-century
> Mâconnais there was no feudal pyramid, no 'feudal system'.[5]

Although Duby never specified precisely when the customary practices
of fief and vassalage appeared, he clearly implied that they had
existed well before the transformation of a Carolingian society in the
Mâconnais into a feudal one.

Duby's revisionist positions on both feudalism in the legal sense of
the word and the place of this form of feudalism in early feudal
society in the Mâconnais foreshadowed several later critiques of the
same concept of feudalism as a theoretical construct, including his
own pointed observation in *The Three Orders* that 'the fief' had nothing

---

[3] Duby (1953) 163–4. I follow the translation in G. Duby (1968) 144–5. Preceding
this revisionist discussion of feudal institutions was a relatively conventional treatment of them, *ib.* 149–58. Duby later acknowledged that in studying the Mâconnais,
"I found precious little evidence concerning the fief before the time of Philip
Augustus". Duby (1994) 51.
[4] Duby (1968) 165–7; see also Duby (1980) 49, 58.
[5] Duby (1968) 164; Cheyette (1968) 144.

to do with what he then saw as a European-wide feudal revolution in the mode of production in c. 1000.[6] However, unlike his account of the collapse of Carolingian public institutions in the county, the formation of the *seigneurie banale*, and establishment of a new class structure in rural society, his views on feudalism did not significantly influence subsequent regional studies of the establishment of feudal society and, in fact, were flatly contradicted by Pierre Bonnassie's findings about the transformation of a Romano-Visigothic public order in Catalonia into a feudal society. In this part of the old West Frankish kingdom, Bonnassie maintained, the development of feudo-vassalic institutions created by feudal contracts was an integral part of a feudal revolution that also involved the establishment of a feudal mode of production. Like the transformation in the Mâconnais between 980–1030 that Duby had traced, the Catalan feudal revolution in c. 1020, according to Bonnassie, overthrew the antecedent system of public order maintained by the count of this region, established private banal lordships as units of seigneurial exploitation of peasants, and replaced a slave mode of production with a feudal one. Moreover, in Bonnassie's Catalonia, unlike Duby's Mâconnais, the feudal revolution also led to the establishment of truly feudal institutions and creation of a feudal system, that is, feudalism in the legal sense of the word.[7]

Before 1020, Bonnassie contended, there was no "true feudalism" in Catalonia. "The fief remained a strictly public institution, a public property granted by the count to reward public service", while "the vassalic network seems to have been confined to the count's own followers", whom Bonnassie identified as public officials, not private dependents of the count.[8] From c. 1020 onwards, however, feudalism was established in Catalonia, as one could see from the proliferation of documents called *convenientiae*, in which a lord and a man "agreed between them, freely and without the intervention of any public or private jurisdiction, the definition of the obligations binding one to

---

[6] Duby (1980) 153. On the connections between Duby's revisionist views on feudalism, a concept that he never fully abandoned, and later critiques of this concept, see Cheyette (1968) 1–10; Brown (1974) 1063–88; White (1996) 223–30; White (forthcoming a); and Cheyette (forthcoming), which I thank the author for graciously allowing me to read and cite in advance of its publication.

[7] See Bonnassie (1991) 170–94, which lucidly and concisely sets out Bonnassie's position on Catalan feudalism. For other versions of this argument see (1991) 149–69; 104–32; (1976) 2:735–80; and (2000) 2:569–606.

[8] Bonnassie (1991) 187.

the other, and guaranteed their execution by solemn agreement".[9]
Convenientiae, according to Bonnassie, appeared at a time when Catalan
society was experiencing "a rapid development—even a veritable revolution—of which the *convenientiae* constitute one of the most spectacular
evidences".[10] The totality of such agreements constituted a system
that Bonnassie identified as "the basis of social relations and, especially, of feudal relations in eleventh-century Catalonia".[11] In contrast to the early feudal society that Duby portrayed in his study of
the Mâconnais, early feudal society in Catalonia was organized into
a feudal system, in which vassalage and the fief were regulated by
feudal contracts that created and legitimated new legal relationships,
instead of simply organizing relationships "already imposed", as Duby
had put it, "by an unequal division of wealth and power". In arguing that "true feudalism" had not existed in Catalonia before 1020
but suddenly came into being thereafter as part of a feudal revolution, Bonnassie established a new paradigm for studying feudalism,
the feudal revolution, and feudal society in the southern regions of
the old West Frankish kingdom, and elsewhere in southwest Europe.[12]
In their important study, *The Feudal Transformation (La mutation féodale)*, Jean-Pierre Poly and Eric Bournazel deployed a version of
Bonnassie's paradigm for the purpose of analyzing an even larger
territory of Europe.[13]

Bonnassie's paradigm now provides the starting-point for Thomas
N. Bisson's recent, highly original argument that in the northern parts
of old West Frankish kingdom, which he calls northern Francia for
the sake of convenience, the proliferation of fiefs in c. 1000 triggered
'a crisis of fidelity' marking the transformation of Carolingian political structures, based on the principle that fidelity and service to
public officials was a public obligation, into feudal political structures,
based on feudal agreements under which private lords could secure
fidelity and service from vassals only by giving them fiefs.[14] As a
result of this revolution in political structures in c. 1000, according to
Bisson, northern Francia, not to mention the rest of Europe, became,
for the next two centuries "a place even less like ours than it had

---

[9] Bonnassie (1991) 170.
[10] Bonnassie (1991) 187.
[11] Bonnassie (1991) 184.
[12] Bonnassie (1991).
[13] Poly and Bournazel (1991).
[14] Bisson (1994) 21–8.

been".[15] In a subsequent article Bisson acknowledges that in different regions, "feudalization", as he calls it, took different forms, proceeded at different rates, and did not necessarily involve either a feudal revolution or the complete overthrow of Carolingian political structures. But he still identifies the proliferation of fiefs and feudalization generally—and not the transformation of a slave mode of production into a feudal one—as the motor driving the transformation of the regional societies in northern Francia.[16] In emphasizing the importance of Bonnassie's conclusions about Catalan feudalism for the study of feudalism in northern Francia, Bisson sharply criticizes Duby for failing to see how important the proliferation of fiefs in c. 1000 was for an understanding the feudal revolution.[17] Bisson also criticizes unnamed 'critics of feudalism' for overlooking the findings of "specialists familiar with the sources", who had discovered in the South "concrete realities of lordship, vassalage, and feudal tenure that were wholly exempt from conceptual anachronism".[18] These critics, according to Bisson, were "false prophets", who had forgotten and had induced their readers to forget that "if 'feudalism' is dispensable in medieval history, lordship, vassalage, feudal tenure, homage, and fealty assuredly are not", since they are, as he put it, "documented realities".[19]

To document the reality of a crisis of fidelity in c. 1000 in the North, Bisson cites several late tenth-century episodes from Richer's *History of France*, in which he sees "the tension between old public order and the new vassalic régime [flaring] into visible conflict"; letters of Gerbert of Aurillac, "whose writings are full of anxiety about fidelity and its violation"; and the chapter "On the king's fidelity" in Abbo of Fleury's *Canons*.[20] Bisson also cites the well-known letter on fidelity by Fulbert of Chartres from c. 1021, which, as he reads it, shows "concretely how benefices and rewards were muddying the waters of good faith" between *fideles* and their lords; and the Conventum of Hugh of Lusignan (late 1020s), in which Bisson finds evidence of the collapse of public order and public fidelity in early eleventh-century Poitou and the advent of a new vassalic régime closely resembling the feudal system that been established, according to Bonnassie, in early

---

[15] Bisson (1997) 225.
[16] Bisson (2000) 1:389–439.
[17] Bisson (1994) 23.
[18] Bisson (2000) 391.
[19] Bisson (2000) 437–8.
[20] Bisson (1994) 24–5.

eleventh-century Catalonia.[21] All of these texts, as Bisson reads them, document "a crisis of fidelity in the millenial generation . . . Without ceasing to be a public obligation, fidelity, or more exactly its sworn content, was being tainted by a vassalage more demanding than it had been in Carolingian times—and far more prevalent".[22]

In the following brief comment on one part of Bisson's argument about feudalism, I consider two main questions: first, does the model of the old Carolingian public order that underlies his account of a crisis of fidelity in c. 1000 accurately represent Carolingian political practice? Second, do Fulbert's letter on fidelity and the Conventum of Hugh of Lusignan clearly document the collapse of that order and the advent of a new vassalic régime in which good faith between *fideles* and their lords had been corrupted by gifts of fiefs?[23]

I

Recent work on Carolingian politics, including Susan Reynolds's important critique of the concept of feudalism, calls into question the stark contrast that historians of France since Duby have made between Carolingian public order and the private régime of feudalism. Brilliantly synthesizing this work, Janet L. Nelson tacitly rejects the assumption that Carolingian rulers maintained a kind of public order that was untainted by the kinds of "gifts and rewards" that Bisson associates with a corrupted form of the old Carolingian order and with an emergent vassalic régime.[24] On the contrary, Nelson interprets "patronage in the form of [royal] land grants" from conquered territories, the royal fisc, ecclesiastical estates, and "estates confiscated from the faithless" as ordinary instruments of Carolingian royal power.[25] Land grants to followers, she further explains, were also instruments of aristocratic power, including the power of counts, who, far from act-

---

[21] Bisson (1994) 26–7. See *The Letters and Poems of Fulbert of Chartres* (1976), no. 51; and Beech, Chauvin, and Pon (1995) 123–38 with French and English translations at pp. 139–47 and pp. 147–53 respectively. For another edition of the *Conventum* with facing English translation, see Martindale (1997) chap. VIIb.

[22] Bisson (1994) 27.

[23] For my comments on other aspects of Bisson's argument in 'Feudal Revolution', see White (1996) 205–23.

[24] Nelson (1995) 383–431 and the bibliography 951–8. Prof. Nelson bears no responsibility for the interpretation I have placed on her work.

[25] Nelson (1995) 384, 386–7, 392–5, 412–5.

ing as accountable public officials of the Carolingian state, "used
their own lands to build up what would later be called affinities of
men (often kinsmen) holding land from them and dependent on their
patronage".[26] Because "political crisis", she finds, "can be documented
by a fall in numbers of grants, the defusing of crisis by a marked
rise as the ruler rewarded supporters", the exercise of political power
must have depended on the effective use of patronage and the ability to confiscate the estates of their former supporters for "treason,
and disloyal service" and grant them out to supporters.[27] If so, then
the lands that Carolingian kings and other lords gave to *fideles* cannot have been discretionary rewards for service. On the contrary,
such gifts should be seen as instances of the necessary generosity of
lords to their supporters without which Carolingian expansion would
have been impossible.

By the same token, *fideles* cannot have been faithful to lords purely
as a matter of public obligation, untainted by the expectation of
rewards, including, in some cases, rewards in the form of land grants.
Instead of being precisely dictated by the specific terms of the oath
of fidelity, political relations between lords and *fideles* were evidently
negotiated, in Susan Reynolds's terms, with reference to two conflicting
norms, one privileging the claims of lords on their *fideles* and the
other privileging the "mutuality of obligations" as between lords and
their *fideles*.[28] Whereas lords could back up their claims to the loyalty and support of their *fideles* with the threat of confiscating their
lands, *fideles* could sometimes back up their claims to rewards from
their lords, Nelson's argument implies, by deserting them, rebelling
against them, or threatening to do one or the other. Although Nelson
regards "ideas of shared participation in public duties and benefits,
of generalized commitment" as "essential elements of Carolingian
government", she treats the inculcation of such ideas, not as an
accomplished fact, but as an unfinished political project of particular rulers and advisors, who attempted to legitimate public claims of
the kind that Bisson's model of Carolingian politics treats as legally
binding and automatically efficacious.[29]

---

[26] Nelson (1995) 412.
[27] Nelson (1995) 392, 386.
[28] Reynolds (1994) 34–5. On oaths of fidelity, see Reynolds (1994) 86–9, 127–30;
Magnou-Nortier (1969) 115–42; Cheyette (1999) 166–77; and Cheyette (2001) 187–247.
[29] Nelson (1995) 426, 429, 430.

As Nelson explains, moreover, Charlemagne incorporated

> into his own rulership . . . notions of lordship, freedom and reciprocal
> duty that would have universal appeal. When he demanded an oath
> of fidelity from "'all", according to a capitulary dated between 787
> and 792, he also "sent *missi* to explain that he was well aware that
> many complain that their law had not been kept for them; and that
> it is totally the will of the lord king that each man should have his
> law fully kept." What *lex sua* meant can be reconstructed from two
> later statements. A further oath of fidelity in 802, Charlemagne said,
> meant that each was thereby obliged not to harm "the *honor* of the
> realm" but to be faithful "as a man in right ought to be to his lord"
> [*sicut homo per drictum debet esse domino suo*].[30]

In a section of capitulary dated 802–803, moreover,

> Charlemagne forbade anyone to abandon his lord have once accepted
> the symbolic lordly gift of a shilling "unless"—and here follow four
> conditions: "unless his lord seeks to kill him, or assaults him with a
> stave, or debauches his wife or daughter, or takes away his allodial
> property". Life, personal immunity from degrading physical violence,
> patriarchal rights in his female dependents, patrimony: these consti-
> tuted a man's *lex*, and at the same time, by setting limits on what a
> lord could do, provided legitimate grounds for rejecting lordship.[31]

Further evidence that the obligations of lord and *fidelis* were assumed
to be reciprocal, even if the reciprocity in question was unbalanced,
can be found in later capitularies. "In 843"—Nelson writes—"Charles
the Bald elaborated on his grandfather's words: while his *fideles* promised in turn to uphold the king's *honor*, Charles promised to keep
for each his due law in each rank and status . . . and not to deprive
anyone of his *honor* without just cause".[32] For evidence of the same
kind of reciprocity between Charles and his *fideles* one can look to the
oaths that the former and the latter exchanged in 858 and in 876.[33]

---

[30] Nelson (1995) 425. For the capitulary of 787/792 see *MGH*, I, no. 25 (787/792),
c. 4, p. 67. For the oath of 802, *ib.* I, no. 34, p. 101, which reads: *Sacramentale
qualiter repromitto ego: domno Karolo piissimo imperatori, filio Pippini regis et Berthane fidelis
sum, sicut homo per drictum debet esse domino suo ad suum regnum et ad suum rectum. Et illud
sacramentum quo iuratum habeo custodiam and custodire volvo, in quantum ego scio et intellego,
ab isto die in antea, si me adiuvet Deus, qui coelum et terram creavit et ista sanctorum patrocinia.*

[31] Nelson (1995) 425, citing *MGH Capit.* I, no. 77 (802/03), c. 16 (p. 172), which
is quoted below in n. 46, along with another passage to the same purpose from
another capitulary, this one dated 801–813.

[32] Nelson (1995) 425, citing *MGH Capit.* II, no. 254 (843), c. 3, p. 255.

[33] Boretius (1883) *Capit.* II, no. 269 (858), p. 296; and *Capit.* II, no. 220 (876),
p. 100.

Because Nelson's argument shows that no system of public order and fidelity untainted by expectations of reciprocity between ruler and *fidelis* or by rewards, including land grants, had ever existed during the Carolingian era, it obviously conflicts with Bisson's contention that this same system either underwent a terminal crisis in c. 1000 or was transformed more slowly through a process of feudalization. Moreover, by rejecting the static model of Carolingian public order that provides a backdrop for arguments that a longer or shorter process of feudalization transformed and privatized this public order and by replacing it with a dynamic model of Carolingian politics that highlights political contradictions, conflict and change, Nelson's work also raises doubts about whether further political changes in the years around 1000 necessarily involved any kind of radical, epoch-making transformation in aristocratic politics.[34]

II

Did this change involve the establishment of a vassalic régime in which benefices and rewards undermined good faith between *fideles* and their lords? Bisson's argument for this position rests largely on his readings of the Conventum of Hugh of Lusignan and the famous letter of bishop Fulbert of Chartres to William, duke of Aquitaine, the same William who appears in the Conventum as the count of Poitou and the lord (*senior*) of Hugh of Lusignan. Reading the bishop's letter as an authoritative explication of a contractual or quasi-contractual agreement between a lord and his *fidelis*, Bisson uses it as evidence of how, during the years around 1000,

> benefices and rewards were muddying the waters of good faith. A *fidelis*, [Fulbert] wrote (at Duke William's request) must not only "abstain from wrong [but also] do what is right if he is to deserve his *casamentum*." This term, while evidently synonymous with *beneficium*, suggests that Fulbert had knights as well as magnates in mind. It is the word that he had applied to the holdings of his sub-vassal knights at Vendôme and Chartres in 1008, in letters that mark the earliest known of a lord to define the substance of (lesser) knightly fealty. By 1020 Fulbert was known for his concerned authority in such matters.[35]

---

[34] Nelson (1994) 163–9; and Nelson (1986) 45–64. For a broad attack on so-called *mutationnisme*, see Barthélemy (1997). For references to other critiques of the same argument, see White (forthcoming b).

[35] Bisson (1994) 26.

To identify the *casamentum* just mentioned as the *fidelis*'s *casamentum* is to assume that it was not a benefice or reward of the kind that a Carolingian *fidelis* might have received from his lord, but rather a fief, which the lord had already given to the *fidelis* and in return for which the *fidelis* was obliged to "do what is right", instead of being obliged to do right to his lord as a matter of public obligation.[36]

If, however, we do not base a reading of Fulbert's letter on the unsubstantiated assumption that it was an authoritative interpretation of a new kind of agreement between a lord and his *fidelis*, we can interpret it as a gloss on a man's oath of fidelity to his lord, one that Fulbert sent to William as a friend, *fidelis*, and political ally in order to counsel him faithfully about the legal basis of the claims that lords, including both William and Fulbert himself, could legitimately make on their *fideles*, including those who held benefices from them and those who did not.[37] In other words, Fulbert's letter provided the makings of what Pierre Bourdieu has called an "officializing strategy" that lords could use to show that their claims on their *fideles* were legitimate, being based on the binding oaths of fidelity that these men had sworn to them.[38] To be sure, ancient texts such as Cicero's *De inventione* provided the phraseology of the introductory part of Fulbert's letter; but when it came to explicating the oath of fidelity that a *fidelis* was supposed to swear to his lord, the bishop used terms identical or similar to the ones used during the years around 1000 in surviving oaths of fidelity from Occitania and, as we shall see, in

---

[36] In certain respects, Bisson's reading of Fulbert's of the letter resembles that of Ganshof, according to whom the letter presented "a remarkable definition of the obligations created by the contract of vassalage" and who translated a critical passage from the letter as follows: "It is only right that the vassal should abstain from injuring his lord in any of [the ways just mentioned]. But it is not because of such abstention that he deserves to hold *his* fief" (Ganshof, 1964, 83; italics added). For other examples of this conventional way of translating Fulbert's letter, see Guillot and Sassier (1994) 192; Boutruche (1959) 369–70. Ganshof's chronology of the history of feudalism, however, differed significantly from the one Bisson now proposes. Arguing that "the legal union of vassalage and benefice" took place in Charlemagne's reign or, at the very latest, in the reign of Charles the Bald, Ganshof asserted that "the disintegrative effects" of vassalage became evident in the ninth century (*ib.* 42–3, 50, 56–9). On the "union" of vassalage and benefice (or fief), see White (forthcoming a).

[37] The discussion here owes much to the valuable comments on Fulbert's letter in Reynolds (1994) 20, 23, 38, 127–8; also 35, where she neatly identifies Fulbert as "that supposed theorist of feudo-vassalic values."

[38] On 'officializing strategies' see Bourdieu (1977) 40.

the Conventum of Hugh of Lusignan.[39] In several respects, the oath of fidelity that Fulbert glossed in the letter resembled both Occitan oaths of fidelity from the years around 1000 and oaths of fidelity sworn to Carolingian rulers such as Charlemagne and Charles the Bald, who, as Nelson shows, acknowledged their obligations to their *fideles*, sometimes by swearing reciprocal oaths to them, as does the lord in Fulbert's letter to William of Aquitaine.[40] Finally, the oath of fidelity to a lord that Fulbert commented upon in his letter to William evidently indicated, as did Occitanian oaths, that the *fidelis*'s violation of the terms of the oath amounted to perjury.[41]

Fulbert began his letter to William by stating that "he who swears fidelity to his lord should always keep the six terms in mind: safe and sound, secure, honorable, useful, easy, possible".[42] The bishop then explained these terms as follows:

> Safe and sound, that is, not to cause his lord any harm [*dampnum*] with respect to his body [*de corpore suo*]. Secure, that is, not to cause him harm [*dampnum*] with respect to his secrets or his fortresses [*municionibus*] through which it is possible for him to be safe. Honorable [*honestum*], that is, not to do anything that would cause harm [*dampnum*] with respect to his rights of justice or to other matters pertaining to his honor. Useful, not to cause him any harm [*dampnum*] with respect to his possessions [*possessionibus*]. Easy and possible, not to make it difficult for his lord to do something that would be of value to him and that he could otherwise do with ease, or to render it impossible for him to do what was otherwise possible.[43]

---

[39] On Fulbert's borrowings from Cicero, see Carozzi, "Introduction" (1981) lxiv–lxviii.

[40] While noting that Occitanian oaths of fidelity taken by lords to their men are very rare, Magnou-Nortier notes that, in other respects, they resembled Carolingian oaths (1969) 16–19.

[41] Magnou-Nortier (1969) 122–23; possible penalties for perjury also included cutting off right hand, according to Poly and Bournazel (1991) 149–50.

[42] Fulbert, *Letters*, no. 51: *Qui domino suo fidelitatem iurat, ista sex in memoria semper habere debet: incolumne, tutum, honestum, utile, facile, possibile.* Here and elsewhere, my translation of this letter largely follows that of Frederick Behrends in Fulbert, *Letters*, no. 51 (90–93).

[43] Fulbert, *Letters*, no. 51: *Incolumne uidelicet, ne sit dampnum domino de corpore suo. Tutum, ne sit ei in dampnum de secreto suo uel de municionibus per quas tutus esse potest. Honestum, ne sit ei in dampnum de suo iustitia uel de aliis causis quae ad honestem eius pertinere uiderentur. Vtile, ne sit ei in dampnum de suis possessionibus. Facile uel possibile, ne id bonum quod dominus leuiter facere poterat faciat ei difficile, neue id quo possibile erat, reddat ei impossibile.* In sharply distinguishing between the *fidelis*'s negative obligations not to harm to his lord, on the one hand, and his positive obligations to give his lord aid and counsel, on the other, historians of feudal institutions have overlooked the positive dimensions of

Having shown that a *fidelis* should not harm his lord in any of these ways, Fulbert then explained what the *fidelis* needed to do in order to be rewarded with a *casamentum* and not, as Bisson and other commentators would have it, to merit "his *casamentum*", that is land that he had already received as part of a feudal agreement with his lord.

> That a *fidelis* should avoid inflicting injuries on his lord [with respect to the six matters just mentioned] is just, but not in this way does he earn a *casamentum*; for it is not enough to abstain from evil [*a malo*], it is also necessary to do good [*bonum*]. So it remains for him to give his lord counsel and aid [*consilium et auxilium*] faithfully with respect to the same six matters if he wishes to be seen as worthy of a *beneficium* and to be secure as to the fidelity [*de fidelitate*] that he has sworn.[44]

In conclusion, Fulbert wrote,

> The lord, in his turn, ought to treat his *fidelis* similarly with respect to each of the six matters [just mentioned]. If he does not do so, he will rightfully be considered to be of ill-faith [*malefidus*], just as the *fidelis*, if he is caught violating any of them by his own actions or by giving counsel [to others], will be considered perfidious [*perfidus*] and perjured [*periurus*].[45]

As this way of rendering Fulbert's letter indicates, the bishop did not state or imply that the relationship between a lord and his *fidelis* was created by a feudal agreement or contract under which the lord granted a man a *casamentum* in return for which the man then became the lord's *fidelis* by swearing an oath of fidelity obligating him not only to abstain from doing wrong to his lord in the six ways already mentioned but also to do what was right, namely give his lord aid and counsel with respect to the same six matters. Instead, the letter simply represented the lord's gift of a benefice to the *fidelis* as being contingent on the *fidelis* earning it by fulfilling the terms of his oath

---

the *fidelis*'s so-called "negative" obligations, which, in a world where political neutrality was virtually impossible to maintain, effectively required the *fidelis* to dissociate himself totally from anyone who was not his lord's friend and active supporter.

[44] Fulbert, *Letters*, no. 51: *Ut fidelis haec nocumenta caueat iustum est, sed non ideo casamentum meretur. Non enim sufficit abstinere a malo, nisi fiat quod bonum est. Restat ergo ut in eisdem sex supradictis consilium et auxilium domino suo fideliter prestet, si beneficio dignus uideri uult, et saluus esse de fidelitate quam iurauit.* The last phrase could have been construed so as to indicate that a *fidelis* had so-called 'positive' obligations to his lord, whether or not he had received a benefice from him.

[45] Fulbert, *Letters*, no. 51: *Dominus quoque fideli suo in his omnibus uicem reddere debet. Quod si non fecerit, merito censibitur malefidus, sicut ille, si in eorum preuaricacione uel faciendo uel consenciendo deprehensus fuerit, perfidus et periurus.*

of fidelity to his lord—a position that hardly amounts to a dramatic change from Carolingian patronage practices. The *fidelis*, according to Fulbert, would not be considered worthy of a *beneficium* or be discharged of his obligations under the oath of fidelity he had sworn to his lord unless he faithfully counseled and aided his lord with respect to the same six matters mentioned above. If he were to be caught violating any of these obligations, he would be judged unfaithful and perjured, in which case, by implication, his lord would be entitled, at the very least, to confiscate his *beneficium* and give it to others. While construing the obligations of the *fidelis* to his lord very broadly, the letter also indicated that under the terms of an oath that the lord evidently swore to his *fidelis*, the lord had parallel obligations to *fidelis*, whom the lord was obliged not to harm with respect to the same six matters. Under one reading, the letter also implies that that the lord was obliged "to give his [*fidelis*] counsel and aid faithfully" with respect to these same matters. Nevertheless, the letter treats the lord's obligations to his *fidelis* as being weightier than the *fidelis*'s obligations to his lord by implying that penalties for violating the former were more serious than were the penalities for violating the latter.

In stating that the lord had obligations to his *fidelis* that were virtually identical to the *fidelis*'s obligations to his lord but that the *fidelis* evidently had no legal way of enforcing, Fulbert does not appear to have been proposing a novel interpretation of a lord's obligations to his *fidelis*. From a comparison of Fulbert's general statement of these obligations with statements from two capitularies of Charlemagne's, one of them discussed by Nelson in a passage cited above, about the specific obligations whose violation gave a man grounds for abandoning his lord, one can see that all of the obligations mentioned in the two capitularies can be subsumed under the general categories of harm (*dampnum*) that lords swore not to cause their *fideles* and that *fideles* swore not to cause their lords. According to the capitulary of 802–803 discussed by Nelson, a man had grounds for abandoning his lord if the lord had tried to kill him or assault him with a stave [i.e. tried to harm him with respect to his life or members], or had tried to violate debauch his wife or daughter [i.e. tried to harm him with respect to his honor], or had deprived the vassal of part of his patrimony [i.e. harmed him with respect to his possessions or fortresses]. A man could also abandon his lord, according to a passage in another capitulary, this one dated 801–813, if the lord had tried to reduce

him to servitude unjustly [i.e. tried to harm him with respect to his
honor and possessions], plotted against his life [i.e. tried to harm
him with respect to his body or members], committed adultery with
his wife [i.e. harmed him with respect to his honor] intentionally
fallen on him with his unsheathed sword [i.e. tried to harm him
with respect to body], or had failed to defend him as the lord ought
to have done after the vassal had commended himself to his lord
with his hands [had failed to give him aid faithfully].[46] What distinguishes Fulbert's statement about a lord's obligations to his man
from the two passages just cited is that it was vague, as the two
capitularies were not, about the possible consequences of the lord's
violating his obligations to his men.

By privileging in this way the obligations of the *fidelis* to his lord
over the latter's obligations to the former and by treating the *fidelis*'s
right to a *beneficium* as being contingent on his being faithful to his
lord in the ways that the letter explicates, Fulbert's letter shows that
a traditional oath of fidelity could be interpreted so as to legitimate
the lord's broad claims on his *fidelis*, while making it difficult if not
impossible in practice for the *fidelis* to call the lord to account for
failing to observe his own obligations of fidelity to his *fidelis*. Under
this reading, the letter does not document the appearance of a new
vassalic régime, much less the establishment of so-called classical feudalism; nor does it show that gifts of fiefs were undermining the
fidelis's fidelity to his lord or that lords were being forced to assume
new obligations to their *fideles*. Instead, the letter provided William—
and, by extension, other lords—with a template for making very serious claims on the loyalty of any *fidelis* to whom a lord had given a
benefice and for threatening him with confiscation of the benefice
and possibly other sanctions for any violation of his many demanding obligations to his lord.

---

[46] *Quod nullus seniorem suum dimittat postquam ab eo acciperit valente solido uno, excepto si
eum vult occidere, aut cum baculo caedere, vel uxorem aut filiam maculare, seu hereditatem ei
tollere* (*MGH Capit.* I, no. 77 [802–3], c. 16 [p. 172]). *Si quis seniorem suum dimittere
voluerit et ei approbare potuerit unum de his criminibus: id est primo capitulo si senior eum iniuste
in servitio redigere voluerit; secondo capitulo si in vita eius consiliaverit; tertio capitulo si senior
vassalli sui uxorem adulteraverit; quarto capitulo si evaginato gladio super eum occidere voluntarie
occurrerit; quinto capitulo si senior vassalli sui defensionem facere potest postquam ipse manus
suas in eius commendaverit et non fecerit, liceat vassallum eum dimittere. Qualecumque de istis
quinque capitulis senior contra vassallum suum perpetraverit, liceat vassallum eum dimittere*
(*MGH, Capit.* II, no. 104 [801–813], c. 8 [p. 215]). On these two texts, see Ganshof
(1969) 31; and Boutruche (1959) 1: 190–2 and 364–5.

Two other letters of Fulbert's provide examples of the kinds of claims on his *fideles* that a lord could make by construing the oath of fidelity as he did in his letter to William. Consider, first, Fulbert's letter to Bishop Reginald of Paris:

> This is what I require of you: assurance as to my life and limbs and the land which I have or shall acquire with your advice, as to your aid against all men saving the fidelity you owe [king] Robert, and as to the handing over of Vendôme castle for me and my *fideles* to use, for which they will give you surety; the commendation of your *milites*, who hold a *beneficium* from our *casamentum*, saving the fidelity they owed you; justice as to the complaint of Sanctio and Hubert, as to the complaints of the canons of our church, and as to the laws of our court.[47]

Here, Fulbert demands, in effect, that Reginald observe the terms of his oath of fidelity to Fulbert by not harming Fulbert's body, his fortifications, his possessions or his powers of justice. Fulbert also demands that Reginald aid him against all men except king Robert and counsel him faithfully with respect the land that he holds or will acquire through Reginald's counsel.[48] Another letter of Fulbert's, this one to the nobles in the Vendômois who held land from the church of Saint Mary of Chartres by the gift of bishop Reginald, illustrates both the claims that, under the terms of Fulbert's letter to Duke William, a lord could make on *fideles* of his who held land from his church and the sanctions that the lord could threaten to impose on them. Summoning and admonishing them to do service to the church of Chartres or else present a legal argument for not doing so, Fulbert wrote that if they did neither, he would excommunicate them, lay an interdict on the castle of Vendôme and its territory, give the lands they held from the church of Chartres to others, and never make any settlement with them about these lands.[49]

Despite the obvious differences between some of the powers that Fulbert wielded as a bishop and the ones that Duke William of Aquitaine wielded as a lay magnate, the authority that Fulbert represents himself as having over on his *fideles* is virtually identical to the authority that duke William, according to the Conventum, exercised or tried to exercise over Hugh of Lusignan when he broke

---

[47] Fulbert, *Letters*, no. 9 (1008).
[48] For another reading of Fulbert's letter, see Poly and Bournazel (1991) 148–50; and Bournazel (1998) 409.
[49] Fulbert, *Letters*, no. 10 (1008), pp. 20–3.

agreements with Hugh, blocked Hugh's agreements with other lords, and refused to make settlements that he had promised to make for Hugh. The count also demanded the hostages that Hugh had taken in disputes with other lords, demanded control over fortresses to which Hugh had claims by right of inheritance, and ordered Hugh to become the man of other lords.[50]

As Hugh's lord, was William legally entitled to exercise authority over Hugh in these ways? Bisson assumes that he was, at least under Carolingian principles of public fidelity and that Hugh could have had no normative basis for contesting the authority that William exercised or tried to exercise over him. William's 'problem', he writes,

> was that Hugh lord of Lusignan could not be content with a fidelity of submission that left the count free to alter agreements bearing on Hugh's interest without consulting him. When Hugh did the same in reverse, as if his armed and ambitious clientele entitled him to an equal claim to his lord-count's good faith, there was trouble: vengeful seizures and devastations over alleged violations of good faith and sworn commitments relating to the control or inheritance of castles and lordships. All that is left of public order here is the tenacious recognition that complaints should be pleaded openly and procedurally.[51]

Here, Bisson posits the existence of an old, moribund Carolingian public order, for which Nelson finds no evidence, and an emerging vassalic régime, for which Duby found no evidence in the eleventh-century Mâconnais and which he and other historians have criticized as an inadequate model for analyzing eleventh-century aristocratic politics.[52] If we read the Conventum against the two oaths of fidelity that Fulbert discusses in his letter to William of Aquitaine, roughly contemporaneous oaths of fidelity from Occitania, and the ninth-century Carolingian texts pertaining to fidelity that Nelson has discussed, the Conventum appears in a totally different light from the one Bisson places it in. Representing the dispute between William and Hugh from the latter's perspective, the Conventum shows, as I have argued elsewhere, that whereas Hugh faithfully fulfilled the terms of his oaths of fidelity to William, William was a traitor who

---

[50] See White (1993) 147–57; and Beech (1995) 123–38.

[51] Bisson (1994) 26–7.

[52] In addition to criticisms of feudalism in the legal sense of the word that are found in works cited elsewhere in this paper, see Barthélemy (1997a) 321–41; and *idem* (1993) 621, where Barthélemy argues that in the Vendômois, kinship and vassalage constituted "a double system of solidarity (or confrontation)."

had consistently acted in bad faith in his dealings with Hugh. The Conventum achieves this rhetorical effect, not by baldly asserting Hugh's power to act as he did or by citing new-found feudal principles, but rather by repeatedly using words and phrases from the oaths of fidelity that William and Hugh had evidently exchanged and that also provided the basis for the statements in Fulbert's letter to William about the obligations of a *fidelis* to his lord and a lord to his *fideles*. Unlike Fulbert's letter to William, however, the Conventum invokes the terms of this oath in such a way as to justify Hugh's claims on his lord William and his decision to defy his lord and wage a *guerra* against him. In this way the Conventum gives greater weight than does Fulbert's letter to the kind of reciprocal good faith between lord and *fidelis* for which Nelson finds evidence in ninth-century Carolingian texts.[53]

The rhetorical strategy that the author of the Conventum deployed for the purpose of justifying Hugh's conduct vis-à-vis his lord William presupposes that William had sworn oaths of fidelity to Hugh that resembled the oath that Fulbert glossed in his letter to the same William, the Occitanian oaths that men swore to their lords during the years around 1000, and, in several respects, Carolingian oaths of fidelity. As we have seen, Fulbert's letter indicates that the lord swore not to do evil (*malum*) to his *fidelis* by causing him harm (*dampnum*) with respect to his body (*corpus*), fortresses, or possessions or by making it difficult or impossible to accomplish something that would be of value to the *fidelis*. Under one interpretation of the letter, moreover, the lord swore to give his *fidelis* counsel (*consilium*) and aid (*auxilium*). Since, according to the same letter, the lord's oath of fidelity to his *fidelis* was identical in most respects to the *fidelis*'s oath to the lord, it is reasonable to suppose that it resembled Occitanian oaths of fidelity to a lord, which, in turn, resembled Carolingian oaths of fidelity sworn by rulers to their *fideles*, as well Carolingian oaths sworn by *fideles* to their rulers. In Occitanian oaths of fidelity, the *fidelis* swore faithfully (*per directam fidem*) that from this hour forward (*de ista ora in antea*) he would not harm his lord with respect to his body or his possessions, including fortresses, and would be a helper (*adiutor*) to his lord and be faithful (*fidelis*) to him without evil trickery (*sine malo ingenio*), as a man ought to be to his lord (*sicut homo debet esse ad*

---

[53] See above at pp. 15–16; see also Magnou-Nortier (1969) 117.

suum seniorem). The man also swore that unless he was absolved (*absolvere*) from his oath (*sacramentum*), neither he nor anyone acting in consultation (*consilium*) with him would cause loss (*dampnum*) to his lord (*senior*), make him lose (*perdere*) anything, take (*tollere*) property from him, injure him by evil trickery (*malum ingenium*), take certain specified actions without consulting him (*sine consilio*), or make an agreement (*finis*) or alliance (*societas*) with any man or woman who took (*tollere*) property from the lord.[54] As Magnou-Nortier has pointed out, ninth-century oaths of fidelity use a number of similar words and phrases, including *ab ista die in antea, vobis adiutor ero, sicut homo per drictum debet esse domino suo, sine fraude et malo ingenio, consilio et auxilio.*[55]

For the purpose of demonstrating that William had betrayed (*tradere*) Hugh's faith (*fides*) in him, the Conventum repeatedly deploys many words and phrases identical with, or similar to, words and phrases used in oaths of fidelity, including: *fidelitas* (8 times), *fides* (9), *fidelis* (2); *damnum* (5); *malum* (14); *consilium* (13); *(ad)juvare* (10) and *auxiliari* (1); *promittere* (7); *ingenium* (5); *finis* (14), *conventus* (22), and *convenientia* (1); and *tollere* (8), as well as *capere* (8), *apprehendere* (4), *auferre* (1), *ferre* (3).[56] These words, along with others that invoke oaths of fidelity, are woven into the story of Hugh and his lord William in such a way as to justify the former's complaints against the latter. When Hugh aided his lord and obeyed his commands, he repeatedly incurred harm (*dampnum*) and evil (*malum*) for which he received no compensation from William. Although William was obliged to give aid (*adjutorium*; also *auxilium*) to Hugh, under the oath of fidelity William had sworn to him, and explicitly promised (*promittere*) to do so, the aid William promised Hugh was never forthcoming. On several occasions, William promised to take counsel (*consilium*) with Hugh before undertaking actions that had bearing on Hugh's interests, including his claim to hold a *castrum* that had been his father's; but in each case William acted without consulting with Hugh. Hugh acted out of trust, fidelity, and love for his lord William, who reciprocated by breaking his promises to Hugh and treating him with evil trickery

---

[54] On the terms of Occitanian oaths, see Magnou-Nortier (1969) esp. 119–26; and Cheyette (2001) 187–92. For examples of oaths see Devic and Vaissette (1872), nos. 139 (c. 985; cols. 301–2), 148 (c. 989; cols. 312–14); 179 (c. 1020; cols. 372–74); 185 (c. 1025; cols. 381–82); 202 (c. 1034; cols. 406–11); 204 (c. 1035; cols. 412–14); 209 (c. 1036; cols. 425–6).

[55] Magnou-Nortier (1969) 119.

[56] See Beech (1995) 'Index du *Conventum*', 171–81.

(*per malum ingenium*). Finally, William insulted and dishonored Hugh by claiming him as "his", asserting his power to make Hugh the man of a *rusticus*, and ordering his men to beseige a fortress where Hugh's wife resided. In short, the Conventum demonstrated that in exercising his authority over Hugh in the ways already mentioned, William harmed Hugh with respect to his body, his agreements with others, his fortifications, his possessions, his honor, and various interests of his that William had made it impossible for him to achieve.

By situating the dispute between the two men in a political world that Fulbert's letter to William totally excludes from view, while legitimating the authority of lords living in that world, the Conventum also shows implicitly that Hugh was entitled to many of the gifts of land that he sought from William by right of inheritance or conquest or by virtue of the agreements Hugh had made with William or others. In the course of demonstrating that William was a traitor, the Conventum specifies normative grounds on which Hugh may have sought redress at William's court for the injuries that William had caused him in violation of William's own oath of fidelity. When he received no justice there, for renouncing his fealty to William except for William's person and his city of Poitiers. When William responded by seizing a benefice of Hugh's, Hugh retaliated, at which point William agreed to come to an agreement with him. In the narrating this story, the Conventum, in contrast to Fulbert's letter to William, treats a *fidelis*'s limited renunciation of fidelity to his lord and direct attacks against him as appropriate sanctions against a lord who was a traitor.[57]

Even though the Conventum obviously represented the dispute between Hugh and William tendentiously, just as Fulbert tendentiously represented the claims of lords over their *fideles*, the Conventum shows that it was thinkable in the early eleventh century to justify a *fidelis*'s claims on his lord by invoking traditional terms of oaths of fidelity and to do so without deviating from Fulbert's interpretation of them, which, with only a little tinkering, could have legitimated Hugh of Lusignan's claims against his faithless lord.[58] Though written in such a way as to privilege the lord's claims on the fidelity of his *fidelis*,

---

[57] See White (1993); see also *idem* (1996) 223–30. Important recent studies of the Conventum include Martindale (1997) chap. VIII; and Barthélemy (2000).

[58] The Conventum also echoes the words of the capitulary cited above in n. 36 by complaining that William tried to make Hugh a serf.

the letter still acknowledged what Reynolds calls the 'mutuality' of obligations between lords and their *fideles*. If we supplement the letter with the postulate that a limited feud was an appropriate sanction for a *fidelis* to use against a lord who had violated his obligations to his man and also denied him justice, we arrive at a clear justification for Hugh's conduct, as the Conventum both represents and justifies it.

In order to explicate the Conventum and Fulbert's letter of fidelity, we need not assume that either of these texts provides evidence of the establishment of a new vassalic régime that came into being in northern Francia in the years around 1000 through a process of feudalization that corrupted an old Carolingian system of public order. Instead, both texts represent a political world in which it was not feudal contracts or the feudal institutions of fief and vassalage, but rather oaths of fidelity, whatever precise form they took, that provided the key terms of a discourse in terms of which nobles, both lay and ecclesiastic, legitimated their own conduct and that of their *amici*, as they represented, evaluated, and tried to control political relations between lords and *fideles* in different ways and from different positions in a political field. This discourse, I believe, can be meaningfully characterized as 'feudal'; but, given the misunderstandings that the use of this term inevitably creates, there are certainly good reasons to call it a 'culture of fidelity', as Cheyette proposes, or a discourse of fidelity.[59]

As Duby pointed out in his study of the Mâconnais, fiefs and vassalage did not constitute the primary basis of social relations within the eleventh-century nobility; and to represent political relations between lords and *fideles* or lords and vassals in this way is deeply misleading. As Cheyette pointed out in 1967, "If a historian approaches medieval society primarily in terms of fief and vassalage, he must make an important empirical assumption, [namely] that fief-holding and vassalage were in fact of primary importance in medieval society, indeed, that they determined its nature". Rejecting this assumption, along with the assumption that the fief and vassalage were legal institutions, historians since Duby have found alternative ways of analyzing what Cheyette identified as the relationships of "dominion and dependence, command and obedience, fellowship and service" that had "traditionally

---

[59] See Cheyette (2001) chaps. 10–13. On feudal discourse, see White (2002) 127–141; White (2000) 169–88; White (1994) 173–97; and White (forthcoming a).

been explained in terms of vassalage" and, in some cases, the fief.[60] In pursuing these lines of inquiry, these historians have not ignored the "documented realities" of fief and vassalage. Instead, after abandoning the conventionalized historiographical practice of reading texts such as Fulbert's letter to William, the Conventum of Hugh of Lusignan, and oaths of fidelity as though they were transparent legal documents providing evidence of legal institutions, they have found that such texts take on new significance, as Cheyette observed, if they treat them as evidence of discursive practices rather than reading them through the lens of feudalism or feudal institutions.[61]

Bibliography

Barthélemy, D. (1993) *La société dans le comté de Vendôme de l'an mil au XIVe siècle* (Paris: 1993).

—— (1997) *La mutation de l'an mil a-t-elle eu lieu? Servage et chevalerie dans la France des Xe et XIIe siècles* (Paris: 1997).

—— (1997) "La théorie féodale à l'épreuve de l'anthropologie (note critique)", *Annales: Histoire, Sciences Sociales*, 52 (1997), 321–41.

—— (2000) "Autour d'un récit de pactes ('Conventum Hugonis'): La seigneurie châtelaine et le féodalisme, en France au XIe siècle", in *Il Feudalismo nell'Alto Medioevo*, 2 vols., Settimane di Studio del Centro Italiano di Studi sull'Alto Medioevo, vol. 46 (Spoleto: 2000) 1:447–89.

Beech, G.; Chauvin, Y.; Pon, G. (1995) *Le conventum (vers 1030): Un précurseur aquitain des premières épopées* (Geneva: 1995).

Bisson, T.N. (1994) "The 'Feudal' Revolution", *Past and Present* 142 (1994) 6–42.

—— (1997) "Debate: The 'Feudal Revolution': Reply", *Past and Present* 155 (1997) 208–25.

—— (2000) "Lordship and Tenurial Dependence in Flanders, Provence, and Occitania (1050–1200)", in *Il Feudalismo nell'Alto Medioevo*, 2 vols., Settimane di Studio del Centro Italiano di Studi sull'Alto Medioevo, vol. 46 (Spoleto: 2000) 1:389–439.

Bonnassie, P. (1976) *La Catalogne du milieu du Xe à la fin du Xe siècle: croissance et mutations d'une société*, 2 vols. (Toulouse: 1976).

—— (1991) "Feudal Conventions in Eleventh-century Catalonia", in idem, *From Slavery to Feudalism in South-Western Europe*, trans. Jean Birrell (Cambridge: 1991) 170–94.

—— (1991) "The Formation of Catalan Feudalism and Its Early Expansion (to c. 1150)", in idem, *From Slavery to Feudalism in South-Western Europe* (Cambridge: 1991) 149–69.

—— (1991) "From the Rhône to Galicia: Origins and Modalities of the Feudal Order", in idem, *From Slavery to Feudalism in South-Western Europe* (Cambridge: 1991) 104–32.

---

[60] Cheyette, "Introduction", 5, 7; see also Cheyette (1996), 998–1006.

[61] For a brief but brilliantly devastating critique of Ganshof, *Feudalism*, see Guerreau (1980) 78–80.

—— (2000) "Sur la genèse de la féodalité catalane: nouvelle approches", in *Il Feudalismo nell'Alto Medioevo*, 2 vols., *Settimane di Studio del Centro Italiano di Studi sull'Alto Medioevo*, vol. 46 (Spoleto: 2000) 2:569–606.

Boretius, A. (1883) *Monumenta Germaniae Historica, Leges*, Sectio II, *Capitularia Regum Francorum*, 2 vols. (Hanover: 1883).

Boutruche, R. (1959) *Seigneurie et féodalité*, vol. 1, *Le premier âge des liens d'homme à homme* (Paris: 1959).

Bourdieu, P. (1977) *Outline of a Theory of Practice*, trans. Richard Nice (Cambridge: 1977).

Bournazel, E. (1998) "La royauté féodale en la France et en Angleterre", in E. Bournazel and J.-P. Poly, eds., *Les féodalités* (Paris: 1998) 389–510.

Brown, A.R. (1974) "The Tyranny of a Construct: Feudalism and Historians of Medieval Europe", *American Historical Review* 79 (1974) 1063–88.

Carozzi, C. (1981) "Introduction," in Adalbéron de Laon, *Poème au roi Robert*, ed. and trans. C. Carozzi, *Les Classiques de l'Histoire de France au Moyen Age* (Paris: 1981) ix–clviii.

Cheyette, F.L. (1968) *Lordship and Community: Selected Readings* (New York: 1968).

—— (1996) Review of Susan Reynolds, *Fiefs and Vassals: The Medieval Evidence Reinterpreted*, in *Speculum*, 71 (1996) 998–1006.

—— (1999) "Women, Poets, and Politics in Occitania", in T. Evergates, ed., *Aristocratic Women in Medieval France* (Philadelphia: 1999) 138–77.

—— (2001) *Ermengard of Narbonne and the World of the Troubadours* (Ithaca: 2001).

—— (forthcoming) "Georges Duby's Mâconnais: A Memoir", *Journal of Medieval History* (forthcoming).

Devic, C. and Vaissette, J. (1872) *Histoire générale de Languedoc*, vol. 5 (Toulouse: 1872).

Duby, G. (1953) *La société aux Xe et XIIe siècles dans la région mâconnaise* (Paris: 1953; rpt. 1971).

—— (1968) "The Nobility in Eleventh- and Twelfth-Century Mâconnais", trans. in F. L. Cheyette (1968) *Lordship and Community: Selected Readings* (New York: 1968) 137–155.

—— (1980) "The Evolution of Judicial Institutions: Burgundy in the Tenth and Eleventh Centuries", in idem, *The Chivalrous Society*, trans. Cynthia Postan (Berkeley, CA: 1980) 15–58.

—— (1980) *The Three Orders: Feudal Society Imagined*, trans. Arthur Goldhammer (Chicago: 1980).

—— (1994) *History Continues*, trans. Arthur Goldhammer (Chicago: 1994).

Ganshof, F.L. (1964) *Feudalism*, 3rd English ed. (New York: 1964).

Guerreau, A. (1980) *Le féodalisme: un horizon théorique* (Paris: 1980).

Guillot, O. and Sassier, Y. (1994) *Pouvoirs et institutions dans la France médiévale: Des origines à l'époque féodale*, vol. 1, O. Guillot, *Les origines de la France (de la fin du Ve siècle à la fin du Xe)* (Paris: 1994).

The Letters and Poems of Fulbert of Chartres, ed. and trans. F. Behrends (Oxford: 1976).

Magnou-Nortier, E. (1969) "Fidélité et féodalité méridionale d'après les serments de fidélité (X^e–début XIIe siècle)", in *Les structures sociales de l'Aquitaine, du Languedoc et de l'Espagne au premier âge feudal* (Paris: 1969) 115–42.

Martindale, J. (1997) "Conventum inter Guillelmum Aquitanorum comitem et Hugonem Chiliarchum", in idem, *Status, Authority and Regional Power: Aquitaine and France, 9th to 12th Centuries* (Aldershot, Hampshire: 1997) 541–548.

—— (1997) "Dispute, Settlement, and Orality in the *Conventum* . . .: A Post-script to the Edition of 1969", in idem, *Status, Authority and Regional Power*, chap. VIII.

Nelson, J.L. (1986) "Dispute Settlement in Carolingian West Francia", in W. Davies and P. Fouracre, eds. *The Settlement of Disputes in Early Medieval Europe* (Cambridge, UK: 1986) 45–64.

—— (1994) Review of T. Head and R. Landes, eds., *The Peace of God: Social Violence and Religious Response in France around the Year 1000* (Ithaca, NY: 1992), *Speculum*, 69 (1994) 163–9.

—— (1995) "Kingship and Royal Government", in R. McKitterick, ed., *The New Cambridge Medieval History*, vol. 2, *C. 700–900* (Cambridge, UK: 1995) 383–431.

Poly, J.P. and Bournazel, E. (1991) *La mutation féodale, X^e–XIIe siècle*, 2nd ed. (Paris: 1991).

Reynolds, S. (1994) *Fiefs and Vassals: The Medieval Evidence Reinterpreted* (Oxford: 1994).

White, S.D. (1993) "Stratégie rhétorique dans la *Conventio* de Hugues de Lusignan", in *Mélanges Georges Duby*, vol. 2, *Le tenancier, le fidèle et le citoyen* (Aix-en-Provence: 1993) 147–57.

—— (1994) "The Language of Inheritance in *Raoul de Cambrai*: Alternative Models of Fief-holding", in Garnett, G. and J. Hudson, eds., *Law and Government in the Middle Ages: Essays in Honour of Sir James Holt* (Cambridge, UK: 1994) 173–97.

—— (1996) "Debate I: The 'Feudal Revolution': II", *Past and Present*, 152 (1996) 205–23.

—— (1996) "The Politics of Fidelity: Hugh of Lusignan and William of Aquitaine", in C. Duhamel-Amado and G. Lobrichon, eds., *Georges Duby: L'écriture de l'histoire* (Brussels: 1996) 223–30.

—— (2000) "The Politics of Gift-exchange. Or, Feudalism Revisited", in E. Cohen and M. de Jong, eds. *Medieval Transformations* (Leiden: 2000) 169–88.

—— (2002) "Giving Fiefs and Honor: Largesse, Avarice, and the Problem of 'Feudalism', in Alexander's Testament", in D. Maddox and S. Sturm-Maddox, eds., *The Medieval French Alexander* (Binghamton, NY: 2002) 127–141.

—— (forthcoming a) "Fiefs for Service or Service for Fiefs", in G. Al-Gazi, B. Jüssen, and V. Groebner, eds., *Négocier le don* (Göttingen: forthcoming).

—— (forthcoming b) "Tenth-Century Courts and the Perils of Structuralist History" in W. Brown and P. Górecki, eds., *Conflict in Medieval Europe* (London: forthcoming).

JUDICIAL RHETORIC AND POLITICAL LEGITIMATION IN MEDIEVAL LEÓN-CASTILE

Isabel Alfonso

Instituto de Historia, CSIC (Madrid)

Royal assemblies—variously referred to as *concilia, curiae,* or *cortes* in contemporary documents—have often been studied in their guise as the forerunners of their better developed institutional descendants, be they parliaments, royal tribunals, or royal consultative assemblies.[1] Those who have studied them have therefore for the most part concentrated on evaluating the king's capabilities or limitations with respect to the judicial, legislative, and governmental tasks that the development of those institutions demanded.[2]

This area of investigation, which has usually been approached from decidedly traditional analytical angles, proves richly rewarding when seen from a novel perspective, from which royal assemblies are perceived as public spaces in which the distribution of political power was debated and legitimized; in which certain behavioural models concerning the transmission and maintenance of power and the functions of those who wielded it were enacted and consolidated while others were—either explicitly or by implication—rejected; in which reputation, prestige, honour, and dignity, as well as their opposite qualities, received public expression; in which political relations were competitively negotiated and defined; and in which participants were educated in the practices upon which that political competition was based.[3]

---

[1] This paper was originally presented at the University of St. Andrews in March 2001 at one of the sessions of the symposium entitled *Political Discourses and Processes of Legitimation,* held jointly by the Consejo Superior de Investigaciones Científicas, Madrid, and the Department of Medieval History of the University of St. Andrews. I am very grateful to the members of that department for their criticism and suggestions for improvements, and to Julio Escalona, Stephen White, Susan Reynolds and Paul Fouracre for their useful comments on its most recent draft.

[2] See for example the collection of studies published in *El Reino de León en la Alta Edad Media, I. Cortes, Concilio y Fueros* (1988) (León: 1988); *Las Cortes de León y Castilla en la Edad Media* (1988) vol. I, (Valladolid: 1988) and *Las Cortes de Castilla y León. 1188–1988* (1990) (Valladolid: 1990) and the bibliography that is cited there.

[3] For a discussion of the political sphere as an area in which rivals competed over resources, see: Alfonso (2002).

I shall adopt this perspective in order to examine the processes of legitimation that developed in the context of royal judicial assemblies and the discourses that these generated. I shall pay particular attention to those royal gatherings presented by the sources as courts at which a king heard and resolved disputes. An important aspect of this investigation concerns the ways by which the king's own image and authority, as well as the nature of his power are constructed before the community of lay and ecclesiastical aristocrats attending royal judicial assemblies. Indeed, it was the dialetic interaction between king and aristocratic groupings that provided the yardstick whereby individual monarchs' authority and the effectiveness of its imposition were measured: through which, in other words, their power was legitimized.

It is not the purpose of this article to comment on the means whereby royal courts were convoked or the nature of those who attended. Neither is it to describe the disputes that were heard there. Suffice it to say that these assemblies are presented in our sources as royal gatherings whose most exalted members often enjoyed close ties to the king. They are generally depicted as solemn and magnificent affairs which we might classify as public spectacles of a ritual type, ideally suited to the ideological representation of royal authority.

Careful analysis of these gatherings reveals much, not only about the official discourses of legitimation that were developed there, but also about the mechanisms whereby royal judicial assemblies were transformed into spaces of legitimation in their own right. The analysis of those mechanisms is another of the principal aims of this investigation.

The records of certain court cases brought before the kings of León and Castile in the eleventh and twelfth centuries by some of the most important religious institutions of those kingdoms provide the documentary basis upon which this investigation is constructed.[4] These texts touch upon three different issues. The first concerns the documents themselves, which as records of royal justice not only contained important expressions of power, but also served as a fundamental tool in its creation. The second concerns the idea that

---

[4] The documentary collections used are those of the Cathedrals of León (Ruiz Asencio, 1987 and 1990; Fernández Catón, 1990 and 1991) and Astorga (Cavero and Martín, 1999) and the monasteries of Celanova (Andrade, 1995) and Sahagún (Herrero, 1988; Fernández Flórez, 1991), together with some editions of royal charters (Fernández del Pozo, 1984; González, 1943 and 1944; Gambra, 1998). For the purposes of this article, documents will be identified according to their year of issue, the name of the collection in which they can be found, and their number.

royal courts were important environments of socialization where cultural values were transmitted and learned. The third concerns the concept of legitimation as a social, political and cultural process.

Bearing in mind the comparative framework within which this study has been conceived, it is worth reflecting briefly on the nature of the documents on which it is based to interpret them, and the ways in which their analysis has been approached. It is also worth emphasizing the need to deepen our knowledge regarding their production, conservation, and functions. The predominantly ecclesiastical nature of these sources obviously conditions the information they contain to such an extent that their origin must be kept constantly in mind by anyone attempting their interpretation. It is therefore very important that we take into account their function with respect to the institutions that issued them, and the context that lent credibility to their contents, though this, of course, is not necessarily described by the texts themselves. It is also essential to note that most of our sources concerning this period are not in fact originals, but later copies that were preserved in twelfth-century cartularies. The implications of this fact are in urgent need of further investigation.[5] Finally, we must examine closely those aspects of our sources that might be identified as topoi of the formulation of legal narrative. Rather than simply representing procedural formalities or conventional formulae, I will argue that these constituted communicative and representative strategies designed to dress the claims and resolutions made at royal judicial assemblies in a cloak of justice and, in the final analysis, legitimacy.[6]

Most of the documents examined here concern legal suits brought before the king by ecclesiastical institutions intent on reclaiming property that had been seized from them or jurisdiction that had been usurped. Although they describe judicial processes that took place within the context of royal assemblies, they are not necessarily the work of legal scribes who recorded the business transacted there for strictly administrative purposes. Instead, they are for the most part narratives formulated by ecclesiastical litigants who, despite recording

---

[5] See Lucas Álvarez (1999) for a study of the diplomatic of royal documents, and Fernández Florez (2002) on the production of documents in the Christian kingdoms of Western Iberia.

[6] On the nature and classification of procedural documents see: Prieto Morera (1992) 386–89. For an interesting discussion of the character of judicial narratives in the context of Italian communal justice, see Wickham (2000).

the arguments put forward by their adversaries, presented a version
of events that was invariably conditioned by a desire to enhance the
legitimacy of a ruling that found in their own favour. However, our
sources' obvious partiality should not blind us to the fact that their
assertions with respect to the functions of the Crown, justice and
criminality, rights and obligations and the proper means whereby
these should be transmitted were understood (and possibly even shared
despite being disputed) by the political community to which they
were directed and within which the disputes with which they were
associated took place. Just as Martin has said of heroic narratives,
one might say that the language of these sources establishes models
of both 'good' and 'bad' behaviour.[7]

We know very little about the process whereby these documents
were written and made public. However, some of them contain evidence suggesting that they were issued after the passing of judicial
decisions in order that they might then be read out and publicly
ratified before the assemblies that had contributed to and witnessed
the debates and resolutions they recorded. The documents themselves therefore did not, as is commonly assumed, simply represent
an official record of judgements that could be presented in the event
of future legal challenges. At a more fundamental level, they also
served as vehicles for the communication of the means whereby those
decisions had been made, and the social networks that had been
activated in the process. In this sense, these documents were themselves the fruit of a process of political legitimation, and should be
considered as social constructs in which language and practice were
inextricably linked. It is for this reason that we must pay especially
close attention to the processes whereby our sources were created.
Although they certainly do not conform to any single diplomatic
model and their contents vary widely, they nevertheless display certain common elements that deserve comment.

The term 'legal rhetoric' is employed here in reference to the existence and significance of discourses developed to represent the royal
activities of judging and settling disputes, or even simply presiding
over judicial processes. This specific term is used because the discourses in question clearly had an audience. By examining the 'judicial rhetoric' used in our sources, it is possible to identify those
elements within them that contribute most significantly to the fulfill-

---

[7] Martin (1997) 150.

ment of their function as self-reinforcing social and political instruments. As proposed by Miller, such rhetoric, far from merely representing discursive convention, is in fact intricately bound up with both power and violence.[8] It is worth noting that the very production of the documents on which this study is based presupposed the recognition of royal power and represented a declaration of its validity and a glorification of royal justice. In this respect, I shall argue that the nature of royal authority was to a great extent defined and consolidated within the context of royal justice, which constituted what Maurice Bloch would term 'practical political ideology'.[9]

In the judicial sphere, royal legitimation was promoted through the employment of diverse rhetorical devices. These deserve careful analysis, as they served not only to define the dynamics of power, but also to establish moral portraits of those who wielded it. In examining them, I will focus first of all on those discourses that emphasized the restoration of social order, and then on the rhetoric of truth that is to be found within them.

Judicial Rhetoric and the Politics of Restoration

In 1018, the Abbot of Sahagún, one of the most powerful monasteries in the Kingdom of León, requested Alfonso V's help in rectifying the damage it had suffered during the king's minority due to the unlawful entry of royal officials (*scurrones*) into monastic settlements and the unjust and unprecedented demands they had made of them. This request was framed by an appeal to common knowledge of how Sahagún had been founded and endowed by the king's ancestors:

> A multis quidem est notum et non a paucis manet declaratum eo quod edificauit rex domnus Adefonsus et coniux eius domna Xemena arcisterium, uocabulo Sancti Facundi et Primitiui, super crepidinis aluei Ceia; et ad ipsum monasterium concederunt uillas et omnes habitantes in eas ab integro, secundum quod in eius testamentum resonat. Tenentes fratres de hunc locum iam taxatum tempore ipsius regis, postea frater eius Raimirus rex uel qui post eos succeserunt in regno usque ad dies Adefonsi, prolis Ueremudi principis, adhuc permanente in puericia, ingressi fuerunt scurrones in eius uillulis et fecerunt in eis quod illis

---

[8] Miller (1990) 3.
[9] Bloch (1975).

> non decebat. Dum uiderunt se ipsi fratres, una cum abbate eorum
> Egilani, in angustia positi et que faciebant super eos quod ab antiquis
> temporibus usualem non abuerant.[10]

This complaint was heard in the Monastery of Sahagún itself by the
king who, we are informed, had been guided there along with his
wife the Queen Elvira, by the will of God once Alfonso had attained
his majority. The document recording the event employs direct speech
to report the plea made by the abbot and monks as they lay pros-
trate at the king's feet: "Our lord and great prince! Lend your ears
to hear and your heart to understand this document that was issued
by your grandparents":

> et ipse principe, plenum intellectum et uera intelligendum, duxit eum
> Deus, una pariter cum coniuge eius gloriosa regina Geluira, ad ipsum
> domum et corpos sanctos; et collegerunt eos, cum susceptione et omni
> gaudio et letitia plene. Sedentes intus monasterii, ipse abbas qui rege-
> bat hunc monasterium cecidit, una pariter cum collegas suos, ad pedes
> ipsius principis et dixerunt: "Domnus noster et princeps magne! Pone
> aurem ad audiendum et cor ad intelligendum et audi hunc scriptum
> que fecerunt aui tui".

Moved to mercy by this outburst, Alfonso V had the testament that
the monks had presented to him read out in the presence of all of
the magnates of his court, after which he recognized its validity and
confirmed it before the assembled company, with the words: "Let
this pact, which was custom in ancient times, be confirmed and
strengthened":

> Ille, uero, motus misericordia, ordinauit coram omnes magnates palacii
> legere ipsum testamentum et dum agnouit ueraciter factum dixit coram
> omni concilio: "Abeat roborem et firmitatem pactum istum quod ab
> antiquis temporibus fuit usum".

The narrative is then continued in the first person by the king who,
appealing to divine mercy and to the memory of his grandparents,
issued a charter of restoration exempting the monastery's settlements
from the dues that had allegedly been wrongfully demanded of them,
these were taxes that were habitually mentioned in royal concessions
of fiscal immunity like fines for homicide, theft, and kidnapping, and
confirming the integrity of the monks' jurisdiction:

---

[10] 1008, *Sahagún*, doc. 404. A twelfth-century copy in *Becerro Gótico de Sahagún*,
f. 8v.

Ob inde, sub misericordia Domini, ego Adefonsus, in solio auorum meorum fultus, uobis domno Egila abba uel omnium Santorum Facundi et Primitiui facio uobis scriptum restaurationis ut amplius et deinceps non faciant uobis ullam, in omnes uestras uillas, inquietationem, que uestra ordinacione discurrunt: non pro omicidio, nec pro furto, nec pro roixo, nec pro aliqua causa, sed sana et integrata maneat sub dicioni uestre.

It is remarkable how this document establishes an association between royal greatness and policies aimed at the restoration of monastic dominions in three distinct ways. In the first instance, it does so by describing in great detail the *ad hoc* transformation of the cloister into a forum of royal justice: the monastery, which is the scene of the action, is presented as a sacred space to which kings are guided by divine providence, and a fundamental point of contact between secular and spiritual powers.[11] Secondly, it contrasts periods of political order and political disorder, and links them to both the weakness or strength of individual monarchs and the fortunes of the monastery itself. In connection with this, it also describes a specific type of royal legitimacy which it links explicitly to the protection of monastic property. It thus relates the history of the foundation and endowment of the monastery by Alfonso V's royal ancestors in such a way as to emphasize his descent from the illustrious kings Alfonso III, who reigned during the second half of the ninth century, and Ramiro, who is not further identified. It goes on to state that the monastery had enjoyed its endowments in peace from the time of those kings until Alfonso V's own minority, omitting any mention of other reigns and events that were detrimental to the monastery, of which we are informed by other sources. In this case such an omission seems to have been made in order to contrast more clearly the two distinct phases into which the royal career of the king before whom they were airing their grievances was divided.[12]

---

[11] On the construction of spaces of power, see De Jong & Theuws (2001).

[12] The references to kings made in this document are vague enough to lend themselves readily to erroneous interpretations. Indeed, its identification of Ramiro as the king's brother supports Isla's theory that the Alfonso mentioned in the document was in fact Alfonso IV the Monk: Isla (1997: 47). However, the document's own identification of Alfonso and his wife as the monastery's founders leads me to believe that it in fact refers to Alfonso III. This is also the opinion of Herrero, who has edited the document: Herrero (1988). It is of course possible that the original version of the charter, written by the famous Sampiro (monk, priest, bishop, and royal notary), referred to and distinguished additional kings, and that the twelfth-century scribe who copied it, acting in accordance with different interests from those

The documents recording the numerous disputes brought before
Alfonso V, even before he attained his majority, by the powerful
Galician monastery of Celanova contain discourses of legitimacy that
were rather more complex and multi-faceted than those found in
the Sahagún documents. The sheer abundance of legal battles waged
by Celanova can perhaps be attributed to its being under the patronage of the most powerful member of the Galician nobility, Count
Gutierre Menéndez and the proximity that that nobleman's position
as regent granted him to the king's own person. His status and political position may also have lain behind the fact that some of the
monastery's judicial records can be seen as both monastic and familiar chronicles, as it were. By establishing genealogical connections
between the house of the Galician count and the royal family, these
narratives effectively emphasized the legitimacy of both, since explicit
statements of kin connections, far from being neutral, are heavily
loaded with meaning.[13]

The surviving documentary record of a Celanovan case of 1007
is typical in this respect.[14] The arguments put forward to justify the
claims of Celanova's abbot are developed in the context of a long
and complex narrative relating the history of the territories under
dispute in connection with the authority of the families of both king
and count, whose genealogies and continuity are shown to be closely
interlinked. We are informed that the property was confiscated by
Alfonso III from its original owner, a rebellious *dux* called Vitiza,
and given instead to Count Hermenegildo Gutierrez, who had loyally quashed the duke's uprising. The count and his descendants,
among whom the document cites Bishop Rosendo, the founder of
Celanova, were confirmed in their possession of the confiscated property by all of the kings who followed Alfonso. These confirmations
are mentioned in the course of the narrative, as are the uncertain-

---

of the original author, edited them out, retaining only the idea of Alfonso V's
restorative efforts and his ties to Sahagún's great royal founder. Indeed, Herrero's
study indicates that the preambles of many earlier documents were suppressed when
they were copied for inclusion in the *Becerro* (*ib.* xxx–xxxvii). It is possible that the
King Ramiro who is mentioned in the document was in fact Ramiro II, given the
favourable attitude displayed by Sampiro in his chronicle towards that monarch,
which is discussed by Isla in the work cited above (1997: 45).

[13] Bourdieu (1991) ch. 2, 267 ff.
[14] 1007, *Alfonso V*, doc. IV. A twelfth-century copy in *Tumbo de Celanova*, ff. 4v–5r.

ties that threatened the property's integrity due to hereditary divisions made by Count Hermenegildo himself. The document also identifies a section of the property that was donated to Celanova by Bishop Rosendo and the *dux* Froila, who were the children of Count Gutierre Menéndez and therefore also direct descendants of Count Hermenegildo, but also the text states that the monastery had no problem in holding onto the territory until after the brothers had died.[15] Thereafter, we are told, outsiders with no local connections

---

[15] *In nomine Dei . . . Dubium quidem non est sed a cunctis compertum manet et cognitum et quod Uittiza dux, in superbia elatus et mala cupidicia ductus, erexit se turgide aduersus ueritatem et mentiendo atque superbiendo composuit se in rebelium, et ueritatem contradicendo, in diebus regis domni Adefonsi et regine domne Scemene, et stetit in ipsa superbia et in ipsa contradictione, Deo et sepe dicto rege, quod ei non licebat, annis VIIm. Et mandauit ipse iam dictum princeps suo comite nomine Hermenegildus Guttiherriz, qui et ipse comes regio generi de propinquus erat, ut quod ad una re se in exercitu cum omnibus militibus palatii et gentis sue et ueniret ad dextruenda superbia iam dictis rebellionis Uittizani, et adprehenderet eum et deportaret in presentia iam dicti regis; et omnem terram quam ille superbiendo possidebat, ipse Hermenegildus comes sibi obtinenda uindicaret et posteritati sue, per iussionem ipsius principis inreuocabiliter obtinenda relinqueret, quanto tempore semen ducis ipsius uiueret per secula nunquam finienda. Et Deo annuente atque iubente, agmina bellatorum circumseptus, ipse dux, precedente ei diuina pietas, uenit ad iussionem regis, implendo ipsam rebellem adprehendit, et eius presentiam in Oueto deportabat, et in iuditio regis eum obtulit, et rex eum carcere trudi precepit, ibique ipse superbus homo uitam finiuit. Et sicut iam supra scribtum est, omnem terram quam ipse rebellis obtinuerat, supra dicto duci uel posteritati eius, rex ad perhabendum concessit. Post obitum uero dicti regis, confirmauit eam filius eius rex domnus Ordonius ad prefatum ducem Hemengildum. Post obitum autem domni Hordonii principis, confirmauit eam filius eius, rex domnus Ranemirus, ad ducem domnum Guttiherrem, Hermenegildi filium. Completis autem diebus domni Ranemiri, confirmauit filius eius, serenissimus princeps domnus Hordonius, ad pontificem domnum Rudesindum episcopum. Rex uero domnus Hordonius fine uite completo, aduero in sedem regiam frater eius rex domnus Santius et soror eius domna Giluira regina, et confirmauerunt ad prefatum antistitem quod auii et parentes et frater eius confirmauerunt. Defuncto autem domno Santio rege, succesit pro eo regnare filius eius domnus Ranemirus, et confirmauit ille et mater eius domna Tarasia regina ad domun Domini Saluatoris monasterii Cellenoue et abbati Manillani. Ut autem compleuit rex domnus Ranemirus annos uite sue, successit in regnum rex domnus Ueremudus, prolis Hordonii, iterum confirmauit ad prefatum monasterium et ad supra dictum abbatem quod priores reges fecerant. In hoc ergo tempore regum, nullus homo inde commissorium aut hereditatem ibi habuit. Ipse uero supra memoratus dux Hermenegildus, per regis iussionem et uoluntatem, filiis suis obtinenda diuisit, et per ipsam diuisionem uenit in portionem filii eius Guttiherri Menendi mandationem de Ablucinos cum Barrra et Bubalo, et homines habitantes nominati trans fluuio Baruantes et alias mandationes plurimas quas hic non scribsimus, et obtinuit eas ipse Guttiher Menendiz omnibus diebus uite sue absque alio herede, non quomodo de comissorio sed quomodo de prima presura. Et iterum ille diuisit de Baruantes usque in Ambas Mestas, ubi se Syle infundit in Mineo, duobus filiis suis domno Rudesindo episcopo et frater eius Froylani duci; aliis autem filiis suis dedit in partes alias suam hereditatem, sicut et istis duobus supra nominatis. Obtinuerunt autem eas domnus Rudesindus episcopus et frater eius, supra nominatus Froyla, cunctis diebus uite sue, nullum alium hominem ibi hereditatem possidentem preter ambos germanos, et dum uenerunt ad extremum diem, que cunctis uiuentibus inreuocabiliter hereditas est, relinquerunt ipsas hereditates mandationem in iure monasteriorum suorum Cellenoue et Uillenoue, nullum illis heredem uel possessorem ibi relinquentes.*

usurped this monastic property, thereby incurring not a few but many ills (*disturbationes . . . non paruae sed multe*) and provoking the first of many disputes about it to be brought before a royal court—this time that of Vermudo II (982–999), who ruled that the property should be returned to the monastery and the order of his royal ancestor respected. Together with the bishops and magnates of his court, Vermudo also confirmed the bequests made to Celanova by Bishop Rosendo. However, we are told that after his death, *raptores et extranei homines* once again seized the disputed territories.[16]

The narrative continues by introducing Alfonso V, who had been called upon to arrange the latest resolution of the dispute, of whom it paints the most magnificent of pictures. Born by God's will, he was said to have been raised to the throne of his forefathers in the royal seat of León with the unanimous approval of a great council that had gathered there and also with divine approval:

> Et defuncto autem supradicto rege domno Uerremudo (*sic*), suscitauit Deus semen illius regem domnum Adefonsum et collecto concilio Castelle, terre Forinseze, Galleciense uel Asturiense, leuauerunt eum regem super cathedram auorum et parentum suorum in sede regia Legionense, omnes una uoluntate Deo laudes reddentes et gratias agentes.

The document then proceeds to list the king's many qualities (*et rex supra dictus imperator iam sciens omnia, et diuidens cuncta et prout opus erat recte diiudicans universa*)[17] by way of introduction to the subject of the old dispute that had been brought before him and Count Menendo González by the abbot and monks of Celanova.[18] The count is de-

---

[16] *Post obitum uero supra dicti pontificis et iam memorati ducis, intrauerunt in ipsas mandationes homines de extraneis partibus, quorum auii uel parentes aut propago numquam ibi hereditatem habuerunt, nec grandem nec modicam, et fecerunt ibi hereditates quod eis non licuerat non paruas sed multas, unde orte disturbationes et supradicta monasteria, non paruae sed multe; et fecerunt inde querimoniam fratres, qui ipsa monasteria possidebant, in Concilio uel presentia regis domni Ueremudi, et mandauit ipse rex ipsas hereditates prehendere et tornare in iure supra dicti monasterii, etiam et quod auii eius fecerant, et iussionem regis domni Adefonsi non conuellerent nec irrumperent. Ille, mente deuota, Deo obediens, pro animabus preteritorum regum uel pro anime sue remedio, et cum conibentia et consilio episcoporum et magnatorum palatii, confirmaui, per seriem testamenti, ipsam mandationem Ablutinus cum Barra et alias que in testamento resonant, secundum eius obtinuit supra dictus pontifex domnus Rudesindus episcopus, post partem Redemptoris mundi et ipsius monasterii Cellenoue et abbatis Manillani et Didaci et fratribus sub eorum regimini ibi degentibus. Post obitum uero regis domni Ueremudi, qui hoc mandauerat et firmauerat, addiderunt ipsi raptores et extranei homines manum et ipsas hereditates quas tenebant non dimiserunt et alias adhuc obtinendas presumpserunt.*

[17] Andrade reads *dividiens* (1995: 15).

[18] The association made here between Alfonso V and David has been identified by Isla (1998: 96).

scribed as the divinely appointed regent and tutor of the king and also as governing the region of Galicia by divine will and royal command:

> Iterum facit ipse supradictus Manilla abbas, et fratres supradicti monasterii, querimoniam ante prefatum et serenissimun principem in multis locis, et ante eum sedentem comes magnus Menindus Gundisaluit, qui ex sub divino nutu creator et nutritor erat et omnem terram Gallecie, sub Dei et ipsius imperio regis, iuri quieto obtinebat.

The description of the hearing, which took place in a Galician village, contains a detailed account of the count's genealogy, through which he is linked to the original aristocratic owner of the disputed territories. His family history is then used to justify the court's decision that the disputed bequests should be returned to the monastery without delay and thenceforth enjoyed by the monks in peace, as they had been held 'without truth' by its adversaries:

> Et rex in uilla Gomarici sedens et ipse iam dictus du Menendus Gundisaluit, qui ex semine supra memorati Hermegildi comitis descendit et neptus supra dicti pontificis et ab eo sanctificatus et benedictus abebatur, elegit rex et ipse comes iudicem de palatio Pelagium, Aroalui filiium, qui iudex erat constitutus a rege, ut ueniret in medio terre supradicte mandationes et uenirent ante eum omnes infanzones et homines qui ipsas hereditates sine ueritate tenebant, siue de comparatione, uel de quacumque petitione uel de obitum supradicti pontificis usque nunc tempus, relinquerunt eas post partem monasterii absque alia dilatione et sine aliqua postea irruptione uel disturbatione.

In the event, however, this decision was never imposed as the king, moved to mercy together with the count and the abbot of Celanova, renegotiated the conditions under which these men, who had originally been described as thieves and foreigners but were now identified as members of the lower nobility (*infanzones*), were either to return the property in question or continue to possess it as monastic tenants:[19]

> Et misericordia motus, ipse serenissimus princeps, et ipse comes et ipse Manillani abbas, ordinauerunt ad ipsos qui ipsas hereditates tenebant uel possidebant, ut ornarent eis medium pretium, de parte ipsorum monasteriorum unde fuerint homines uiui, unde fuerint autem mortui careant omnia ab integro et tornet se totum post partem monasterii.

---

[19] It is interesting to note that it was in fact *infanzones*, as representatives of local power groups, who were the principal claimants and occupants of monastic property. I have examined the tensions that existed between these groups and monastic institutions in various different areas and periods, Alfonso (1993), (1997), (2001) with further bibliography.

The questions raised by this document are too numerous and wide-ranging for us to attempt to answer them all within the context of the present study. There are, however, a few whose relevance to our topic deserves special emphasis. It is clear, for example, that a narrative such as this, in which the continuity of a royal line of descent is stressed while interruptions in its genealogical history are quietly swept under the carpet, was not constructed merely to record the result of a monastic land dispute.[20] Through their account of the history of these disputed lands, the monks of Celanova presented their claim as having a certain status that was linked to both the fortunes of the monarchy and the relationship of their own patrons with the king. The process whereby the monks thus consolidated their status also served clearly to reinforce the foundations on which Alfonso V's own power rested as this, just like the possession of land, was legitimized through proof of inheritance. What is more, the passage of time is marked in this narrative by successive royal confirmations of an original donation to the monastery in such a way as to present royal policy as one of continuous protection of ecclesiastical patrimony. Finally, the document's depiction of this public legal ritual in such a way as to emphasize the historical continuity of the monastery's patronage by the king's royal forefathers must also be interpreted as an affirmation of a kind of inherited symbolic capital, which was the collective fruit of all of the individual alliances through which its subjects' blood, prestige, and superiority were exalted before the political community in the assembly. Both trials described in the document, the one heard by Vermudo II and the other brought before Alfonso V, are presented in such a way as to negate the possibility that the monastery's adversaries might have had any worthwhile arguments with which to defend their claims against Celanova. Instead, they are depicted as acts of restitution of property over which the Church held unchallengeable rights.[21] Although this is clearly a biased account,

---

[20] One might, for example, examine the very object of the dispute, as the terminology used to describe it varies greatly throughout the document (*omnem terram, mandationes de . . . et homines habitantes, hereditates mandationem*).

[21] The phrase *cunctis uiuentibus inreuocabiliter hereditas est* is especially interesting in this respect, as it is reminiscent of the terms used to express the concept of absolute ownership 'against the world' identified by Milson as a constituent part of the property law that was imposed in England by Common Law (Milson, 1976, 1981). A critique of the rigidity of his interpretation of these terms, which in my view is justified, can be found in White (1987). However, the appearance of this phrase may be the result of interpolations made in the twelfth century copy of the document in which it appears.

it nevertheless hints at the difficulties faced by this Galician abbey when it came to imposing their exclusive dominance on areas in which they had to compete with other power groups.

This ecclesiastical discourse thus employs the rhetoric of restoration to legitimize royal justice and presents royal genealogies in such a way as to emphasize their positive aspects while totally suppressing other less savoury ones. This is most evident in the case of Fernando I (1037–1065), whose assumption of the throne of León as a result of his marriage is presented as following smoothly and directly on from the reign of his father-in-law, Alfonso V. What this version of events fails to reveal is that his path to the throne was in fact rather bloody and led to the death of his brother-in-law and rival Vermudo III on the battlefield on which the two clashed. In this case it is particularly interesting to note that the position of a king who was, according to general opinion, the founder of a new dynasty was legitimized through his representation as the continuator of the ideals and spirit attributed to the reigns of his wife's most illustrious royal ancestors.[22] This is illustrated in the lengthy preamble to one of Fernando I's judgments.[23] The stated aim of this introductory narrative, in which Fernando I addresses the assembled court in the first person, is to render a faithful account of the events that led up to the ruling in question. In his speech, the king makes an explicit link between his own political agenda concerning the restoration and protection of Church property to that of his father-in-law, Alfonso V (who is also described as 'Great' in the document), which had been cut short by the celebrated king's death. This document, which was drawn up in 1046, is among those most often cited as evidence of Fernando I's reconstructive policies. It is therefore also extremely relevant with respect to the 'rhetoric of legitimacy' that we have been discussing. Its preamble begins with an account of how Fernando, king by the grace of God, gathered his faithful subjects together at a royal council. There he, together with his wife Queen Sancha, celebrated the good deeds of his predecessor Alfonso V, who, after defeating the Muslims, had summoned a council at which he had ordered the restitution of ecclesiastical property and enlarged the holdings of the Church in general:

---

[22] A more generalized overview of these reigns can be found in Isla (1998).
[23] 1046, *Catedral de Astorga*, doc. 306. copia del siglo XVII en BN. ms. 1195b, ff. 14–15.

> Sub ipsius imperio et illius genitricis Sanctae Mariae semper virginis. Fredinandus, gratia Dei rex, una cum uxore mea Sanctia, Regina, scire atque nosse facere curauimus fideli concilio regni nostri ut presentes et qui postea ad synodum posteritatis nostrae nascendo venturi sunt ut vere sciant et intelligant, atque certe agnoscant eo quod in diebus domini Adefonsi principis, soceri nostri, quanta et qualia bona fecerint regioni suae qui omni tempore vitae suae gentem muzleimitarum detruncauit, et ecclesias ampliavit et val de omnibus bonis suis ditavit et omnes homines fideliter ad synodum congregauit, atque unus quisque hereditatem suam habere precepit tam ecclesiis seu cunctis magnis, vel minimis regni sui provinciis.

The narrative continues with an account of the anarchy that followed Alfonso V's death, with special reference to the damage done at that time to ecclesiastical property and the kingdom's faithful as a result of the armed conflicts that broke out among its subjects:

> Post mortem vero ipsius divae memoriae gloriossissimi et serenissimi regis, surrexerunt in regnum suum viri peruersi, veritatem ignorantes et extraneaverunt atque vitiauerunt hereditates ecclesiae et fideles regni ipsius ad nihilum redacti sunt. Proter quod unusquisque ipsorum unus inter alio gladio se tracidauerint.

It is onto this bleak background that the subject of the new king's project of ecclesiastical restoration is introduced once, as is also the case in the previous narratives we have examined, the divine approval in which his ascent to the throne was shrouded has been emphasized, combined in this case with the acceptance of 'the faithful', who are also identified here as victims of the political turmoil described:

> Post plurimis namque temporibus, diuina procurante clementia et eius misericordia protegente, dum nos apicem Regni concedimus, et tronum gloriae de manu Domini et ab universis fidelibus accepimus.

We are then informed that the king had inherited his reconstructive policies from his royal ancestors, and that these consisted in ordering royal enquiries into ecclesiastical holdings, appointing bishops in every see, for them to restore churches and make the Christian faith recover, so that, by his authority, they maintain both within the framework of the Church:

> . . . iussimus perquirere haereditates ecclesiae, sicut ab antecessoribus nostris et prioribus regibus facta cognovimus fecimus ordinare per illas sedes episcopos ad restaurandum ecclesias et recreandum fidei christianae, per nostrum nanque auctoritatem illius diocessis et haereditatibus fideliter acquississent et sub potestate eclesiae firmiter subiugassent . . .

It was in precisely this restorative context that Fernando I sent out one of his faithful royal officials (*sayon*) to investigate the rights claimed by the bishopric of Astorga over certain properties. The mission must have been a rather difficult one, as the unfortunate royal official to whom it was entrusted met his death at the hands of the inhabitants of the disputed settlement while on the job. The king subsequently summoned a legal assembly at which he, *caelum veritatis eligentes*, invoked both Canon Law and Gothic legal codes before establishing exemplary punishments for the rebellious peasants and ordering the restitution of their village to the see of Astorga. The document recording these events is extremely well known due to its relevance to the history of peasant uprisings and their suppression, and deserves much more detailed analysis than I can undertake here.[24]

Astorga's cathedral archives also contain another, later document in which a similar narrative is employed to highlight Fernando I's efforts at ecclesiastical restoration.[25] Just like its forerunners, this charter also makes much of the general disorder that followed the death of Alfonso V, whom it describes as *princeps magnus*. Unlike the documents we have just been looking at, however, it also mentions his successor, Vermudo III, under whom, it blandly states, that no property was restored to the church. It then goes on to contrast what is identified as a general decline under Vermudo III with the improvements made by the current king, Fernando I, who is also described as *magnus*, through the restitution of bishops to their sees and the granting of legal protection to Church property:

> Permansit ibi plures annos secundum in testamento resonat, tenuerunt illum iuri quieto abbates, monachos vel sorores, sub potestate episcopi sedis astoricensis, et fecerunt ex eo servitum et obedientiam, secundum illos ordinaverint omnes episcopus astoricensis more pacifico usque dum rapuit mors ad principe magno rex domino Adefonso, et tunc soliciti fuerunt omnis adversariis ecclesiae in omnem terram que regebat ille princeps iam de super nominato. In illis vero diebus, antequam regnum accepisset prolem eius, rex domino Bermudo, subrexit Ero Salidiz et

---

[24] This document has been studied by both Pastor (1980) and Cavero (1995). In a recent article, Larrea (1999) questions both of their theses and disputes the existence of the political transformations that have been associated with the repression of this peasant community. This disagreement, however, forms part of a broad and longstanding debate over the transition of medieval Christian Iberia to feudalism into which we cannot enter here.

[25] 1057, *Catedral de Astorga*, doc. 353. A seventeenth-century copy of this document is in BN. ms. 1195b, f. 633.

filios ejus, per violentia, ut presumpserit ipso monasterio de ipsos mona-
chos et abbates de Sancta Maria, qui ibidem erant permanentes fecerunt
illos esse ex torres de ipso monasterio. Ad aliquanto tempore, princeps
magno rex Fredinando, in Legione principato regente, cum uxore sua
regina domina Sanctia, iussio Dei et illius, annuit mens spontanea
ordinare episcopo in sedis astoricensi domino Didaco quamvis indigno,
sicuti et fecerunt, et dederunt illi licentia ut exquireret omnem debitum et veritatis huius sedis astoricense qui proprium est debitum ibidem servire.

The family of usurpers described here were members of the local
nobility who gave up their claims to ownership of the disputed
monastery and acknowledged its belonging to the bishopric:

> Ipse autem princeps magnus iussit venire in eius presentia Ero Salitiz
> et suos filios. Tunc calumniavit eos episcopus dominus Didacus et vol-
> untarie desideravit super illum facere iudicium et cum plures secun-
> dum ille ordinaverit, et ipse rex et eorum judices, seu et illos iam
> suprataxatos reunxerunt facere judicium cum illo episcopo super ipso
> monasterio et cognoverunt quod erat proprium debitum de Sancta
> Maria et domos de ipsa sede.

The bishop and canons of Astorga were not alone in lamenting the
loss of ecclesiastical property which they reclaimed through royal courts.
The archives of the aforementioned Leonese monastery of Sahagún,
to cite one more example, contain a document which records a longstanding dispute concerning such property. Once again, churchmen
can be seen to have added weight to their claims by associating the
stability of their own holdings in particular, and that of the Church
in general, with the strength and glory of royal authority:

> . . . orta fuit intemtio . . . ante serenissimo rege domno Fredenando,
> cuius regnum et imperium sit in benedictione. Dicebat ipse abbas
> domno Ecta, cum collegio fratrum de Santo Facundo, pro Uilla
> Antoniano et suas hereditates de suis terminis antiquis, sicut in suo
> testamento antiquo resonat; et quomodo eam iurificarunt fratres in
> diebus serenissimi regis domni Ranemiri, usque dum peruenit terra
> sine rege et ecclesia sancta non habebat ueritatem.[26]

On visiting Sahagún, Fernando I also issued another charter at the
monks' request in which he restored to them the jurisdiction they
had exercised over some settlements in a nearby region, after rec-

---

[26] 1048, Sahagún, doc. 514. A twelfth-century copy in *Becerro Gótico de Sahagún*,
ff. 190v–191r. We shall comment further on the contents and eloquence of this
document at a later point.

ognizing the written evidence that they had read out before him as truthful and legitimate:

> Vt cognoui quia ueridica essent testamenta et legitima, sub misericordia Domini, ego, iam dictum Fernandus rex, una cum coniuge mea Sancia regina, facimus uobis scriptum restauracionis.[27]

It has been suggested by the editor of Sahagún's cartulary that this document may in fact have been modeled on another, earlier, diploma dating from the reign of Alfonso V which we have already discussed. She also suggests that the issues of restoration and confirmation that are highlighted in these and other documents represent repetitions of borrowed diplomatic formulae.[28] Although diplomatic similarities certainly do exist between these documents, they do not contradict my proposition that the language represents more than the mere repetition of conventional topoi. Indeed, not only do the documents in question display significant variations—like for example the uncharacteristic absence of any allusion to the judicial assembly which reached the decision recorded in the last of them—but the rhetoric of restoration also appears in other contemporary documents that fall into different diplomatic categories. This provides a clear indication that our sources' employment of justificatory discourses that described royal policies that were favourable to the Church can be attributed to motives that went far beyond mere compliance with diplomatic convention. This is further indicated by the presence of such discourses in the documentation of other religious institutions of the period.

The points of reference employed in the development of these discourses changed over time. For example, a document issued by Alfonso VI in 1068 attributes his restorative activity with respect to Sahagún to the same motives as had purportedly inspired Alfonso III before him. However, on this occasion Alfonso III was not identified as the monastery's founder but rather as its restorer; the monastery's adversaries were more vaguely described, as was the chronology of their aggression; and in the final analysis all damage done over the years to the monastery's property was attributed to the devil himself:[29]

---

[27] 1049, *Sahagún*, doc. 534. A twelfth-century copy in *Becerro Gótico de Sahagún*, f. 11v.

[28] Herrero (1988) XL–XLI.

[29] It is worth noting that weight is added to the monastery's claims in this case when the document in which they are recorded specifies that on this occasion the

A multis namque temporibus transmisit Deus in corde principis Adefonsi, una cum coniuge sua domna Xemena, regina, ut restauraretur hoc uenerabile locum et ut redderet illi, de omnibus bonis quod illi Dominus dederat, quod habebatur in suis scriptionibus et tuebatur in menbranis que fuerant scripta ab antiquis pictoribus, per precepta regum priorum permitente Dei uoluntate, et iussit ut omnes suas hereditates et suas uillas illesas et intactas stabilirent ad ipsum sanctum et uenerabile locum. Tunc demum, surgente in omnibus iniquitate et refrigecente multorum caritate, detractum est hoc opus et non permansit sicut in superioribus scripcionibus habebatur. Modo uero, annuit serenitas nostris principis Adefonsi, filii Fredinandi imperatoris, permisit in eum Dominus sapienciam et sciencientiam (sic) atque intelligenciam et currentes omnes congregationis fratres ipsius loci, una cum abate Gundisaluo nomine suggerentes regi et procurante diuina pietate et honorificentia ipsius regis iterum ut aliquid de rebus suis restauraret hunc locum. Rex magnus, pius et misericors, una cum omnes magnati palatii, ut omnes suas uillas, elegit cum toth hominess qui ibi habitant uel posmodum ad habitandum uenerint, permaneant illesas ut nullus eas inquietet, sicut prius solebant, in iuri regio.[30]

In this case the restorative activity of a king who is presented as great, pious, merciful, and divinely endowed with wisdom, knowlege, and intelligence, takes the form of a royal confirmation of the monastery's fiscal and jurisdictional immunity.

We can take this argument further. Some later Castilian-Leonese reigns also provide documents concerning some of the same religious institutions mentioned above, in which discourses of legitimation similar to those we have already encountered are employed. Although this is not always explicitly linked to royal assemblies, its connection to environments where royal justice was administered can usually be inferred. These diplomas date from the twelfth century and, although penned by ecclesiastical clerks, were undoubtedly issued by royal chanceries,[31] yet the rhetoric they deploy is very much the same.

One such document, issued in 1126 by the 'divinely inspired' (diuina inspiratione inflamatus) Alfonso VII, contains a confirmation of the monastery of Sahagún's holdings and its immunity from royal taxation.[32]

---

king restored to the monastery all the possessions listed in its charters and protected by documents drawn up by ancient scribes (pictoribus).

[30] 1068, Sahagún, 680. A twelfth-century copy can be found in BGS, ff. 4v–5r.

[31] This period is generally believed to have witnessed the birth of the Royal Chancery in León-Castile. Fernández Flórez (2002) 123 ff.

[32] 1126, Sahagún, doc. 1227. ed. Escalona, Historia, doc. 153.

Just as his predecessors had done before him, the king used this document to establish a connection between his protection of the monastery and the continuity and legitimacy of his royal family line. In it, he emphasizes the activity of his grandparents (*misericordia Dei fultus in solio auorum meorum*), who had been great benefactors of Sahagún, and whose generosity he wanted to both emulate and surpass.

> Ego rex Adefonsus, comitis Raymundi et regine Urrace filius, ad honorem ipsius sponsi, uidelicet, Christi filii Dei eiusdemque sponse sante, uidelicet, Ecclesie, mee fragilitatis memor, misericordia Dei fultus in solio auorum meorum, spe uite eterne et pro remisione peccatorum meorum et pro animabus parentum meorum, decreui munire et sublimare regia munificentia, simul et auctoritate, monasterium sanctorum martirum Facundi et Primitiui. Idcirco, diuina inspiratione inflamatus atque precibus Bernardi, abbatis supradicti monasterii, totiusque monachorum conuentus permotus, munio, regia auctoritate, quandam decaniam predicti monasterii que uocatur Cofinniale . . .

The document makes no mention of the conflict-ridden reign of the king's mother, Queen Urraca. This is, however, alluded to in another royal diploma issued only months before, which describes the disasters that were visited on the *regnum Hyspanum* during the seventeen years that followed the death of his grandfather, Alfonso VI, when he himself was young and ignorant and bereft of illustrious parents and the land suffered due to the internecine fighting of its magnates:

> Ego Adefonsus, Dei gratia tocius Hyspanie rex et dominus, comitis Reymundi et Urracce regine filius, domno Bernardo, abbati, et omnibus monachis, tam presentibus quam futuris, in cenobio quo est Dompnis Sanctis regulariter uiuentibus, in Domino Deo aeternam salutem. Postquam auus meus dompnus, uidelicet, Adefonsus uiam tocius carnis est ingressus, qui monasterium Santi Facundi largis et magnificis ditauit muneribus remansi ego puerulus et inscius, duobus clarissimis orbatus parentibus, et regnum Hypanum decem et septem annorum temporibus innumeros sustinuit casus, a propriis conculcatum proceribus, inter se, pro se, dimicantibus.[33]

This charter continues with a first-person narrative in which the king relates that he had been entrusted to the guardianship of the abbot and townsmen of Sahagún during those tempestuous years in order that he might be spared the wicked influence of the faction that had supported his mother (*Qua tempestate, ab abbate et a burgensibus in uilla*

---

[33] 1126, *Sahagún*, doc. 1226.

ad tutelam tantarum calamitatum sum receptus, ubi a matre eiusque partes defen-
satibus acriter sum sepe infestatus).[34] He thus establishes a framework to
justify the detailed confession that follows, in which he describes his
contributions to the damage suffered by the monastery during the
disturbances. These included seizing gold, silver, and other monastic possessions for himself and his knights, without respect to the
monastery's jurisdiction and grants, both royal and papal, imposing
a royal official on the town of Sahagún, replacing its old customs
with new laws, and sharing out monastic settlements and other possessions among his knights:

> Vnde, multis neccessitatibus coangustatus et leui adolescentie sensu agi-
> tatus, supradicto abbati et monachis multa iniuste, ut modo iam meliori
> sensu recognosco, intuli; aurum et argentum et substantiam monas-
> terii, ad meum et meorum militum sumptum, accepi; cautum et regalia,
> necnon Romana priuilegia, infregi; uille prefectum, contra ius et fas,
> imposui; consuetudines antiguas, nouas inducens, immutaui; uillas
> ceterasque possessiones, intus et extra, mihi militantibus, distribui.

By the time this document was issued, we are reassured, the kingdom had been pacified and the king had repented of his actions and
decided, in the interests of his own salvation and the stability of the
kingdom, to repair the damage that had been done. He therefore
confirmed the monastery's independent lordship and immunity from
royal jurisdiction:

> Nunc, uero, quia tantam procellam, Dei gratia aliquatinus sedauit, reg-
> numque in parte male diuisum bene coadunauit michique meliorem
> aetatem, intellectum, honorem prestitit, ad me reuersus, mala supra-
> dicta emendare disposui. Correptus, ergo, timore et amore Dei uen-
> eratione sanctorum martyrum Facundi et Primitiui, necnon et reuerentia
> aui mei bone memoriae Regis Adefonsi, ibidem sepulti, omnes hered-
> itates et possessiones, a me et ab aliis ui direptas, monasterio, abbati
> et monachis restituo; cautum, consuetudines, priuilegia, tam regalia
> quam Romana, et kartas a quibuslibet Deum timentibus, rite factas,
> absque ulla diminutione, confirmo; uillas, etiam, cunctas que in toto
> regno meo uestri iuris fuerunt uel esse debent, cum aecclessis et par-
> rochiis, intra uel extra cautum, longe uel prope populatas uel deser-
> tas, secundum priscos usus, uobis redintegro. Et ut nichil aliud uel
> aliter quam auo meo, regi bone memoriae Adefonso, antecessores uestri

---

[34] It is clear that the author of this document, the king's chaplain, who was
standing in for the chancellor on this occasion (*regie domus capellani, cacellarii uice fru-*
entis), employed the term '*infestatus*' in a negative sense to mean 'politically manipulated'.

> caritatiue exhibuerunt, a uobis uel a loco isto exigam, itidem, confirmo. Pro remedio, quoque, anime mee et mei regni stabilitate, prefectum a uilla tali tenore excludam ut deinceps ulla occasione in illa nec in aliis omnibus nullum alium dominum, nisi abbatem et monachos preferam, nec alicui terram Sancti Facundi ulterius in prestamine concedam. Promitto, etiam, et promittendo confirmo, ut nulla alterius monasterii persona, nisi quam concors congregatio predicti cenobii elegerit, in ibi abbas substituatur; nec alicui, unquam. ex proieniae regum, sit licitum monasterium Sancti Facundi uel aliquam partem ex suis hereditatibus, pro seculari heredite, requirere, uel in eis aliquod ius secularis hereditacionis seu terrene subiectionis dominium possidere.

Although there is no space here to embark on the detailed analysis such rich source material clearly deserves, a brief consideration of its language and contents serves to illustrate the typical readiness with which a discourse concerning the royal defense of ecclesiastical property was adopted in this and other diplomas of Alfonso VII. This king, who at his most explicit declared himself '*de quiete et utilitate ecclesie Dei sollicitus*',[35] seems to have taken to heart the saying of the Church Fathers that kings should endow and patronize the Church because 'He who builds the house of God builds for himself', with which he introduced one of his donations to the Cathedral of León

> Antiqua sanctorum patrum institutio terrenis regibus precipit ut ecclesias Dei hereditent et amplificent. Scriptum quippe est "qui domum Dei hedificat semetipsum hedificat", quam institutionem doctrine conperiens, ego Adefonsus gratia Dei Yspanie rex dono . . .[36]

It is clear that the defense and protection of the patrimony and privileges of the Church were both attributed to and demanded of the king. Furthermore, his greatness and majesty were defined in relation to his ability to fulfill these tasks. This is well illustrated in the preamble to one of Alfonso VII's most generous concessions to Sahagún:

> Regie maiestatis interesse, et iam minus eruditis certum est, ecclesias et sacra loca non solum ab iniuria tueri et defendere verum eciam elemosinarum et beneficiorum in Dei obsequium . . . uisitare, fouere et honorare.[37]

This discourse of legitimation was not, moreover, simply limited to the use of the rhetoric of social restoration with which each successive

---

[35] 1140, *Sahagún*, doc. 1269. Original.
[36] 1132, *Cathedral of Leon*, doc. 1404. Original.
[37] 1131, *Sahagún*, 1248. Copy of 1411.

monarch affirmed his hold on the crown, and was in turn affirmed in his position by those powers on whom his own authority depended. It also employed a different rhetoric of good government through which royal protection of the Church was linked to the guardianship of the peace, health, and stability of the kingdom.[38] This effectively legitimized the king's authority by distancing it from his power as an individual and presenting it as both public and superior in nature. In this way, a model of good kingship was developed through a process of which we are still largely ignorant. It demanded love for, and defense of, justice, respect for old laws and new legislation, and the resolution of conflicts. According to this model, a good king was supposed to be the source of all good things and offer protection against all evils. It is a model whose development is worth charting as it eventually came to represent the foundation of a political culture whose effects were extremely far-reaching and whose constituent parts represented means of legitimation that could be employed in a wide range of different contexts and situations.

The preambles of a number of diplomas issued by Fernando I, by emphasizing that those kings who enjoy divine assistance from the Holy Trinity promote all that is good and reprove all that is bad (*Sub diuino et caelesti auxilio sancta et indiuidua Trinitas . . . eligens quod bonum est et quod malum est reprobans . . .*), precede and justify the king's decisions. Thus, the restoration of bishops to their sees and their subsequent maintenance, chief among the good deeds attributed to good Christian kings, opens Fernando I's aforementioned diploma of 1046 to the see of Astorga.[39] Likewise, the exemplary generosity of the Christian king heads a document drawn up one year later recorded the donation of an estate to the Bishop of León.[40] This image of good kingship had in fact already been formulated as early as 992 in Sahagún's scriptorium by Sampiro, its most famous chronicler and royal notary, by way of introduction to a grant made to

---

[38] The formula *Pro remedio, quoque, anime mee et mei regni stabilitate* certainly predates the period under discussion. Although I have not been able to find it among the diplomatic formulae that Amancio Isla has identified in connection with early medieval Iberian kingships, it occurs in Merovingian legislation (I thank Paul Fouracre for this information). However, what interests us here is the moment in which it is revived and once again assimilated into the royal documents that we are commenting.

[39] 1046, *Cathedral of Astorga*, doc. 306. A seventeenth-century copy is in BN. ms. 1195b, ff. 14–15.

[40] 1047, *Sahagún*, doc. 505. A twelfth-century copy is preserved in the *Becerro Gótico de Sahagún*, ff. 80v–81r.

that monastery by Vermudo II.[41] On that earlier occasion, a king's subjection of his rebellious subjects was also celebrated as model royal behaviour inasmuch as the donated goods provened from confiscation of the rebels' property. This model was clearly of Isidoran inspiration, and a reflection of a biblical ideal of kingship which Sampiro himself celebrated in the chronicle he penned at the beginning of the eleventh century.[42]

By representing their royal subjects in the context of judicial assemblies through which they imposed order and harmony on the litigants, these documents also established a clear association between their royal person and the establishment of peace. The year 1089 both witnessed a rather peculiar hearing which is particularly interesting in this respect and because it concerns the formulation of norms in the context of a judicial assembly.[43] On that occasion the bishop of León, trusting in the justice of his lord the king, brought a case against the king's own sister, Urraca. In the document recording this event the king, Alfonso VI, confesses that it was his desire to put an end to the confusion and disorder that afflicted his kingdom that moved him to judge the case. The king is thus presented as a peacemaker taking charge of law and order in his kingdom with the consent and advice of the members of his curia.

Orta fuit intencio inter infantam domnam Urracam, filiam Fredinandi regis, et Legionensem episcopum domnum Petrum super hereditates et uillanos Sancte Marie de Legione. Infantissa enim domna Urraca leuauat illos uillanos cum sua hereditate que pertinebat ad Sanctam Mariam, et pro ista causa episcopus domnus Petrus tenebat grandem calumniam, et dicebat quod, si ipsa infantissa leuabat illos uillanos, non debebat leuare illas hereditates, quas reges et alii per hereditatem Legionensi ecclesie dederant, ut eas in perpetuum sine contradictione haberet. Tunc episcopus, confidens de iusticia domini suis regis domni Adefonsi, fecit grandem querelam de hoc coram ipso rege. Postea uero domnus Adefonsus rex, cum esset in Uilla Alpando, uolens tollere grandem confusionem et grandem baraliam de regno suo, uocauit ad se germanas suas, infantem domnam Urrakam et infantem domnam Geloiram, et illis autorizantibus et affirmantibus per iudicium et consilium comitum, baronum suorum et maiorum de sua escola et meliorum de sua terra, cunctis uocatis ad suam curiam, fecit istum plazum [o placitum]

---

[41] 998?, *Cathedral of León*, doc. 1244. Preserved in a copy of 1020.

[42] The Isidoran inspiration of these documents is noted by Isla in his comparison of the virtues attributed to these kings. Isla (1998) 81–88.

[43] 1089, *Cathedral of Leon*, doc. 1244. Preserved in a twelfth-century copy.

> et affirmauit hoc scriptum . . . Hoc scriptum fecit fieri rex domnus Ade-
> fonsus et affirmauit in toto suo regno, et statuit ut si ille aut aliquis de
> genere suo aut de genere comitum aut nobilium hoc suum scriptum
> infringere temptaret, maledictus et anathemizatus esset in hoc seculo
> et in futuro cum Iuda Domini traditore in inferno lueret penas inferni
> et pro temeritatis ausu duplet quantum inquietauerit et ad partem regis
> mille marchas argenti persoluat et hoc scriptum firmum permaneat.

It is also interesting that this document refers to a legal battle of a
distinctly aristocratic nature, in which the bishop of a powerful see
confronted a member of the kingdom's highest nobility over the possession of territory and dependent peasants. In this case the king's
credentials as peacemaker are promoted through a description of a
regulation that he attempted to impose universally (*affirmauit in toto
regno suo*) on the transfer of property, through which he prohibited
property transfers between different modes of lordship (royal, ecclesiastical or the two kinds of lay noble lordships).[44]

Rhetoric such as this, which emphasizes the re-establishment of
social order through the proper exercise of royal justice—which in
this case is specified as the formulation of regulations dedicated to
the maintenance of a peaceful society—is to be found in various
guises throughout the documentation of twelfth century León and
Castile. It is, however, in the description of the great royal assembly that was summoned to attend Alfonso VII's coronation in León,
to be found in the *Chronica Adefonsi Imperatoris*, that it receives its most
ritualized expression.[45] On that occasion, we are told, archbishops,
bishops, and abbots, counts and princes, dukes, and judges all gathered in the royal city to await the day of the king's crowning (. . . *concilium apud Legionem civitatem regiam cum archiepiscopis, episcopis et abbatibus,
comitibus et principibus, ducibus et iudicibus, qui in illius regno erant, . . .*), on
which they were joined by the queen and the king's sister as well
as the king of Pamplona, and a great multitude of monks, priests,
and common people (*Venit autem et maxima turba monachorum et clerico-
rum, necnon et plebs innumerabilis ad videndum sive ad audiendum vel ad
loquendum verbum divinum*). The proceedings lasted three days. On the
first, the spiritual wellbeing of the kingdom was dealt with at a meeting that took place in the Cathedral of León. On the second, with

---

[44] I have pointed out elsewhere the lack of attention to the general character of
these legal dispositions despite the fact that they clearly set a precedent for those
that were formulated at the Court of Nájera one century later. Alfonso (1997) 951.
[45] 1135, *Chronica Adefonsi Imperatoris*, 69, 70, 71.

great ceremony Alfonso VII was crowned and received the title of Emperor, also in the city's cathedral. Then, on the third and last day, the focus shifted to the royal palaces (*palatiis regalibus*), where all gathered together (*iuncti sunt*) in order to legislate on those issues that touched on the health of all Spain (*quae pertinent ad salutem regni totius Hispanie*). Interestingly enough, the series of legal acts passed on this occasion faithfully reflected those made by many previous rulers on their accession to the throne.

Through the first day, the king issued legal codes for the whole of his kingdom in accordance with those that had been in use in his royal grandfather's time (*deditque imperator mores et leges in universo regno suo, sicut fuerunt in diebus avi sui Regis domni Adefonsi*). This served to legitimize his authority not only by presenting him in the role of lawmaker, but also by reminding his subjects of the continuity of his royal inheritance and his continuation of the good government of his royal ancestors.

The second consisted of an order that the churches of his kingdom be given back all the dependents that had been taken from them unlawfully and without a trial (*iussitque restituere universis ecclesiis omnes habitatores et familias, quas perdiderant sine iuditio et iustitia*). In this case this particular aspect of Alfonso VII's general policy of restoration, which was explicitly and exclusively concerned with the defense of the patrimony and jurisdiction of the Church, was presented not as a purely ecclesiastical matter, but as an issue that affected the health of the entire kingdom.

In the third day, the king ordered the restoration of all the lands and settlements that had been destroyed by war (*praecepitque villas et terras, quae fuerant destructae in tempore bellorum, populare, et plantare vineas et omnia arbusta*). Thereafter, he ruled that his judges should judge righteously in order to put an end to the crimes of those men, both rich and poor, who had been discovered acting unjustly and who had contravened rules made by kings, princes, magnates, judges, and other authorities (*iussitque omnibus iudicibus stricte vitia eradicare in illis hominibus qui contra iustitiam et decreta regnum et principum et potestatum et iudicum invenirentur, et illi alios in lignis suspendentes, alios truncatis manibus aut pedibus relinquentes: non divitibus vel generosis plusquam pauperibus parcentes, sed totum secundum modum culpae discernentes, iuste iudicaverunt*). In addition to this, the king invoked the biblical mandate *ne patieris maleficos* and ruled that 'evildoers' be condemned to exemplary execution. Then, to show that he was in earnest, he hung a few wrongdoers in the presence of the assembled company (*Praeterea iussit nullomodo suferri maleficos, sicut Dominus dixit Moysi "Ne patieris maleficos", et in conspectu omnium, capti sunt aliqui operarii iniquitatis et suspensi sunt in patibulis*). The last of this series of royal decrees was addressed to the municipal authorities of the regions of Toledo and Extremadura, who were directed to make war on the infidel each year in order to avenge God and protect Christian laws.

This detailed description of the great assembly that gathered for Alfonso VII's coronation, written by an anonymous twelfth-century chronicler, is undoubtedly unique as far as our sources are concerned. Despite its singularity, however, it is infused with the same rhetoric that we have discovered in all of the other documents examined so far, which elaborates on the image of the king as the guardian of the kingdom's health, the restorer of ecclesiastical patrimony, the rectifier of the ravages of war, and the administrator of exemplary justice.

Alfonso VII's diplomas offer many more examples through which this image of royal greatness is promoted. One of them describes the king's Lenten meditation in the leonese monastery of Sahagún—in whose scriptorium a large proportion of his documentary output originated—and relates the king's desire to encourage good deeds and stamp out evils in his kingdom (*curandum summopere nobis est ut queque honesta in regno nostro succrescant et inhonesta atque iniqua consulte extirpetur*).[46] Another describes how he replaced the bad old laws of the town of Sahagún with a new, improved, charter after mediating in the resolution of a conflict.[47]

If we pause to consider just one more document, we will have proved beyond doubt the continuity in our twelfth-century sources of the association of restorative royal power with the image of model kings who combined the functions of judge, legislator, and peacemaker. It was issued by Alfonso VII's Leonese successor, Fernando II, in order to record the ruling he made in favour of the Bishopric of Lugo against the *cives* of that cathedral city in 1161.[48] Its preamble contains a royal exaltation of the judicial process in which kings are attributed the tasks of maintaining justice, banishing evils, protecting the rights of churches and upholding Canon Law, and confirming and extending royal donations to religious institutions:

---

[46] 1136, *Sahagún*, doc. 1256. Original.
[47] 1152, *Sahagún*, doc. 1314. Original.
[48] 1161, *Fernando II*, doc. 6. Twelfth-century copy in Madrid, BN. ms. 1195b, ff. 14–15.

Regum est officium iustitiam colere, mala extirpare, bona bonis tribuere, et iura ecclesiastica lege canonum et regum donatione instituta conseruare, conseruataque in melius propagare. When legislating in favour of the see of Lugo and against that town's municipal authorities, Fernando II claimed to do so by divine inspiration (*Dei gratia . . . diuina inspiratione monitus*), in order to put an end to the many wrongs (*multa facinora et quamplures iniurias*) that had been done to that church, and because he desired all concerned to live together in peace (*omnes enim uolo uiuant in pace*).[49]

Our brief foray into the archives of the religious institutions of eleventh and twelfth-century León and Castile has demonstrated that the political activities of the kings of those kingdoms were legitimated through the development of a discourse that contrasted order with disorder, and good deeds with bad. A firm association was also thus developed between divine and secular power through the repeated affirmation that the latter was entrusted to kings by the will and grace of the former. It was a discourse that represented a fundamental component of the political ideology transmitted by kings through the legal arena that provided the physical setting for the administration of royal justice. Any discussion of the rhetoric employed in the development of this discourse would be incomplete if it avoided the controversial issue of the way in which texts reflect reality, since the use of the term 'rhetoric' itself implies that the texts are not to be taken at face value. We must therefore be aware of the dangers of accepting without question our sources' accounts of the reconstructive efforts they attribute to their various royal subjects. In other words, we should be wary of interpreting the discourse of restoration that they promote as anything other than a resource of legitimation.[50] Above all, we must accept that tool of legitimation as an important element of medieval social reality and strive to learn more about its construction and employment, and development over time.

---

[49] A 'discourse of peace' is also employed by Fernando II's successor, Alfonso IX, who, having heard that his *regnum ualde turbatum erat per malefactores* in the first year of his reign, acted to banish those *uiolentias et iniurias* from his kingdom by issuing some extremely interesting decrees, although their dating and content are strongly debated. 1188, *Alfonso IX*, doc. 12. See Pérez Prendes (1988).

[50] The long persistence of discourses based upon restorative power, the improvement of justice and order, as well as the recreation of historical memory and legitimacy by those who hold such a power has often led historians to take those narratives at face value, as descriptions of real events. Centuries later, the old rhetoric still writes its effects on its readers.

Judicial Rhetoric and the Politics of Truth

We must now turn our attention to another fundamentally important aspect of the development of the legitimacy attached to judicial
places. This concerns the relationship that is established between justice and truth, terms whose synonymy is established through the presentation of the judicial process as a process of truth. This connection
between the two concepts endowed the courts with which they were
associated with unimpeachable credentials as forums of legitimation.
They were thus promoted as environments in which a certain 'truth'
was identified and presented in the form of 'justice', and where rights
were both defined and legitimized. In the process, the ownership of
land was elevated to a level where it also became synonymous with
the 'truth'. Semantically speaking, therefore, 'justice' (*iustitia*), came
to encompass both 'truth' (*veritas*) and 'right' (*directum*) in our sources.
In this context, the pursuit of a legal claim became the conceptual
equal of the pursuit of both truth and justice.

   In 1043, Fernando I and his wife Queen Sancha responded to a
claim made by the Bishop of León to an estate that had been lost
to his see since *tempore persecutionis* by commissioning a legal investigation into the "truths" of their kingdom's churches in order that
they might confirm their rights accordingly: *iussimus perquirere ueritates
ecclesiis et precepimus eas stare per directum sicut ab antecessoribus permanser-
ant.*[51] In keeping with the restorative rhetoric of such proceedings,
the royal couple went on to state that, while they heard the 'truth',
they also understood that he who restores is more worthy than he
who builds: *dum audiuimus ueritatem . . . intelleximus quia melius est qui
restaurat quam qui hedificat.*

   As we have already seen, this discourse promoted the mutual support of church and monarchy to such an extent as to make the two
institutions inseparable. The dependence of religious institutions on
a favourable monarchy is most eloquently expressed in the aforementioned document recording the claims made by the Abbot of
Sahagún on the lordship of an estate.[52] In that document, the abbot
is reported to have claimed that the property in question had belonged
to his monastery from the time of Ramiro III until that time when

---

[51] 1043, *Cathedral of León*, doc. 1007. Preserved in a twelfth-century copy in the
Tumbo Legionense, f. 22r–v.m.
[52] See p. 66.

the land was without king and the Holy Church without 'truth' (*peruenit terram sine rege et ecclesia santa non habebat ueritatem*). This was a reference to the disorder associated with the reign of Vermudo II which, according to this document, lasted until Alfonso V took up the rule and the Church was able to recover the 'truth' (*ecclesia Dei habere cepit ueritatem*). In a similar vein, a document issued by the Cathedral of León praises Fernando I for ordering an investigation into all the rights and 'truths' of the bishopric (*ut exquireret omnem debitum et veritatis hujus sedis*).[53]

This association between justice and truth established through legal proceedings is apparent before the reign of Fernando I. One document of 1012, for example, tells of a dispute between the monastery of Celanova and a layman who was the nephew of one of its monks.[54] The case was brought before Alfonso V, who ordered one of his royal officials to take control of the disputed property until both parties to the quarrel had attended his council and each had arrived at the 'truth' of the matter (*usque quando devenissent ad concilium et abuissent unus cum alios veritatem*). The king also ordered one of his counts to give them the truth until the cause of the truth had been defined in his presence (*que dedisset veritatem . . . usque definessent inde ante eum causam veritatis*). The count in turn delegated the job to another, whom he ordered to be a truthful judge of the case and to deliver to its litigants both judgment and the truth in such a way as to decide with which side the truth lay, and then to grant that side the undivided possession of the disputed property (*et ordinavit ad Pelagio Strofediz ut fuisset suo vicario et iudice verifico de ista actione, et dedisset inter eos iudicium et veritatem, et cui dedisset veritas ipsa hereditas possidisset omnia iuri quieto absque alio herede ita et fecit*). In the event, the property was granted to the monastery because the defendant recognized 'in truth' the 'truth' of the document presented by the monks to support their case (*agnovit . . . in veritate quia erat ipsa scriptura verifica et debent semper robore abere pro quo ipsam hereditatem obtineant iuri quieto*). In other cases, compromise agreements (*convenientiae*) were implemented to settle disputes when their judges found that both litigants "were in possession of the truth" (*ueritatem tenebant*).[55]

---

[53] 1057, *Catedral de Astorga*, doc. 353. A seventeenth-century copy is in BN. ms. 1195b, f. 633.

[54] 1012, *Celanova*, doc. 548. A copy is preserved in *Tumbo de Celanova*, ff. 188r–188v.

[55] 1048, *Sahagún*, doc. 514. A twelfth-entury copy is preserved in the *Becerro Gótico de Sahagún*, ff. 190v–191r.

Such inquiries into the 'truth' referred primarily to ecclesiastical patrimony and were justified through their representation as obedient responses to expressions of divine will. Thus at the 1017 Council of León, Alfonso V supported his legislation by claiming that the law stated that whoever "made truth" did so in compliance with God's will, and that he who denied the truth defrauded God: *inquiramus ueritatem sicut lex docet, quia legem dicit ut qui ueritatem facit Dei uoluntatem adimplet. Deo enim fraude facit qui ueritatem resindet.*[56] In this way, the taking of royal decisions is presented by our sources in such a way as to emphasize the desire of kings to deliver decisions that were just, legal, and accordance with truth and right. Thus in the aforementioned 1046 diploma Fernando I is said to have been moved by *caelum veritatis* when judging the case of the rebellious peasants of the village of Matanza, whom he defeated and imprisoned before deciding that according to both Canon Law and the Visigothic Law they should be re-incorporated into the jurisdiction of the bishopric that they had rejected.[57]

How was this 'truth' ascertained? On which foundations did its authority rest? The search for the 'truth' which is described in that León code as both legal mandate and divine will was in practice pursued through inquisitive mechanisms such as judicial inquiries. The evidence presented at such inquiries was often of a written nature, and the documents in which it was recorded were authenticated by the testimony of the litigants themselves. The case brought before Alfonso V in 1014 by the Portuguese monastery of Guimaraes illustrates not only this process, but also the way in which the practice it represents predated the legal norms from which it was com-

---

[56] 1017 *Alfonso V*, doc. 19a. A thirteenth-century copy is in the *Liber Fidei* de Braga, f. r–v. Another clause of the same code applies the same method of inquiry to seignurial contexts: *qui habuerit debitum uadat ad domino suo pro accipere sua ueritate et si noluerit eam dare in uoce det duas uel IIIes de ipsa uilla qui uideant ueritas et postea pergant ante ipsos iudices qui in concilio electi sunt et dent illi sua ueritate.* Compare with the version of these same laws recorded in the twelfth-century copy *Liber Testamentorum* (ff. 54v–57r; *ib.* 19b).

[57] *Nos vero caelum veritatis eligentes et horum taliam superbiam prosternentes iussimus comprehendere ipsi homines et in ergastuli mittere, ut aliquid ex facto suo presenti in vita recipiant, et ceteris in hac opinione exemplo fiat. Elegimus etiam ex eis quidquid in santissimum canonem et goticam legem inuenitur de rebelionibus et contradictoribus regis, siue de facultatibus eorum sicut in libro secundo et in eius titulo constitutum vel exaratum a prioribus santis patribus scriptum esse decernitur.* 1046, *Catedral de Astorga*, 306. Seventeenth-century copy in BN. ms. 1195b, ff. 14–15.

monly assumed to have proceeded.[58] The document recording this case relates that the monks of Guimaraes, who had had all of their documents authenticated at the court of every new king since the foundation of their monastery, had been challenged by 'wicked slanderers' who claimed those documents to be false (*surrexerunt omnes inique et maliciantes contra ipso monasterio Vimaranes, narrauerunt ei quomodo non erant ipsos testamentos uerificos*).[59] It also tells that the monks testified to the veracity of their documents after they had been read out before the assembled council and the truth of their contents had been investigated. This process resulted in a new royal ratification of the disputed monastic documentation, which could be produced as a guarantee of the monastery's possessions in the face of future attacks on its patrimony. One needs look no further than the preamble of the charter that contained this ratification to discover the function that was attributed to the documents to which it refers, as it most explicitly states that it was written in order that all might be informed that the narrative it relates was a 'true account' (*Ambiguum quidem non est sed multis plerisque manet connitum atque notissimum in ueritate*).

In this context, it is fitting to consider cases in which false documents were burned in order that the 'truth' might be established, as the identification of falsifications and their destruction were among the functions attributed to judicial assemblies.[60] Indeed, it is impossible to overstress the importance of written documents in the legal contexts we have been discussing. The written word was such an important legitimizing weapon in the battle to impose and gain recognition for any single version of past events, that protecting the documents that recorded them was of the utmost importance. What they most needed protecting from were fires, both those that started accidentally and those that resulted from more sinister causes. It is not surprising, then, to find that some royal confirmations were clearly

---

[58] 1014, *Alfonso V*, doc. 15.

[59] It would be worth investigating this claim with respect to the types of documents to which it refers (*testamentos, agnitios, notitias . . .*) in order to discover more both about the nature of monastic archives and how these supported their owners' claims to credibility.

[60] This occurred in a case in which the charters produced by one of the sides to a dispute were found to be falsifications and were ordered to be burned (*posteriores et falsas et aborrendas mandarunt eas cremare et fuissent inualidas*). *Diplomata et chartae*, I, n. 25. Cited by Prieto Morera in his commentary on the dispute. Prieto Morera (1992) 479.

drafted in response to the needs of those who had lost documents through fire.[61] Although the causes of those fires, which were generally perceived as divine punishment, were rarely specified, the destruction of the charters of one's adversaries clearly represented a recognized strategy of political aggression. This is well illustrated by a document, issued in 1058, recording a case brought before Fernando I by the bishop of Astorga in an attempt to reclaim some villages that had been usurped by men who, like preying wolves, had attacked his see by seizing all of its documents, which they had then burned at the devil's own prompting (*surrexit Ecta Rapinatiz et filiis suis sicut lupis super hanc sedem et aprehenderunt omnes scripturas et cremaverunt eas zelo diaboli ductus*).[62] The case was resolved when the accused men personally recognized the truth of the allegations leveled against them before a council at which many 'good men' who lived in the disputed area were present (*agnoverunt se in veritate . . . cum propia sua lingua in hoc concilio, necnon et multorum filii bonorumque hominum ibidem stantium atque residentium*).[63] This public recognition was to be maintained in the memory of all those present, but was also committed to the written record and preserved in the cathedral's archives to serve as a more permanent guarantee of the see's property.

In 1063, Fernando I dealt with another dispute, this time between two monasteries. In this case, he ordered his 'most faithful deputy' (*fidelissimum vicarium*) Fernando Osoriz to summon all the nobles and wise men who "were familiar with the truth" to judge the case (*convocassent omnes nobiles et sapientes qui bene nouerant veritatem ut discernerent iustitiam inter utrosque monasterios*). The *iudices et nobiles magistratus* who had been summoned to the task duly ordered one of the disputing parties to provide witnesses to testify as to the 'truth' regarding their monastery during the reign of Alfonso V (*testes ydoneos que iurassent qui erat uel que fuerat ueritas*). The document recording this case details the sworn testimony of the witnesses presented (*ita verifice iuramus quia est ueritas*), and then describes the division of the disputed goods, made

---

[61] 1007, *Alfonso V*, doc. 6, is a request for a royal confirmation of privileges that had been destroyed by fire; 1027, Alfonso V, 33, is a confirmation of the diplomas belonging to the cathedral of Lugo that had been kept in its *scriniis et tesauris* and had been lost through fire.

[62] 1058, Catedral de Astorga, doc. 361. Eighteenth-century copy in *Tumbo Negro*, f. 42r.

[63] Later, when returning the disputed property, these men confessed that they did so '*secundum leges et judices elegerunt in hoc concilio et nos in veritate fuimus conscios sic facimus . . .*'.

and confirmed in the king's presence, which it states was made publicly in order to ensure its stability (*Omnia taxata vel divisio firmata publice exaravimus, et coram Regis presentia adstabiliendum vel confirmandum protulimus*).[64] The 'truth' about the property of the Church was thus gradually incorporated into the documentary registers of religious institutions.

The preamble to a charter we have already discussed provides an emphatic example of the ecclesiastical imposition of the value of written evidence as a guarantee of rights gained through disputes brought before judicial assemblies. It contains a commandment that the resolutions of those assemblies, which it describes using the term *agnita*, should be committed to writing in order that they might always be remembered by the people and therefore never lose their force:

> Antiqui enim patres atque doctores de preterita presentia atque future agnitionem scribere docuerunt, ut agnita in memoria semper esse ut et presentes scirent, et scienda cuncta posteris relinquerent et confirmata firmiter et inreuocabiliter tenerent.[65]

In the same vein, the preamble to yet another legal narrative relates its committal to the written record to the maintenance of the 'truth' as it had been defined and recognized in the context of royal justice:

> Hoc autem scriptum facimus et cartula decernimus ut quisquis legeret vel audierit vera esse fateatur agnitionem veritatis plenam habeat firmitatem.[66]

According to these documents, this method of ascertaining and defining past events was well established in León and Castile well before the influence of Roman Law made its way into those kingdoms. A hundred years later, at the end of the twelfth century, we see it again being employed by Fernando II, another Leonese monarch, who stated unequivocally in the preamble to a judicial settlement that when judgments were not committed to writing, they were consigned to oblivion instead (*Plerumque contingere solet ut ea que per iuditium diffiniuntur nisi in scripto redigantur posteris obliuioni tradantur*).[67] This document of

---

[64] 1063, *Celanova*, doc. 260. A twelfth-century copy in *Tumbo de Celanova*, f. 95v. This monastery also brought another dispute before Fernando I, during which the king ordered that *quantum erat sua veritate* should be ascertained through the testimony of witnesses in a council *ubi fuerunt non modica multorum filii multorum benenatorum*. *Ibid.* doc. 300.

[65] 1007, *Alfonso V*, doc. IV. Twelfth-century copy in the *Tumbo de Celanova*, ff. 4v–5r.

[66] 1057, *Catedral of Astorga*, doc. 353.

[67] 1186, *Sahagún*, doc. 1423. Original.

1186 records a dispute in which the authorities of a powerful royal town confronted the oft-cited monastery of Sahagún before the king and his curia (*coram rege et eius curia*). It employs very refined language and presents its subject in a notably formal and institutionalized light. It states that the sentence handed down by the king in this case was based, not on consideration of the law, but on the truth as it had been ascertained by a royal inquiry: *In qua causa iudi-tiali sententia deffinitum est: ut, datis exquisitoribus, ueritas inquireretur et qui in diebus imperatoris et ad mortem eius hereditatem illam tenebat ipse eam libere possideret.* This sentence was in fact a compromise solution reached in the interests of peace (*pro pace conformanda*) that, temporarily at least, resolved the quarrel. As we have already seen, such negotiated resolutions were sometimes reached because the judges ruled that both parties to a dispute were "in possession of the truth".

The documents we have been discussing demonstrate the process whereby the truth was effectively objectified in the judicial arenas whose business they record.[68] This process was a circular one through which legal decisions acquired the status of truth as a result of the authority invested in the methods with which that truth had been ascertained, which in turn derived from the power that ordered the implementation of those methods, which was itself legitimized in the process, along with the forum in which the whole process unfolded. This process and its circularity were described by Foucault when he examined the relationship between power, law, and truth in an attempt to identify the source of the authority that can bestow the status of truth on a given version of events.[69] The relevance and interest of his aim to apply historical analysis to what he termed 'the politics of truth' through the examination of historical judicial practices cannot be doubted. Indeed, leaving aside his contradictory and widely questioned assertions concerning the model of political development that should have accompanied the establishment of the truth through inquiries and the innovation that would have implied in terms of judicial convention, we can agree with Foucault that this type of judicial inquiry in effect represented a 'means of exercising power'.[70]

---

[68] We are in fact far from the "zealous search for an objective truth" or the "material rather than formal truth" which Prieto Morera associates with these documents. Prieto Morera (1992) 435, 480.

[69] Foucault presents a consideration of this problem, which underlies his work in its entirety, in *Microfisique du pouvoir* Barcelona: 1979 (2nd ed. in Spanish), and *La verdad y las formas jurídicas*, Barcelona, 1995 (4th ed. in Spanish).

[70] Foucault proposed that the revival of this method of judicial investigation, which

The evidence of the judicial narratives we have been discussing allows us to extend this argument one step further, as the way in which they represent royal power has more to do with its legitimation than its exercise. Their function was not only to record actions based on established truth, but also to use that truth, and the methods by which it was ascertained, to justify the power that imposed it. It is between the lines of this dialectical relationship between the exercise of power and its legitimation that I believe one can discern the process whereby the superiority of royal power and jurisdiction were established. It is a process in urgent need of further investigation.

Translated by Carolina Carl

Bibliography

Alfonso, I. (1994) "Resolución de disputas y prácticas judiciales en el Burgos medieval", en *Burgos en la plena Edad Media. III Jornadas Burgalesas de Historia* (Burgos: 1994) 211–243.
—— (1997) "Litigios por la tierra y 'malfetrías' entre la nobleza medieval castellano-leonesa" in I. Alfonso (coord.) *Desarrollo legal, prácticas judiciales y acción política en la Europa medieval, Hispania*, 197 (1997) 917–995.
—— (2001) "Conflictos en las behetrías" en C. Estepa y C. Jular (eds.), *Los señoríos de behetría* (Madrid: 2001) 228–259.
—— (2002) "Venganza y Justicia en el Cantar de Mio Cid" en *El Cid: de la materia épica a las crónicas caballerescas*, ed. C. Alvar, F. Gómez Redondo and G. Martin (Alcalá de Henares: 2002) 41–69.
Andrade, J.M. (1995) *O Tombo de Celanova: Estudio introductorio, edición e índices (ss. IX–XII)* 2 vols. (Santiago: 1995).
Bloch, M. (1975) *Political Language and Oratory in Traditional Society* (London and New York: 1975).
Bougard, F. (1997) "La justice dans le royaume d'Italie aux IXe–XIe siécles" in *La giustizia nell'alto medioevo (secoli IX–XI)* (Spoleto: 1997) I, 133–178.
Bourdieu, P. (1991) *El sentido práctico* (Madrid: 1991, orig. 1980).
Cavero, G. (1995) *Astorga y su territorio en la Edad Media (s. IX–XIV): evolución demográfica, económica, social, político-administrativa y cultural de la sociedad astorgana medieval* (León: 1995).

accompanied the recovery of Roman Law in the twelfth century, signified the demise of previous magical or irrational judicial practices in which the function of a trial was not so much to establish the truth, but to decide which party to a dispute was the strongest. It was his opinion that the re-introduction of the judicial inquiry transformed those previous legal practices and led to the development of new forms of justice. ('La verdad': pp. 60–85). For the challenges that have been made to others who have shared Foucault's opinion see: Reynolds (1997); Davis & Fouracre (1986); the articles by Bougard (1997), Wickham (1997), and Nelson (1997) in Spoleto; and those of Alfonso (1997) and White (1997) in the dossier in *Hispania*.

Cavero, G. y Martín, E. (1999) *Colección documental de la Catedral de Astorga*, I *(646–1126)* (León: 1999).

Davies, W., Fouracre, P., eds. (1986) *The Settlement of Disputes in Early Medieval Europe* (Cambridge: 1986).

De Jong M. de and Theuws, F. eds. (2001) *Topographies of power in the early Middle Ages* (Leiden: 2001).

El Reino de León en la Alta Edad Media, I. *Cortes, Concilio y Fueros* (León: 1988).

Fentress, J., Wickham, Ch. (1992) *Social Memory* (Oxford: 1992).

Fernández Catón, J.M. (1990) *Colección documental del archivo de la Catedral de León (775–1230)*, V *(1109–1187)* (León: 1990).

—— (1991) *Colección documental del archivo de la Catedral de León (775–1230)*, VI (León: 1991).

Fernández Florez, J.A., (1991) *Colección documental de Sahagún (857–1230)*. IV *(1110–1199)* (León: 1991).

—— (2002) *La elaboración de los documentos en los reinos hispánicos occidentales (ss. VI–XIII)* (Burgos: 2002).

Fernández del Pozo, J. (1984) "Alfonso V, rey de León. Estudio Histórico-Documental", in *León y su historia*, V (León: 1984) 9–264.

Foucault, M. (1979) *Microfísica del poder*, (Barcelona: 1979), 2ª ed. in Spanish.

—— (1995) *La verdad y las formas jurídicas* (Barcelona: 1995), 4ª ed. in Spanish.

Fouracre, P. (1995) "Caroligian justice: the rhetoric of improvement and contexts of abuse" in *La giustizia nell'alto medioevo (secoli V–VIII)*, (Spoleto: 1995) 771–803.

Gambra, A. (1997, 1998) *Alfonso VI, Cancillería, Curia e Imperio*, 2 vols. (León: 1997, 1998).

González, J. (1943) *Regesta de Fernando II* (Madrid: 1943).

—— (1944) *Alfonso IX*, 2 vols. (Madrid: 1944).

Herrero de la Fuente, M. (1988) *Colección diplomática de Sahagún (857–1230)*, II *(1000–1073)*; III *(1073–1109)* (León: 1988).

Isla, A. (1997) "La monarquía leonesa según Sampiro" in *Historia social, Pensamiento historiográfico y Edad media. Homenaje al Prf. Abilio Barbero*, ed. M.I. Loring (Madrid: 1997) 33–58.

—— (1999) *Las realezas hispánicas del año mil* (La Coruña: 1999).

Larrea, J.J. (1999) "Villa Matanza" in *Les sociétés méridionales à l'âge féodal: Espagne, Italie et sud de la France Xᵉ–XIIIᵉ s. Hommage à Pierre Bonnassie*, textes réunis par H. Débax (Toulouse: 1999) 223–228.

Las Cortes de León y Castilla en la Edad Media, vol. I, (Valladolid: 1988).

Las Cortes de Castilla y León. 1188–1988 (Valladolid: 1990).

Lucas Álvarez, M. (1995) *Cancillerías reales astur-leonesas (718–1072)* in *El Reino de León en la Alta Edad Media*, VIII (León: 1995).

—— (1993) *Cancillerías reales (1109–1230)* in *El Reino de León en la Alta Edad Media*, V (León: 1993).

Martin, G. (1997) "Le récit héroïque castillan (formes, enjeux sémantiques et fonctions socio-culturelles)" in *Histoires de l'Espagne médievale (Historiographie, geste, romancero)* (Paris: 1997) 139–152.

Miller, W.I. (1990) *Bloodtaking and Peacemaking: Feud, Law, and Society in Saga Iceland* (Chicago, Illinois: 1990).

Milsom, S.F.C. (1976) *The Legal Framework of English Feudalism* (Cambridge: 1976).

—— (1981) *Historical Foundations of the English Common Law* (London: 1981, 2nd ed.).

Nelson, J. (1986) "Legislation and Consensus in the reign of Charles the Bald", in *Politics and Ritual in Early Medieval Europe* (London: 1986) 91–111.

—— (1995) "Kingship and royal government" in *The New Cambridge Medieval History*, Volume II *c. 700–c. 900* (Cambridge: 1995) 383–430.

—— (1997) "Kings with Justice, Kings without Justice: an Early Medieval Paradox" in *La giustizia nell'alto medioevo (secoli IX–XI)* (Spoleto: 1997), II, 797–826.

Pastor, R. (1980) *Resistencias y luchas campesinas en la época del crecimiento y consolidación de la formación feudal. Castilla y León, siglos X–XIII* (Madrid: 1980).

Pérez Prendes, J.M. (1988) "La potestad legislativa en el reino de León. Notas sobre el *Fuero* de León, el *Concilio* de Coyanza y las *Cortes* de 1188" in *El Reino de León en la Alta Edad Media*, I. *Cortes, Concilio y Fueros* (León: 1988) 495–545.

Prieto Morera, A. (1992) "El proceso en el Reino de León a la luz de los diplomas" in *El Reino de León en la Alta Edad Media*, II. *Ordenamiento jurídico del Reino* (León: 1992) 383–520.

Reuter, T. (2001) "Assembly politics in Western Europe from Eighth Century to the Twelfth" in *The Medieval World*, ed. P. Linehan and J.L. Nelson (London: 2001) 432–450.

Reynolds, S. (1997) *Kingdoms and Communities in Western Europe, 900–1300* (Oxford: 1997, 2nd ed.).

Ruiz Asencio, J.M. (1987) *Colección documental del archivo de la Catedral de León (775–1230), III (986–1031)* (León: 1987).

—— (1990) *Colección documental del archivo de la Catedral de León (775–1230), IV (1032–1109)* (León: 1990).

Sánchez Belda, L. (1950) *Chronica Adefonso Imperatoris* (Madrid: 1950).

White, S. (1987) "Inheritances and Legal Arguments in Western France, 1050–1150", *Traditio*, 43 (1987) 55–103.

—— (1997) "La traición en la ficción literaria. Derecho, hecho y ordalías en la narrativa y la épica en francés antiguo" in I. Alfonso (coord.) *Desarrollo legal, prácticas judiciales y acción política en la Europa medieval, Hispania*, 197 (1997) 957–980.

Wickham, Ch. (1997) "Justice in the Kingdom of Italy in eleventh century" in *La giustizia nell'alto medioevo (secoli IX–XI)* (Spoleto: 1997) I, 179–256.

—— (2000) *Legge, pratiche e conflitti. Tribunali e risoluzione delle dispute nella toscana del XII secolo* (Roma: 2000).

LEGITIMATION, DESIGNATION AND SUCCESSION TO THE THRONE IN FOURTEENTH-CENTURY ENGLAND

Chris Given-Wilson
University of St. Andrews

Generically speaking, kings and kingdoms required little by way of legitimation during the middle ages. History, the Bible, and current practice all taught that kingdoms were 'natural' units of government, and, if there were going to be kingdoms, then it followed that there must be kings. Not only was kingship an almost universally-accepted mode of government, it was also a divinely-ordained one: it had always existed, and—so it seems to have been assumed—it always would. Jesus Christ, after all, was—and still is—commonly referred to as a king.

Individual kings, on the other hand, might often find themselves in need of legitimation, and they sought it from various quarters: God, marriage, kinship, prophecy, conquest and 'election' might all be— and at times were—cited. Whenever possible, however, kings sought to legitimate their right to rule through blood inheritance, for, as is well known, this was the most powerful and widely-accepted way in which land, title and authority were transmitted. Exactly *how* the blood inheritance of a kingdom ought to be transmitted—whether by strict male primogeniture, for example, or through a female line— was, of course, a much more complex, and frequently a highly controversial, question, but not one with which we are directly concerned here. The aim of this paper is to ask one quite specific question about the ways in which it was believed that someone might legitimately succeed to the English throne during the middle ages, with particular reference to the later fourteenth century. That question is: in cases where there was more than one plausible candidate to succeed him, what influence might a reigning king hope to exert by designating his heir?

It is, as it happens, quite a topical question. Some five years ago, in a lengthy and stimulating article on the succession to the crown in fourteenth- and fifteenth-century England, Michael Bennett published a document dating from the last year of the reign of Edward

III (1327–77) which he had discovered in the British Library.[1] The
document in question is severely damaged, and substantial parts of
it are illegible. To judge by those parts which are legible, however,
Bennett argued convincingly that it is a deed whereby King Edward
designated his grandson Richard II as his successor and stipulated
that, should Richard die without producing a son, the crown should
subsequently pass to each of his (Edward III's) sons, and their male
heirs, in order of age. In other words, he created an entail of the
crown in the male line, or, as it is sometimes called, a tail male. As
Bennett demonstrated, there is no real problem in dating Edward's
deed: it was drawn up at the king's favoured manor of Havering-
atte-Bower, in Essex, probably in early October 1376.[2] Nor, indeed,
is there any great difficulty in understanding its context, for, as a
number of contemporary sources make clear, various rumours were
circulating in both England and France at this time about the question of the succession to Edward III, and it was pretty clear that
the king had to clarify the situation.

Edward III had five sons who survived infancy: Edward the Black
Prince (born in 1330); Lionel of Clarence (born 1338); John of Gaunt
(born 1340); Edmund of Langley (born 1342); and Thomas of
Woodstock (born 1355). Lionel of Clarence had died in 1368, leaving only one child, his daughter Philippa, who was married to
Edmund, earl of March. However, while Lionel's death may well
have induced some degree of uncertainty about the future inheritance of the crown, it was the death on 8 June 1376 of Edward the
Black Prince which really brought the succession question to the
forefront of English politics (see Table I). The potential consequences
of the premature deaths of the king's two eldest sons were twofold:
firstly, that in the short term, Edward III's eldest surviving son (John
of Gaunt) might succeed him, rather than his grandson by his first
son (Richard II). Secondly, that in the long term, should Richard
II succeed him but fail to produce an heir of his own body, he in
turn might be succeeded by a descendant of Lionel's daughter Philippa.
It is worth remembering in this context that it was through the
female line that, half a century earlier, Edward III had claimed the
French throne. There was, therefore, some cause for concern, and

---

[1] Bennett (1998). The document in question is British Library, Cotton Charter
XVI 63.

[2] Bennett (1998) 590.

Table I

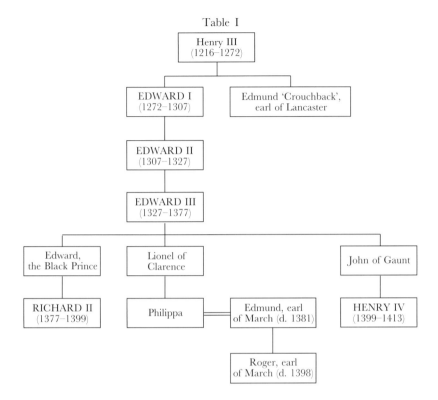

a certain amount of manoeuvring for position. According to Thomas Walsingham, the chronicler of St. Albans abbey, this began within days of the Black Prince's death, when Gaunt, "puffed up with pride and haughtiness", paid a visit to a meeting of the parliamentary knights (for the prince had died in the middle of the Good Parliament), and asked them whether they might consider the question of who ought to inherit the kingdom of England following the death of the king and the prince's son.

> And he begged moreover that, following the example of the French, they might enact a law (*legem statuerunt*) to the effect that no woman could be heir to the kingdom; for he was well aware of the great age of the king, whose death was approaching, and the youth of the prince's son (whom, so it was said, he planned to poison if he could not acquire the kingdom in any other way); because if these two were to be removed from his path, and a law of this sort were to be approved in public parliament (*communi parliamento*), he himself would subsequently be the closest heir to the realm. For no male had a closer proximity than him to the realm. These matters were being spoken of by everyone at that time.

It was, according to Walsingham, the earl of March whom Gaunt
especially feared, because "to him pertained the hereditary right to
the kingdom (*ius regni hereditarium*), should the only son of the prince
die without an heir". But the knights simply fobbed Gaunt off: there
were more important matters to be discussed, so they said, and in
any case it was perfectly possible that Edward III might outlive them
all. "And even if the king should die", Walsingham has them saying,
"then as long as the son of our lord the prince [i.e. Richard], who
is now aged ten, is alive, we shall not lack an heir." And so Gaunt
retired, "confusus".[3]

It is difficult to know how much of this one ought to believe. Walsingham was notoriously hostile to John of Gaunt, and—especially
during the last year or so of Edward III's reign—was prepared to
believe almost anything which reflected badly on him.[4] And, although
the discovery of Edward III's entail certainly makes Walsingham's
story more rather than less believable, it can hardly have happened
as Walsingham describes it. In particular, the idea that the knights
of the shire might have any say in the matter is distinctly improbable.
Yet, true or not, Walsingham's account and Edward's entail, taken
together, touch upon most of the issues which had in the past surrounded, and would continue to surround, the succession question.
Firstly, that is, the question of the validity of the 'representative principle'—namely, the right of a grandchild through a senior line over a
child through a cadet line. Secondly, the rights of females and their
offspring. And thirdly, the question with which we are chiefly concerned here, the right of a reigning monarch to designate his heir.

Various entries in the anonymous chronicle known as the *Eulogium
Historiarum* are also of relevance to this last point. The *Eulogium* is a
problematic chronicle, not least because of its extremely confused
chronology, of which there is no more celebrated example than its
much-quoted statement that in the parliament of 1385 Richard II
declared the earl of March to be his heir. The passage is worth
quoting in full:

> Also in the same parliament, in the public hearing of all the lords and
> of the commons, the king had had it publicly proclaimed (*publice fecerat*

[3] *Chronicon Angliae 1328–1388*, ed. Thompson (1874), 92–3.
[4] Gransden (1982) 129, 136–8.

proclamari) that the earl of March should be the next heir after him to the crown of England; which earl was killed in Ireland a short time afterwards (*modico tempore post*).[5]

Now, this entry comes immediately after a list of comital promotions which are said to have been made in the parliament of 1385, but which includes promotions which were in fact made both before and after that year—in 1377, 1388, and 1390. Since it records March's death, moreover, it was obviously written after 1398, for that was when he died. It needs to be compared with another passage in the same chronicle, placed by the chronicler in the parliament of 1396— which presumably means that of January 1397, since no parliament met in the new-style year 1396. This latter passage reads as follows:

> In this parliament the duke of Lancaster asked that his son Henry be adjudged heir to the kingdom of England (*iudicaretur haeres regni Angliae*); to which the earl of March disagreed, claiming that he was descended from Lord Lionel, the second son of King Edward. The duke, by way of reply, said that King Henry III had two sons, Edmund the elder and first-born, and Edward. But this Edmund had a broken back, and because of this he adjudged (*iudicavit*) him to be unfit for the crown, as a result of which their father made them agree as follows (*eos sic componere fecit*): that Edward should reign, and after him the heirs of Edmund; and he gave Edmund the earldom of Lancaster; and from him descended his son Henry, by right of his mother, who was the daughter of this Edmund. To which the earl replied that this was not

---

[5] *Eulogium Historiarum sive Temporis*, ed. Haydon (1863), III.361. One or two other later chronicles repeated this story, but the *Eulogium* seems to have been the source for it. Pugh (1988) 73–4 (where the March claim to the throne is discussed) thought that the story was a later (c. 1430–1440) fabrication by the Yorkists, and it is certainly telling that Adam Usk, who was patronised by the earls of March, made no mention of it in his chronicle, as surely he would have had he known anything about it. However, the Welsh poet Iolo Goch wrote a poem which anticipated March becoming king of England once he had become prince of Wales: *Cywyddau Iolo Goch ac Eraill*, ed. Lewis, Roberts and Williams (1972) 45–8. Also the Scottish chronicler Walter Bower, writing in the 1440s, reported that at the Shrewsbury parliament of January 1398 Richard II had proclaimed March as his heir: Walter Bower, *Scotichronicon*, ed. Watt (1987) vol. VIII, 20. Tuck (1973) 205, said that Tout had 'disposed of the myth' that Richard proclaimed March as his heir in 1385, but in fact all that Tout said was that the *Eulogium* included "a mass of gross errors, including the imagined recognition of the earl of March as heir to the throne", offering no evidence in support of this: Tout (1920–33) III.396, n. 1. See also the comments of Bennett (1998) 595. A major problem lies in determining exactly when the different sections of the *Eulogium* were written: although not compiled in its final form until about 1430, it is likely that much of it was in fact written about a quarter of a century before this.

true, "but Edward was the first-born, and Edmund was a noble and most elegant knight, as is clearly stated in the chronicles." The king, however, told them to be silent.[6]

This is the well-known 'Crouchback legend' (so-called from Edmund's allegedly 'crooked' back), which is also mentioned in the chronicles of John Hardyng and Adam Usk, and for the use of which there is therefore plenty of contemporary warrant. Usk said that Henry convened a committee of "doctors, bishops and others", of which Usk himself was a member, in order to determine whether there was any truth in the Crouchback story, but it concluded that there was not. Hardyng even said that, in order to try to prove the truth of the legend, Gaunt had "an untrue chronicle . . . fabricated during the time of King Richard II . . . whereby he hoped to make his son Henry king".[7] However, it is not very easy to believe that Gaunt would have raised the question of the Crouchback legend publicly while Richard II still reigned, because, among other things, it invalidated Richard's own title to the throne. Far more likely is Usk's statement that it was Henry, searching in September 1399 for grounds upon which to claim the throne, who brought it up. If, on the other hand, as the author of the *Eulogium* claimed, there was indeed some kind of public debate over the succession between Gaunt and March during Richard's reign, it is most likely to belong to the years between 1394 and 1397—that is, after the childless death of Richard's first queen, Anne of Bohemia, in 1394, but before March's own death in 1398—rather than to the 1380s.

However, although the chronology of the *Eulogium* is not to be trusted, it nevertheless preserves some interesting ideas. What Richard either did, or was asked to do, according to the chronicler, was to designate his successor: he had it publicly proclaimed (*publice fecerat proclamari*) that March should be his heir. And Henry III, so the chronicler thought, had acted in similar fashion: he adjudged (*iudicavit*) Edmund to be unfit for the crown, and made his two sons agree to a compromise (*eos sic componere fecit*). There is no suggestion—not, at any rate, in the way that the chronicler tells it—that either king sought any kind of consent for his decision: each of them simply decreed to whom his kingdom should pass after his death. Whether either Richard or Henry did in fact do what the chroni-

---

[6] *Eulogium Historiarum*, III.369–70.
[7] *Chronicles of the Revolution 1397–1400*, ed. Given-Wilson (1993) 161, 195.

cler claims they did is certainly an interesting question, but, for present purposes, a subsidiary one: the point at issue is the fact that he
believed that they had the authority to act in this way. A passage
in the 'Record and Process', Henry IV's sanitized version of the procedure according to which Richard II was deposed, is also relevant
here. It is recorded on the Rolls of Parliament, where it follows
immediately after the enrolment of Richard's formal act of renunciation, and reads as follows:

> And immediately the same king added to this Renunciation and Cession
> in his own words that, were it in his power, the duke of Lancaster
> should succeed him in the realm (*si esset in potestate sua, dictus dux Lancastrie*
> *succederet sibi in regno*). Yet, since his power to decide such things, so he
> said, was minimal (*quia hoc in potestate sua minime dependebat, ut dixit*), he
> asked the aforesaid archbishop of York and bishop of Hereford, whom
> he also appointed as his spokesmen to convey and announce his Cession
> and Renunciation to the estates of the realm, that they should declare
> his will and intention in this matter to the people. And as a sign of
> his will and intention he publicly removed from his finger his golden
> signet ring, and placed it on the aforesaid duke's finger, declaring that
> he wished this deed of his to be made known to all the estates of the
> realm. When this had been done, all who were there bade him farewell
> and left the Tower to return to their lodgings.[8]

What Richard seems to have been saying here—or at least what he
was alleged by Henry to have said—was not that a king had only
"minimal" power to designate his successor; on the contrary, it was
that, since he had just resigned and was now no longer a king, his
say in the matter was much less than it would have been were he
still king. Otherwise, why would Henry have bothered to mention it
at all? In fact, Henry made considerable play with the idea that Richard
had named him as his successor, repeating it to the assembled estates
at the time of his formal claim to the throne in Westminster hall.[9]

The evidence from the 1390s suggests, therefore, not only that
Richard, while he still reigned, was regarded as having a say in
determining who his successor should be, but also that Henry regarded
the designation of his predecessor as a factor which might add weight
to his own title to the throne. And if it is true that Richard had

---

[8] *Rotuli Parliamentorum 1278–1503* (6 vols., London: 1783), III.417.
[9] *Chronicles of the Revolution*, 186 (Cf. also pp. 163–4). See also Sayles (1981) 266:
Item voluit et declaravit quod renunciavit regimen regni, ita quod, quantum in eo fuerat, dominus
Henricus, dux Lancastrie, proximo sibi succederet in regno.

first nominated March, but later—under compulsion—recognised Henry instead, then it is hardly surprising that the early years of the Lancastrian dynasty were regularly punctuated by attempts of various kinds to assert the right of the young earl of March.[10] For there were, after all, a number of occasions in England's earlier history when something quite similar had occurred.

Most obviously, there was the precedent of 1066. The question of William the Conqueror's claim to the throne has been much debated, and although George Garnett has convincingly shown that William's claim to have been designated by Edward the Confessor in 1051 is supported by "not a shred of pre-Conquest English—or for that matter Norman—corroboration", it remains true, as he has pointed out, that it was on the basis of Edward's alleged designation that William asserted his claim to the English throne.[11] Since designation of the ducal heir was customary practice in Normandy, this is hardly surprising—it was, in Garnett's words, "a ducal designation ceremony retrospectively imposed upon England in 1051". What is also interesting is that, despite the fact that there is "very little evidence for anything akin to designation in Anglo-Saxon England", nevertheless the Anglo-Saxon Chronicle also picked up the idea: "Earl Harold succeeded to the kingdom of England", declared the E (Godwinist) version of the chronicle, "as the king [Edward the Confessor] granted it to him and as he was elected thereto". The C and D versions say that Edward "did . . . entrust his kingdom to a man of high rank, to Harold himself".[12] This was, it seems, simply a case of answering like with like: Harold's claim to have been designated by Edward on his death-bed was probably no truer than William's claim to have been designated fifteen years previously. Nevertheless, the result of the propagation of these competing claims appears to have been that henceforward greater significance came to be attached to the role of designation in influencing the succession.

---

[10] The plausibility of the young earl of March's claim to the throne was a constant worry both to Henry IV and—during his first few years—to Henry V. The Percy rebellion of 1403, Archbishop Scrope's rising of 1405, and the 'Southampton Plot' of 1415 all had as their declared aim the overthrow of the Lancastrian dynasty and the recognition of March as king. The kidnap from house arrest of March and his younger brother in 1405 was also widely believed to be the first move in a plot to put March on the throne. See Pugh (1988) 73–4.

[11] Garnett (1997) 62–9; see also Garnett (1986).

[12] *The Anglo-Saxon Chronicle*, ed. and trans. Garmonsway (1972) 195–7.

As is well known, there were several further cases of disputed succession to the throne of England over the following century and a half (see Table II): in 1087, for example, when the Conqueror divided his lands between his sons, and in the 1120s and early 1130s, when Henry I tried to secure the succession for his daughter Matilda. Although by no means decisive, designation by the reigning monarch was, in both cases, certainly influential. How likely was it, one might ask, either that William II would have succeeded to the English throne in 1087 in preference to his elder brother Robert, or that Matilda would have secured the support of many of the English nobles after 1135 (and eventually seen her son, Henry II, become king in 1154) had they not been designated as heir by their respective fathers? Equally problematical was the situation which arose in 1199 at the death of Richard I. As in 1399, there were two entirely plausible candidates for the throne: Arthur of Brittany, Henry II's

Table II

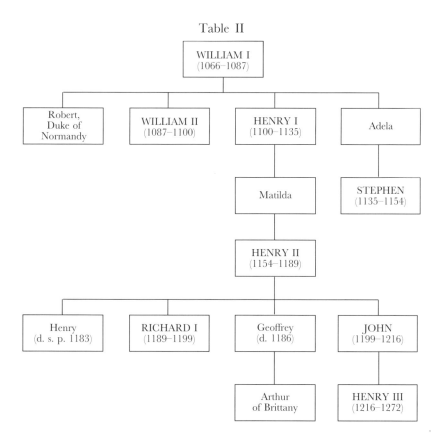

grandson through his third son Geoffrey, and John, Henry II's fourth and youngest son. What is more, confusion had marked Richard's own pronouncements on the subject. In October 1190, while at Messina in Sicily on his way to crusade in the Holy Land, Richard had declared the four-year-old Arthur to be his heir, apparently on the grounds that he was less likely than John to become a focus for opposition during the king's absence. John's reaction was predictable: he rebelled, and at a council meeting in 1192 he compelled all those present to take an oath of fealty to him as his brother's heir.[13] Later, following Richard's return and John's submission to him in 1194, this oath was presumably disregarded, but as he lay on his death-bed in the Limousin in April 1199, Richard nevertheless decided to change his mind and designate John as his heir to England. The chronicler Roger of Howden describes the scene:

> When, therefore, the king had despaired of his life, he bequeathed (*divisit*) the kingdom of England to his brother John, together with all his lands; and he made those who were present pledge their fealties (*fidelitates*) to the aforesaid John, and ordered that all their castles should be handed over to him, and three quarters of his treasure; and he bequeathed (*divisit*) all his jewels to his nephew Otto, the king of the Germans.[14]

Howden's use of the word *divisit*—that is, devised, or bequeathed—is reminiscent of Garnett's comment on the presentation in the Norman sources after 1066 of Edward the Confessor's alleged designation of William in 1051, namely that it "treated the kingdom as if it were a piece of land or a chattel, left in a will"—which, as he points out, was a point of some importance in the Norman concept of kingship.[15] And, as it turned out, it proved to be good enough for John, although like Henry IV it took him some years to silence the dissenters, and only by eliminating Arthur physically—that is, by murdering him—was he able to eliminate his nephew's claim. However, as James Holt has shown, the decision of 1199 did not go unnoticed by the legal profession, so that over the next fifty years or so the plea rolls "reveal a confused, unsettled situation", with judgments in cases of disputed inheritances going sometimes to uncles (such as John), and sometimes to nephews (such as Arthur).[16] By the mid-thirteenth

---

[13] Warren (1978) 39–44.
[14] *Chronica Magistri Rogeri de Hovedene*, ed. Stubbs (1868–71) IV.83.
[15] Garnett (1997) 69.
[16] Holt (1990) 21–42.

century, however, the common law had been clarified: Bracton was
in no doubt that "the representative grandchild [e.g. Arthur] was the
nearer heir", and Henry III, despite the uncomfortable reality of his
own father's claim to the throne, was evidently of the same opinion.[17]

The next occasion in English history when a reigning king felt
obliged to choose between potential successors to his kingdom was in
1290. On 17 April of that year, Edward I (1272–1307) held a gathering of his family at Amesbury in Wiltshire to prepare for the forthcoming marriage of his daughter Joan to Gilbert de Clare, earl of
Gloucester (they were married on 30 April). Two months later, her
younger sister Margaret was to be married to John, duke of Brabant.
They were the first and second of Edward's children to be married.
His queen, Eleanor of Castile (who would herself die later in the year),
had borne Edward at least eleven children, but five of them had
already died before even reaching the age of twelve, and of the six
that were left, only one, the future Edward II, was a son. With such
a devastating mortality rate, only one direct male heir, and two
daughters about to take husbands, it is hardly surprising that the king
recognised the urgency of making some declaration on the succession.
The terms of that declaration survive only in a letter sealed by the
earl of Gloucester and—as guarantors—the archbishop of Canterbury
and five other bishops.[18] There is no evidence that Edward issued
a written proclamation on the matter—a further indication of the
informal way in which medieval English kings sometimes sought to
provide for the succession. It was a private matter, a family affair.

The terms to which Gloucester was asked to 'swear on the saints',
in the presence of fourteen witnesses, were that, following Edward
I's death, he would recognise as king his son (the future Edward II),
and after him his children (male or female). If, however, the king
died without leaving a son—that is, if the younger Edward prede-
ceased his father, as three of his brothers had already done—the
throne was to pass to his eldest daughter Eleanor and any children
that she might have, failing which to Joan (Gloucester's future wife)
and their children, and so on in turn "from daughter to daughter,
and from heir to heir" (*de filie en filie, e de eyr en eyr*), in order of age.
This was what the king had "willed and ordained" (*voyt et ordeyne*).

---

[17] Holt (1990) 39.
[18] Gloucester's letter is printed in *Foedera, Litterae, Conventiones*, etc., ed. Rymer
(1816–30) I (part 2) 742.

The chief point, it seems, was to ensure that Gloucester—whom the king did not fully trust, notwithstanding the fact that he was about to become his son-in-law—would respect the as-yet-unmarried Eleanor's rights in the event of the younger Edward's death. In legal terms, the king was simply applying standard common law to the question of the succession. He had, as Maurice Powicke put it, "disposed of his kingdom as a feudal estate. . . . There was no suggestion that the magnates might have a say in the matter".[19]

Nor, despite his reputation as a legislator, is there any suggestion that Edward was 'legislating' or in any way trying to establish long-term principles according to which the succession to the English throne ought to be governed. He was issuing instructions to cope with a short-term problem; had he wished at some later date to change his mind, it is difficult not to believe that he would have done so— as Richard I had done before, and as Richard II is alleged to have done afterwards. Indeed, it is worth asking how many people were even aware of what had been agreed at Amesbury in April 1290, especially once Gilbert de Clare had died in 1295—but then the same question might be asked of the deed of entail which Edward III drew up in the winter of 1376–7. The entail of 1376–7 is, in fact, a rather strange document. Although described as a letter patent,[20] it is not like other letters patent, for it includes a list of witnesses and is written in French; nor does it seem to have been enrolled in chancery. Furthermore, no fourteenth-century copy of it is known to survive, and there is no external evidence that anyone in late fourteenth-century England knew of its existence.[21] Claiming the throne in 1399, for example, Henry Bolingbroke made no mention of it, although it might have added weight to his claim. Nevertheless, while its form is a puzzle, and despite the fact that the only surviving copy of the text—which dates from the second half of the fifteenth century—is fire-damaged to the point that much of of it is irrecoverable, both its tone and its purpose are reasonably clear. "We have ordained to declare our will" (*avons ordeignez a declarer nostre voluntee*), pronounced Edward III, which was that he should be succeeded in the first

---

[19] Powicke (1947) II.

[20] In line 34: Bennett (1998) 609.

[21] This includes the chroniclers: for example, the monk of Westminster remarked around 1390—quite innocently, apparently—that if Richard were to die childless the succession would devolve upon the Mortimer family: *The Westminster Chronicle, 1381–1394*, ed. Hector and Harvey (1982) 192–4.

instance by his grandson, Richard II, and by Richard's male heirs, failing which the succession should devolve in turn, in order of age, upon each of his surviving sons and their male heirs. "This definitive declaration of our will" (*cest adecertes declaracion de nostre voluntee*), as Edward called it, was preceded by some quite personal musings on the king's part in relation to his great age, his dead eldest son, and his hopes of eternal life.[22] In one important respect, however, it differed significantly from the arrangements put in place by Edward I in 1290, for it made no mention of the king's surviving daughter (Isabella, countess of Bedford, who died in 1379) or of any of his descendants or potential descendants through female lines—most notably, of course, his grand-daughter Philippa, wife of the earl of March.

This can only have been deliberate. Whatever others might have been saying about the March claim to the throne, Edward III apparently regarded it as a non-starter—which means either that he was unaware of what his grandfather had done in 1290, or that he felt free simply to disregard it. Yet, while the exclusion from the line of succession of his daughter and the female descendants of his sons might seem like a triumph for John of Gaunt, this should not lead us to ignore what must at the time have been seen as the most significant aspect of Edward's entail: namely, that it designated Richard as the immediate heir to his grandfather, thereby scotching any hopes that Gaunt might have had of emulating his namesake in 1199 and succeeding to the throne directly following Edward III's death. It is primarily in this context, surely, that Edward's entail ought to be viewed: both its timing and its nature suggest that its principal purpose was to act as a check on the—alleged—ambitions of Gaunt. Whether or not they were true, the rumours that he intended to seize the throne were widespread, and indeed, why not? The situation was, after all, remarkably similar to what had happened in 1199, and Gaunt's position vis-à-vis Richard was remarkably similar to that of King John vis-à-vis Arthur. Despite the fact that Edward III's entail would—in theory, though not apparently in practice—have lent weight to Henry Bolingbroke's succession in 1399, it can have given Gaunt little cause for satisfaction.[23]

---

[22] Though surely not about the moon, as Bennett (1998) 583 suggests: *les reules de lune* . . . in line 5 sounds very much like the first half of that much-used phrase *de lune et lautre* (the rest of the line has been rendered illegible by fire).

[23] Compare Bennett (1998) 584–7, 591.

Edward III's decision in 1376–7 to designate his male descendants as his heirs should also be seen within the context of the general drift among the English nobility during the fourteenth century towards settling their estates in tale mail,[24] just as it is arguable that the clarification of the common law on succession during the thirteenth century might have had some influence on Edward I's family settlement of April 1290. Yet, if these kings were indeed influenced by the legal developments of their age, they seem to have thought nothing of overturning—or simply ignoring—the pronouncements which their predecessors had made on the succession. Indeed, the overriding impression to be gained from a study of those occasions between the eleventh and fourteenth centuries when English kings engaged in some form of 'designation' of an heir is of the informality which they did so. Given the momentous political consequences of such decisions, this point requires some emphasis. Of course, designation was never more than a makeweight in the political balance. The range of choices with which kings were faced was extremely limited—although the very fact that they took the trouble to nominate their successors, or even that they were alleged to have done so indicates that it did count for something.[25] The pronouncements which they made were, however, little more than short-term expedients, private agreements imposed upon plausible contenders, guaranteed—if at all—not by law or the "common assent of the realm" but by the oaths or seals of small numbers of witnesses. If circumstances changed, kings might change their minds; and future generations do not seem to have regarded them as in any way binding.

It is worth noting finally, however, that this was soon to change. Within a few years of succeeding Richard II, Henry IV decided that the time had come to make his own pronouncement concerning the inheritance of his kingdom, and what is striking—and quite different

---

[24] McFarlane (1973) 271–4.

[25] As it may also have done in Scotland: during the 'Great Cause' of 1291–2 to decide who should be king of Scotland, one of the arguments put forward by Robert Bruce 'the competitor' (the grandfather of King Robert Bruce) was that he had been designated as his heir by King Alexander II in the event that Alexander failed to produce any children of his own. Although he claimed that this had been put in writing, the fact that Bruce was unable to find the document in question suggests that, if it was true, it must have been done in a fairly informal manner. John Balliol, Bruce's rival for the throne, claimed that even if it was true, any such designation had been invalidated as soon as Alexander's heir was born. And it was Balliol, of course, who was chosen to be king: Stones and Simpson (1978) II.145, 170, 178, 318.

from what had gone before—is the fact that it was by parliamentary statute that he chose to do so. In fact, not one but two statutes regulating the succession were passed in the Long Parliament of 1406. Their principal purpose was not so much to designate his eldest son (the future Henry V) as his successor—this had already been agreed in the parliaments of both 1399 and January 1404—as to determine the order of succession in the event of the young Henry predeceasing his father or dying without having produced any children of his own. The first act "for the inheritance of the crown", passed in June, restricted the succession to the king's four sons, in order of age, and their *male* descendants; the second, passed in December, restored the succession to the king's sons and their heirs general (male or female), as had been agreed in January 1404. The commons, at whose request the statute was (said to have been) enacted, declared that the June act "in excluding the female sex, greatly restricted that which they by no means intended to diminish but rather to increase", and that by restoring the rights of their heirs general the prince and his brothers would have "a better and firmer claim to succession by right to your crown"—although it is worth noting that in neither of the two statutes of 1406 were Henry IV's two daughters even mentioned, despite the fact that that of December 1406 apparently envisaged the possibility of the succession of one of the king's grand-daughters.[26]

The reasoning behind this change of mind has been much debated: it almost certainly had more to do with the rise to power during the Long Parliament of the prince of Wales, and of his concern for the future status of any children that he might have, than with any abstract principles about the rights or wrongs of female inheritance of the crown.[27] However, the real point of interest for present purposes is not the content of the statutes but their form. They were passed—or at least they were said to be—"at the request and by the assent of the lords and commons in parliament"; they were witnessed and sealed by each of the lords individually and by the Speaker

---

[26] *Rotuli Parliamentorum*, III.525 (January 1404); 574–6 (June 1406); 580–3 (December 1406).

[27] The decision in June 1406 to exclude female descendants may have been intended as some kind of retrospective justification for Henry's succession in 1399, and certainly the claim to the throne of the earl of March was not mentioned. By December, however, the prince of Wales seems to have put his foot down and insisted that all his potential heirs must be included in the line of succession. Cf. McNiven (1982) 470–88; Bennett (1998) 600.

on behalf of the commons; they were summarised as letters patent; and they were formally enacted as statutes, the December act being enrolled on the Statute Roll (7 Henry IV, cap. 2).[28] Much of this was unusual: statutes were not normally sealed with private seals, nor did they carry witness lists. The fact that Henry IV needed statutes, seals, witnesses and letters patent to buttress his dynasty's claim was, as the duke of York observed in 1460, an infallible sign of its weakness.[29] What it does *not* mean, however, is that parliament now had the right to determine the succession to the throne. What was being sought in parliament was, in reality, the public confirmation of a private deed of conveyance which was already a *fait accompli*. Despite all this dressing-up in public form, it was, as Stanley Chrimes remarked, "notions of private property law [which] were active and uppermost in the minds of the parties".[30] If we return, then, to the original question—what influence might a reigning king hope to exert by designating his heir?—the answer would appear to be that, although it was unlikely to be decisive, and although the choices that faced him were extremely limited, the *belief* that a king could influence the succession by an act of designation seems to have been quite widely held, and there may even have been times when that belief was justified. What he clearly could not do, however, was to exert any influence from beyond the grave on longer-term developments. The succession to the throne was a family affair, to be settled by each generation in turn.

Bibliography

Chronica Magistri Rogeri de Hovedene, ed. W. Stubbs (4 vols., Rolls Series, London: 1868–71).
Chronicles of the Revolution 1397–1400, ed. C. Given-Wilson (Manchester: 1993).
Chronicon Angliae 1328–1388, ed. E.M. Thompson (Rolls Series, London: 1874).
Cywyddau Iolo Goch ac Eraill, ed. H. Lewis, T. Roberts and I. Williams (Cardiff: 1972).
Eulogium Historiarum sive Temporis, ed. F.S. Haydon (3 vols., Rolls Series, London: 1863).
Foedera, Litterae, Conventiones, etc., ed. T. Rymer (20 vols., Record Commission, London: 1816–30).
Rotuli Parliamentorum 1278–1503 (6 vols., London: 1783).
Statutes of the Realm (11 vols., Record Commission, London: 1810–28).
The Anglo-Saxon Chronicle, ed. and trans. G.N. Garmonsway (London: 1972).

---

[28] *Statutes of the Realm* (11 vols., Record Commission, London, 1810–28), II.151. It was repealed by the Yorkists in 1460 (*Rotuli Parliamentorum*, V.379).
[29] *Rotuli Parliamentorum*, V. 379.
[30] Chrimes (1936) 25, 61.

The Westminster Chronicle, 1381–1394, ed. L.C. Hector and B.F. Harvey (Oxford: 1982).

Walter Bower, *Scotichronicon*, ed. D.E.R. Watt (Vol. VIII, Aberdeen: 1987).

Bennett, M. (1998) "Edward III's Entail and the Succession to the Crown, 1376–1471", *English Historical Review*, CXIII (1998) 580–609.

Chrimes, S.B. (1936) *English Constitutional Ideas in the Fifteenth Century* (Cambridge: 1936).

Garnett, G. (1986) "Coronation and propaganda: some implications of the Norman claim to the throne of England in 1066", *Transactions of the Royal Historical Society*, Fifth Series, XXXVI (London: 1986), 91–116.

—— (1997) "Conquered England, 1066–1215", in *The Oxford Illustrated History of Medieval England*, ed. Nigel Saul (Oxford: 1997) 61–101.

Gransden, A. (1982) *Historical Writing in Medieval England II: c. 1307 to the Early Sixteenth Century* (London: 1982).

Holt, J.C. (1990) "The *casus regis*: the law and politics of succession in the Plantagenet dominions 1185–1247", in *Law in Mediaeval Life and Thought*, ed. E.B. King and S.J. Ridyard (Sewanee: 1990), 21–42.

McFarlane, K.B. (1973) *The Nobility of Later Medieval England* (Oxford: 1973).

McNiven, P. (1982) "Legitimacy and consent: Henry IV and the Lancastrian title", *Mediaeval Studies* XLIV (1982), 470–88.

Powicke, F.M. (1947) *Henry III and the Lord Edward* (2 vols., Oxford: 1947).

Pugh, T.B. (1988) *Henry V and the Southampton Plot of 1415* (Cambridge: 1988).

Sayles, G.O. (1981) "The deposition of Richard II: three Lancastrian narratives", *Bulletin of the Institute of Historical Research*, LIV (1981) 259–271.

Stores, E.L.G. and G.G. Simpson (1978) *Edward I and the Throne of Scotland 1290–1296* (2 vols., Oxford: 1978).

Tout, T.F. (1920–1933) *Chapters in the Administrative History of Medieval England* (6 vols., Manchester: 1920–33).

Tuck, A. (1973) *Richard II and the English Nobility* (London: 1973).

Warren, W.L. (1978) *King John* (2nd ed., London: 1978).

THE KING'S FACE ON THE TERRITORY: ROYAL OFFICERS, DISCOURSE AND LEGITIMATING PRACTICES IN THIRTEENTH- AND FOURTEENTH-CENTURY CASTILE

Cristina Jular Pérez-Alfaro
Instituto de Historia, CSIC

It was the bailiff Herman Gessler who began the private nightmare of William Tell.[1] Not precisely characterised by his understanding and equanimity, Gessler demanded that all the inhabitants of the village of Altdorf should perform an obligatory act of reverence to his hat. Conveniently placed in a visible location, the public square, on a pole that enhanced its prominence, the object became a symbolic reference. With this act, the bailiff transformed the nature of power from notion to reality, from episodic occurrence to permanent presence; he exploited the collective space *par excellence* and personalised power by elevating himself as the very embodiment of an authority that, in reality, he enjoyed merely by delegation. Gessler orchestrated the stage, the timing, the actors and the audience for the theatre of power. William passed by the hat, nonchalantly, without any sign of reverence; the slight had been made, and the challenge to power set in motion. The arrival of the protagonist, the preordained victim, completed the scene. The drama could now begin.[2]

The first step in the history of power is the study of the human subjects embroiled in the workings of authority. In this case, William Tell and Gessler form the principal axis of the action, but in addressing the two individuals we face very different situations. Since 1901, the tale of Tell has not been presented in Swiss textbooks as being historically true, and we now know that he was a legendary figure. Nevertheless, investigation of this character has produced the more significant results in historical scholarship, being considerably more fruitful than research relating to Gessler. The bailiff, for his part, has

---

[1] I am grateful for the comments and suggestions of I. Alfonso, J. Escalona, F. Rodríguez Mediano and S. Doubleday.
[2] Balandier (1994).

many parallels, broadly speaking: for instance, the sheriff of Nottingham, who as loyal servant of King John shaped the destiny of Robin Hood in medieval English *gestes*, or the bailiff who imprisoned Joan of Arc's brother-in-arms Étienne de Vignolles. Finally, there is the *merino* Pedro Núñez de Guzmán, who despite repeated royal warnings long continued to obstruct the rights of the city of León without being removed from office.[3] As delegated agents of a superior authority, intermediaries and instruments of political action, these men were among the many Herman Gesslers of medieval community life. The remoteness of the king or emperor, as far as the majority of his subjects were concerned, meant that the network of agents established across the land constituted the basic element in the exercise of power.

The discussion in the following pages is concerned with exploring the complex role of these agents in order to understand the justification, mechanisms, discourses and practices that such officials (*baillis*, *bayles*, sheriffs, *merinos*, seneschals—representatives and intermediaries of power—present in medieval political culture. This type of official has been chosen precisely because they do not work within the central apparatus of government, in the strict sense, but rather transpose these political structures onto a broader geographical plane. They represent not merely a basic link between governors and governed but also the territorial face of monarchy. This article will rest on a conception of medieval political culture as a sphere that encompassed a great many individuals, rather than a small circle containing only a few agents of power, allegedly isolated from the masses, who silently suffered the actions of government or at best resisted and rebelled. This is not to say that we should think of a medieval world in which everyone could act politically. Medieval societies were of course hierarchical, unequal, and extremely discriminatory, as a number of historians have masterfully shown,[4] but we will only weave the public into the fabric if we consider it to be involved from the beginning. Returning to our Swiss story, we know today that in 1291 a peasant from Uri murdered a bailiff of the Habsburg family, and that castles were burned. As a result of these events, Rudolf von Habsburg assured the inhabitants of the valleys that they would henceforth be judged not by external bailiffs but by officials from within the communities themselves. Dependency on the crown, inter-

---

[3] Jular (1990), 294–308.
[4] Hilton (1978) and (1986), Pastor (1973) and (1980). As I write these lines, I am saddened to hear of the passing of Prof. Hilton.

connection between local and central powers, the political identity of the intervening groups, the collective action of the local community, and a process of negotiation: all are to be found in the genesis and development of the conflict and the solutions that were adopted.[5] The representation and practice of power into which the central-medieval monarchy entered were not merely prescribed, but engaged in dialogue with other members of the political community. Interaction was sought, created and achieved.[6] It is now worth asking on what terms, to what extent, and with what degree of attention these different elements of society were involved.

I will address these questions on two levels: one relating to the formal structures of power, the other exploring specific micro-political factors, above all concerning the kingdom of Castile to the north of the Duero in the thirteenth and fourteenth centuries. Until the 1980s, the study of territorial officials—and indeed the history of medieval power—was undertaken in Spain principally by historians of institutions and historians of law. It was not particularly pursued by the new school of social history that was then gathering steam, or by historians trained in historical materialism, who found more urgent priorities and research agendas.[7] But this approach was reflected later in the works of second- or even third-generation historians with an interest in social organisation, the structures of power, and their territorial formation.[8] One should also point out that there is now a renewed interest in power, influenced by French research, and particularly in the monarchy and issues relating to representation, ritual and ceremony. These are works that, in my view, are still in a transitional and exploratory phase rather than having achieved synthesis or completion.[9] The theme plays a significant role in my own research

---

[5] There is a comparative study of the peasantry dependent on the king in Castile and in the Germanic world, including Switzerland, in Estepa (2001), and an overview of Swiss federalism, critical of traditional historiography, in Chevallaz (1989–1990).

[6] Alfonso (1997) and the monograph issue of *Hispania* (1997) which she also coordinated, with articles by I. Alfonso, J. Hudson, S. White, C. Wickham, J.Mª. Salrach and D.L. Smail.

[7] A comprehensive analysis in Monsalvo (1995).

[8] García de Cortázar (1985, 1988), Estepa (1989, 1990), Martínez Sopena (1985). Peña (1999), Álvarez (1993, 1996), Escalona (2000). The forthcoming work of C. Estepa, *Las behetrías castellanas*, will be an essential reference in future research on the kingdom of Castile.

[9] The most complete research projects have been conducted by Nieto Soria (2000). On the thematic links with the 'Origins and Formation of the Modern State', see the interesting critical analysis in Monsalvo (1998).

projects, which reflect this evolution.[10] Here, I will organise the analysis in three sections—king, officials, and community—in the hope of
interrogating different sources and, above all, asking different questions
in each case. In the first section, the main focal point will be the
central-medieval monarch and his principal source of legitimation (the
sphere of jurisdiction); in the second, the territorial officials and their
horizontal and vertical relationships will be examined, making use of
case studies. The third section, dedicated to the role of the community,
will be suggestive more than definitive, providing a basis for addressing
more recent historiographical concerns and a greater range of sources.
The three parts correspond to avenues of research that have so far
been more separated than fused; the article will ultimately suggest
the need for a unified perspective on these issues.

The King:
Ideal Models of the Territorial Official

Positive and Negative Approaches in the Making of Legitimation

Adelantados and *merinos*, as we have said, represented the king's face
on the territory. What kind of monarch did they represent, and what
was their relationship with their superior authority? The first space
for the discourse of legitimation is institutional. Legitimation can take
the form of justification of official action in terms of rights, responsibilities and obligations associated with office; it can also present
justification of the position that a certain office or institution occupies within a more global order. The sphere of law, the construction of normative standards, is therefore the natural starting point
for legitimation. The Castilian monarchy of the thirteenth century
is extraordinarily dynamic in this sense. Not only is it not unlettered

---

[10] In Jular (1990), I attempted a general reconstruction of the adelantamiento of
León from the second half of the twelfth century to the fifteenth. Jular (1991) and
(1994) are concerned with political and territorial concepts (*alfoz, tierra, honor*), in a
comparative framework, in the kingdom of Castile and León. See also Jular (1993)
on family y clientage relationships; Jular (1996), lordship and clientage; Jular (1997),
conflict with royal officials; Jular (1999), monarchy, property and power; Jular (2001),
nobility, clientage and power. Currently I am developing a research project on
'Kings, Patrons and Clients', within the Programa Ramón y Cajal, funded by the
Spanish Ministerio de Ciencia y Tecnología.

but, quite to the contrary, it develops ambitious and complex legal texts in writing. The thirteenth-century king is articulate, produces discourse, creates means of self-legitimation, and apportions legitimacy by developing a scheme of order. Within this scheme, he produces an ideal model of the territorial official: his own image transposed onto the territory. In the lines that follow, I will analyse aspects of what I will call the 'positive' model, arising directly from the normative standard, and without opposition—at least of the explicit kind. Yet in the world of applied politics, the real political world, the discourse of legitimation can also be stimulated when officials are accused of breaking the law, or when they face principled opposition to their decisions, their policies or their actions.[11] Confronted by overt protest, the king then turns to a discourse of legitimation, either adjusted or affirmed without modification, which I will refer to as 'negative' by virtue of having arisen from a challenge. Both routes to the same theoretical model are configured particularly during the thirteenth century and the first half of the fourteenth century.

The kingdom of Castile experienced a marked advance in the process of monarchical centralisation in the thirteenth century: a process whereby the king gradually mutated from being a lord among equals to being a supreme lord with distinct institutional resources. There are four elements allowing us to observe this dynamic, which redounded to the benefit of the monarchy and the progress of regal supremacy.[12] Firstly, the king's capacities for military leadership above and beyond the feudal retinues, a phenomenon derived from the special conditions of the Iberian peninsula. Second, the development of a centralised fiscal system that gradually came to fill the royal coffers not with rents but with forms of income closer to the concept of taxation, including *monedas* and *servicios*.[13] Thirdly, we may observe the extension of royal justice, again generalised across the kingdom and above seigneurial jurisdictions. The final element, and one that established the framework of action, was territorial demarcation: the configuration of great administrative districts entrusted to royal officials. These are the *merindades mayores* (in the case of León and Asturias, Galicia and Castile) and the *adelantamientos* (Andalucía, 'Frontera' and Murcia) which

---

[11] Dijk (1999) 320.
[12] Álvarez (1993) and (1996).
[13] These two are the earliest and clearest examples of direct tributes to be rendered by everyone throughout the kingdom.

were controlled respectively by the *merinos mayores* and *adelantados* under the aegis of the king, who had the exclusive right to nominate and dismiss such officials.[14] Certainly, there is evidence from before the thirteenth century of men who received delegated royal authority over territory. These were noblemen who, generally speaking, had a patrimonial presence in those areas to which they also received authority ceded by the king. We also know of *merinos* and *adelantados* from before the thirteenth century. But the normative establishment of these officials at the head of *adelantamientos* and *merindades* occurs especially during the reigns of Fernando III (1217–1252) and Alfonso X *el Sabio* (1252–1284). During Fernando's reign, this was a consequence of the extraordinary territorial expansion arising from conquest and the union of the kingdoms of Castile and León from 1230; in the reign of Alfonso X, a result of the juridical projects developed by the monarchy.

Before entering into juridical matters, a few words are needed about the terms *adelantado* and *merino*. There are nuances between the two, discussed at length by institutional historians.[15] Essentially, the *adelantado* had greater capabilities for immediate military action; the *merino* was more dependent in this sense on the king. For this reason, the high nobility tended to be nominated to the former position, more than to the latter.[16] The most notable difference lies in the greater development of the position of *merino* both vertically (*merinos mayores, merinos menores,* and local *merinos*) and horizontally (royal *merinos* and seigneurial *merinos,* who should in turn be distinguished from the municipal *merinos* dependent on the town council or *concejo*). In other words, the term *merino* has a political usage much broader than that relating to royal representation. Yet it is the royal *merino*—and *adelantado*—who plays the key role in the discourse of legitimation for the central medieval Castilian monarchy. Here I will be concerned with the net-

---

[14] Pérez-Bustamante (1976) offers the basic outline.

[15] To my knowledge the most recent and complete work is that of MacDonald (2000), which concerns both the territorial *adelantados* and *merinos* and the *adelantado de la Corte* (or *sobrejuez*), whom I will not address in this article. I examined the differences in Jular (1990) and consider that this line of inquiry is now exhausted. Terminology is not as important as the question of the resources and attributes that corresponded to these positions. There are other offices, such as that of *prestamero*, which like the merinos have a territorial basis but which did not produce formal normative models. On the prestamería there is no work of synthesis, but there are details in Jular (1996, 1999 and 2001), Estepa (1994), and Escalona (2001).

[16] MacDonald (2000).

work of *merinos* directly dependent on the king, the *merinos* for whom regal discourse created normative standards in the thirteenth century. *Adelantados* and *merinos* constitute a key component in the construction of royal pre-eminence. As legal agents of 'good order', watchmen of privilege and seigneurial interest, always directly dependent on the principal figure of power, they are envisioned as the ideal instrument for the king to reach the population and demonstrate his presence. In contrast to mere force and the imposition of authority in accordance with the 'laws of nature', the legitimating discourse of the king, an artifice achieved through the written word, plays a persuasive rhetorical role. A complex core of arguments involving the transfer of royal power, the search for effective government, and the conceptual development of the phenomenon of delegation, it crystallises notions of the relationship between the king and his immediate agents.[17]

Alfonso X is undoubtedly the protagonist in these events, although the king's role will be important in this section less as an individual—and certainly not as one with plenipotentiary powers to direct historical change—than as a focal point for the discourse of legitimation. There are three principal juridical works with Alphonsine inspiration and composition: the *Fuero Real*, the *Especulo* and the *Siete Partidas*.[18] Together they express a political programme with varying results in their projected spheres of influence. The *Fuero Real* was intended for the *concejos* of Castilla Vieja and Castilian Extremadura, and did not include Toledo, Andalucía, Murcia or the kingdom of León. Redacted by 1255, its enforcement was significantly affected by the crisis of the nobility that began in 1272. Meanwhile, the *Especulo* was a legal synthesis intended for universal application across the realms, although this project was cut short: it was neither completed nor remitted to all the towns as initially planned. Several researchers have related this interruption of the work to the events known as the *fecho del imperio*: to Alfonso's quest for the title of Holy Roman Emperor and his aspiration to a jurisdictional work more in keeping with his imperial pretensions.[19] Nonetheless, the legal material that had been prepared still served the royal court in orienting

---

[17] Senellart (1995) analyses the evolution of medieval political thought from the apex of power in depth.

[18] For the *Fuero Real* I have used the edition of Martínez Díez (1988), for the *Especulo* that of the same author (1985), and for the *Partidas* the edition of the Real Academia de la Historia (1972).

[19] Martínez Díez (1985).

judges, officials and other governors of the realm. It was also used for the redaction of the great new work, the *Partidas*, a legal code based on the earlier work of compilation and written within the framework of Roman law as conceived in the juridical school of Bologna. The programme of the *Partidas*, which has generated an extensive bibliography and animated debate corresponding to its importance,[20] did not have the force of law until the fourteenth century, after the legal primacy established by Alfonso XI (1312–1350) in the Ordenamiento de Alcalá (1348). There are clear traces of the *adelantados* and *merinos* in this Alphonsine trilogy. I will address three relevant aspects of the royal legitimating discourse: the presence and importance of territorial officials; the presentation of the relationship between king and officials; and finally, certain elements in the normative configuration of the office which allow us to define features of its political and social identity.

The *Fuero Real* does not contain many allusions to *adelantados* and *merinos mayores*, and has precious few references to the merinos *menores* established as executive agents in the towns, be they either seigneurial or royal.[21] As the legal code with the most restricted territorial application of the three, it does indicate the proximity of these officials to local communities through the daily exercise of power, dealing with accusations, summonses, oaths, grants or sales of property, and debts. Local *merinos*, permanently attached to the king, lord, judge, or *alcalde*, are mentioned without special emphasis. They are a standard presence, parallel in each type of lordship. There is no real debate regarding the genesis and allocation of these offices, and a lack of involvement on the part of the nobility or royal court in regard to the construction of a territorial model. But we do find the pre-eminence of the king explicitly expressed in the *Fuero Real*, which presents the monarch as the very image of divine majesty, as supreme authority over an earthly court that mirrors the celestial:

---

[20] An overview of Alfonso X's legal production in Pérez-Prendes (1985). Alfonso's policies are an inexhaustible vein of historical scholarship. Cfr. Gómez Redondo (1998–99), for whom the second *Partida* must be seen as a knightly model imposed to the king by the nobility, and Martin (forthcoming), for whom the *Partidas* represent the royal model of dominance over the nobility. See also Bermejo (1970) for applications of the *Partidas* before their definitive enforcement. For Alfonso X, the nobility and the *fecho del imperio*, see Estepa (1984) and (1997) and O'Callaghan (1993).

[21] Its 550 laws, distributed over four books, mention *merinos* on pages 199, 206, 243, 252, 257, 362, 387, 392, 393, 394, 414, 425, 429, 475 y 486 of the edition mentioned above.

Our Lord Jesus Christ firstly made his celestial court, and placed himself at the head and beginning of the angels and archangels and wished and commanded that they love and keep him as beginning and guardian of all things. And afterwards he made Man in the manner of his court; and just as he had placed himself as head and beginning, he placed Man as head of the body and gave this head reason and understanding of how it should guide the other members and instruct them how they should serve and guard the head more than themselves. Thus he ordered the earthly court in the same guise and in the same manner as the celestial court was ordered, and he placed the king as the head and beginning of the whole people just as he had placed himself as the head and beginning of the angels and archangels, and gave him power to guide the people and ordered that the whole people, each and every man, should receive and obey the commands of the king and that they love and keep him, in fame, in honour. and in body (. . .). Because just as no member of the body can be healthy without the head, so neither the people nor any one of the people could be well without their king, who is their head, and placed by God to advance virtue and to avenge and prevent evil.[22]

The perception of the organisation of the here-below as an imitation of the hereafter is of course a permanent feature of medieval thought. But it is important to note—as suggested by Berges[23]—the variations in the symbolic use of this mental structure, and in its use in specific contexts. The notion of the king as an *adelantado* of God in human affairs is replicated in the model of the king's official *adelantado* in his territory.

The *Especulo* and especially the *Siete Partidas* are both more profound in addressing the king's relationship with his most immediate delegates. The *Especulo* was characterised by its universalising aspirations,

---

[22] *Nuestro Sennor Ihesu Christo ordenó primerament la su corte en el ciello e puso a ssí mismo por cabesca e començamiento de los ángeles et de los archángeles e quiso e mandó quel amassen e quel agardassen como a començamiento e garda de todo. Et depués desto fizo el omne a la manera de su cort; e como a ssí auíe puesto cabeça e comienço, puso al omne la cabesca en somo del cuerpo e en ella puso razón e entendimiento de cómo se deuen guiar los otros miembros e cómo deuen seruir e guardar la cabeca más que a ssí mismos; e desí ordenó la corte terrenal en aquella misma guisa e en aquella manera que era ordenada la suya en el cielo, e puso al rrey en su logar cabeca e comienço de todo el pueblo assí como puso sí mismo cabeça e comienço de los ángeles e de los archángeles, e diol poder de guiar su pueblo e mandó que todo el pueblo en uno e cada uno omne por sí recibiesse et obedeciesse los mandamientos de su rrey e que lo amassen e quel temiessen e quel guardassen tan bien su fama e su ondra como su cuerpo mismo; (. . .) ; ca assí como ningún miembro non puede auer salut sin su cabeca, assí ni [el] pueblo ni ninguno del pueblo non puede auer bien sin su rey que es su cabeca et puesto por Dios por adelantar el bien e pora uengar e uedar el mal. (Fuero Real, I, Titulo 2 (de la guarda de los reyes e de su sennorío), law 2, pp. 189–191).*

[23] See comments in Senellart (1995) 148.

its bureaucratic character, and its exclusivity. It aspired to universal validity in the realm of Castile. It was bureaucratic in the sense that each town was to receive a copy, authenticated with the royal leaden seal, with the original to be kept in the royal court. And it was exclusive by virtue of aspiring to be the only legal point of reference, ending the legal force of any other text and serving as a basis for the insertion of future royal provisions that might complement it. A program as ambitious as this incorporated a hierarchical schema of offices and subjects and wove into itself the complex web of inter-locutors between the king and his people. Apart from the *letrados* and the legal experts, it explicitly states the obligation of the high clergy, nobility and other members of the court and kingdom to give counsel. And among its 650 laws, the hierarchical pyramid of *ade-lantados* and *merinos* occupies a significant place.[24] The *Especulo* places these officials within a semantic context revolving around the king. The monarch is the unquestionable focal point of the discourse, and just as he must watch over property he must watch over men. Lordship, castles-towns-fortresses, houses-storehouses-estates, and rents and harvests, are elements that must be protected and guarded care-fully along with the men who correspond to them. The discourse of legitimation is constructed on the basis of indisputable, primordial authority, a mirror of the principal political figure, the king. An order is imposed on clerics and on laymen; the latter are born into a hierarchy.[25] Among the major officials, after the royal *alférez* (respon-sible for military matters) and the royal *mayordomo* (chief administra-tive officer, both within and beyond the royal household) we find the king's *adelantados mayores* and the royal *merinos*.[26] These officials are therefore high in the global structure and—this is emphasised—personally dependent on the king. These officials exist because the king exists, with the obligation of maintaining the king's temporal

---

[24] In its five books—of the seven that were projected—there are specific men-tions in Libro II, Título XIII, laws III and IV; Libro IV, Título II, laws III, V, VI, XI, XII, XIII, XVII, XIX, [XX], XXI, XXII; Libro IV, all of Título III. In Martínez Díez (1985), these references correspond to pages 157–158, 160–161, 240, 241–242, 244–258, 259–269, 271–274, 288–289, 397–398.

[25] Among the clergy, it includes the *capellanes mayores, cancilleres*, notaries and *los otros clérigos del rey que son en consejo del rey*, ending with the king's scribes: Libro II, Título XII, leyes I–VI.

[26] They are followed by *el alguacil de casa del rey, los caballeros de la mesnada del rey, alcalles que judgan en la corte del rey, los de criazón del rey*, ending Libro II, *De la guarda y honra del rey, de sus cosas y de sus oficiales.*

interests, and are to be honoured and respected. The rhetoric of regal pre-eminence still inherits elements relating to the imposition of power, but indicate the arrival of a more genuinely political community to which the normative discourse is directed. Officials are considered to occupy a *bona fide* office. The *Especulo* therefore accentuates this notion of pre-eminence, empowers the body of agents acting across the territory, and establishes a basis for the image of delegated royal authority with respect to the community of the governed.

The *Siete Partidas*, also including *adelantados* and *merinos* among the highest magistrates of the kingdom, take this normative discourse of legitimation considerably further.[27] They entrust the organisation of the palace and the administration of the kingdom to three types of officials: secret agents, advisors, and those responsible for territorial administration, among whom are *adelantados* and *merinos mayores*. The 'king's men' are therefore presented according to eminently functional criteria. The *adelantados* and *merinos* in turn oversee a substantial body of *merinos menores* and other supporting officials in their territory:

> *Adelantado* means a man placed ahead in some action specified by the king's own hand, and for this reason the man who in earlier times was placed at the head of some territory, known in Latin as *praeses provinciae*. This office is very great, because the *adelantado* is placed by the king's hand above all the merinos, including those from the *cámaras* and the *alfoces*, and all the merinos from the towns. . . .[28]

The *Partidas* go further than the *Especulo* by indicating the personal qualities that the leading officials should possess (and those they should avoid) and by placing some limits on their position, for instance by indicating the need for accountability during and after their mandate. The *adelantado* should be of good lineage, loyal to the king, and knowledgeable in war and law. He should be neither arrogant nor seditious, nor should he be burdensome on those places he visits

---

[27] The *Siete Partidas* encompass 2.751 laws and the 37 *reglas del derecho*. The key texts on *adelantados* and *merinos* are *Partida II*, tít. I, ley II; tít. IX, leyes XII, XVI, XIX, XXII y XXIII; *Partida III*, tít. IV, ley I y tít. XVI, ley I; *Partida*, tít. XIV, ley II; *Partida V*, tít. V, ley V, which states that *Cómo los adelantados nin los jueces ordinarios non pueden comprar ninguna cosa en aquella tierra do han poder de judgar*; and *Partida VII*, tít. I, ley II and ley V.

[28] *Adelantado tanto quiere decir como home metido adelante en algunt fecho señalado por mano del rey, et por esta razon el que antiguamente era asi puesto sobre alguna tierra, llamábanlo en latin* praeses provinciae*: et el oficio deste es muy grande, ca es puesto por mano del rey sobre todos los merinos, tambien sobre los de las cámaras et de los alfoces, como sobre todos los otros de las villas . . . (Partida II, Titulo IX, ley XXII).*

during his tours of duty. He cannot act as prosecutor in a trial since he is part of the body of representatives of justice; he must be answerable, and must recognise the right to appeal his actions to the king, both during and after his term of office. Thus there is more nuance here to the construction of a 'positive' discourse of legitimation, and a degree of specificity in the model of official behaviour that represents a step towards the official's autonomy in regard to the king. No longer is service conceived as a matter of blind respect for authority, the result of natural submission, obligation or coercion. This remains a theoretical model, of course, as is well indicated by the fact that the *Partidas* prohibit the purchase of property by an *adelantado*, or even the taking of a wife, within his jurisdiction during his term of office, in order to prevent the possibility of coercion. This could not be further from actual practice. But we are still faced with a new level of presentation of the political structure: alongside royal pre-eminence, dependence of the officials in relation to the king, and a pyramidal hierarchy of responsibilities, we also have an advance in the degree of autonomy within the apparatus of the state. The question of 'agency' becomes one of 'agents'. The *adelantado*'s responsibilities encompass the punishment of crime, the achievement of general public order, and finally providing the king with the information that he needed:

> Furthermore, he [the *adelantado*] must travel the land for three reasons: firstly, to chastise evildoers, secondly, to grant justice to the people, and thirdly to keep the king apprised of the state of the land....[29]

We are no longer dealing with a king with indisputable and primordial authority deriving from his role as divine delegate and transposing the heavenly plan onto his body of executive agents. Neither are we facing a king who amalgamates royal court with seigneurial household. We are facing a just king, distributor of favour and punishment, and an informed king, knowledgeable about his kingdom. This professionalization places us in a more advanced stage of the discourse of legitimation. Just as in John of Salisbury's comparison between the *res publica* and the human body, different functions are assigned to the different instruments of government.[30] The king's judicial and

---

[29] *Otrosi debe [el Adelantado] andar la tierra por tres razones: la una por escarmentar los malfechores, la otra por facer alcanzar derecho a los homes, la tercera para apercibir al rey del estado de la tierra...* (*Partida* II, título IX, ley XXII).

[30] "The clergy are the soul, the king the head, the royal council the heart of the

territorial agents are likened to the distinct human organs: eyes to see, ears to hear, and tongues to speak, means of communication between governor and governed. The 'king's face on the territory' becomes physical presence.

Before examining the officials more directly, it is important to say a few words about the next source we will be using, the *Cuadernos de Cortes*. The documentation of the Cortes falls halfway between the kind of source we have been concerned with up to now and those we will be using in the remainder of the article. By virtue of establishing legislation, it also has a normative character, but it embodies concrete governmental action rather than theory. We do not have records of the daily sessions but rather of the answers given by the king to the petitions of the urban representatives in the Cortes, as well as some of the *ordenamientos* resulting from issues discussed in these sessions. The *ordenamientos* and royal responses were subsequently sent to the towns and other bodies with representation in the Cortes, to diffuse the official nature of government, not just in these particular places but across the realm. A close analysis of these meetings of the Cortes indicates a phase of pivotal importance for the history of *adelantados* and *merinos* between the middle of the thirteenth century and the first half of the fourteenth. Most crucial in this respect were the Cortes of Valladolid (1293), Valladolid (1312), Carrión (1317), Madrid (1329), Alcalá de Henares (1348), Valladolid (1351) and Toro (1371). The affairs discussed in these meetings bring us to the kind of official model that I have designated 'negative'.

The Cortes material contains a good deal of information about the *adelantados* and *merinos*: their actions (hypothetical or concrete), their emoluments and the means of acquiring them; the qualities and conditions needed for the office, as well as their obligations. They indicate sources of support for the official and measures of protection and respect, and articulate their relationship with other authorities. And, of course, in this world of applied politics, in which institutional power is sometimes challenged, there are formal complaints and denunciations about their behaviour, both individualised and generalised.[31] This partly occurs in the meetings of the Cortes themselves:

---

political body; the judges and administrators of the provinces are the eyes, ears and tongue; the administration of finances occupies the belly; the soldiers are the hands; peasants, artists and merchants, the feet" (cit. Senellart (1995) 141 n. 2).
[31] Jular (1990) 431–441.

a forum for criticism from which the *adelantados* and *merinos* are certainly not spared, particularly because of the onerous expenses they placed on the towns and villages in their jurisdiction. They are accused of taking greater *yantares* than they were entitled to, and of doing so more than once a year, without personally appearing in the place.[32] But the complaints are critical without being destructive and—like the king's responses—ultimately reinforce the model of legitimacy established in the royal legal codes. Conflicting interests provide material for the construction of the same normative model. It is time now to look more closely at the officials themselves.

The Officials:
Social Identity, Political Identity, Collective Identity

Among the questions that need to be addressed in regard to the officials are the following: did the *adelantados* and merinos constitute a homogenous body of officialdom? Did they pursue a well-defined strategy? Did they express a group culture? Did they represent and maintain a collective political identity? Here I will note some of the problems this line of inquiry presents, and will propose some suggestions. Townspeople, merchants, clerical elites and *letrados* have been more intensively studied than royal administrative agents and officials. Equally, *adelantados* and *merinos* have been examined more as individuals than as a collective, and sometimes even the analysis of the individual is problematic: there are, for instance, difficulties for prosopographical reconstruction.[33] The lists of names of *adelantados* and *merinos* are becoming fuller but are not complete enough to allow comparative studies. Reconstruction of their careers is often demoralising and time-consuming. The lower levels of *merinos* on the regional, district and local level—far more numerous, far more changeable, yet far less visible in the documentary sources—are difficult to trace over time.

---

[32] The basic salary of the *adelantados* and *merinos* is related to this concept of movement: *yantar* are *posada* are effectively board and lodging, due to the official on entering office, once a year, and everytime they move into the area where their presence is requested. The same concept applies to other areas (cf. Grava, 1994) and is based on the imitation for royal agents of what is otherwise known for kings themselves (Autrand, 1994).

[33] National historiographies vary much, but the relative lack of Hispanic studies is apparent in Genet and Lottes (1996).

When they do appear in the sources, they seem always to be subjected to the strategies that their superiors dictate. Studies of these officials—and the limited debate—have been focussed above all on the *merinos mayores*. They have attempted the categorisation of their attributes and responsibilities, their loyalty or disservice to the king, and the way they used the position to develop their seigneurial power, rather than seeking evidence of internal bonds, dialogue or interrelations. Nor have they fully explored the interaction with the broader community.

Let us focus the discussion for a moment on the higher officers. Do they generate their own discourse, or are they permanently dependent of that of the monarchy? True, it is widely held that the office was a desirable and useful means of upward social mobility,[34] and that the monarchy developed alliances through the distribution of positions whereas the acquisition of authority over a territorial district was greatly coveted by the nobility. It would be simplistic, though, to present the relationship between the nobility and the crown as one of mere antagonism or 'natural conflict' and, especially, to overlook the dynamic changes in the competition between both. The central medieval monarchy, a constantly developing apparatus, could not function without the collaboration of the dominant social class, the feudal nobility, which in turn managed to advance by modifying its relationship with the king. There was in fact a dialogue over the resources of power, which now reflected a new element in the discourse of legitimation: the direct intervention of the voice of the dominant class. One key moment in which this development can be observed was the Castilian noble revolt of 1272–1273.[35] The people allied against the king were the principal powers of the kingdom: the *infante* Felipe, brother of the king, the heads of the three leading noble families in the realm—Lara, Haro and Castro—and *alii multi barones, infanciones et nobiles*: a broad coalition of disaffected nobles. There was a substantial programme of complaints and demands, one that indicates the existence not merely of an aristocratic voice but also evidence

---

[34] The complexities of '*officier versus burgeoisie*' relations have been addressed by Bulst (1996), on the basis of the États Généraux from the fifteenth century onwards.

[35] See González Jiménez (1998) for a thorough presentation of the events, with a corrected chronology, and Doubleday (2001), especially for the pivotal role of the Laras in the revolt. A new reassessment of the whole episode in Alfonso (2002) and Escalona (2002). The revolt would in fact last far longer than two years, reviving—with very much the same arguments—in the rebellion of the future Sancho IV (1284–1295) against his father.

of a real policy of state in noble discourse.[36] The platform of protests places under discussion various aspects of royal policy in regard to finance, repopulation and jurisdiction. The nobles criticise the increase of the extraordinary *servicios* imposed by the king, as well as problems relating to counterfeit coin and high prices resulting from changes in royal monetary laws. They complain about the generalisation of laws, overruling their own private legal norms, the lack of specific *alcaldes* for trials of *hidalgos* in Castile, and the expansion of royal *fueros* to towns adjacent to those under noble jurisdiction, with consequent pressures for the application of the same law. Above all, they resent the suppression of the old *fuero* in favour of the *Fuero Real*. Their protests also relate to the king's officials, and the harm done by merinos and tax collectors, and they also discuss the distribution of offices which, according to written norms, was the exclusive privilege of the king. The rebels demand that the king substitute the royal *merinos* with *adelantados*, a request from which one can gather the higher social standing and greater degree of autonomy enjoyed by the *adelantados* and, more generally, the nobles' anxiety not to be subsumed under the iron apparatus of royal control. They wished to participate actively in this system, and to share influence in political responsibility over the land. The nobility, as a collective, thus expressed its real political consciousness as a group.[37]

This kind of debate in the highest spheres of power can probably be related to the construction of the five *Leyes de los Adelantados Mayores*. A difficult text by virtue of its fragmentary nature, its unknown authorship and its unclear date of redaction (between 1258 and 1448), it has been analysed by several historians, among whom Benito Fraile has suggested its link to this moment of conflict.[38] Largely drawing

---

[36] Escalona (2002).

[37] Undoubtedly we need to be very cautious about evaluating noble alliances and presuming the existence of a collective consciousness among the nobility (Pastor et al., 1994). But this is suggested by the presence of *alii multi barones, infanciones et nobiles*, indicating the coalescence of different strata of the nobility. On the exceptional reasons with this unity was imposed over firmly established aristocratic party strategies, see Escalona (2002), and also the discussion by Carlos Estepa, in chapter 6 of this same volume, for events taking place within the two next generations.

[38] For some time these laws were attributed to Alfonso X, but Pérez Prendes (1962) broke with this historiographical tradition, and, by suggesting the possibility of its being a private elaboration based upon a text of royal provenance, he paved the path for further research: Jular (1990), 419–424, Benito Fraile (1996)—especially on the political context of its composition. See, more recently the legal analysis of this source by MacDonald (2000).

on the *Especulo*, the *Leyes de los Adelantados Mayores* systematically sub-stitute the term *merino* with that of *adelantado*, modify details relating to the responsibilities of the official and his authority over his sub-ordinates, and try to establish a clearer hierarchy in relation to different types of lordship. The notion that these laws were related to the noble revolt seems entirely plausible. Whether the laws were prepared by the king in response to the noble protests, or whether they were developed by the nobles themselves, we are clearly looking at two sides of the same legitimating discourse: that of the dominant class in relation to the community of the governed. But now there is a greater articulation of opinion and action, and new voices are introduced. Aristocratic discourse demands from the king respect for the seigneurial order and direct participation in the apparatus of royal government. And government has, to a significant degree, come to revolve around the appointment of officials. Good officials make for good kingship; poor officials undermine royal authority. Yet, a distinct concept of the 'rightful exercise of office', neatly distinguished from its practice by individual officials existed, and played a major role in shaping notions of 'good' and 'bad' noble behaviour. Witness to it the complaint in the *Chronicle of Fernando IV* about the king-dom's main magnates:

> It is difficult to distinguish the lord of Lara, Haro, Alburquerque, or the *infante* don Juan; they come to terms, they rebel, they conciliate again, and once more they rise up. They are cruel, mean, jealous of power and thirsty for wealth; neither is religion their polestar, nor is monarchy their faith. They believe ion nothing but themselves, and have no higher end than their personal profit. Neither have they won a laurel leaf for the crown, nor a crest nor a coat of arms for their shield. Unfortunate king, unfortunate times, and unhappy kingdoms.[39]

Were these offices indeed desirable? At the higher levels, the position of *adelantado* or *merino mayor* allowed access to information about the situation of the realm: a powerful position, therefore, from which to act. These officials used their own seals, had a chancellery adequate for issuing direct written commands, and had the assistance of *alcaldes*,

---

[39] *Trabajo cuesta distinguir a Lara, a Haro, a Alburquerque o al infante don Juan; se aco-modan, se rebelan, se vuelven a avenir, tornan a alborotarse; son crueles, bajos, ambiciosos de poder y sedientos de riqueza; ni la religión es su norte, ni la monarquía su fe; ni creen mas que en sí mismos, ni tienen más fin que el de sus ganancias; ni una hoja de laurel han ganado para su corona, ni un timbre, ni un blasón para su escudo: desgraciado Rey, desgraciados tiempos e infelices reinos.* Benavides (1860) 280.

judges, *letrados* and legal experts to ratify their decisions. They had the support of executive agents and in fact the towns and villages in their jurisdiction: they ate and lived at the expense of the places that hosted them on their tours of duty. With greater or lesser limitations, they are entitled to access to all kinds of seigneuries: *realengo, abadengo, solariego o behetría*.[40] In their role as 'the king's face on the territory'—as observers of any development in the territory and as guarantors of good order—they enjoyed a privileged position in regard to regional sources of information and to the political situation, and had exceptional opportunities—by comparison to the officials of central government—to develop webs of patronage of intense territorial influence. At this point, the broader community enters the picture, as part of this network as well as a public for the actions of government.

The Community:
Public and Political Agent

We began with the tale of Herman Gessler, ostentatiously displaying his hat in the public square of Altdorf. The visual manifestation of this symbol of authority was aimed at a wide audience, whose active involvement in daily acts of administration I will now address, focussing on records of legal cases. In this field there have been promising advances in Spanish historical research. I will use the concept of community in a broad sense to refer to a set of individuals embodying a range of interests much fuller, and more complex, than those of the dominant aristocratic elite, and capable of developing certain levels of organisation. I will also provide examples of local *communities*, in the plural, to refer to specific nuclei of organisation and action. My hope is to illustrate that political dynamics were not dictated solely from above. Rather, in the Central Middle Ages, there was also space for dialogue and negotiation; agreements were reached with the governed, whether they came through action from below or through the ini-

---

[40] These are the standard words for the four main forms of lordship in central medieval Castile, respectively, royal direct lordship, that of the Church, that of lay noblemen and a complex system of collective secular lordship (*behetría*). Royal officers are entitled to act on any of them when major crimes are at issue (treason, manslaughter, assault, robbery, rape . . .); morover, they represent the king in courts where a great number of lawsuits dealing with disputes between lords are heard. On seigneurial categories, see Álvarez (1993; 1996); Estepa (1989; forthcoming); Estepa and Jular (2001).

tiative of higher authorities.[41] The community imposes limits on domination: it is dynamic, as it seeks out authority, it has a voice (both
oral and written) and it has an opinion, expressing its grievances.[42]
From this perspective, I will make some suggestions regarding the
role of the *merinos* and other territorial officials.

The community of the realm was emphatically a community in
motion. In 1234, Fernando III determined the manner in which
judges, *alcaldes* and *jurados* were to be appointed in the city of Oviedo;
the arrangement was then confirmed in Burgos, after the visit of
representatives of both the bishop and chapter of Oviedo and the city
concejo. Some men from Cacabelos (in the modern province of León)
and a royal official subsequently went to see the king in Valladolid
in 1238 to give testimony regarding the obligation to provide animals
for the royal army. As the result of a dispute, representatives of the
concejo of León and the bishop and chapter of that city similarly went
before the king in León in 1241; and men from the Asturian councils
of Oviedo and *Nora a Nora* visited the royal court in Burgos in May
1242. But the king could be at significantly farther reach. Fernando
III received Lucas, bishop of Tuy and various canons representing
the cathedral chapter, along with some *omes buenos* sent to represent
the *concejo* of this Galician city, to discuss some wide-ranging matters
in Seville in July 1250.[43] Two days later, the king received the archbishop of Santiago, don Juan Arias, two archdeacons representing
the cathedral chapter of Compostela, and four other men acting as
representative delegates of the city *concejo*. Later in the month the
royal chancellery issued a number of documents presenting a resolution
of the case between the archbishop and the city council.[44] From
Oviedo to Burgos, from Cacabelos to Valladolid, and above all from
Tuy to Seville, the distances involved are very considerable. Oviedo,
Burgos, León, Valladolid and Seville are leading towns of the kingdom, and therefore important centres of the itinerant royal court.
Cacabelos and *Nora a Nora* are relatively minor settlements, but are
nonetheless swept up in the process of motion. Various social strata
are involved; and, as the final case in the list illustrates, several days

---

[41] Alfonso (1994).
[42] Cf. Bisson (1998).
[43] González (1986), docs. 539, 635, 682, 699 and 794.
[44] González (1986), docs. 795, 796, 798, 799, 800 and 801, 6, 8, 9, 10 and 12
July 1250.

might be dedicated to their disputes. Ecclesiastical representatives changed according to necessity, and equally a new urban *procurador* might be added, as the matter required, so more members of the community were involved than it initially appears.[45] Preliminary organisation required preparation and heavy expenses, difficulties that were aggravated if the case dragged on. These kinds of phenomena, indicated by Grava and Hébert in the context of fourteenth-century Provence, suggest dynamics that have barely been examined in Spanish scholarship and that involved daily practices clearly affecting the action of government.[46] These legal practices should not be separated from the activities of royal officials if we are to reach a full understanding of their role. A good deal of the burden of these practices must in fact have fallen on the royal *merinos*, intended as intermediaries between the king and the community and as a network avoiding the need to visit the king directly. In 1239, the sons of *Ruy Faian* of Sigüenza made their case before the king against the monastery of Oña, because it had occupied the hamlet of *Villiela*, which they claimed to be theirs. And it was the responsibility of Don Moriel, *merino mayor* of Castilla, to publicise and implement the judgement.[47] In a number of the examples cited above, the territorial officials are present, because they were involved in the investigations preceding the judgement of the royal court, because they are mentioned in the final decision about the distribution of rights, or because it is the *merino* who finalises the process. One structure (king-*merinos*) certainly does not substitute the other (community of litigants-royal court), but it runs in parallel, and creates problems for officialdom. Territorial officials require additional funds, in order to support litigants during their visits and expenses during their movements, and so forth. Equally, the community continues to solicit the king's personal presence, maintaining direct channels of information, communication and movement to the royal court. Thus the question of legitimising royal officials needs to take into account pressure from below, as well as the program of government that was attempted from above.

The community was also an articulate community: reading, writing,

---

[45] Don Martin de Tudela, don Sancho Ibáñez, don Pedro Núñez y don Martín Cabeza—note their title—are the usual representatives, but are substituted by *Martin de Larenço, por si* and Juan Estébanez, his son and other butchers when matters relating to their trade are broached.
[46] Grava (1994), Hébert (1994).
[47] González (1986) doc. 646.

and recalling. Let us return once more to the legal record. In the face of a problem such as the occupation of an estate, for example, an aggrieved party might hypothetically take his or her case to the *merino* or the *alcalde* and might wish to gather the material necessary to pursuing his case. The authority would then order an inquest (*pesquisa*) to ascertain the facts, with the result that the process would come to involve a significant proportion of the community. It is the community, after all, that is the repository of social and political memory,[48] and the community that consequently affects the operation of government. I will give three examples. The first dates from a period before the establishment of the *merinos*, so that we can see the contrasts. In 1194, the men of Ledigos submit a plea to the king against Gutierre Fatah, *que tenie Saldana en honor.*[49] Don Gutierre had allegedly taken animals, axes and other booty from Ledigos to Saldaña. Discussion of the jurisdictional limits of Ledigos and Saldaña implied a conflict between the archbishopric of Santiago, upon which the village of Ledigos was dependent, and the lay lord, who was also a temporary delegate of royal authority (a combination of interests that will not recur in the later examples). The king, after listening to the information submitted, ordered a public inquiry of the frontiers, to be undertaken in Ledigos itself. Eighteen people give testimony, coming from a number of different places to give witness before Don Velasco and Pelayo Ibáñez, the royal delegates. Among them were at least three knights and an *alcalde*. Second example: In May 1217, Fernando III of Castile addresses a dispute regarding pasture rights between the *concejos* of Riocerezo and Hurones, on the one hand, and the monastery of San Cristóbal de Ibeas, on the other. The case is heard before the king in Burgos. Fernando orders Don Gonzalo Pérez de Arniellas, *merino mayor*, to look into the case. The official, who is now an outsider to the lordships involved, must send investigators to the two villages in order to inquire into the previous use of pastures in his grandfather's reign. These investigators are a royal *portero* and the

---

[48] Cf. D. Smail's notion of public 'archives of knowledge'. Smail (1997).

[49] González (1960) doc. 632. In the twelfth century, right before the system of territorial administration based upon *merinos* and *adelantados* was introduced, the *in honor* formula indicates lay tenancy, that is to say a lord receiving territorial administrative responsibilities delegated by the king. This subject was traditionally explained as a reflection of the non-feudal nature of medieval Castile (Grassotti, 1969), but more recent approaches further explore its complexities. Rodríguez (1994), Álvarez (1993) 99–138, Barton (1997), Peña (1999) and Doubleday (2001). For the kingdom of León, see Jular (1990).

merino of the district of Burgos. Both men visit at least four places: the concejos of Rubena, *Uillaurmyos* and Cótar, and to the road *que uiene de Riocerezo y va a Riouena*. They seek testimony from the different *omes buenos* from the villages involved: two priests and four labourers from Rubena; a priest, a knight, his two sons and two labourers in *Villaurmyos* priest and four labourers in Cótar. The seventeen witnesses, having sworn on the Gospels, describe the frontiers in minute detail.[50] Third and final case: the inquiry ordered by Fernando González, *merino mayor* of Castile, into the right of the abbot of Santa María de Aguilar de Campóo (Palencia) to demand *yantar* from his vassals in San Quirce.[51] The case is entrusted to two people: one religious (the prior of Santa Cruz de Monzón) and one lay (Don Garci Téllez de Naberos), probably a local *hidalgo*. This time, there are eight witnesses, all from San Quirce itself or from nearby Barrio de Alba. All but one (a cleric from San Quirce) are laymen; three are referred to as *Don*, one a knight, one a royal *jurado*, and one— the only one to declare his dependent status—a *vasallo del obispo*.

The first example, a case between different lords, involves a significant complication: the lay party combined private interests with the political authority that legitimated his actions (the taking of property). Two additional delegates are therefore needed in order to hear the testimony. In the later examples, whether we are dealing with different lordships (second case) or a single lordship (third case), the apparatus of royal inquiry is external to the lordships involved and one may presume a different level of objectivity. But now let us look at the other parties necessary for obtaining the 'truth': in the first case, eighteen witnesses, in the second, seventeen, in the third, eight. As many as a hundred witnesses were heard in the inquiry undertaken in the last third of the thirteenth century as a result of a conflict between the Castilian monastery of San Salvador de Oña and the concejo of the royal town of Frías.[52] The important thing is not the number, but the involvement of people of a variety of ages, status, and social back-ground. These people saw, heard, and knew: the eyes, ears and tongues which functional criteria attributed to the *merinos* had a very real equivalent in the community itself. It is fair to assume

---

[50] Garrido (1983) doc. 505.
[51] Archivo Histórico Nacional, *Clero*, carp. 1664, doc. 3, which may be dated to the years 1249–1255.
[52] See Alfonso and Jular (2000) for details.

that there would have been a significant change in the daily atmosphere of the local communities during the hearing of the case and even afterwards.

The inquiries are not merely 'objective' procedures for verifying the truth; they can also be seen as mechanisms correcting the basic pattern of domination. There is no inquiry without the intervention of the community. In the thirteenth and fourteenth centuries, it is normal for the royal *merinos* to become involved in the investigations, but they are not alone. There was a wide range of other investigators, with varying seigneurial conditions, and there might even be simultaneous inquiries into the same matter. This was the case with the inquiries conducted in 1225, by royal order, into the obligation of the inhabitants of Lences to pay taxes to the monastery of San Salvador de Oña, the Hospital, or the king himself. The first inquiry was entrusted to the archpriest of Frías, the second to Gonzalo Pérez de Arnillas, *merino mayor* of Castile. The reports of each investigation were to be submitted to the king, who after appropriate comparison would resolve the matter.[53] The respective seigneurial rights became clear after conflating the results of the inquiries; in this case it does not seem that here was disagreement between the two reports. But in other instances, there was. The Cacabelos case of 1238, mentioned earlier, involves the action of a royal official who has demanded a payment from the villagers, specifically the lending of animals for the royal host; he was therefore presumably acting on behalf of the king. Both parties—the official and the men of Cacabelos—present their arguments before the king. The official alleges that the animals had been provided in the reign of the previous king, but the villagers dispute this, claiming that they had never done so. The king ordered inquiries to be conducted by Pedro Fernández, archdeacon of Astorga, and his chaplain, and García Rodríguez, his *merino*, who was subsequently substituted by another *merino*, Rodrigo Isidori. Both men undertook an investigation encompassing other figures such as the *comendador* of Peneros, Fray Juan, from the monastery of Villabona, and Guillermo Pérez de Ponferrada. The resulting document, written and sealed, was returned to the king. On this occasion, we do not know the names of the witnesses, but some stated that although the animals had been demanded in the time of Alfonso IX, they had not been given, while many others confirmed that they had

---

[53] González (1983) doc. 201.

never been granted. The king decided to support this view, and accepted that the provision of animals—demanded by his own official—should not be demanded.[54] The appearance of the men of the town before the king had therefore had positive results for the community and even fosters a second favourable decision, just a few days later in that same month, relating to the action of the *merino mayor* within the town limits. The king forbade the *merino mayor*, García Rodríguez, and his subordinate Rodrigo Isidori, from demanding taxes from Cacabelos and Trabadelos, and ordered these payments to be returned if they had been taken.[55] Thus deep-rooted mechanisms like the public inquiry function as a corrective mechanism for the system of royal power. Local communities are fully involved in these practices.

Towards a Conclusion

The vision of alien normative systems imposed on a community from above is therefore questionable. The Castilian monarchy of the central Middle Ages introduced order and rationality into the legal procedures, but this is only one part of the story. Royal *merinos* seem to have been 'designed' as intermediaries between king and subjects, creating a degree of proximity that camouflaged the desire for absolute social control, but the community actively used the law, and in the interaction of discourse and practice, a space opened up for dialogue and negotiation. A legal case brought before the king set in motion many complex mechanisms; instruments of proof; arguments over authority; individual and collective participation; physical movement; written communication, oral testimony, replies and counters; scrutiny of arguments. Certainly, the dominant class was rhetorically dominant, too, but inasmuch as persuasion goes hand in hand with social dominance, the rhetoric of persuasion also implied a need to convince and therefore to negotiate, and this opened a door for communities to engage

---

[54] ... *Et ego inspexi [inquisitionem et inueni] quod aliqui ex ipsis que [dede]runt testimonium dicebant quod bestie fuerant demandate tempore patris mei set nunquam fuerunt date, et plures illorum dicebant quod nunquam fuerunt date. Et quia ego inueni per ilam inquisitionem quod homines de Cacauellis nunquam dederant bestias tempore patris mei, statuo et firmiter mando quod de cetero non dent eas, et defendo firmiter quod aliquis non sit ausus demandare ipsas bestias, quia qui faceret incurreret iram meam, et pectaret mihi in cauto centum morabetinos, et ipsis hominibus de Cacauellis dompnum duplicatum.*

[55] 30 November 1238. González (1986) doc. 642.

in the process in their own right. In this context, it cannot be by
chance that the central medieval monarchy typically emphasised
negotiated solutions. Among the cases cited, the conflict between Tuy
and the bishop, which had become violent and which now led the
action to unfold before the king in Seville, is paradigmatic.[56] 'They
came before me'—says the king, referring to the representatives of
both parties—'. . . I heard the complaints of both sides . . . I had them
written down . . . When I heard the reasons I deemed it necessary
to conduct an inquiry . . . The two parties agreed that the inquiry
be conducted . . . I ordered investigation of the complaints . . . I sent
the record of grievances inside the letter in which I ordered the
inquiry . . . They conducted the inquiry and sent me the report . . . and
the two sides were instructed to come before me at Pentecost'—a
bishop, an archdeacon and a canon came from the ecclesiastical party;
and for the town council, a judge with written power of attorney.
'After I saw the report, I ordered the archbishop of Santiago and
the bishops of Palencia and Segovia and my *alcalde* Pelayo Díaz'—
that is, the king, three high ecclesiasts and a royal officer—'also to
examine it . . . At the hearing, it was agreed in advance that my
judgement should be final, whether I found for one party or ordered
both sides to negotiate an agreement[57] . . . And I consulted with my
son, the *infante* Alfonso, and with the archbishop of Santiago, and
with the bishops and *ricos hombres* who were with me . . .' Only after
all these steps had been taken did the king consider the case and
pass judgement. And his long judgement involves a number of distinct
arguments with different solutions to each problem. On the one hand,
violent misdeeds are punished: he explicitly condemns the aggressors,
and sentences them to pay restitution. On the other hand, instead of
the mere imposition of the dominant elite, the whole process—when
carefully deconstructed—suggests a dense complexity in the practice
of power in which the community has real political agency: this
could not be ignored by royal official in the exercise of their duty.

If our script does not include all the actors we will not comprehend
the play. In every political system there are agents of power; and
they usually attract criticism. Order and debate, conflict and negotiation are all basic to medieval society. But we are more prepared,

---

[56] González (1983) doc. 788.
[57] *et ante que la pesquisa judgasemos avinieronse el obispo et los personeros del cabildo et el
personero del concejo de meter el pleyto todo en mi mano, et que estuviesen por quanto yo mandase,
quier por judicio quier por avenencia, quier por otra manera qualquier que yo toviese por bien.*

in some instances, to understand protest than to appreciate the subtle, intricate links binding us to authority, and historians are partly responsible for this problem. William Tell and Robin Hood seem familiar to us. The actions of William Tell consecrated the 'legitimate' direct confrontation of authority, and his example led to the emergence of the Pact of Swiss Confederation, which allowed the 'liberty of the collective' in the face of the 'imposition of authority'. The heroic and mythologised model of Robin Hood ultimately shaped the models of the 'bad king deposed' and the 'just king restored'.[58] As interpreters of history, we have mythologised certain figures in great measure by demonising others. The medieval era itself knew the efficiency of rhetorical construction, the power of binary images. Yet the positive and negative presentations of royal officials are merely two sides of the same coin: an affirmation of the necessity of authority. All that changes is the discourse and practice of legitimation, the capabilities and limits of power. In the central medieval world, protagonism in the political theatre is granted to the dominant class, but this does not mean that the community is excluded.

This is the principal idea I have attempted to explore in this article. Within the complex political culture of the medieval world, negotiation and conflict modify the relations between community, intermediaries, and power as much as the imposition, coercion and domination inherent in feudal authority. *Acuerdo, placito, convenientia, asensu, compositio, abenencia, consensu,* and *beneplacito* imply the possibility of *compensatio, enmienda, defensa.* Mechanisms such as *inquisitio, informatio, demostratio, pesquisa* can correct the problems that underlie the *querella, causa, desafuero, contienda, controuersia, contentio,* or *discordia.* William Tell and Gessler, Robin Hood and the sheriff of Nottingham, should help us to appreciate the rather less Hollywood-appealing cases of royal officials such as Pedro Núñez de Guzmán,[59] or Bernat de Blas.[60] The

---

[58] Holt (1989). On the rhetorics of the 'restoration of good government', see the chapter by I. Alfonso in this same volume.

[59] In the fourteenth century, the *concejo* of León led a plaid against the royal *merino mayor* of León, Pedro Núñez de Guzmán, who extorted from the citizens of the town a considerably higher quantity of goods than those to which he was entitled. Once the case had been heard before the royal court, and he had been accused officially of rebellion and required to compensate the city from his own wealth, he remained persistently defiant, but this did not make him immediately lose his office. Instead, it was his desertion from the king's army that triggered his fall. After his loyalty was discredited, he was no longer necessary, and was dismissed. Jular (1990) 294–308.

[60] Bernat de Blas, bailiff of Gerona, was threatened and wounded along with his

complexities of the local articulation of central power in medieval societies cannot be explained only through kings and royal agents. 'The King's face on the territory' must the studied through the dialogue between monarchy, intermediaries and communities.

Translated by Simon Doubleday
(Hofstra University, New York)

Bibliography

Primary Sources/History of Law

Archivo Histórico Nacional, Sección *Clero*, Carpeta 1664.
Ballesteros-Beretta, A. (1984, 2nd ed.) *Alfonso X el Sabio* (Barcelona: 1984).
Benavides, A. (1860) *Memorias de D. Fernando IV de Castilla*, 2 vols. (Madrid: 1860). Tomo I: *Contiene la crónica de dicho rey, copiada de un códice existente en la Biblioteca Nacional, anotada y ampliamente ilustrada por D. Antonio Benavides, individuo de número de la Real Academia de la Historia, por cuyo acuerdo se publica* (Madrid: 1860).
Benito Fraile, E. de (1996) "En torno a las Leyes de los Adelantados Mayores", *Cuadernos de Historia del Derecho* 3 (1996) 287–312.
Bermejo Cabrero, J.L. (1970) "En torno a la aplicación de las Partidas. Fragmentos del Espéculo en una sentencia real de 1261", in *Hispania* 114 (1970) 169–177.
Garrido Garrido, J.M. (1983) *Documentación de la Catedral de Burgos (1184–1222)* (Burgos: 1983).
González, J. (1960) *El reino de Castilla en la época de Alfonso VIII*, 3 vols. (Madrid: 1960).
—— (1980, 1983 y 1986) *Reinado y diplomas de Fernando III*, 3 vols. Vol. I: *Estudio* (Córdoba: 1980); Vol. II: *Diplomas, años 1217–1232* (Córdoba: 1983); Vol. III: *Diplomas, años 1233–1253* (Córdoba: 1986).
González Jiménez, M. (ed.) (1998) *Crónica de Alfonso X* (Murcia: 1998).
MacDonald, R.A. (2000) *Leyes de los Adelantados Mayores. Regulations, Attributed to Alfonso X of Castile, Concerning the King's Vicar In the Judiciary and in Territorial Administration* (New York: 2000).
Martínez Diez, G. (1985) *Leyes de Alfonso X. I: Especulo, edición y análisis crítico* (Ávila: 1985).
—— (1988) *Leyes de Alfonso X. II. Fuero Real. Edición y análisis crítico* (Ávila: 1988).
Pérez-Bustamante, R. (1976) *El gobierno y la administración territorial de Castilla (1230–1474)*, 2 vols. (Madrid: 1976).
Pérez-Prendes, J.M. (1962) "Las Leyes de los Adelantados Mayores", *Hidalguía* 51 (marzo–abril 1962) 365–384.
—— (1974) "'Facer justicia'. Notas sobre actuación gubernativa medieval", *Moneda y crédito* 129 (1974) 17–90.
—— (1985) "Las leyes de Alfonso el Sabio", *Revista de Occidente* 43 (1985) 67–84.

men in 1331 by armed clerics because he protected the city ordinances concerning the Jews. He too was an important official, delegate of superior power, agent of executive authority; but now the community necessarily take account of this dialogue between monarchy, intermediaries and community. Nirenberg (2001) 296–302, 312–316.

Sinués Ruiz, A. (1954) *El merino* (Zaragoza: 1954).
Las Siete Partidas del rey don Alfonso el Sabio, cotejadas con varios códices antiguos por la Real Academia de la Historia, III vols. (Madrid: 1972).

Bibliography

Alfonso Antón, I. (1994) "Resolución de disputas y prácticas judiciales en el Burgos medieval", in *Burgos en la Plena Edad Media. III Jornadas Burgalesas de Historia* (Burgos: 1994) 211–243.
—— (1997) "Litigios por la tierra y "malfetrías" entre la nobleza medieval castellano-leonesa" y Presentación del Dossier monográfico: "Desarrollo legal, prácticas judiciales y acción política en la Europa medieval", *Hispania* 197 (1997) 917–955 y 879–883.
—— (1997) "Campesinado y derecho: la vía legal de su lucha (Castilla y León, siglos X–XIII), *Historia Agraria* 13 (1997) 15–31.
—— (2001) "Conflictos en las behetrías", in C. Estepa Díez and C. Jular Pérez-Alfaro (Coords.) *Los señoríos de behetría* (Madrid: 2001) 227–259.
—— (2002) "*Desheredamiento* y *desafuero,* o la pretendida justificación de una revuelta nobiliaria", *Cahiers de linguistique et de civilisation hispaniques médiévales,* 25 (2002) 99–129.
Alfonso, I. y Jular, C. (2000) "Oña contra Frías o el pleito de los cien testigos: una pesquisa en la Castilla del siglo XIII, *Edad Media* 3 (2000) 61–88.
Álvarez Borge, I. (1993) *Monarquía feudal y organización territorial: Alfoces y merindades en Castilla: Siglos X–XV* (Madrid: 1993).
—— (1996) *Poder y relaciones sociales en Castilla en la Edad Media. Los territorios entre el Arlanzón y el Duero en los siglos X al XIV* (Salamanca: 1996).
—— (1998) "Nobleza y señoríos en Castilla la Vieja meridional a mediados del siglo XIV", *Brocar,* 21 (1998) 55–117.
—— (Coord.) (2001) *Comunidades locales y poderes feudales en la Edad Media* (Logroño: 2001).
Autrand, F. (1994) "L'allée du roi dans les pays de Languedoc 1272–1390", in *La circulation de nouvelles au Moyen Âge* (París: 1994) 85–97.
Balandier, G. (1994) *El poder en escenas. De la representación del poder al poder de la representación* (Barcelona: 1994. [Orig.: *Le pouvoir sur scènes,* Paris: 1992]
Barton, S. (1997) *The Aristocracy in Twelfth-Century León and Castile* (Cambridge, Eng., 1997).
Bisson, T.N. (1998) *Tormented Voices: Power, Crisis and Humanity in Rural Catalonia, 1140–1200* (Cambridge, Mass., 1998).
Blanchard, J. (ed.) (1995) *Représentation, pouvoir et royauté à la fin du Moyen Âge* (París: 1995).
Bulst, N. (1996) "Les officiers royaux en France dans la deuxième moitié du XVe siècle: bourgeois au service de l'État", in J.Ph. Genet and G. Lottes (Eds.) *L'État moderne et les élites, XIIIe–XVIIIe siècles. Apports et limites de la méthode prosopographique* (Paris: 1996) 111–121.
—— (1996) "Objet et méthode de la prosopographie", in J.Ph. Genet and G. Lottes (Eds.) *L'État moderne et les élites, XIIIe–XVIIIe siècles. Apports et limites de la méthode prosopographique* (Paris: 1996) 467–482.
Chevallaz, G.-A. (1989–1990) "L'histoire de la Confédération suisse: une démarche en contrapoint", in *Les défis des années 1990: position et stratégie internationale de la Suisse, Annales d'études internationales,* Volume 17 (1989–1990).
Demurger, A. (1996) "Carrières normandes: les vicomtes (1350–1450)", in J.Ph. Genet and G. Lottes (Eds.) *L'État moderne et les élites, XIIIe–XVIIIe siècles. Apports et limites de la méthode prosopographique* (Paris: 1996) 97–109.
Dijk, Teun A. (1999) *Ideología. Una aproximación interdisplinaria* (Barcelona: 1999) [Orig.: London: 1998].

Doubleday, S. (2001) *The Lara Family: Crown and Nobility in Medieval Spain* (Cambridge, Mass., 2001).

Escalona Monge, J. (2000) *Transformaciones sociales y organización del espacio en el alfoz de Lara en la Alta Edad media* (Madrid: 2000). Ph.D. dissertation, CD-Rom edition.

—— (2000) "De 'señores y campesinos' a 'comunidades locales y poderes feudales'. Elementos para definir la articulación entre territorio y clases sociales en la Alta Edad Media castellana", in I. Álvarez Borge (coord.) (2001) *Comunidades locales y poderes feudales en la Edad Media* (Logroño: 2001) 117–155.

—— (2001) "Unidades territoriales supralocales: una propuesta sobre los orígenes del señorío de behetría", in C. Estepa Díez and C. Jular-Pérez-Alfaro (Coords.) *Los señoríos de behetría* (Madrid: 2001) 21–46.

—— (2002) "Los nobles contra su rey. Argumentos y motivaciones de la insubordinación nobiliaria de 1272–1273", *Cahiers de linguistique et de civilisation hispaniques médiévales*, 25 (2002) 131–162.

Estepa Díez, C. (1984) "Alfonso X y el fecho del imperio", *Revista de Occidente*, 43 (1984) 43–54.

—— (1989) "Formación y consolidación del feudalismo en Castilla y León", in *En torno al feudalismo hispánico. I Congreso de Estudios Medievales* (León: 1989) 157–256.

—— (1990) "El realengo y el señorío jurisdiccional concejil en Castilla y León (siglos XII–XV)", in *Concejos y ciudades en la Edad Media Hispánica* (León: 1990) 465–506.

—— (1994) "Estructuras de poder en Castilla (siglos XII–XIII). El poder señorial en las merindades 'burgalesas'", in *Burgos en la Plena Edad Media. III Jornadas Burgalesas de Historia* (Burgos, 1994) 245–294.

—— (1997) "Alfonso X en la Europa del siglo XIII", in *Alfonso X. Aportaciones de un rey castellano en la construcción de Europa* (Murcia: 1997) 11–29.

—— (2001) "Labradores del Rey y Königsbauern. Planteamientos y perspectivas para una comparación", in Álvarez Borge, I. (Coord.) (2001) *Comunidades locales y poderes feudales en la Edad Media* (Logroño: 2001) 157–201.

—— (2003) Las behetrias castellanas (Valladolid: 2003).

—— and Jular Pérez-Alfaro, C. (coords.) (2001) *Los señoríos de behetría* (Madrid: 2001)

García de Cortázar, J.A., coord. (1985) *Organización social del espacio en la España medieval. La Corona de Castilla en los siglos VIII al XV* (Barcelona: 1985).

—— (1988) "Organización social del espacio: propuestas de reflexión y análisis histórico de sus unidades en la España Medieval", *Stvdia Historica. Historia Medieval*, VI (1988) 195–236.

Genet, J.-Ph. y Lottes, G., (eds.) (1996) *L'État moderne et les élites, XIIIᵉ–XVIIIᵉ siècles. Apports et limites de la méthode prosopographique* (París: 1996).

Gómez Redondo, F. (1998–1999) *Historia de la prosa medieval castellana*, 2 vols. (Madrid: 1998–1999).

González Jiménez, M. (1993) *Alfonso X* (Palencia: 1993).

Grassotti, H. (1969) *Las instituciones feudo-vasalláticas en León y Castilla* (Spoleto: 1969).

Grava, Y. (1994) "Les ambassades provençales au XIVᵉ siècle et les enjeux de la communication", in *La circulation de nouvelles au Moyen Âge*, XXIVᵉ (París: 1994) 25–36.

Hébert, M. (1994) "Communications et société politique: les villes et l'État en Provence aux XIVᵉ et XVᵉ siècles", in *La circulation de nouvelles au Moyen Âge*, XXIVᵉ (París: 1994) 231–242.

Hilton, R. (1978) *Siervos liberados. Los movimientos campesinos medievales y el levantamiento inglés de 1381* (Madrid: 1978).

—— (1986) "La société paysanne et le droit dans l'Angleterre médiévale", in "Le droit et les paysans", *Études rurales* 103–104 (1986) 13–18.

Hispania (1997) 879–1078. Special issue on *Desarrollo legal, prácticas judiciales y acción política en la Europa medieval*. Articles by I. Alfonso, J. Hudson, S. White, C. Wickham, J.M.ª Salrach and D.L. Smail.

Holt, J.C. (1989) *Robin Hood* (London: 1989).

Jular Pérez-Alfaro, C. (1990) *Los adelantados y merinos mayores de León (siglos XIII–XV)* (León: 1990).

—— (1991) "*Alfoz* y *tierra* a través de documentación castellana y leonesa de 1157 a 1230. Contribución al estudio del dominio señorial", *Studia Historica. Historia Medieval* IX (1991) 9–42.

——(1993) "La participación de un noble en el poder local a través de su clientela. Un ejemplo concreto de fines del siglo XIV", *Hispania* 185 (1993) 861–884.

—— (1994) "Aproximación a la terminología territorial de la monarquía feudal. El *Honor* en la documentación regia de León y de Castilla en la segunda mitad del siglo XII, in *Burgos en la Plena Edad Media. I Jornadas Burgalesas de Historia* (Burgos: 1994) 609–621.

—— (1996) "Dominios señoriales y relaciones clientelares en Castilla: Velasco, Porres y Cárcamo (ss. XIII–XIV)", *Hispania* 192 (1996) 137–171.

—— (1997) "Conflictos ante tenentes y merinos en los siglos XII–XIII ¿contestación al poder señorial o al poder regio?", *Historia Agraria* 13 (1997) 33–63.

—— (1999) "Los bienes prestados: estrategias feudales de consolidación señorial", *Historia Agraria* 17 (1999) 3–28.

—— (2001) "Nobleza y relaciones clientelares: el caso de los Velasco", in C. Estepa Díez and C. Jular-Pérez-Alfaro (Coords.) *Los señoríos de behetría* (Madrid: 2001) 145–186.

Maddicott, J.R. (1984) "Magna Carta and the Local Community 1215–1259", *Past and Present*, 102 (1984) 25–65.

Martin, G. (Comp.) (2000) *La historia alfonsí: el modelo y sus destinos (siglos XIII–XIV)* (Madrid: 2000)

—— (forthcoming) "Violencia, autoridad, consenso. La caballería según Alfonso X el Sabio", in *Lucha política: condena y legitimación en las sociedades medievales* (París: forthcoming).

Martínez Sopena, P. (1985) *La Tierra de Campos Occidental. Poblamiento, poder y comunidad del siglo X al XIII* (Valladolid: 1985).

Monsalvo Antón, J.M.ª (1986) "Poder político y aparatos de Estado en la Castilla bajomedieval. Consideraciones sobre su problemática", en *Stvdia Historica* vol. IV, nº 2 (1986) 101–167.

—— (1995) "Historia de los poderes medievales, del Derecho a la Antropología (el ejemplo castellano: monarquía, concejos y señoríos en los siglos XII–XV)", in C. Barros (ed.) *Historia a Debate. Medieval* (Santiago de Compostela: 1995) 81–149.

—— (1998) "Crisis del feudalismo y centralización monárquica castellana (observaciones acerca del origen del "Estado moderno" y su causalidad)", in C. Estepa/ D. Plácido (coords.) and J. Trías (ed.) *Transiciones en la antigüedad y feudalismo* (Madrid: 1998) 139–167.

Moreta, S. (1978) *Malhechores feudales. Violencia, antagonismos y alianzas de clases en Castilla, siglos XIII–XIV* (Madrid: 1978).

Nieto Soria, J.M. (2000) "Cultura y poder real a fines del medievo: la política como representación", in *Sociedad, culturas e ideologías en la España bajomedieval* (Zaragoza: 2000) 7–31.

Nirenberg, D. (2001) *Comunidades de violencia. La persecución de las minorías en la Edad Media*, Barcelona, 2001. [Orig.: *Communities of Violence: Persecution of Minorities in the Middle Ages*, Princeton University Press, 1996].

O'Callaghan, J. (1993) *The Learned King: The Reign of Alfonso X of Castile* (Philadelphia, 1993).

Pastor Baños, R.; Estepa Díez, C.; Alfonso Antón, I.; Escalona Monge, J.; Jular Pérez-Alfaro, C.; Pascua Echegaray, E.; Sánchez León, P. (1994) "Baja nobleza: aproximación a la historiografía europea y propuestas para una investigación", *Historia Social* 20 (1994) 23–45.

Pastor, R. (1973) *Conflictos sociales y estancamiento económico en la España medieval* (Barcelona: 1973).

—— (1980) *Resistencias y luchas campesinas en la época de crecimiento y consolidación de la formación feudal. Castilla y León. Siglos X–XIII* (Madrid: 1980).

Peña, E. (1999) "Alfoces y tenencias en La Rioja", in García de Cortázar, J.A. (ed.) "Del Cantábrico al Duero. Trece estudios sobre organización social del espacio en los siglos VIII al XIII" (Santander: 1999).

Rodríguez López, A. (1994) *La consolidación territorial de la monarquía feudal castellana. Expansión y fronteras durante el reinado de Fernando III* (Madrid: 1994).

Senellart, M. (1995) *Les arts de gouverner. Du regimen médiéval au concept de gouvernement* (Paris: 1995).

Smail, D.L. (1997) "Archivos de conocimiento y la cultura legal de la publicidad en la Marsella medieval", *Hispania* 197 (1997) 1049–1077.

THE IMPORTANCE OF BEING EARNEST:
URBAN ELITES AND THE DISTRIBUTION OF POWER IN CASTILIAN TOWNS IN THE LATE MIDDLE AGES

José Antonio Jara Fuente

Instituto de Historia, CSIC

In Oscar Wilde's masterpiece *The Importance of Being Earnest*, Victorian society is depicted with acidic humour. The very title of the play introduces the audience to the central theme of Wilde's play and the pivotal point of its social critique: the importance of social status deriving from the class structure. What evidently mattered in Victorian society was not *how* but *who*. Social standing in Victorian society was principally based neither upon the behaviour of the individual nor upon his character: surprisingly, perhaps, since good deeds and moral probity were much-vaunted ideals in the puritanical world of Victorian England. Victorian society appraised the external signs that help to define the individual; the adornments that embellish—rather than comprising—the personality. In Victorian society, such adornments functioned as social codes of identification that helped to differentiate one individual from another, one social group from another, in relation to the broader class structure. Within this culture, a Jeeves could never aspire to integrate in the elite of Victorian society. In the best case scenario, he would be considered and treated as a *parvenu*. Thus, the importance of the Victorian individual is determined by a coded set of relationships to the broader structure of society.

There are many similar codes of identification in other societies and systems, and the Middle Ages were no exception to the rule. In a period in which images had such an important role, these codes of identification were pervasive in everyday life. Some were easily intelligible and accessible by elemental processes of social decoding. Clothes were perhaps the most conspicuous and rapidly decipherable code; and, being susceptible to abuse by medieval *parvenus*, required strict regulation. In Castile, for example, sartorial sins constituted one of the grievances expressed to the king in the Cortes held in the town of Palenzuela in 1425. The urban representatives asked the king to enforce the laws dictated by his predecessors and to forbid common people to dress like nobles. They emphasised the difficulty of distinguishing between noblemen and commons and the fact that many noblemen, not so wealthy as some artisans and merchants, could not afford to compete with them in dress.[1]

Another code commanding attention was that of the instruments of war, and especially horses and swords. These distinctive elements gradually came to identify the knight, the *defensor christianitatis*, and, by a process of association between dignity and nobility, it finally came to signify the nobleman.[2] In Castile, this is a more complicated process because of the incorporation of a new social category, that of the urban *caballeros*.[3] This social group is fundamental in understanding the process of *Reconquest* undertaken by the Castilian monarchy. The vast territories conquered from the Spanish Muslims in the twelfth and thirteenth centuries, and the lack of a population adequate for restructuring that space, gave primacy to the inhabitants of villages, but especially those of cities and towns, who could afford and make use of a war-horse and weapons.[4] This group constituted the elite of every city and town, especially in frontier areas where they protected Christian-ruled territory from Muslim raids and where they took part in, or directly organised, campaigns against the Muslims. Their centrality in the towns was explained, and ideologically justified, as much by their defensive role as by their superior social and economic position. The group's consolidation at the heart of the dominant class was based on military services rendered to the monarchy and on the booty won in war. Nevertheless, the urban *caballeros* did not

---

[1] *Vid Cortes* (1866), vol. III, Cortes held in Palenzuela, in 1425, bill number 31.

[2] The development of this process in Castile is fascinating. In the fifteenth century, there were two schools of thought on the related themes of dignity (knighthood *inter alia*) and nobility, one of them supporting their equivalence and the other denying it. On these questions see Rodríguez Velasco (1996) and Jara Fuente (2001).

[3] I have preferred to translate *caballeros villanos* as urban *caballeros*, to preserve a sense concealed in the term *caballeros villanos* that many of them were not noblemen or knights, though in time a good part of those *caballeros* will enter into the low nobility.

[4] In the fifteenth century, when "civil" wars provided a perfect arena for social climbing, many people rose into the low nobility by joining the royal retinue as a result of royal promises of knighthood. Most were merchants, traders, or artisans who, besides their wealth and social aspirations, had a taste for adventure, though not always a corresponding ability to use the tools of their new trade: war-horse and weapons. Their incompetence was a constant concern for the urban representatives in the Cortes, which urged the kings to assure them of such men's ability before granting any privilege. *Vid Cortes* (1866), vol. III, Cortes held in Ocaña, in 1469, bill number 6; and vol. IV, Cortes held in Madrigal, in 1476, bill number 19.

at first experience a change in their juridical status paralleling their socio-economic (and ultimately political) role. There was no confusing these *caballeros* with the class of knights, never mind the nobility, even though some of them might belong to the *hidalguía*, the lesser nobility.

This situation began to change by the mid-thirteenth century, when two partially contradictory interests converged in the urban sphere. On one hand, there were the interests of the urban *caballeros*, non-nobles in most cases, who, after the conquest of Córdoba and Seville and the stagnation of the Reconquest, lost one of the integral elements of their process of social reproduction: war and the attendant possibilities of booty and land. This group now turned its attention to the urban resources of the towns themselves. On the other hand, there were the interests of the monarchy, that of Alfonso X of Castile and León (1252–1284), concerned with a political project to overcome the latent tensions existing between the different mechanisms integrated in the Castilian crown. Royal primacy over the other elements that configured it—the Church, the nobility, and the towns—rested mainly on a fiscal system free from the interference of the nobility or the urban elite themselves. In order to achieve that goal, an agreement between the king and the urban elite seemed desirable and almost indispensable. This was true firstly because royal incomes depended heavily on the urban areas; and secondly because of the support that towns, and especially their militias, could give in the monarchy's struggle against the aspirations of a nobility that had also suffered from the stagnation of the Reconquest. Alfonso X therefore obtained the support of the urban elites and, by way of compensation, granted numerous privileges to the members of those elites, analogous to those of the blood-nobility. He also supported the elite's control of the municipalities, undermining the role of the urban assemblies as a collective instrument for the decision-making processes of local government.[5]

---

[5] On this general process in the thirteenth century, in regard to its effects on the towns, see Barrios García (1984), Monsalvo Antón (1990) and Asenjo González (1987). The privileges granted by the monarchy to the urban *caballeros* are similar from town to town. For those of Cuenca, they included the receipt of wages when called to join the royal retinue and the distribution of the *fonsadera* collected in Cuenca and its jurisdiction. (The *fonsadera* was paid to the king by those wishing to avoid service in the royal retinue, and it was confirmed by Alfonso XI in 1322). Other privileges in Cuenca included the right to be compensated for a horse lost in battle; exemption from tours of duty in royal castles (confirmed by Alfonso X in 1268) and from royal taxes (granted by Alfonso X in 1272). Further, the *caballeros*

In the fourteenth century, Alfonso XI (1312–1350) developed this process further, sanctioning, with the introduction of the *regimientos,* the consolidation of an urban elite. The *regimiento* was intended to be the supreme institution of urban government. It presupposed the exclusion from direct participation in government of an ample part of society. These functions were then assigned to the most prominent urban *caballeros,* implying a partial closing of the power subsystem, although there was nonetheless a certain amount of social mobility to and from the core of this subsystem. Alfonso XI drastically modified the nature of the urban *caballeros,* making membership of this group compulsory for all those with a certain level of wealth, established at a different level in every town. In this way, to endow oneself with a war-horse and weapons was no more a voluntary decision, but an obligation born of economic position. At the same time, the possession of these items sanctioned the right to participate in the urban power subsystem, constituting a code of identification that was not merely social but also political. Nevertheless, it should be stressed that the consolidation of these urban elites, by means of the introduction of the *regimiento,* did not imply the solution of the problems of municipal government. There were dysfunctional consequences in practically every town, causing a plethora of conflicts between the second half of the fourteenth century and the first third of the fifteenth century. It is precisely at this moment, the first decades of the 1400s, that local pacts and agreements concerning the operation of urban government were reached throughout the towns of Castile.[6]

It is on the urban *caballeros* that this article will focus, in a period, the fifteenth century, in which most of these *caballeros* came to form powerful elites in Castilian towns. In the following pages, I will

---

enjoyed the rights to extend their exemption to their servants (granted by Fernando IV in 1302), and to transfer these privileges to their widows and sons. Finally, they received the *montazgo* in Cuenca (three heads of every thousand cattle crossing the jurisdiction of Cuenca, granted by Sancho IV in 1293 and enlarged to five by Alfonso XI in 1322). Cfr. Cabañas González (1980) 28–46.

[6] An analytical model of these functions can be found in Jara Fuente (2000), esp. 129–135. Not all these agreements were the result of pacts directly reached by the parties in conflict; sometimes they were the consequence of arbitration. Examples of those agreements, among many others, are the pacts of 1320–21 in Valladolid, 1371 and 1433 in Segovia, 1395 in Guadalajara, 1419 in Alcalá de Henares, 1419 and 1499 in Zamora, 1426 in Burgos, and the one of 1495 in Medina del Campo. See Rucquoi (1987a) 241–243, Ladero Quesada (1996) 147–160, Asenjo González (1986a) 415–417, Martínez Moro (1985) 148–149, Sánchez León (1998) 85–86, Bonachía Hernando (1978) 123–124, and Val Valdivieso (1994) 41–58.

analyse the models of power that they worked within, and the codes of identification that emerged from those models. In many cases, these models extended their benefits to the whole of urban society. One crucial premise is that whenever this system was predisposed to, and capable of, harnessing broad social participation, this participation consolidated the stability of the paradigm being legitimated. Thus processes of legitimation in the urban sphere can be investigated and revealed through the study of the construction of paradigms of power.

My contribution begins (Section I) with a logical assumption, that people—as social actors—must be the fundamental concern in any study on power. The mechanisms whereby a model of power emerged in a specific place and time cannot be understood if they are not related to the social agents that gave them life, that operated and benefited, or suffered, from them. Most scholars tend to view power as a simple face-to-face confrontation, forgetting that power is ultimately the result of negotiated social relations. Thus, in section II, I will argue that power in the urban world of Castile was not merely the consequence of conflict, whose existence I do not pretend to deny or underestimate, but also—and primarily—an achievement reached through agreement. Informal, unwritten, pacts were widely granted by the king and the most prominent lineages in every town (lineages that, *de facto* and in time *de iure*, controlled urban power resources). Social peace was the most fundamental consequence of these pacts, and those located deep in the subaltern class were often those who most benefited.

Section III explains how urban citizens participated in the construction of this power model. In this section, domination is viewed not only as the imposition of a superior class position but also as the result of negotiations around the profits that each element within the dominant class and even the lineages or individuals in the upper echelons of the subaltern class could enjoy. This is a theoretical approach that revolves around the notion of system and especially around the concept of a subsystem of resources and its related pair of double assumptions: disposable/non-disposable resources and control over/ access to the subsystem. These are important tools for understanding how people were stratified and categorised, and the social, economic and political advantages that domination allowed them to share. The relationship between the system's recognition of class positions and individuals' level of satisfaction helps to explain the evolution of urban power models and the degree of social violence or peace.

Finally, in section IV, the theoretical analysis undertaken in the preceding chapter is put to the test. The members of the dominant class are analysed according to three key concepts: the elite of power, the elite of participation, and a minor element, lesser in terms of power.[7] The social mechanisms that governed the incorporation of lineages or individuals into any of these categories, and their respective roles in the benefits of domination, are fundamental considerations in understanding the emergence and development of urban power models. In order to test these theories, I have taken the city of Cuenca as a case study. This city is located to the south of the river Duero, in an area where the importance of the territory conquered from the Muslims and the lack of men to populate it determined royal grants of large hinterlands to the towns and the emergence of important groups of urban *caballeros*. This analysis is based on a prosopographical work of the city of Cuenca that covers the years 1417 to 1480, and comprises 6,495 individuals and approximately 300,000 data of different types.[8]

I. Social Agency and Models of Domination

In 1979, in a now classic work, G. Therborn discussed the approaches whereby power was usually analysed by scholars and affirmed the irrelevance of the question of *who* as opposed to the matter of *how* power is exercised.[9] Though this is neither the place nor the moment to discuss this proposition in depth, it seems obvious that a *how* without a *who* lacks real meaning. Instruments of domination and their related operating mechanisms (Therborn's *how*) are predicated on a single person or a collectivity. This, in turn, implies two mirror

---

[7] In this theoretical model of class organisation inside the dominant class, the notion of a power elite—developed by Mills (1956)—is reserved, following his proposal, to the powerful minority that composed the central core of domination.

[8] The database is built around two main blocks of data: those related to the texts themselves, and those related to the social actors. The first combines diplomatic data with short summaries of the document, organised around key words. The second involves entries concerning information on the person's name, professional and public offices and activities, information on his patrimony, family and other relations, status, residence, etc. This information allows us to reconstruct their lives as completely and faithfully as the documents permit.

[9] See Therborn (1979).

images: people viewed as active social agents, either conscious or not of that role; and people viewed as passive social agents, again either conscious or not of their role. Thus, ignorance of the social agents involved in the exercise of power undermines all possibility of understanding the mechanisms through which power is realised and operates. (Therborn, of course, was well aware of these problems; his error should be understood as a question of emphasis, unbalanced in favour of the *how*). The discursive model or models that legitimated and shaped a concrete model of domination are best understood through the examination of the *behaviour* of the social agent. This is especially relevant when examining the construction of a power model in the Castilian urban subsystem.[10] Here, the traditional thesis affirmed the existence of urban oligarchies that exercised power in a monopolist or quasi-monopolist way. This view emphasises the notion of "oligarchy" in the singular, for every city, town or village municipal government. In this study, however, I will reject the term "oligarchy" in favour of the term "elites", using the plural form advisedly.

Successful integration in the elites implies, of course, recognition of one's own status.[11] Around 1499 or the beginning of 1500, the Tribunal of Cuenca accused Diego de Alcalá of judaizing. This man belonged to the upper echelons of Cuenca's dominant class and to one of the two most prominent and powerful lineages in the town: those of Alcalá and Álvarez de Toledo. Once he discovered who had testified against him, Diego proceeded to answer the charges and suggested his own witnesses to the court. Clearly understanding that the best method of defence is attack, he opened his plea by unleashing a series of allegations against the witnesses brought by the public prosecutor, saying that:

---

[10] The notion of system is fundamental to this sort of analysis, when considering towns as an integrated whole of instruments, mechanisms and processes in permanent interaction. The use of this notion in urban historiography was first introduced by Yves Barel (1981) in his classic work, *La ciudad medieval. Sistema social-Sistema urbano.* This work, intended as a study in which the analysis of the urban world would revolve around the notion of system, in fact fails to accomplish this goal, but nonetheless popularised the notion of system. In Spain, Monsalvo Antón (1988), and Guerrero Navarrete and Sánchez Benito (1994), have used this notion as a model for the analysis of the town councils of Alba de Tormes and Cuenca. More recently, I have adopted this analytical framework for the study of a concrete part of the urban subsystem, the power subsystem in the city of Cuenca. *Vid* Jara Fuente (2000).

[11] On individual and group consciousness and external recognition, see Centers (1961) 75, and Chaussinand-Nogaret (1991) 302.

the aforesaid witnesses that have made depositions against me, had incurred faults as a result of which they cannot and should not be accepted as witnesses, for they are perjurers, men of poor reputation, excommunicates, feeble-minded, drunkards, poor persons and women, avowed enemies of mine, of my sons, wife, brothers and the rest of my kinsmen, and that they acted jointly to plot against me.[12]

I will not attempt to trace the violence (moral or physical) inherent in this and other self-legitimating actions. Rather, I wish to observe how this is linked to a position of class power, and how opposition to the conduct of others implies an attack on their status, and, even more importantly, their lineage's position in the urban subsystem. Diego de Alcalá had to respond to the charges aggressively in a criminal case in which he was apparently the only accused; in reality, it was the weight of the lineage of Alcalá that was at stake. Evidently, a large proportion of prosecution witnesses was comprised of members of second-tier lineages, pressing hard on the heels of the families (like that of Alcalá) that controlled the town, and making use of the most valuable instrument available, the Inquisition. Diego depicted his "avowed enemies" in a very crude manner. This, no doubt, satisfied his violent instincts, but it simultaneously pointed to the core of what mattered in that place and time.[13] Three elements of his response, all related to the importance of being *someone*, are worth particular emphasis. Firstly, the positive evaluation of his own lineage, implicit in the discrediting of the witnesses. Secondly,

---

[12] Archivo Diocesano de Cuenca (ADC.), Inquisición (Inq.), Judicial process against Diego de Alcalá and others, leg. 698, exp. 10.

[13] Diego's domineering nature emerges clearly from the criminal records and, though the accusations were probably exaggerated in order to present the court with Diego's worst face, they still stand as examples of the abusive use of his power and position. One, in particular, incites repulsion (if also a certain wry amusement). This is the case of Alonso Guijarro, servant to Diego's brother, Alonso Álvarez de Alcalá. In his trial, Diego explained his reasons for rejecting all the depositions made against him, invariably alleging the witnesses' enmity towards him. In the case of Alonso Guijarro, he alleged that this man, quite apart from his low condition of being a servant, had to live every day with the infamy of being cuckolded by his wife and by Diego himself, and proclaimed that Alonso's horns were a matter of public knowledge. When Alonso, unable to tolerate the situation any further, dared to upbraid his wife in the presence of Diego, the latter—so he claims—feeling injured by Alonso's insolence, ordered his servants to beat him up. He also asked his brother to throw the man from his home—the house which Alonso Álvarez had provided him—because he, Diego, could not permit such an offence and was obliged to re-establish his outraged honour. Alonso's destiny was evidently to live without honour, a complaisant cuckold and a silent servant. ADC., Inq., Judicial Process against Diego de Alcalá and others, leg. 698, exp. 10.

the very resort to lineage in a trial in which only one of its members—Diego himself—actually stood accused. And finally, there is the attribution of blame to members of enemy lineages.[14] This can be seen more clearly in Diego's response to the deposition of Juan del Espinar, of whom Diego stated that

> he was the chief of the prior's kinsmen, friends and servants when disputes occurred at times between the aforesaid prior and his kinsmen and mine.[15]

Diego de Alcalá did not answer in quite the way as others, in his same position, did. On 11 May 1514 Juan Álvarez de Toledo, senior, also prosecuted by the Inquisition for judaizing, discredited the witness Lope de Priego, saying that he was a *light-minded man, fearful, inconstant and mentally weak*.[16] Verbal violence, sometimes accompanied by physical violence, was the result, on one hand, of the compulsions of the power or class positions achieved within the urban subsystem. On the other hand, it was also the result of the perceived need to legitimate high social status, and an elite class position, in the face of those that did not share it. It is in this context that the development of a power model in Cuenca, or in any other city or town, should be understood.

II. *Power Positions / Class Positions:*
Conflict and Agreement

What were the key elements of that elite class position, and what did it imply? Sadly, for the fifteenth century there are not many documents in which the protagonists speak to us as openly and frankly as in the preceding cases. Nevertheless, the exhaustive use of documents running from 1417 to 1480 and an extensive use of prosopography allow us to reconstruct those elements.

The trials of Diego de Alcalá and Juan Álvarez de Toledo, senior, shed light not only on their position as individuals and members of

---

[14] Following the well-known Roman aphorism, *causa causae, causa causati est.*

[15] ADC., Inq., Judicial Process against Diego de Alcalá and others, leg. 698, exp. 10.

[16] ADC., Inq., leg. 698, exp. 13. Note that Juan Álvarez de Toledo's use of the term mentally weak, goes far beyond the mere affirmation of Lope de Priego's stupidity, implying insanity.

lineages, but also on the nature of the power subsystem itself. In the course of the fifteenth century, this partially open subsystem tended to solidify around the lineages that in the middle of the century formed the core of the dominant group, closing the mechanisms that allowed access by individuals rising from other sectors of the dominant class. This process was sporadically but bitterly contested, and there is no doubt that by the end of the century it had reached a critical point. By this stage, there was little room for social or political negotiation. But the anti-Semitic measures of the Crown in the last years of the century (including the expulsion of the Jews from Castile and the arbitration of the Inquisition courts to address accusations of false conversion) gave fresh grounds for opposing lineages with Jewish blood, like Alcalá and Álvarez de Toledo. Diego's deposition, in which he accused the prior of Belmonte and his kinsmen of a variety of evils, must be understood as the emergence of dysfunction in the power model in Cuenca. By the end of the fifteenth century, this model was unable to distribute power resources among the members of the dominant class, causing instability in the power subsystem and, consequently, giving rise to open conflict.

As will already be clear, conflict was endemic in this period. Much of the time, it was a silent and dormant process, only erupting into open violence, on a limited number of occasions: in 1442, 1465 and around 1475. On the last of these occasions, a sector of the dominant class, which may be called the elite of participation, tried and failed to modify the political constitution of the city in order to gain greater protagonism.[17]

Nevertheless, in spite of these occasional conflicts (especially those at the end of the century), what is most surprising in the construction of the urban subsystem in Cuenca is the ability of many lineages to avoid conflict and to reach agreements. These agreements were based on diverse strategies for the occupation of positions in the urban subsystem and the diversification of the positions attained by every lineage—that is to say, multiple members of those lineages—within the urban resources subsystem and the mechanisms developed to distribute those resources. It is in the development of the urban subsystem itself that we must seek a discourse of domination that, far from being based on aggression and conflict, was largely based on unwritten pacts addressing the distribution of those resources.

---

[17] See Jara Fuente (1999) 113–136.

How, then, did this power model function? What were the propo-
sitions and mechanisms at the root of its construction? And what
was the final expression of the urban political constitution, begun in
the eleventh century—with the emergence of the urban *caballeros*—
but developed and articulated in the fifteenth century?

When, sometime between 1359 and 1362, Alfonso XI of Castile,
granted Cuenca the *regimiento*, he was promoting a form of government that had spread swiftly and with no opposition throughout
Castilian towns from the 1340s. It had been granted to Segovia,
Burgos and León in 1345, Astorga and Zamora by 1345, Ávila and
Plasencia before 1346, Madrid in 1346, Ciudad Rodrigo and Ledesma
in 1350, Soria by 1351, Palencia in 1352 and Valladolid before
1360.[18] Everywhere both the commons and the upper echelons of
the dominant classes greeted this development with relief. In fact,
royal grants fulfilled two objectives. On one hand, the formal recognition of the superior power of several lineages in each city and
town pacified these lineages and ended a period of confrontation
that had sometimes become openly violent. This was welcomed both
by the victorious lineages and by the commoners who had gradually lost access to urban power, *de facto* and *de iure*, and who simultaneously had suffered the consequences of the struggle between the
lineages of the dominant class. On the other hand, by reducing the
number of those occupying office in the subsystem, the king secured
a clearer and easier access to urban power and to the dominant lineages. He bound these lineages to his person, with less conflict, by
means of several processes: grants of public offices, privileges, and
so on. This policy proved to be highly effective, especially in the
second half of the fifteenth century, when the monarchy was engaged
in a struggle against a "turbulent" nobility, and both needed and
obtained urban support.

Thus, the introduction of the *regimiento* in Cuenca implied a logical development rather than a novelty in the broader context of
Castile. Moreover, in practice, as in other Castilian towns, the lineages formally empowered by the *regimiento* had already acquired
functions of power, independently of what the urban political constitution authorised. Well before the *regimiento*, in Cuenca and elsewhere in Castile, urban government had rested on a set of public

---

[18] *Vid* Monsalvo Antón (1990).

Graphic I. Urban Public Offices

offices authorised by the *fueros* (charters) that had been granted to every town, generally soon after their foundation or reconquest. In the case of Cuenca, the conquest took place in 1177 and the charter had been granted by 1190. The *fueros* made provision for the annual election, by all the neighbours, of a set of offices, different in every town but usually involving a number of judges or mayors, bailiffs, jurors and others. Such officials constituted the nerve centre of government in every town.[19] With the introduction of the *regimiento*, the principal governing functions that those officials had exercised, were transferred to and assumed by the *regidores* (the members of the *regimiento*), while *fuero* officials were reduced to the accomplishment of strictly technical functions directly related to their offices. As is shown in Graphic I (Urban Public Offices), the binding of the *regidores* to other power subsystems (especially the monarchy and high nobility) was the key that helped them to gain control of the entire urban subsystem, relegating *fuero* officials to subordinate positions of authority. From the mid-fourteenth century, a moment in which *regimental* offices are established, the *regidores* were able to concentrate in their hands all the main instruments of urban power, leaving merely secondary functions to the *fuero* officials. Finally, on the lowest rungs of the apparatus were some auxiliary offices that gave basic

---

[19] For the *fuero* de Cuenca see Ureña y Smenjaud (1935) preface, Barrero García (1982), González González (1975) 63–64, and Powers (2000). For a more general treatment of Castilian towns, see Martínez Llorente (1990).

support to this two-tiered government (*regimiento* and *fuero*). These offices, referred to in Graphic I as municipal offices, scarcely had any projection over the decision-making process.

III. Shaping a Power Model Through Consensus: Power Resources and their Distribution

Who could gain access to the different corridors of power in the city? Who could be a *regidor*, a *fuero* official or a minor municipal officer? And, to return to Therborn's terminology, *how*? Through what means and mechanisms was their incorporation into the structure of power recognised or formalised? Unlike many medieval English towns, in Castilian towns there was not typically what could be properly called a *cursus honorum* that dictated the phases of political climbing in the town.[20] Anyone properly qualified could aspire to the *regimiento* without having served as a *fuero* official, let alone having exercised the minor municipal offices.

The king appointed the *regidores*. From the very beginning of this process, these appointments served as recognition of the political primacy that some lineages had already reached in every town. In due course, many of the *regimental* lineages developed the inter- and intra-urban power relationships indispensable to exercise sufficient control over the mechanisms that governed admission to the *regimiento*. In many towns, these lineages could negotiate with the king their perpetuation in the supreme governing institution in town, closing access to the *regimiento* from the many other lineages that, in other circumstances, might have disputed the benefits of domination. From that moment on, the monarchy simply sanctioned the appointments favoured by the town's *regimiento*s, though when the king absolutely needed it, he was able to depart from these strictly urban interests and designated *regidores* better disposed to serve royal interests.[21]

On a second rung in the power apparatus, the *fuero* offices had always been open to the whole citizenry of the town. It had been entirely in these offices that the town's political representation and decision-

---

[20] There are several exceptions. Though not affirming the existence of a true *cursus honorum*, Ruiz Povedano has depicted for Loja, Baza, Almería and Málaga (towns in the kingdom of Granada) a process of selection of urban officials very close to it. *Vid* Ruiz Povedano (1991).

[21] *Vid* Guerrero Navarrete (1997).

Graphic II. Urban Resources Subsystem

making had lain. The introduction of the *regimiento* put an end to this, bringing a modification not only of their authority but also of those who could aspire to serve in these offices. In those towns where the most important lineages had gradually achieved nobility and acquired the means to intervene cohesively in the urban power subsystem, this process evolved towards the emergence of guilds of noble lineages, well organised and able to project their power over the entire urban subsystem. These guilds not only reserved for their members the *regidurías* but even the *fuero* offices, distributing them among their members with more or less success and greater or lesser levels of conflict.[22] Conversely, in towns like Cuenca, where this process was much less developed, the *fuero* offices remained open to an ample group of individuals, the so-called *cuantiosos*. Any male *vecino*, neighbour, married and owner of a house in the town, and wealthy enough to provide himself with a war-horse and weapons, was automatically considered a *cuantioso*.[23] Every year in September, at Michaelmas, all

---

[22] On the process of emergence of guilds of noble lineages, see the cases of Segovia, Valladolid, Alba de Tormes, and Soria, among others. *Vid* Asenjo González (1986a), Rucquoi (1987a, 1987b), Monsalvo Antón (1988) and Diago Hernando (1993).

[23] The monarchy also legislated on the quality of the war-horse and weapons, establishing their categories and evaluating them in *maravedises*. In Cuenca, the war-horse was valued in the town's charter, by 1190, in 20 *maravedises* (mrs.), in 1422 in 1000 mrs., in 1456 in 2000 mrs., and in 1521 in 5000 mrs. *Vid* Cabañas González (1980) 51. Those figures were not exorbitant for most members of the dominant class. In fact, between 1417 and 1480, one hundred and fifteen lineages in Cuenca,

qualified *vecinos* went to the town hall to register themselves, voluntarily, before the town clerk in the district in which they lived: there were fourteen such districts, called *collaciones*. After registering, two drawings were made by the judicial officials and the *regidores*. The first was to draw the *fuero* office for which each district would be responsible that year: there also were fourteen *fuero* offices. The second was to draw from among the *cuantiosos* registered in every *collación* the individual who would serve in the corresponding office.[24] Though these drawings could take place at other moments of the year, as it happened sometimes in Cuenca, the process was quite similar elsewhere.[25]

Finally, there were the municipal offices, which played a minor supporting role in the tasks of government undertaken by the *regidores* and the *fuero* officials. The social prestige of such offices, in general, was rather low and they were filled with people from the subordinate class. Town criers, messengers, porters and the other minor offices were not drawn by lot but were in general directly nominated by the city council.[26] There were several exceptions, however. Some offices, among them the town clerkship and the receivership, were more relevant to the town's interests and also better paid. They were used by the *regidores*, more clearly than other officers, to reward loyalties and to bind together a select group of lesser elite lineages that could participate in the benefits of the system.[27]

---

besides the *regidores* and noble lineages, could afford to endow themselves with one or more war-horses and weapons. *Vid* Jara Fuente (2000) 198–230.

[24] The fourteen *fuero* offices were assigned to four mayors or judges, one notary, one bailiff, one ward of weights and measures, one market-bailiff, four mounted guards of the town's jurisdiction and two assistants to the mounted guards.

[25] This was the case of Astorga, under the lordship of the bishop and, with several restrictions, when it was bestowed to the count of Trastámara in 1465; and it was also the case of Burgos, Madrid or Talavera. *Vid* Martín Fuertes (1987), Bonachía Hernando (1978), Gibert y Sánchez de la Vega (1949) and Suárez Álvarez (1982).

[26] Ordinances decreed by the regent of Castile, Fernando de Antequera, in 1411, and by the town council in 1417, 1463, 1468 and 1479. *Vid* Cabañas González (1982), and Archivo Municipal de Cuenca (AMC.), Libros de Actas (LL.AA.), leg. 185, exp. 1, 10v–11v; leg. 196, exp. 1, 13r; leg. 198, exp. 2, 25r–27r; and leg. 201, exp. 2, 87r–89v and 90r.

[27] In most towns, the clerkship was an office held for life and elected by the town officials (usually the *regimiento* and the justice officers). Its function was basically to keep the town records, and the fact that the office was granted for life explains its importance to the town and its dominant class, and the use that the latter made of it as a space in which to locate its supporters. The same can be said of the receivership, whose interest for the town rested in the fact that, since the officer was charged with the management of the town finances, he was obliged to put his wealth at the town's disposal. This, no doubt, implied in theory a heavy burden on the receivers but it was not so in practice, if we consider that they earned relatively

What is most striking in this power apparatus is the fact that the *cuantiosos* could scarcely aspire to a role in the *regimiento*. Firstly, the number of *regidores* was fixed, although the monarchy and elite lineages of power did not invariably observe this limit.[28] Secondly, the appointment of new *regidores* was proposed to the king by the *regimiento* itself, thus limiting the king's initiative to promote new members. Moreover, those nominations and promotions took place only when a *regiduría* was vacant, usually due to their holder's death. In Cuenca and other Castilian towns, the *regimiento* and the king tended to reserve the vacant offices for the lineages that had served them most loyally, to the point of sanctioning their transmission in life from father to son, which made the incorporation of new lineages more difficult.[29] It is true that the crown sometimes acted with more freedom and independence from the *regimiento*, decreeing the appointment of new *regidores* as a reward to members of the nobility or the urban elites not integrated in the *regimiento*. But access to these subsystems, monarchy and nobility, an access whose advantages were clear, was not easy for the *cuantiosos*, the great majority of whom could not rise beyond the benefits inherent to the privileged position they occupied in the urban power subsystem. Only a minority could acquire the qualifications necessary for contesting the power space of the *regidores*.

On the other hand, *regimental* lineages invariably enjoyed the status of *cuantiosos*, and therefore benefits beyond the mere profits that domination afforded them. They could also contest the ground occupied by other lineages of *cuantiosos*. It is evident that this model of participation and distribution of power could be, at least on first sight, highly conflictive. The limitations on social mobility for those *cuantiosos* whose members could scarcely aspire to integration in the dominant class, and the fact that *regidores* could contest the benefits of other *cuantiosos* tended to feed this conflict. Such conflict had been widespread in Castilian towns. The case of Segovia is paradigmatic.

high wages and participated in the town's power subsystem from a privileged position. Thus, the receivership was an important political tool in the hands of the dominant class, and, as an annual office, it was usually granted year after year by the *regidores* to the same individuals.

[28] At the time when the ordinance of Fernando de Antequera was decreed, Cuenca had twenty-four *regidores*, whereas the *regimiento* had established its number at nine. Fernando de Antequera ordered its reduction to six *regidores* and forbade new appointments until such time as that number were reached. This order was never adhered to either by the monarchy or by the lineages of the *regimiento*.

[29] On this process, see González Alonso (1981) and Tomás y Valiente (1970).

Here, the *regimental* lineages had emerged from a guild of noble lineages, from the political organisation built by the lineages located in the upper echelons of the dominant class. In time, those regimental lineages cut their links with the guild, usurping some of the benefits shared with it: benefits that derived from the control over the town exercised by both the *regimiento* and the guild. This attitude encouraged a union *contra natura* between the guild lineages and the commons, jointly opposing the *regimental* lineages, and even sometimes even resulted in open street fighting.[30]

Did the urban subsystem in Cuenca evolve as it did in other towns? And did competition for the benefits bring conflict, even armed clashes, between the different sectors of the dominant class and the commons? Conflict certainly did not disappear in this period. Nevertheless, what it is more important was the ability of the social agents involved to reach agreements, at least on a basic level, concerning their participation in the domination of the city. These unwritten and informal pacts shaped the distribution of the resources of domination, and implied acceptance of the distinct class positions pertaining to every lineage and individual. Thus, though the urban political constitution in Cuenca did not contemplate the existence of a *cursus honorum* ruling the way in which the lineages could participate in the urban power subsystem, in social practice this was a system that gradually, informally developed.

The discursive model in Cuenca, and indeed the way that the dominant class was structured, revolves around a "resources subsystem". This subsystem implies both access to and profit from the subsystem, and from power positions and class positions in the urban subsystem as a whole. It is evident that the resources subsystem had to be open to an ample participation in order to avoid the worst consequences of conflict, such as occurred in other Castilian towns. However, at the same time, it is also evident that not all the lineages could aspire to benefiting from those resources in the same degree. This fact could have evolved into a conflictive power model in Cuenca. In reality, however, it stimulated the emergence of a cohesive power model, based on the recognition of different power positions, and class positions. This was possible because of the concurrence of a set of rules that governed the urban power subsystem.

---

[30] Asenjo González (1986a) 307–308.

The first rule was related to the way the subsystem itself operated and the nature of the resources involved in the process of distribution. As Graphic II (Urban Resources Subsystem) shows, two kinds of resources converged on the subsystem: the so-called disposable and non-disposable resources. Non-disposable resources emerge from subsystems other than the urban context: the Church, the nobility or the monarchy, which controlled an ample set of resources (offices, rents, dignities, among others) that could be disposed and distributed at will. From the point of view of these other subsystems, these were resources that could be freely disposed. For the urban subsystem, meanwhile, they were non-disposable resources, because access to and profit from them were determined by other subsystems. Conversely, the urban subsystem benefited from a set of resources of its own: a set of resources similar to those existing in other subsystems, and over which the town exercised complete power. These were disposable resources for the town, because it did not depend on other subsystems to determine access to, or profit from, the resources. The distinction between disposable and non-disposable resources is crucial. In first place, it drew an invisible line between a major group of lineages unable to access to the non-disposable resources, and a select group able to do so successfully. This had important consequences in terms of power because it determined the existence of a reduced group of lineages that enjoyed an open access to other subsystems, giving them primacy in the town's power subsystem. Secondly, the consequences were apparent to all and were well known to members of the dominant class. They were conscious that a substantial part of the *regimental* lineages' political weight rested on the social networks they had woven in other power subsystems (especially those of the monarchy and high nobility) and that, in order to assimilate to them, they would have to use the same instruments. Thus, nobody disputed the importance of the influence over the town of the non-disposable resources. This avoided conflicts with the other power subsystems and reduced urban tension.

The second rule concerned the way disposable resources worked in the urban resources subsystem. At least in theory, and often in practice, the resources subsystem was an open circuit. It was assumed that any person with a certain level of wealth—that which was necessary to provide oneself with a war-horse and weapons—could participate in this subsystem. Indeed, certain minor areas of the subsystem could also be opened for those not being qualified as *cuantiosos*, thus opening in theory the subsystem to the entire social structure.

A third rule derived from the different sort of participation that the subsystem allows. Participation in the resources subsystem implies a positioning inside the urban power subsystem, not only in terms of the individual but also in terms of lineage. Such positioning took place through access to resources that were not equally open to all and were non-disposable resources in the context of the urban subsystem; through the levels attained in the urban and other subsystems; and through the capacity to take part in the resources subsystem.

The fourth and final rule functioned as a mechanism for deciphering social and political codes of relationship to sectors in the dominant class. The urban power subsystem learned to recognise the class positions reached by every self and lineage, and to satisfy the aspirations born from access to those positions. For their part, lineages learn also to recognise the subsystem, the set of rules that governs it, and to accept the benefits so gained.

This set of rules complements the notion of power resources, understood as every instrument and mechanism (ideological or material, formal or informal, institutional or not) directed to produce and reproduce the urban power subsystem and the social groups present in it. This includes those groups that occupy contradictory class positions that locate them simultaneously in the dominant and subjugated classes. As we see again in Graphic II, those instruments and mechanisms can emerge directly from the town or from other power subsystems. The notion of power resources is based on two clear distinctions: that between disposable and non-disposable resources, and between control over access and distribution of resources, on the one hand, and the right to benefit from them, on the other (see Graphic III, Urban Resources: Control and Distribution). In the traditional analytical model, this last distinction is not made because the "oligarchy" in each town allegedly controls and profits from power resources. These "oligarchies" are widely seen as a minority that monopolistically controlled and operated the subsystem exclusively in its own benefit. But not all urban elites in the Middle Ages acted in this way. In fact, it is more probable that they tended to act as urban aristocracies; this was certainly very much the way their urban contemporaries saw them.[31] In Cuenca, the importance of consensus and participation is fundamental. The urban subsystem and the

---

[31] In Spanish historiography there is not yet a proper debate on this theme, but there are some contributions worthy of notice. *Vid* Valdeón Baruque (1990, 1995), Ferrer Navarro (1990), Rucquoi (1995).

lineages within it assume that in the dominant class there is a superior sector able to control power in the town and its hinterland.
They work within this subsystem as long as it is able to recognise
the class positions reached by every individual and lineage.

A minority controls the subsystem and in a sense determines who
can benefit from the resources. But at the same time, a majority, recog-
nising the superior position of that minority, gains the recognition
of its own position and, therefore, the right to participate and benefit
from the power resources. In other words, those who control, do so
because the rest recognise their right to exercise that control. Moreover,
those who benefit from power resources, do so because they recognise the right of the former to control who can benefit from those
resources. Thus there emerged a balance in the development of the
urban power subsystem, whose success must be measured in terms
of the longevity of the model and the relative absence of conflict.

Graphic III. Urban Resources: Control and Distribution

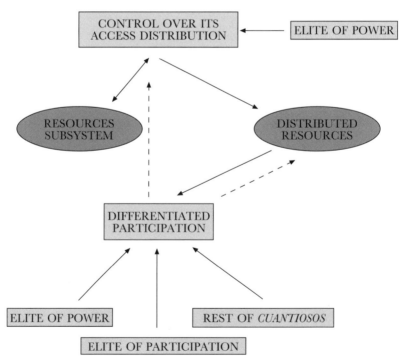

IV. In the Dominant Class:
Recognition of Class Positions

Who composed the dominant class, and what did membership of this class imply? As we have already seen, the construction of an urban power model cannot be separated from the social actors that breathe life into it. *Who* and *how* are so closely connected that separated study only makes sense when breaking down the constituent elements and establishing relationships within the system as a whole. This becomes even more relevant when we are examining the process whereby lineages become abstract units of social classification, or class sectors. The social action of the individual cannot be separated from the actions of other individuals or from the rules that organise the system.[32] The individual's success, or failure, in acquiring a concrete social position within the system cannot be separated from the broader context determining the system in which the self acts.[33] The question of *who* and *how* necessarily implies exploring the way in which lineages produced, and were the product of, a concrete dominant class in Cuenca. Their positioning in the urban subsystem was the result not only of their ability/inability, as individuals or as lineages, to act and take advantages of the system, but also of the very development and functioning of the system.

In this system, lineages within the dominant class accepted the rules of the game, the definition of class sectors, and the sharing of power and its benefits according to the class positions reached within the town. The definition of what I call an elite of power, an elite of participation, and a minor sector (in terms of power) became an integral part of the model of social and political recognition within the subsystem. (See Graphic III, Urban Resources: Control and Distribution).

The elite of power, the leading sector of the dominant class, was comprised of a minority that could access non-disposable resources directly and was able to bind itself to the monarchy, Church and/or the high nobility. This elite could access resources partially or completely closed to the rest of urban lineages, allowing it to share and

---

[32] On these different interactions, *Vid* Blau and Schwartz (1984).
[33] This is a well-known argument in Bourdieu's work. *Vid* Bourdieu (1966) and (1979) 145–146 and 151.

distribute some of the benefits with other lineages in the town, binding the latter to itself. It thereby amplified its social network of relations in the natural space, the town, for the profit, enjoyment and
increase of its power resources. The elite of power's growth as an agent
depended in large measure on its capacity to be recognised as such,
not only within the urban subsystem but by the other subsystems as
well. In brief, its power depended on the kind of services it could
render to the extra-urban social agents but also agents within the
town. Entering into the service of those agents, loaning them money,
fighting with their men in the armies of the crown and nobility, were
the best means of access to a reciprocal system of service and benefit
within those subsystems.[34] At the same time, most of the services
they were able to render implied the previous availability of resources
of their own: wealth in land, cattle, urban and rural properties, money
and men, and the will to risk them on their lord's behalf. Lineages
like Alcalá and Álvarez de Toledo were able to support contradictory
parties (royal and noble) and come out unharmed; others had to
rely on just one, like Beteta, Chinchilla or de la Muela, (which served
the monarchy) or Torres (the high nobility). Their ability in serving
and benefiting from those subsystems naturally had its reward in the
town. They were wealthier, in many respects, than the other lineages.
They counted on the support granted by the leading agents in those
subsystems and were earmarked by those agents as the natural links
between them and the town. If they could transfer some of the
benefits that their position in other subsystems allowed them to access
to other lineages within the dominant class, and as long as they were
perceived as the basic instruments connecting the urban subsystem
to the other agents, half the battle was won. This implied willingness to recognise the right of the other lineages to participate in the
only power space where they could project their interests, the town,
and their readiness to share the resources of the town with them.
This meant that the position of the elite of power, its class and
power position, had to be recognised by those lineages and, therefore, that its control over the entire urban subsystem could not be
questioned. After all, what underlay their mutual pact was a matter
of reciprocity and services that each sector of the dominant class
could render to the other sectors and to the subsystem as a whole.

---

[34] *Vid* Asenjo González (1986b).

The elite of participation was a large group of lineages located on a second tier within the dominant class. Though as a group it could neither access non-disposable resources, nor control the disposable resources, it was able to benefit from participation in the construction of the power subsystem and therefore the resources subsystem itself. The elite of participation was a powerful engine for the power subsystem as it afforded the necessary balance to the power exercised by the elite of power. It fulfilled the necessities of the elite of power and provided the means for the power subsystem to pervade everyday life in the town. Their force rested on the collectivity, on their capacity to act with coherence and solidarity. This, too, obliged them to recognise the position reached by every lineage within the elite of participation and to share with them the privileges and resources derived from that position.

Finally, the minor sector was integrated by a broad group of lineages that occupied an ambiguous class position, as they were simultaneously located at the bottom of the dominant class and at the upper steps of the subordinated class. Though their participation and the benefit they drew from power resources was minimal, it had important political consequences as it guarded against the spectre of social conflict introduced by those who aspired to enter the ranks of the dominant class.

Thus there were three main sectors of this class: the elite of power, the elite of participation, and a minor sector (in terms of power). Categorisation depended firstly, on the level of the social agents' presence in other subsystems (especially those of the monarchy and the high nobility); secondly, on their degree of projection within the urban subsystem; and, thirdly, on recognition of their relative positions and social mobility. Avoidance of high levels of conflict, a permanent hazard to the subsystem, depended, precisely, on the acceptance of the rules governing these processes. Success therefore largely derived from their capacity to establish bonds both within and beyond the urban subsystem, as a lever for social mobility. This implied consensus that not all those who participated in the production of these bonds stood at the same social and political level. The importance of bonds, even those that went beyond the urban sphere, was not a matter of discussion. The most critical agents in this game lay beyond the urban subsystem and access to them was a general aspiration for individuals both in the towns and elsewhere, even though the inherent difficulty of that task was commonly acknowledged.

Although the crown was the master key for opening the gates to power in the towns, the importance of the nobility and the Church should not be understated. The capacity to render valuable services, especially to the king or the high nobility, was at the heart of the process of upward social mobility.

The lineage Álvarez de Toledo, more than any other, exemplified this process. Its story begins with the brothers Alfonso and Pero Álvarez de Toledo, a fine example of the tactics of social and political diversification. They forced their way into Cuenca's dominant class with the backing of Juan II; both were clerks of the Royal Chamber and the former was also a prominent member of the Royal Exchequer (as treasurer and later chief treasurer) and, by 1449, even a counsellor of the Royal Council. Service to the king meant that in 1422 and 1432 respectively the two brothers were promoted by Juan II to *regidurías*, thus entering Cuenca's elites.[35] From 1422 onwards, they played an important political role in the town, based on their ability to be represented within every available power resource area. They appear to have taken an important decision: Alfonso would stay in the court, assuring himself and the lineage of royal favour (he scarcely had any direct participation in Cuenca's government) while Pero would remain in Cuenca, enhancing the lineage's power in the town. Their marriage politics was also an example of political strategy. Alfonso was married to Aldonza Ferrández, daughter of Juan Ferrández de Valera, a member of Cuenca's elites and a *regidor*, an office that, with the king's license, he renounced in favour of his son-in-law.[36] For his part, Pero married María Álvarez de Mendoza, daughter of Diego Hurtado de Mendoza, lord of Cañete (a seigneurial town not far from Cuenca) and one of the most prominent noblemen in the area, closely connected to the king and the high nobility, but also well-established in Cuenca, where he was the king's Warden of the Town since 1419.[37] In this way, the lineage located itself within a complex net of relations and power resources: royal service, the most influential and powerful offices in Cuenca (the *regidurías*) and family connections with the nobility and a member of Cuenca's elites, from the Valera family. Other lineages attempted such a strategy, and in due time most members of Cuenca's elite of power and some of those from the

---

[35] AMC., LL.AA., leg. 186, exp. 4, 2r–v; leg. 188, exp. 3, 1r; leg. 188, exp. 6, 4r–6v; leg. 188, exp. 4, 30r–31r; leg. 191, exp. 6, 91v–92r.
[36] AMC., LL.AA., leg. 185, exp. 1, 28r; leg. 187, exp. 4, 4r–5v; and Archivo Capitular de Cuenca (ACC), siglo XV, c. 3, leg. 14, 206.
[37] AMC. LL.AA., leg. 185, exp. 4, 9r; ADC., Inq., leg. 698, exp. 13.

elite of participation were able to establish similar links. Never, however, did they do so with quite the intensity, or quite the same success in achieving proximity to the core of those other subsystems, as the lineage Álvarez de Toledo.

As Table I illustrates, few lineages were able to attach themselves successfully to the monarchy. In the period from 1417 to 1480, the elites in Cuenca were comprised of 136 lineages, of whom 21 belonged to the elite of power and 115 to the elite of participation. The 32 lineages which did establish links with the monarchy, represent a mere 23.5%, a figure that is reduced to a mere 14.7% if we exclude minor positions in royal service such as the hunting officers. Only a minority of lineages, therefore, was able to render significant service to the monarchy and to obtain, in return, the king's favour. Among them, the Álvarez de Toledo family stood in a privileged position, as is shown by the nature of the offices they held and the fact that they did so both before and after 1450. The same conclusion can be reached in relation to the bonds established with the nobility and the Church (see Table II).

Within Cuenca itself, meanwhile, the urban subsystem also encouraged the emergence of personal bonds. These bonds were based on a multiplicity of possible links, including marriage, lord-servant relations of various types, and landlord-tenant bonds. The Álvarez de Toledo family again serves as a good example. Like other lineages in the town, it diversified its investment policy and, as is characteristic of urban medieval Europe, one of its economic preferences was the acquisition and rental of urban property. This was rather common in Castilian towns and in itself might be seen merely as a sensible economic strategy. But the Álvarez de Toledo family thus became not merely one of the most important landlords in town (after the Church, of course) but the most important one in the two *collaciones* where they lived, San Andrés and San Salvador. The latter was their main residence and a district over which it exercised political control through the rental of houses (350 maravedís annually, on average), as the contracts and the fiscal records of the *collación* make clear.[38]

---

[38] This is what Guerrero Navarrete and Sánchez Benito point out for Cuenca (1994) 20–27. For Valladolid, Álava, Burgos, Gandía and Murcia and their hinterland, see Rucquoi (1987b) 136–147, Díaz de Durana y Ortiz de Urbina (1986) 193–202, Casado Alonso (1985), Pastor Zapata (1992) 181–215, and Rodríguez Llopis (1993).

Internal urban bonds help to explain the importance of the lineages' simultaneous presence in several positions of power: that is, their multi-functionality. Lineages within the elite of power occupied multiple, and potentially contradictory, positions in the subsystem. Loyalties to the king or to the nobility might oblige the elite of power to work against the town's interests or, even worse, to act against its own interests or to take part in the disputes between its masters. When in 1465 a noble faction raised arms against Enrique IV, the great majority of Cuenca's elite of power (including the Alcalá lineage) left the town to fight the king in the count of Buendía's army. Such elite lineages had to follow their lord's lead because they were well connected to the nobility and, at that moment, less closely connected to the monarchy. Their position in Cuenca depended not on the king's grants and favour but on the help provided to them by members of the high nobility. The immediate consequence of their positioning was the loss of public offices, dignities and rents decreed by Enrique IV. But this attached them even more closely to their lords, in the hope that victory would allow them the return of their position or, at least, that an agreement between the nobles and the king would have the same effect (as indeed occurred in 1469).[39]

However, the lineages' multiple positioning in diverse power subsystems, with all the attendant contradictions, was an important instrument of political action, especially for lineages within the elite of power: those best connected to those subsystems. If they had to serve various masters faithfully and loyally, risking their positions of power in the process, they received in return their masters' support, allowing those lineages to increment their power and strengthen their position in town. Certainly, the Alcalá lineage suffered the king's punishment for supporting the rebellion in 1465, but in the end it shared the pardon granted to the count of Buendía and the other rebels and remained as a prominent lineage in Cuenca, just one rung below the Álvarez de Toledo family. Besides, multiple positioning was essential for the town because it presupposed the ability of its governors to deal with other agents of power, thus benefiting the whole urban community through their political influence.

Two main principles lay at the base of this strategy of multiple positioning. On one hand, the importance of power resources within

---

[39] AMC., LL.AA., leg. 198, exp. 3, 45r–v.

the lineage: the lineage's ability to move and thrive in a complex social and power space, and to be present in multiple subsystems of power, had to be recognised. To fail to do so would lead the whole subsystem into conflict with those agents (monarchy and high nobility, but also the Church) responsible for granting many of the resources enjoyed by the lineage. On the other hand, all lineages participating from the power resources had to be called upon to share power in town, according to the weight each had attained through the profits of those resources. Failure to do so would mean conflict not with other extra-urban agents but within the town itself, between the lineages involved in sharing urban power.

Accessing a multiplicity of resources necessarily introduced an element of qualitative evaluation, since not all the resources at the elites' disposal had the same social, political or economic significance. For the lineages best located in the power apparatus (and therefore in the social scale) some could be even disregarded because of their negative social value. That was the case with urban offices such as the ward of weights and measures and the market-bailiff. Both of these offices were rarely performed by members of the elite of power or by members of the regional high nobility. On just six occasions did members of the elite of power become market-bailiffs of the town (from the lineages of Alcalá, Alarcón, Molina and Muela). As for the ward of weights and measures, three members of the regional high nobility (from the lineages of Acuña, Cabrera and Mendoza) and five of the elite of power (lineages of Alcalá, Molina, Muela) occupied this position.[40] The wardship of weights and measures was in fact a truly denigrating office because of the duties involved. Who can imagine the lords of Cañete or Buendía walking the market up and down, carrying a heavy set of weights and measures, contrasting them with those of the merchants and retailers, and suffering the pushes of the crowd and the hardships of the marketplace? Hence this office was always bestowed on men of lesser substance, wishing to access the subsystem of urban offices; lineages in the elite of power usually transferred the office to others, building, like the nobility, new bonds with those who thus benefited.

---

[40] AMC., LL.AA., leg. 187, exp. 5, 14r, 33v and 52v; leg. 188, exp. 1, 45v–48r and exp. 7, 16r–17v; leg. 189, exp. 1, 6r–7v; leg. 190, exp. 2, 13v and exp. 9, 16v–17v; leg. 192, exp. 1, 15v–16r and exp. 4, 12r–13r and 37r; leg. 193, exp. 3, 39v–40v; leg. 194, exp. 5, 9r–10v; leg. 200, exp. 2, 1r–v; leg. 201, exp. 2, 104r–v.

Graphic IV. Royal Rents: Lessees and Collectors

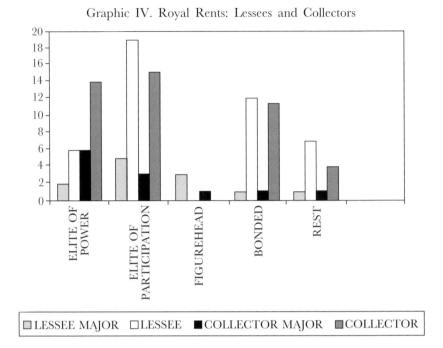

In other cases, the evaluation of resources was based on economic parameters. Royal and urban taxes were the object of such an evaluation. The right to collect these taxes was sold to the highest bidder, at a public auction, in the court or in the town respectively, but they differed in three important aspects. First, the total amount of the royal auction, and the gains that could be obtained, greatly surpassed that of the urban auction. Participating in the royal auction implied risking large sums of money, far more than most members of the urban elites (in Cuenca and elsewhere) could gather or afford to risk. This reduced the possible participation in royal tax farming for members of the elite of power and the wealthiest men in the elite of participation. Secondly, royal tax farming implied contact with officers of the crown (mainly, though not exclusively, those of the Exchequer) and the opportunity to enlarge the lineage's influences at court. And thirdly, urban rents implied a personal involvement in the collecting process, as the urban tax collector had to exact them almost directly from individuals. Royal rents, on the other hand, were for the most part collected indirectly. Royal taxes passed through the hands of tax collectors, to the local tax farmers,

from them to the chief collector and, finally, to the major farmer of
each royal rent. The chain of people involved in the process, in the
case of royal rents, reduced the direct impact of the unpopularity
born of those compulsory payments and of so unequal tax burden.
Whenever they could, lineages in the elite of power always therefore chose royal rents. Besides, most of the time the elite of power
used intermediaries to disguise its own participation in royal rents,
partly because tax farming was forbidden to public officers such as
the *regidores* and partly because using a figurehead created a safer
distance from public reproach.[41]

Graphic IV shows the participation of Cuenca's elites in royal
rents.[42] Though, at a first glance, the elite of participation seems
amply involved in the process of tax farming and collecting royal
rents, several facts have to be taken into account. First, many of the

Graphic V. Distribution of Fuero Offices

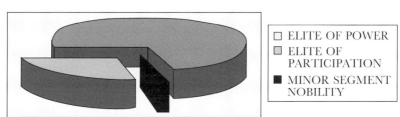

☐ ELITE OF POWER
☐ ELITE OF
PARTICIPATION
■ MINOR SEGMENT
NOBILITY

---

[41] On those prohibitions see the Cortes held in Madrid, in 1433, bill number
35; Toledo, in 1436, bill number 31; Valladolid, in 1451, bill number 39; Burgos,
in 1453, bill number 18; Madrigal, in 1476, bill number 30. *Cfr. Cortes* (1866), vols.
III and IV.

[42] The Figure distinguishes between the elites of power and participation, and it
divides the elite of participation's tax farmers/collectors into several categories that
help to explain their presence in this kind of resources. The figureheads, or intermediaries, are men who we are sure took the royal rents not for themselves but
for their masters in the elite of power. Those with bonds were directly or indirectly
linked to the elite of power, and in many cases it can be presumed that acted as
figureheads though it is not documented. The remainder encompass those cases in
which there is no clear relation between the elite of participation's tax farmer or
collector and a lineage from the elite of power. Cfr. AMC., LL.AA., leg. 185, exp.
4, 21v; leg. 186, exp. 3, 22r–v and exp. 4, 10v–11r; leg. 187, exp. 2, 2r–3r and
25r–v, exp. 3, 52r, 72r–v, exp. 4, 32r–v, and exp. 5, 51v; leg. 188, exp. 3, 7r–8v,
exp. 4, 5v and 8r, 30r–31r, exp. 5, 26r, and exp. 6, 4r–6v; leg. 189, exp. 2, 2r–v,
6r and 73r–74v, exp. 4, 18v, and exp. 5, 18r–19r; leg. 190, exp.1, 32r–33r and
36v, exp. 2, 7r–v, exp. 7, 23v–25r, and exp. 10, 10v; leg. 192, exp. 4, 137r–v; leg.
195, exp. 1, 5r–6r and 17v–18v, exp. 2, 31v, 40v, 41r–42r and 47r, and exp. 4,
76r and 78r; leg. 196, exp.1, 31v–32r and 45r–47r; leg. 197, exp. 3, 18v–19r and
22v–23r, and exp. 4, 51r, 59v; leg. 198, exp. 2, 7r–v; leg. 198, exp. 4, 11r–12v
and 14r; leg. 200, exp. 1, 12r–v.

Graph VI. Distribution of Urban Rents

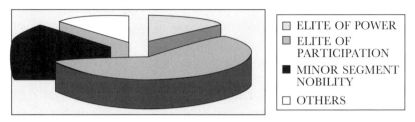

tax farmers and collectors in the elite of participation acted on behalf of members in the elite of power. Second, whenever royal rents could not be sold or the major tax farmers had not already come into town to show their contracts to the urban authorities, the latter, to avoid loss of income, used to sell them in public auctions or to nominate temporary urban collectors. Many of the tax farmers from the elite of participation received these rents in this way.

Conclusion

The model of urban power in Cuenca, quite contrary to what might be imagined, was not oligarchic. The mere fact of occupying superior class position, the importance of being in the elite of power, did not imply a monopoly of power resources. Their access to types of resources closed to the urban subsystem as a whole allowed for a broad distribution of urban resources among the lineages located in the elite of participation and the minor sector in terms of power. As shown in Figures V and VI (Distribution of *Fuero* Offices and of Urban Rents) the elite of power shared these resources with other members of the dominant class, privileging that second tier comprising the elite of participation. The latter was granted ample participation in the power subsystem, and its class position was recognised by those that controlled the subsystem; in return, this control was not questioned.

If, at least in theory, lineages like the Álvarez de Toledo or Alcalá families had access to all possible spheres for the projection of power and achieved control over the entire subsystem, they did so with the consensus of other lineages able to benefit from the available power resources. The documents available are rarely of a discursive nature in themselves. Nevertheless, a discourse of legitimation clearly underlies the construction of this particular power model. This discourse involved two converging elements: a) the affirmation of the privileges of the elite of power in the urban power subsystem and its power resources subsystem; and, b) the claims of other members of the dominant class to participate in the profits of that subsystem. The elite of participation and the minor sector, unlike the lineages in the elite of power, were in most cases at an early stage of development. These lineages were usually reduced to a main line, formed by the household head and his sons. Internal diversification, with the emergence of subsidiary branches, of a kind that allowed multiple positioning and diversification within the elite of power, had not yet appeared within many of those lineages.

In Cuenca, unlike some other towns, the elite of participation and the minor sector accepted the rules of the game. Consensus implied the acceptance and legitimation of the urban subsystem and the elite of power. If their projection beyond a purely urban sphere was difficult, if not impossible, their successful projection within the urban subsystem was certainly within their reach. In turn, the elite of power was intelligent enough, and politic enough, to see the advantages of a pact with the rest of the dominant class. Quite capable of closing access to disposable resources, as had happened in other towns, the elite of power in Cuenca kept it open to the whole of urban society, retaining in its hands merely the right to close it to a specific individual or lineage. The success of the system depended on the non-discussion of the superiority of the elite of power, and on its own acceptance of the need to promote the interests of other lineages of the dominant class, in accordance with their respective importance. This promotion operated exclusively within the urban subsystem, where the elite of power could keep the process under control. Of course, in the long run, this model of power tended towards its own petrification, as the lineages located in the superior level of the dominant class became more entrenched. But that is another story.

Translated by
Simon Doubleday
(Hofstra University, New York)

Table I: Royal Offices

Lineages	Accountant of the Exchequer	Clerk of the Royal Chamber	Royal Counsellor	Crossbowman	Feudatory	Hunting Officer	Officer of Knife	Junior Mounted Guard	Senior Mounted Guard	Physician	Porter Major	Waiter	Warden of Castle
Elite of Power													
Alarcón					◆				◆				
Alcalá					◆				◆				
Álvarez de Toledo	● ◆	●	●		◆				● ◆				
Barrientos					◆				◆				◆
Beteta					◆		●						●
Castillo		◆				◆		◆	◆				
Cherino/Guadalajara					◆					●			
Chinchilla					◆								
Jaraba						●	●						●
Molina		◆											
Muela					◆				◆				
Sacedón					◆								
Elite of Participation													
Anaya											◆		
Bolliga						◆							
Calahorra			●										
Carboneras/Cueva/Emper/Fojero/Huete/Orduña/Titos/Toro/Villarreal						◆							
Madrid						◆			◆				
Olivares						●							
Peñafiel						● ◆							
Requena		◆											
Sevilla				◆									
Torre									◆				
Torrepineda													
Valera					◆				●				

● Office bestowed before 1450
◆ Office bestowed after 1451

Royal offices are shown in alphabetical order rather than in terms of their proximity to the king or the influence and power they might bring. Offices like the hunting officer were of no influence at all; they were bestowed on a large number of people and accomplished just two objectives: to grant an honour and to free the grantee from certain royal and urban taxes. Underlying the Castilian fief, the *lanzas*, was an annual grant, of land but usually of money, given by the king with the condition of the grantee recruiting an established number of horse-men or footmen for the king's army when needed. It was not a royal office in the strict sense, implying royal service but not in the court or in the king's proximity. Nearer to the king were some offices of the royal household attending the royal person, like the officer of the knife, physician, chief porter or waiter; they brought high honour and wages and usually close contact with the king. Also closely connected to him were the men charged with the duty of his physical protection, that is, his bodyguard. The Castilian monarchy developed in the four-teenth and fifteenth centuries several corps of bodyguards, the crossbowmen (mounted and afoot), the *donceles* (the junior mounted guard of the table) and the *guardas* (the senior mounted guard). Probably at the same level of confidence were the wardens of royal castles and, though civil offices, the clerkship and the accountancy. Counsellors (members of the Royal or Privy Council) occupied the highest level of power and influence. For a study of the royal offices, see Salazar y Acha (2000). Cfr. AMC., LL.AA., leg. 186, exp. 5, 60r–61r; leg. 187, exp. 3, 49v; leg. 187, exp. 4, 4r–5v; leg. 188, exp. 4, 30r–31r and exp. 6, 4r–6v; leg. 189, exp. 2, 11r–12v and exp. 4, 20r and 21v; leg. 190, exp. 6, 5v and exp. 9, 12r and exp. 11, 26v–41v; leg. 191, exp. 6, 91v–92r; leg. 192, exp. 4, 4r–25r and 48r–59r and exp. 5, 13r–24v; leg. 193, exp. 1, 18v, 22r–v, 30r and 48r–62r; leg. 194, exp. 3, 17v–18r and exp. 5, 6r; leg. 195, exp. 1, 51r and exp. 2, 25r and exp. 4, 67r–v and 75r–v; leg. 197, exp. 1, 11r–15v and 2r–6v and exp. 3, 13v, 18v–19r and 32r–45r; leg. 198, exp. 1, 13r and 17r–v and exp. 2, 12r and exp. 3, 45r–46v; leg. 200, exp. 2, 30r; leg. 201, exp. 1, 100r–101v and 110v–112r; leg. 203, exp. 2, 244r.

Table II: Bonds with the Nobility and the Church[43]

Lineages	Regional High Nobility	Regional Medium and Low Nobility	Kingdom's High Nobility	Seigneurial Tax Collectors	Ecclesiastical Dignities	Major Offices served for the Bishop	Dignities in Military Orders
Elite of Power							
Alarcón	✚		✚		✚		
Alcalá	●			●	✚		
Álvarez de Toledo	●✚		●✚	●✚	✚		
Barrientos	✚			✚			
Beteta			●				✚
Castillo	✚	✚		✚		✚	✚
Cherino/Guadalajara					✚		
Jaraba							✚
Molina	●				✚		
Sacedón					●✚		
Torres	✚			●			
Elite of Participation							
Alcocer/Barajas/Castro/Esquivel/Pareja						✚	
Anaya/Bordallo/Brihuega/Lorenzana/Moya/Verdejo					✚		
Antezana/Ecija/Montoya/Ochoa/Torralba/Torre/Valdecabras/Velasco	●						
Banda	✚				✚		
Camargo	●		✚		✚		
Cuenca/Ocaña	●				✚		
Deza/Fitero/Olivares/Valera	✚						
León		✚			✚		
Priego			●				
Rojas		✚					
Salas	✚				✚		

● Office served before 1450
✚ Office served after 1451

[43] AMC., LL.AA., leg. 185, exp. 1, 18v–19v and exp. 5, 23r–24r; leg. 186, exp.

THE IMPORTANCE OF BEING EARNEST 173

Bibliography

Asenjo González, María (1986a) *Segovia. La ciudad y su tierra a fines del medievo* (Segovia:\ 1986).

—— (1986b) "Clientélisme et ascension sociale à la Ségovie à la fin du moyen-âge", *Journal of Medieval History*, 12 (1986) 167–182.

—— (1987) "Fiscalidad regia y sociedad en los concejos de la Extremadura castellano-oriental durante el reinado de Alfonso X", in *Homenaje al Profesor Juan Torres Fontes*, vols. 1, Universidad de Murcia-Academia Alfonso X el Sabio (Murcia: 1987) 69–84.

Barel, Yves (1981) *La ciudad medieval. Sistema social-Sistema urbano*, Instituto de Estudios de Administración Local (Madrid: 1981, Grenoble: 1975).

Barrero García, Ana María (1982) "El proceso de formación del Fuero de Cuenca (Notas para su estudio)", in Actas del I Simposio Internacional de Historia de Cuenca, *Cuenca y su territorio en la Edad Media*, September 5–9 1977 (Madrid-Barcelona: 1982) 41–58.

Barrios García, Angel (1984) *Estructuras agrarias y de poder en Castilla: el ejemplo de Avila (1085–1320)*, Universidad de Salamanca-Institución Gran Duque de Alba (Salamanca-Avila: 1984).

Blau, Peter M. and Joseph E. Schwartz (1984) *Crosscutting Social Circles. Testing a Macro-structural Theory of Intergroup Relations* (Orlando: 1984).

Bonachía Hernando, Juan A. (1978) *El concejo de Burgos en la Baja Edad Media (1345–1426)*, Universidad de Valladolid (Valladolid: 1978).

Bourdieu, Pierre (1966) "Condition de classe et position de classe", *Archives Européennes de Sociologie./European Journal of Sociology*, VII, 2 (1966), 201–223.

—— (1979) *La distinction. Critique social du jugement* (Paris: 1979).

Cabañas González, María Dolores (1980) *La caballería popular en Cuenca durante la Baja Edad Media* (Madrid: 1980).

—— (1982) "La reforma municipal de Fernando de Antequera en Cuenca", in Actas del I Simposio Internacional de Historia de Cuenca, *Cuenca y su territorio en la Edad Media*, September 5–9, 1977, Consejo Superior de Investigaciones Científicas (Madrid-Barcelona: 1982) 381–397

Casado Alonso, Hilario (1985) "La propiedad rural de la oligarquía burgalesa en el siglo XV", in Actas del Coloquio, *La ciudad hispánica durante los siglos XIII al XVI*, 3 vols., La Rábida and Seville September 14–19, 1981, Universidad Complutense de Madrid (Madrid: 1985) I, 581–596.

Centers, Richard (1961) *The Psychology of Social Classes. A Study of Class Consciousness* (Nueva York: 1961, Princeton: 1949).

Chaussinand-Nogaret, Guy (1991) "De l'aristocratie aux élites", in *Histoire des élites en France du XVIe au XXe siècle. L'honneur, le mérite, l'argent*, dir. Guy Chaussinand-Nogaret, Editions Tallandier (s.l.: 1991) 217–318.

Cortes (1866) *Cortes de los antiguos reinos de León y de Castilla*, vols. III and IV, Real Academia de la Historia (Madrid: 1866).

1, 1r–v and exp. 4, 23r–24r; leg. 187, exp. 3, 1r–42v; leg. 188, exp. 5, 17r, 18v and 24r and exp. 7, 13v–15v; leg. 189, exp. 1, 14v–15v and exp. 2, 45r; leg. 191, exp. 3, 3v–5v and exp. 6, 86r–v and 94r–v; leg. 193, exp. 3, 51v; leg. 194, exp. 3, 17v–18r, 21r–22r and 37v–38v; leg. 195, exp. 1, 34v, 35r–36r and 51r and exp. 2, 25r and 42v; leg. 196, exp. 1, 48r–v and exp. 2, 109v–112v; leg. 197, exp. 1, 6v–7r, 22r–v and 26r, exp. 3, 17v and exp. 4, 52r; leg. 198, exp. 1, 6v–7r, 13r, 17r–v, 37r and 98v, exp. 2, 7r, 9r–v, 54r– and 56v, exp. 3, 13r, 40r, 43v, 49 r, 137v and 142r and exp. 4, 16v–17r, 46r, 48r–v and 64v; leg. 200, exp. 2, 2r–v and 7r–8r; and leg. 201, exp. 2, 89v–90r.

Diago Hernando, Máximo (1993) *Soria en la Baja Edad Media. Espacio rural y economía agraria*, Universidad Complutense de Madrid (Madrid: 1993).

Díaz de Durana y Ortiz de Urbina, José Ramón (1986) *Alava en la Baja Edad Media. Crisis, recuperación y transformaciones socio-económicas (c. 1250–1525)*, Diputación Foral de Alava (Alava: 1986).

Ferrer Navarro, Ramón (1990) "Las ciudades en el reino de Valencia durante la Baja Edad Media", in Actas del II Congreso de Estudios Medievales, *Concejos y ciudades en la Edad Media hispánica*, Madrid, September 25–29 1989, Fundación Sánchez Albornoz (Madrid: 1990) 175–198.

Gibert y Sánchez de la Vega, Rafael (1949) *El concejo de Madrid, I, Su organización en los siglos XII al XV*, Instituto de Estudios de Administración Local (Madrid: 1949).

González Alonso, Benjamín (1981) *Sobre el Estado y la Administración de la Corona de Castilla en el Antiguo Régimen. Las Comunidades de Castilla y otros estudios* (Madrid: 1981).

González González, Julio (1975) *Repoblación de Castilla la Nueva*, II vols., Universidad Complutense de Madrid (Madrid: 1975).

Guerrero Navarrete, Yolanda and José María Sánchez Benito (1994) *Cuenca en la Baja Edad Media: un sistema de poder*, Diputación de Cuenca (Cuenca: 1994).

——, Yolanda (1997) "Del concejo medieval a la ciudad moderna. El papel de las cartas expectativa de oficios ciudadanos en la transformación de los municipios castellanos bajomedievales: Burgos y Cuenca", in Actas de las III Jornadas Hispano-Portuguesas de Historia Medieval, *La Península Ibérica en la Era de los Descubrimientos (1391–1492)*, 2 vols., Sevilla, November 25–30 1991 (Sevilla: 1997) II, 1013–1024

Jara Fuente (1999) "Sobre el concejo cerrado. Asamblearismo y participación política en las ciudades castellanas de la Baja Edad Media (conflictos inter o intra-clase)", *Studia Historica. Historia Medieval* 17 (1999) 113–136.

——, José Antonio (2000), *Concejo, poder y élites. La clase dominante de Cuenca en el siglo XV*, Consejo Superior de Investigaciones Científicas (Madrid: 2000).

—— (2001) "La ciudad y la otra caballería: realidad político-social e imaginario de los caballeros («villanos»)", in *La chevalerie en Castille à la fin du Moyen Âge: Aspects sociaux, idéologiques et imaginaires*, dir. Georges Martin (Paris: 2001) 27–44.

Ladero Quesada, Manuel Fernando (1996) "Zamora: Formulación y dinámica del poder en un concejo medieval", *Medievalismo. Boletín de la Sociedad Española de Estudios Medievales* 6 (1996) 147–160.

Martín Fuertes, José A. (1987) *El concejo de Astorga. Siglos XIII–XVI*, Diputación Provincial de León-Consejo Superior de Investigaciones Científicas (León: 1987).

Martínez LLorente, Félix Javier (1990) *Régimen jurídico de la Extremadura castellano-leonesa medieval. Las Comunidades de Villa y Tierra (s. X–XIV)*, Universidad de Valladolid (Valladolid: 1990).

Martínez Moro, Jesús (1985) *La tierra en la comunidad de Segovia. Un proyecto señorial urbano (1088–1500)*, Universidad de Valladolid (Valladolid: 1985).

Mills, C. Wright (1956) *The Power Elite*, Oxford University Press (New Jersey: 1956).

Monsalvo Antón, José María (1988) *El sistema político concejil. El ejemplo del señorío medieval de Alba de Tormes y su concejo de villa y tierra*, Universidad de Salamanca (Salamanca: 1988).

—— (1990) "La sociedad política en los concejos castellanos de la Meseta durante la época del regimiento medieval. La distribución social del poder", in II Congreso de Estudios Medievales, *Concejos y ciudades en la Edad Media hispánica*, Fundación Sánchez Albornoz (Madrid: 1990) 359–413.

Pastor Zapata, José Luis (1992), *Gandia en la baixa Edat Mitjana: La Vila i el senyoriu dels Borja* (Oliva: 1992).

Rodríguez Llopis, Miguel (1993) "La propiedad de la tierra en el reino de Murcia durante la Baja Edad Media", in *Señorío y feudalismo en la Península Ibérica (ss. XII–XIX)*, 4 vols., Zaragoza, December 11–14, 1989, Institución Fernando el Católico, eds. Esteban Sarasa Sánchez and Eliseo Serrano Martín (Zaragoza: 1993) I, 315–335.

Rodríguez Velasco, Jesús D. (1996) *El debate sobre la caballería en el siglo XV. La tratadística caballeresca castellana en su marco europeo*, Junta de Castilla y León (Salamanca: 1996).

Rucquoi, Adeline (1987a) *Valladolid en la Edad Media, 1. Génesis de un poder*, Junta de Castilla y León (Valladolid: 1987).

—— (1987b) *Valladolid en la Edad Media, 2. El mundo abreviado (1367–1474)*, Junta de Castilla y León (Valladolid: 1987).

—— (1995) "Las oligarquías urbanas y las primeras burguesías en Castilla", in Actas del Congreso Internacional de Historia, *El Tratado de Tordesillas y su época*, 3 vols., Setúbal, June 2, Salamanca, June 3–4, Tordesillas, June 5–7, 1994, Junta de Castilla y León (Madrid: 1995) I, 345–369.

Ruiz Povedano, José María (1991) "Las élites de poder en las ciudades del reino de Granada", in *Actas del VI Coloquio Internacional de Historia Medieval de Andalucía, Las ciudades andaluzas (siglos XIII–XVI)*, Universidad de Málaga (Málaga: 1991) 357–415.

Salazar y Acha, Jaime (2000) *La casa del Rey de Castilla y León en la Edad Media*, Centro de Estudios Político y Constitucionales (Madrid: 2000).

Sánchez León, Pablo (1998) *Absolutismo y comunidad. Los orígenes sociales de la guerra de los comuneros de Castilla* (Madrid: 1998).

Suárez Alvarez, María Jesús (1982) *La villa de Talavera y su tierra en la Edad Media (1369–1504)*, Universidad de Oviedo-Diputación Provincial de Toledo (Oviedo: 1982).

Therborn, G. (1979) *Cómo domina la clase dominante* (Madrid: 1979).

Tomás y Valiente, Francisco (1970) "Origen bajomedieval de la patrimonialización y la enajenación de oficios públicos en Castilla", in Actas del *I Symposium de Historia de la Administración*, Instituto de Estudios Administrativos (Madrid: 1970) 125–159.

Ureña y Smenjaud, R., *Fuero de Cuenca* (Madrid: 1935).

Val Valdivieso, María Isabel del (1994) "Oligarquía versus común (Consecuencias sociopolíticas del triunfo del regimiento en las ciudades castellanas)", *Medievalismo. Boletín de la Sociedad Española de Estudios Medievales* 4 (1994) 41–58.

Valdeón Baruque, Julio (1990) "Las oligarquías urbanas", in Actas del II Congreso de Estudios Medievales, *Concejos y ciudades en la Edad Media hispánica*, Madrid, September 25–29 1989, Fundación Sánchez Albornoz (Madrid: 1990) 509–521.

—— (1995) "La conflictividad social en Castilla", in Actas del Congreso Internacional de Historia, *El Tratado de Tordesillas y su época*, 3 vols., Setúbal, June 2, Salamanca, June 3–4, Tordesillas, June 5–7, 1994, Junta de Castilla y León (Madrid: 1995) I, 315–324.

PART TWO

DISCOURSES OF POLITICAL LEGITIMATION

THE STRENGTHENING OF ROYAL POWER
IN CASTILE UNDER ALFONSO XI

Carlos Estepa

Instituto de Historia, CSIC (Madrid)

The power of the Castilian crown was substantially reinforced during the years 1325–1337. This development is especially obvious when considered in the context of the extensive phase of internal conflict that preceded it (1270–1325), which reached its climax during Alfonso XI's own minority (1312–1325). In contrast to those unstable times, the period 1325–1337 witnessed significant events and developments that contributed to the consolidation of Castilian royal power. As we shall see, they also indicate the fundamentally harmonious nature of relations between Alfonso XI and the Castilian high nobility.

There are two related narrative sources that describe the reign of Alfonso XI (1312–1350) down to 1344, and which provide the documentary basis for this article: the 'Chronicle of Alfonso XI', and the 'Great Chronicle of Alfonso XI'. The first is generally attributed to Fernán Sánchez de Valladolid, who was a contemporary of the events he described. The second is derived from the first, and is identical to its precursor in all but a few additions. It was written around 1376, towards the end of Enrique II's reign.[1] Fernán Sánchez de Valladolid was a dedicated member of Alfonso XI's political entourage, who eventually rose to occupy the post of the royal chancellor. His generally accepted authorship of the chronicles of Alfonso XI's predecessors Alfonso X, Sancho IV, and Fernando IV[2] also establishes him as the first official chronicler of the Castilian Crown.[3] He most likely came from an affluent urban family that had links to the nobility. Even if this was not the case, moreover, his prox-

---

[1] Catalán (1977) 238–51.
[2] For editions of these chronicles, see Rosell (1953).
[3] On Fernán Sánchez and his historical works, see Gómez Redondo (1999) 1260 ff.

imity to the crown ensured that his status as a landlord was equal
to that typical of the lower ranks of the nobility.[4]

It is vital that we keep this author's background and position in
mind when analyzing his chronicle, which constitutes our principal
source. Indeed, his close identification with the Castilian monarchy
in general, and Alfonso XI in particular, is ever-present in his work,
which contains a very detailed chronological account of events.[5]
Although the author was an eyewitness to the history he relates, and
we do not therefore need to doubt either the existence of the events
he describes or the order he describes them in, we must be aware
that they are inevitably presented from an emphatically royalist perspective. This perspective is most clearly reflected in the structure of
the chronicle, which opens with a description of Alfonso XI's extremely
troubled minority (1312–1325). This is followed by a section detailing
the king's recovery of royal power and subjection of the rebellious
aristocracy. It concludes with a description of two of Alfonso XI's
most important victories over the Muslims in the Battle of the River
Salado (1340) and the Fall of Algeciras (1344) gained when, having
resolved his kingdom's internal problems, he was free to launch himself into the great military campaigns that dominated the latter part
of his reign. The history is underpinned by the concept that the
administration of justice and the waging of war against Muslims constituted the principal duties of a Castilian monarch. In Alfonso XI's
case, Fernán Sánchez clearly believed that the restoration of royal
justice, which had been so badly affected during the king's minority, was not only necessary in meeting the first of those obligations,
but was also a pre-requisite for the fulfilment of the second. The
structure adopted by the author of the 'Chronicle of Alfonso XI'
therefore allowed him to depict Alfonso XI as a king who was able
to deliver his kingdom from the chaotic and conflictive mismanage-
ment of the various regents who oversaw his minority through the
recovery and consolidation of his royal power.

---

[4] In 1352, shortly after his death, it was recorded that he had been the lord of
four settlements (Fuentes de Duero, Olmos de Esgueva, Arroyo de Santa Ana, and
Fuentitaja), and had enjoyed part-lordship over five others (Cubillas de Cerrato,
Villamentero de Campos, Polvorera, Fuensaldaña, and Bambilla). Martínez Díez
(1981) vol. I, 132–267.

[5] The chronicle is generally out by two years in its dating of events. This is corrected in Catalán's edition of the 'Great Chronicle': Catalán (1977).

The period 1325–1337 was dominated by various significant developments that contributed to the recovery of Alfonso XI's royal authority. Although the overwhelmingly royalist perspective of our principal source necessarily colours the information it conveys, it also provides a valuable reflection of the political and ideological premises that informed royal government under Alfonso XI. In this way, the chronicle reveals how royal power, especially with regard to the high nobility, was regarded by the monarch; which mechanisms were employed during this brief but decisive period in order to establish the undisputed superiority of that power; and how the Castilian king balanced his political authority with the highly developed seigneurial prerogatives of a typically feudal monarchy in the consolidation of that superiority. All of the above were of prime importance to the political development of the Crown of Castile. The subjectivity of our source material is therefore not only typical of historical texts of its kind, but also, far from invalidating any analysis based upon it, actually affords us a direct glimpse of royal political activity during a period that was fundamental to the evolution of the Castilian feudal monarchy.

The reign of Alfonso XI (1312–1350) saw the development of a strong and centralized Castilian monarchy. During these years, important milestones were reached in the imposition of the crown's authority over justice and fiscal affairs.[6] They marked a path that eventually led to the proclamation of the 1348 Ordinance of Alcalá, a legal code that was applied generally throughout the kingdom, and which constituted an important expression of the nature and extent of royal power. As we shall see, a brief glance back at Castile's past indicates that Alfonso XI's achievements in fact represented the fulfilment of the objectives of his rather less successful great-grandfather, Alfonso X (1252–1284).

This article focuses on the years 1325–1337, which represented the opening phase of Alfonso XI's majority. At the beginning of this period, the Kingdom of Castile was in a state of extreme turmoil due to the violence and instability that had accompanied the king's minority, during which different and opposing groups of regents had taken charge of royal government. In order to understand the period in question, we must therefore first discuss the king's minority, which

---

[6] Moxó (1975); Ladero (1993).

should in turn be regarded within the broader temporal framework
of the years 1270–1325. Although it is beyond the scope of this article to offer a detailed analysis of the complex conflicts and events
that followed the noble rebellion faced by Alfonso X around 1270,
some relevant background information may serve to enrich our understanding of the political climate of Alfonso XI's minority. In examining the period 1325–1337, we shall focus on those events and
developments that best reflect the bases, both ideological and practical, upon which royal power was consolidated. The king's coronation and his knighting of the Castilian nobility in 1332, the relationship
between the crown and its greatest aristocratic rivals, Don Juan
Manuel and Don Juan Núñez de Lara, and the siege of Lerma,
which resulted in the capitulation of the latter in 1336, will all be
examined in this light.

Alfonso XI's Minority

Alfonso XI gained his majority in 1325 at the tender age of fourteen. In a fascinating passage, the 'Chronicle of Alfonso XI' describes
the state of the realm at this moment as one of total catastrophe.[7]
According to its author, the aristocracy and knighthood were living
on the proceeds of thefts committed with the consent of regents who
depended on their support; the settlements of the realm, both those
that had accepted the rule of a regent and those that hadn't, were
internally divided; in those that had accepted regents, some factions
attempted to overthrow their rule in order to destroy their rivals; in
those that had no regent, the powerful monopolized royal taxes in
order to maintain their followers while at the same time imposing
unlawful duties on the rest of the inhabitants, some of whom rightly
rebelled and killed their oppressors; justice was not done in any part
of the kingdom and the land was in such turmoil that men did not
dare to travel unarmed or dwell in unfortified settlements; most of
the inhabitants of settlements that were walled, both nobles and peasants, lived off the proceeds of theft; and the state of the realm was
so desperate that nobody was surprised to find dead men on the

---

[7] 'Chronicle of Alfonso XI', ch. XXXVII; 'Great Chronicle of Alfonso XI', ch.
XLIX. When both sources coincide we will cite only the first. Extract reproduced
in Appendix I.

roads, nor were the people shocked by theft and destruction. In addition to all that, the regents imposed unlawful taxes and labour duties on the populace each year. Due to this situation, settlements belonging to the crown, the high nobility, and to *caballeros* (lower-ranking knights) had all suffered much destruction. When the king took over government from the regents, he inherited a depopulated kingdom that had been abandoned by its people, who had left their goods behind to seek refuge in Aragón or Portugal.

Although this description is undoubtedly exaggerated (for example in its claims regarding the extent of Castile's depopulation), the chronicle's general outline of events is credible, especially when one considers the precision with which historical events are described in the rest of the text. It describes a situation brought on by a whole series of disasters that affected the power of the crown and the well-being of the Castilian Kingdom, and which unfolded not only during Alfonso XI's minority, but also during previous reigns. Indeed, we would do well to remember that the chronicles of Alfonso XI's predecessors Alfonso X, Sancho IV, and Fernando IV have also been attributed to Fernán Sánchez de Valladolid. It therefore seems logical to assume that their author established the successive disasters that affected the Crown of Castile throughout all of these reigns as a dramatic backdrop before which to glorify Alfonso XI's royal achievements.

Any discussion of Alfonso XI's minority must take into account the attempts of Castile's various regents to control the kingdom. In order to understand the background of those attempts and their authors, we must first refer briefly to the great Castilian aristocratic houses, relations between the crown and the nobility, and the problems associated with the royal succession in an earlier period.

It is generally held that the period 1270–1325 witnessed a great clash between crown and nobility, and that this was reflected in a series of conflicts between the king and his followers on the one hand, and noble factions led by the kingdom's most powerful aristocrats on the other. According to this thesis, a powerful and rebellious nobility rose up against a weak crown during this period, wreaking greatest havoc during the minorities of Fernando IV (1295–1301), and Alfonso XI.[8]

---

[8] Suárez (1975) is the principal proponent of the existence of a conflict between Monarchy and nobility. Although his work mainly concerns the fifteenth century,

It is certainly true that the conflicts of this period were in some way structural, inasmuch as they reflected contradictions between the interests of the crown and those of the nobility. The complaints expressed by the members of the high nobility who rose up against Alfonso X in 1272 are indicative of this. They concern areas such as the creation of new *pueblas* (settlements-specifically royal), the promulgation of the *Fuero Real*[9] (which the king was eventually forced to retract), and other fiscal matters.[10] These problems all derived from the administration of royal justice to the detriment of seigneurial justice; a tendency to superimpose generalized legal codes on the variety enshrined in local territorial jurisdiction;[11] or fiscal demands made of the vassals of the landed nobility. The greatest of these problems was caused by a policy of extending and consolidating the *realengo* (royal direct lordship) in areas that were already highly feudalized, like the Castilian territories to the north of the Duero, which necessarily signified a reduction in the lordly power of the regional nobility.

Although it is important to bear the existence of these issues in mind, however, we should be wary of inferring from them the existence of generalized and opposing royal and noble camps: different factions allied themselves to the interests of the crown at different times according to changing circumstances. There were generally two or three opposing noble factions attempting to control royal politics at any one time during this period, and they did this either by gaining the king's favour, or by controlling his person. It goes without saying that the absence of effective royal power during the minority of a monarch facilitated the latter option.

Before discussing the effect this political context had on the Castilian monarchy, we must first familiarize ourselves with the great noble houses of the kingdom and some relevant members of the royal family.[12] Castile's most powerful aristocrats came from the houses of

---

his ideas have been extended to cover the whole of the late middle ages in defence of the proposition that the Modern State owed its origins to a Monarchy that was forced to compete with the selfish interests of the nobility. For the application of this concept to the period covered here, see González Mínguez (1976).

[9] (explanatory note?)

[10] For a recent detailed analysis of these issues, see Escalona (2002).

[11] Alfonso X embarked on the policy of establishing the '*Fuero Real*' in 1255, shortly after his accession to the crown.

[12] These are discussed in greater detail in Estepa (2003).

Lara[13] and Haro. Nuño González de Lara was one of the leaders of the rebellion against Alfonso X. His son and grandson, Juan Núñez and Juan Núñez II, succeeded him at the head of the family, and clashed with Sancho IV and Fernando IV respectively. Their position with regard to the monarchy was often a function of their animosity towards the Haro family. The latter were important landowners in Castile and Lords of Biscay. Count Lope, one of the family's leading members, enjoyed a close relationship with Sancho IV, whose major-domo he became. However, he fell into disgrace and died at the king's own hands at Alfaro in 1288. His death marked the beginning of a complex dispute over the highly significant lordship of Biscay.

Secondary members of the royal family, who bridged the gap between aristocracy and king, gained importance during the reign of Alfonso X.[14] These were the sons and grandsons of kings, and included: the *Infante*[15] Don Felipe, Alfonso X's brother, who led the rebellion against the king together with Nuño González de Lara; the *Infante* Don Enrique, another of Alfonso X's brothers, who returned to Castile after a long sojourn in an Italian prison at the hands of the Anjou in time to take control of Fernando IV's regency together with Queen María de Molina, the wife of Sancho IV; Alfonso and Fernando *de la Cerda* and their father Fernando, Alfonso X's son and heir who died in 1275 and from whom they inherited their nickname; the *Infante* Don Juan, the brother of Sancho IV; Fernando IV's brothers, the *Infantes* Don Pedro and Don Felipe; Don Juan 'the crouchback', who was the son of the *Infante* Don Juan; and Don Juan Manuel, the son of the *Infante* Manuel, another of Alfonso X's brothers. Both of the latter were important figures during the reign of Alfonso XI.

It is especially important to understand the relationships that bound the great Castilian noble houses to the royal family.[16] For example, Diego López de Haro, Lord of Biscay and brother of the aforementioned Count Lope, married the *Infanta* Violante, Alfonso X's daughter, and was therefore Sancho IV's brother-in-law. Count Lope's daughter María was married to the *Infante* Don Juan, Sancho VI's

---

[13] For a recent study of this family, see Doubleday (2001).
[14] See Fig. I.
[15] The title given to the legitimate children of Castilian kings.
[16] See Fig. II.

brother, who based his aspirations to control the Lordship of Biscay
on the claims of his wife. Finally Juana, the sister of Juan Núñez II
de Lara, married Fernando *de la Cerda* around 1310.

It is also important to bear in mind that whenever these individuals, who represented the most powerful elements within Castilian
society, entered into conflicts, these necessarily also engulfed the
extensive groups of middling and lesser nobles who were tied to
them by bonds of vassalage or patronage.

The Castilian royal succession became problematic on various
occasions during this period. When, for example, the *Infante* Fernando,
son and heir of Alfonso X, died in battle against the Marinids in
1275, the right of succession was disputed among the king's remaining heirs. The claims of Alfonso and Fernando *de la Cerda*, the sons
of the dead prince, were championed by the Lara family and by
their uncle, Philip III of France.[17] Despite their efforts, however,
Sancho, the king's second-born son—who enjoyed the support of the
Haro family—was named heir to the throne. He further complicated
matters by leading a widely supported rebellion against his father in
1282. Despite his broad following, however, his succession continued to be disputed and the claims of his nephews pressed throughout his reign (1282–1295). This succession crisis reached its climax
during Fernando IV's minority, when Alfonso *de la Cerda* was supported in his ambitions by the *Infante* Don Juan, Juan Núñez II de
Lara, much of the Castilian aristocracy, and even the kings of Aragón
and Portugal.[18] For his part, the *Infante* Don Juan attempted to secure
for himself the crown of León, along with the kingdoms of Galicia
and Seville, in what would have represented a wholesale dismem-
berment of the Castilian crown territories. In the long run, however,
the king's position held. In 1300, the *Infante* Don Juan recognized
his title to the throne and renounced his own claims to it. Then, in
1304, the kings of Castile and Aragón signed the Treaty of Tarazona,
through which Alfonso *de la Cerda* renounced his claims to the throne
in return for important lordships for himself and his brother.

The disputes that clouded these two royal successions obviously
cast the legitimacy of individual monarchs into doubt. They did not,
however, represent a challenge to royal authority itself. The author

---

[17] See Fig. I.
[18] Philip IV of France was obliged to keep his distance from the dispute owing
to the promise he had made at Bayonne in 1290 not to support the claims of
Alfonso and Fernando *de la Cerda* against Sancho IV. Jofré de Loaysa (1982) 146.

of the royal chronicles that describe these events was obliged to both accept and defend the legitimacy of Sancho IV's rebellion against his father Alfonso X, which was initially condemned by Aragón, France, and even the Papacy, as Sancho IV was the founder of the dynastic line from which Alfonso XI was directly descended.[19] Despite representing the most insecure years of this long period of instability, Alfonso XI's own minority did not witness any challenges to the young king's legitimacy. Instead, the royal rights of the king and his grandmother, María de Molina (who died in 1321), were universally recognized by those who competed for control of his person and the political power that went with it. It is to the regencies through which this competition was expressed that we must now turn.

The minority of Fernando IV (1295–1301) was supervised by his mother, María de Molina, and the *Infante* Don Enrique. The former was responsible for the king's safety and upbringing (*guarda* and *crianza*), while the latter took over the government of the kingdom.[20] During Alfonso XI's minority, in contrast, the regency was fought over fiercely. Initially, it was uneasily divided between Queen María and the *Infantes* Don Juan and Don Pedro. When both men perished in the Battle of Granada in 1319, it was once again disputed among members of the royal family. The situation was further aggravated by the death of the Queen Mother, after which the *Infante* Don Felipe, Don Juan Manuel, and Don Juan, the son of the *Infante* Don Juan, were all recognized as Regents of Castile.

The division of royal government among various regents during these minorities was reflected in the division of territorial authority. In this way, towns and villages recognized the authority of either Don Juan or Don Pedro during the first phase of Alfonso XI's minority. The Burgos Parliament of 1315 attempted to remedy this situation

---

[19] Gómez Redondo (1988) 976 ff.

[20] Queen María was in charge of the 'safekeeping of the king's person and of the upbringing that she would not give to any other person in the world' ('*guarda del cuerpo del rey é de la crianza que non daria á ninguna persona del mundo*'), while the '*Infante*' Don Enrique was entrusted with the 'safekeeping of the kingdoms' ('*guarda de los reinos*'). 'Chronicle of Fernando IV', ch. I: 95a. The official record of the 1295 Valladolid Parliament mentions an 'Ordinance of Fernando IV' that was issued 'with advice from the queen our mother, Doña María, and with the permission of the "*Infante*" Don Enrique, our uncle and regent' (*Con consseio dela Reyna donna Maria nuestra madre, e con otorgamiento del infante don Anrrique nuestro tio e nuestro tutor*). Cortes (1861) 131.

by decreeing that 'the regency should be all one' (*la tutoria fuese toda una*): it was ruled that although justice should be administered independently by the two regents in different settlements, appeals must be heard by the king himself; that the regents should not have use of their own seals nor make independent donations of lands or rents; and that all such concessions should be authenticated with the Royal Seal and agreed by all three regents.[21] Furthermore, the queen's authority as regent was decreed to be superior to that of the *Infantes* as she was entrusted with the exclusive care of the young king's person.[22]

When the *Infantes* Don Juan and Don Pedro died in 1319, the queen was left as sole regent. She besought Castile's townsmen to save the kingdom from division (*departimiento*) by 'avoiding disputes or alliances with any *Infante* or magnate, or any other powerful man' (*que se guardasen de poner pleyto nin postura con Infante nin Rico-ome nin otro ome poderoso*). Before such a division should take place, she declared that she would call them together—presumably in a parliament—in order that they, together with the prelates and nobility of the realm, might agree the future of the kingdom.[23] In the event, the queen's exhortations went unheeded. The 'Chronicle' informs us that soon after they were made, some towns sought the protection of Don Juan Manuel, who lost no time in devising a new Royal Seal for his own use and declaring himself regent (*fizo un sello nuevo del Rey, et llamóse tutor del Rey*).[24] He competed for control of Alfonso XI's minority with the *Infante* Don Felipe, who had the support of Queen María, and with whom he negotiated the division of the regency. A third contestant for the title of regent appeared in the figure of Don Juan, the son of the late *Infante* Don Juan, who enjoyed considerable support in the north of Castile.[25] His supporters duly clashed with the forces of Don Felipe.[26] Don Juan Manuel was supported by the towns of Extremadura, while Don Felipe gained support in

---

[21] 'Chronicle of Alfonso XI': ch. VIII.

[22] This is already expressed in the 1313 Treaty of Palazuelos. Ibid.: ch. VI.

[23] Ibid.: ch. XIV.

[24] Ibid.: ch. XVII.

[25] He was supported by the towns of the province of Castile, to the north of the Duero, Fernando '*de la Cerda*' (who was related to the Lara family), Don Lope de Haro, and the Galician magnate Pedro Fernández de Castro.

[26] This happened first in León, and then in Campos. 'Chronicle of Alfonso XI': chs. XXII, XXIII, & XXIV.

the regions of Seville and Jaén.[27] The scene was therefore set for a three-way battle over royal government, none of whose protagonists had been recognized by any parliament. The 'Chronicle' lays the blame for what its author considered to be a deplorable situation squarely on Don Juan Manuel, who had used the support of the towns to assume the title of regent. It is in this context that we must understand our source's insistence that Don Juan Manuel should renounce his right to the regency and let Parliament resolve the issue.

By combining the testimonies of our two sources, it is possible to deduce that Queen María summoned the three opposing parties either to a parliament in Palencia in 1321, or to two separate meetings in Palencia and Valladolid.[28] Cardinal William, the Bishop of Sabina, was sent to mediate in Castilian affairs around this time. It seems probable that the queen's death on July 1, 1321 led to the calling of the Parliament of Valladolid in 1322.[29] However, the 'Great Chronicle of Alfonso XI', which is the only one of our sources to mention the Parliament of Valladolid and describe the naming of the three regents that took place there, also states that the queen was present at the gathering:

> At that time Castile was overrun daily by fire and sword, and her soil was rendered barren by the absence of a king and lord who could protect and defend her settlements with the sword of justice. Such destruction and fighting were due to the regency, over which nobody could agree, as some wanted one thing and others another. And the queen, Doña María, ordered that a Parliament be held in Valladolid in order to put an end to such evil and discord. And nobles, knights,

---

[27] The 'Chronicle' presents the latter as a reaction to the support gained by Don Juan Manuel in Córdoba. Ibid.: ch. XXVI.

[28] Chapter XXV of the 'Chronicle' speaks of one meeting in Valladolid, to which Don Felipe and Don Juan Manuel were summoned, and another in Palencia, at which the Castilian towns supporting Don Juan were to be represented. However, it is possible that the chronicle merely refers to the queen's intention of calling these meetings, rather than their actual existence. Later, once Cardinal William had already stepped onto the scene, the 'Chronicle' refers to a parliament that was called at Palencia on April 8th of either 1321 or 1322.

[29] It is interesting that the two documents that refer to what may have been the Parliament of Valladolid concern different dates and different protagonists. The first, dated May 8, 1322, was called by the *Infante* Don Felipe and comprised of those town councils of Castile, León, and Extremadura 'that had not taken a regent' (*que non auian tomado tutor*) and which recognized his authority as such (Cortes (1861) 337 ff.). The second was a piece of legislation directed at the monasteries of Castile dated June 17 and was issued in the presence of Don Juan's following (Ibid., I: 369 ff.).

and representatives of the towns and settlements of the kingdom gathered there; and with advice from the noble queen they appointed those
regents for the king whom they understood to be good and prepared
to undertake great deeds should the need arise. And these were the
Infante Don Felipe and Don Juan, the son of the *Infante* Don Juan, and
Don Juan, the son of the *Infante* Don Manuel. And in this way the
regents were appointed with the approval and permission of the noble
queen and by everybody else, in order that they might follow the
queen's counsel and never disobey her. After their appointment the
regents dissolved Parliament and the people returned to their respective places.[30]

This interpolation emphasizes the queen's concern for the good of
the kingdom while laying the blame for Castile's ills at the door of
the regents. The 'Great Chronicle' goes on to suggest that the evils
unleashed on the realm by its regents after their appointment were
the cause of the good queen's illness and subsequent death:

History tells us that the king's regents roamed the land and instead
of bringing peace and concord to its settlements, they began to quarrel amongst themselves and each one assumed the regency as he
pleased, so that the settlements were worse off than before. And Queen
Doña María, seeing the evil and destruction that was being visited on
the king's lands, fell ill and died. She was buried in the monastery of
Las Huelgas de Valladolid, and may God in his mercy grant her forgiveness and make her heir to his holy kingdom, amen.[31]

It seems that the Parliament of Valladolid adopted the only possible solution to the crisis, which was to sanction the *de facto* existence

---

[30] *En este tiempo fue Castilla metida en gran fuego e corrida de cada dia asi que se ermauan
las tierras por mengua de rrey e de señor que los oviese a manparar e defender los pueblos con
espada de justiçia. E este mal e guerra fue por fecho de la tutorya sobre que se non podian avenir,
los vnos queriendo lo vno e los otros queriendo lo otro. E la rreyna doña Maria por sacar este
mal e discordia que avia entre los pueblos, fizo fazer cortes en Valladolid. E alli fueron ayuntados los nobles e fijosdalgo e procuradores de la çibdades e villas destos reynos; e con consejo
desta noble rreyna dieron al rey tutores, aquellos que entendieron que eran buenos e abtos par se
parar a grandes fechos si menester fuese. E estos fueron el infante don Felipe e don Joan hijo
del infante don Joan e don Joan hijo del infante don Manuel. E ansi fueron fechos los tutores
con plazer e otorgamiento de la noble rreyna e de todos en general e que todos se guiasen por
consejo de la rreyna e le non saliesen de mandado. E desque los tutores fueron fechos derramaron
las cortes e fueronse las gentes cada vno para sus lugares.* 'Great Chronicle of Alfonso XI':
ch. XXXVII.
[31] '*Dize la historia que los tutores del rrey andaron por las tierras y en lugar de poner paz
e avenençia entre los pueblos, qu'ellos començaron aver contiendas e tomaron la tutoria cada vno
como se queria, ansi que los pueblos lo pasauan peor que en el comienço. E la rreyna doña
Maria, veyendo el mal e daño que las tierras del rrey rresçibian, ovo gran pesar, e adolesçio de
vna dolençia de que fino. Y el su cuerpo fue enterrado en las Huelgas de Valladolid e Dios por
su merçed le de perdonamiento e le faga eredera en el su santo rreyno, amen*'. Ibid.: ch. XXXVIII.

of the three regents (Don Felipe, Don Juan Manuel, and Don Juan), and their division of power within the kingdom.[32] This clearly represented a continuation of the situation that had characterized the first phase of the minority. The bitter fighting that raged between the regents until 1325 encouraged violence among magnates, knights, and the lower ranks of the nobility who were invariably allied to one of the three contestants' causes.[33] This theory is borne out by the chronicler's afore-cited description of the desperation of Castile's situation in 1325.

In the absence of effective royal government, the regents not only exercised territorial authority, but also assumed powers that were more decidedly 'royal' in nature. Don Juan Manuel, for example, used a royal seal, made royal appointments, donated royal land-rents, and obstructed legal appeals to the king.[34] For his part, Don Juan, the son of the *Infante* Don Juan, imposed no less than seven new labour duties on the inhabitants of Castile together with Don Fernando, the son of the *Infante* Don Fernando, Don Lope de Haro, and Don Pedro Fernández de Castro when they gathered representatives of the town councils of Castile together at Burgos in 1320.[35] In this way, they assumed the royal prerogative in imposing fiscal burdens which were normally decided by Parliament. In 1324, Don Juan held a council in Burgos at which the creation of five new labour duties for the settlements under his control was agreed.[36]

The dispute that raged over the Lordship of Biscay during most of this period represented a particularly significant factor in the friction between kings and the great noble families of Castile. It also reflected the family ties that linked the two.[37] This conflict, which we shall presently examine, was an enduring one: it existed under Sancho IV, was temporarily resolved under Fernando IV, and then finally resurfaced in the early years of Alfonso XI's reign.

---

[32] Proof of the regents' *de facto* division of royal government is provided in the decree cited in note 28, which was issued 'with the counsel and approval of Don Juan, son of the '*Infante*' Don Juan, my uncle and regent and the guardian of my kingdoms and my deputy and my commander-in-chief on the frontier' (*con conseio e con otorgamiento de don Iohan fijo del infante don Iohan mio tyo e mio tutor e guarda de mios rregnos e mio alfierez e mio adelantado mayor en la frontera*).

[33] 'Chronicle of Alfonso XI': ch. XXIX.

[34] Ibid.: ch. XVII.

[35] Ibid.: ch. XX.

[36] Ibid.: ch. XXII.

[37] See Fig. II.

Count Don Lope, who had once served as the king's mayor-domo, met his end at the hands of his former master, Sancho IV, in 1288 in Alfaro. His son-in-law and ally Don Juan was taken prisoner, and the Lordship of Biscay confiscated by the king. When Don Lope's brother, Diego López, was re-admitted into royal service in 1295, he also recovered Biscay. However, his right to the territory was disputed by the *Infante* Don Juan, whose wife María Díaz de Haro was the daughter of the dead Count Lope and claimed Biscay's tenancy as her rightful inheritance. The dispute between the two developed during Fernando IV's majority, when both were in the king's service. Don Juan and Doña María Díaz officially lodged their claim to the lordship at the Parliament of Medina del Campo in 1305. The dispute was finally resolved three years later, in 1308, along the following lines: Don Diego was to hold Biscay, Orduña, Valmaseda, Las Encartaciones, and Durango during his lifetime, after which they would pass to Doña María, while Doña María was to enjoy all of Don Diego's seigneurial rights outside of Biscay during her lifetime, after which they would pass to Don Lope and the other children of Don Diego, who would thereafter have no title to Biscay.[38]

Don Diego died in 1308 or 1309, taking with him the force of the Haro family's claim on Biscay.[39] Through María Díaz de Haro, this important tenancy passed first to the *Infante* Don Juan, and then to his son, Don Juan 'the Crouchback'. When the latter was executed for treason in 1326, the lordship was, in theory, re-integrated into the crown's possessions. This confiscation was disputed by Juan Núñez III de Lara, who was married to María, the daughter and heir of Don Juan 'the Crouchback'.[40]

The 'Chronicle of Fernando IV' describes this dispute and its resolution under Fernando IV. It's assertion that the supporters of Don Diego López de Haro mistrusted the king, whom they considered to be a partisan (*bandero*) of the *Infante* Don Juan, is most revealing about the king's position with respect to this dispute.[41] According to the chronicler, the king, far from leading his own faction against the high nobility, was actually allied to one of the parties to an exclu-

---

[38] 'Chronicle of Fernando IV': ch. XIV, p. 150a.
[39] The interests of his sons, Don Lope and Don Fernando, were overshadowed by those of Don Juan in the second phase of Alfonso XI's minority.
[40] See Fig. II.
[41] 'Chronicle of Fernando IV': ch. XIII, p. 139a.

sively aristocratic quarrel between two of his kingdom's most powerful families.

The First Phase of Alfonso XI's Majority:
Rebels and Favourites

Alfonso XI took over the government of Castile in 1325 at the tender age of fourteen. The end of the regency was formally expressed
through the summoning of a parliament which met during that same
year, and was attended by Don Felipe, Don Juan Manuel, and Don
Juan.[42] The author of the 'Chronicle of Alfonso XI' presents this
event as one through which the king set about restoring to his kingdom justice, which had suffered so greatly as a result of friction
between the regents and the deeds of evildoers.[43] He also presents
the restoration of royal justice as an essential pre-requisite to the
waging of war against the Muslims.

During this period, the king selected *caballeros* instead of members
of the high nobility as his principal advisors and closest companions.
The most prominent of these were Alvar Núñez Osorio and Garcilaso
de la Vega, both of whom were associated with the *Infante* Felipe.
Although they were not among the kingdom's most powerful men,
however, these were important knights in their own right, who moreover were implicated in the creation of the very situation that the
king now wanted to reverse. The 'Chronicle' does not try to hide
this fact, and is most expressive in stating that although Alfonso XI
knew that these men and their followers had caused harm to his
kingdom, he valued their advice because their extensive experience
of the situation meant that they also knew how best to prevent it's
recurrence.[44]

Despite the king's efforts, the kingdom remained divided between
his own camp and that of Don Juan and Don Juan Manuel, who

---

[42] Cortes (1861) 372. The summoning of this assembly is also mentioned in
'Chronicle of Alfonso XI': ch. XXXVIII.

[43] The 'Chronicle' first mentions this subject with regard to the king's sojourn
in Valladolid, where he dedicated three days out of every week to the resolution
of disputes heard in the Royal Court because he perceived the great harm that
had been done to his kingdom for want of adequate justice, and thought very ill
of those responsible. See Moreta (1978) on the development and contextualization
of the concept of 'evildoers' as described in the 'Chronicle'.

[44] 'Chronicle of Alfonso XI': ch. XXXIX.

claimed to object to the king's favourites, whom they considered to be the creatures of their enemy, Don Felipe. However, the opposition of these, 'the most powerful men in the kingdom' (*los más poderosos omes del su regno*), should in fact be seen as an attempt to prolong the power they had held as regents through their newfound alliance.[45] Alfonso XI attempted to break that alliance by negotiating his own marriage with Constance, the daughter of Don Juan Manuel. However, the nuptials did not take place and Don Juan intensified his opposition to the king by seeking the support of the King of Aragón and rekindling the claims of Alfonso *de la Cerda* to the Castilian Crown.[46] For his part, Don Juan was executed for treason in Toro in 1326 and his estates, Biscay among them, were confiscated by the Crown. Far from solving all of the king's problems, however, his death merely left more room on the Castilian stage for the development of the ongoing struggle between the young monarch and Don Juan Manuel.

Alfonso XI clearly experienced great difficulties in affirming his authority during the early years of his majority. Indeed, his struggle with Don Juan Manuel, which lasted until 1338, represented a significant test for the monarchy. The alliance that Don Juan Manuel established with Juan Núñez de Lara, another of the kingdom's most powerful magnates, resulted in the creation of a noble faction in opposition to the king which fluctuated in size according to changing circumstances. There are certain events that took place during this period that are especially revealing in terms of the intentions that lay behind the consolidation of royal power and the gains that were made in this respect, as well as the reasons behind the rebellions of certain members of the high nobility. It is to a discussion of these that we must now turn.

Alfonso XI worked hard throughout this period to consolidate his alliance with Alfonso IV of Portugal: he not only wed the Portuguese king's daughter María, but also arranged the marriage of his son and heir, the *Infante* Don Pedro, to Blanca, the daughter of the Castilian *Infante* Don Pedro. His own marriage called his pre-nuptial negotiations with the family of Don Juan Manuel to an abrupt halt[47]

---

[45] Ibid.: ch. XLI.
[46] Ibid.: ch. XLV.
[47] Evidently, gaining the allegiance of the King of Portugal was a greater priority for Alfonso XI. The 'Chronicle' justifies the king's breaking off of negotiations with Don Juan Manuel by claiming that the wrecked marriage was to have served

and provided the ex-regent with an ideal pretext for rebellion.[48] He promptly sent messengers to tell the king that he, along with his supporters and vassals, were quitting his royal service and going into exile.[49] Despite his action, however, Don Juan Manuel continued to act as governor of Murcia and The Frontera,[50] and to receive substantial incomes from the fiscal administration of his royal tenancies ('he held from him a large part of the rents of his kingdom').[51] In practice, therefore, this aristocrat's 'exile' simply signified his hostility towards the king, and had no bearing on his administration of important sections of the royal fisc which, as a powerful magnate, he continued to control, and from which he continued to maintain his vassals. Naturally, the king must have been keen to re-incorporate this rebellious and expensive aristocrat into royal service.

The war against the Kingdom of Granada was fundamental to the development of Alfonso XI's political activity. Indeed, we have already seen that the young king stated his intention to carry forward the 'two most important things entrusted to him by God in his Kingdom, the first being justice, and the other the war against the Infidel', in 1326.[52] He attempted to enlist the support of Don Juan Manuel for the second of the two enterprises on various occasions, but always unsuccessfully. The loss of Gibraltar in 1333 represented a pivotal moment in the war on Granada. Alfonso XI's military action against the Muslims of Granada and North Africa is traditionally glorified in hindsight through consideration of his victory at Salado in 1340 and the siege and conquest of Algeciras in 1342–4. These victories are presented by Fernán Sánchez de Valladolid as the glorious conclusion of policies developed throughout the king's reign.

---

the purpose of weakening the alliance between Don Juan Manuel and Don Juan, and had therefore become meaningless on the death of the latter. Ibid.: ch. LX.

[48] However, he had already refused to heed the king's summons in 1326 after Don Juan's execution despite not having a pretext for his action.

[49] . . . se envió despedir e desnaturar del Rey por sí et por todos sus amigos e vasallos. 'Chronicle of Alfonso XI': ch. LX.

[50] Alfonso XI's charters continued to cite him as such. See González Crespo (1985).

[51] tenia dél grand parte de las rentas del su regno. The 'Chronicle' states this to have been the case when Alfonso XI made a petition in preparation for his campaign against Granada in 1327. 'Chronicle of Alfonso XI': ch. LVII.

[52] dos cosas las mas principales que Dios le encomendó en el regno, la una justicia, et la otra la Guerra de los Moros. Ibid.: ch. XLIX.

Alfonso XI's favourites enjoyed mixed fortunes.[53] The most important among them, Alvar Núñez Osorio, rose to attain first aristocratic status and then the title of Count (1327).[54] His immense power
was reflected in his patronage of numerous vassals and his tenancy
of various royal castles and fortifications, and was resented by magnates, knights, and town councils alike. In 1328 he was accused of
embezzling royal rents that were rightly the preserve of the king's
vassals.[55] This accusation proved to be his downfall, as he was first
expelled from the royal household and then physically eliminated by
the magnate Ramiro Flórez de Guzmán. Alfonso XI's other favourite,
Garcilaso de la Vega, was killed in Soria in 1328 when fighting
broke out between rival factions in that town. The king found sub-
stitutes for his two late advisors in Fernán Rodríguez de Valbuena,
the Prior of San Juan, the admiral Alfonso Jofre Tenorio, and Juan
Martínez de Leyva, all of whom came from the lower ranks of the
nobility. However, the section of the 'Chronicle' that describes the
retinue that accompanied Alfonso XI from Burgos to the Kingdom
of Aragón in January 1329 for the wedding of the king's sister Leonor
with the Aragonese king reveals that he did not exclude the high
nobility from royal service, as there were plenty of magnates among
the company.[56] Furthermore, Don Alfonso *de la Cerda* placed himself
at the king's mercy in 1330, recognizing Alfonso XI's authority,
renouncing all claims to the Kingdoms of Castile and León, and
declaring himself the king's vassal. In return, the king granted him
the tenancy of royal lands and settlements and their associated rents
just like he did with all his other vassals.[57]

When the Lord of Lara, Juan Núñez II, died without issue in
Burgos in 1315, his inheritance fell to his sister Juana, who was mar-

---

[53] See Moxó (1975) 255–9
[54] 'Chronicle of Alfonso XI': ch. LXI. The title of Count had fallen out of use
in Castile, the last count, Lope de Haro, having died in 1288. Alvar Núñez's acquisition of this dignity was therefore of the highest significance and marked him out
clearly from the rest of the Castilian nobility.
[55] After rebellions by the towns of Zamora, Toro, and Valladolid, this complaint
was officially lodged by Fernán Rodríguez de Valbuena, the Prior of San Juan, and
the knight Juan Martínez de Leyva. Ibid.: ch. LXX.
[56] Our source cites: Pedro Fernández de Castro; Juan Alfonso de Haro, Lord of
Cameros; Rodrigo Álvarez de Asturias, Lord of Noreña; the Grand Masters of the
military orders of Santiago, Calatrava, and Alcántara; Fernando Rodríguez de
Villalobos; Juan García Marique; 'and the knights of the King's Council and of his
military host' (*et los Caballeros del Consejo del Rey et de la su mesnada*). Ibid.: ch. LXXVIII.
[57] Ibid.: ch. XCII.

ried to Fernando *de la Cerda*.[58] They had a son called Juan Núñez (III) who, according to the 'Great Chronicle of Alfonso XI', was named as heir to the Lara family's inheritance by the nobility of Castile while still a child ('they gave a lord and heir to the house of Lara, and this was Don Juan Nuñez').[59] Around 1330, the Lara family and Don Juan Manuel forged an alliance through the marriage of the latter with Blanca, the daughter of Doña Juana de Lara and Fernando *de la Cerda* (who had died by this time) and the sister of Juan Núñez III de Lara. The Lordship of Biscay was also placed on the negotiating table between the two sides, for although the king had confiscated the territory from Don Juan in 1326, the traitor's daughter Doña María was still generally considered to be its rightful heir. A marriage was duly arranged between the heiress and Juan Núñez III de Lara.[60] The result was that the Lord of Lara also laid claim to the Lordship of Biscay, and his claim was supported by none less than Don Juan Manuel, who declared himself ready to wage war on the king until Biscay was delivered into the hands of Don Juan Núñez and Doña María.[61] This alliance represented a dangerous focal point for the organization of any potential noble faction in opposition to Alfonso XI, and as such represented the greatest single obstacle to the strengthening of royal power during this period.

In this tense context, the crown's political strategy revolved around involving all Castilian nobles in royal service and securing their recognition of the king as their 'natural lord' (*señor natural*). This policy was most successfully achieved through the knighting ceremonies and Royal Coronation that took place in 1332, which we shall examine shortly. As Book III of the 'Great Chronicle' points out, this event marked the end of the brief period that lasted from 1328 to 1332, during which the confidence of the Castilian monarchy was boosted by a series of significant military and political victories, such as the conquest of Teba in 1331, successes in the War of Granada, and the acquisition of the Lordship of Álava with the approval of the region's nobility.[62]

---

[58] See Fig. II.
[59] *dieron señor heredero a la casa de Lara, e este fue don Joan Nuñez*. 'Great Chronicle of Alfonso XI': ch. IX.
[60] See Fig. II.
[61] 'Chronicle of Alfonso XI': ch. LXXXI.
[62] 'Chronicle of Alfonso XI': ch. XCLVII.

The Royal Coronation of 1332

Alfonso XI's coronation was an event of the highest symbolic significance. As such, it is depicted in the two versions of the 'Chronicle' in ways that reflect most valuably the way in which crown-nobility relations were perceived by Alfonso XI and his biographers. By combining his coronation with a knighting ceremony, the king introduced the idea that none of the nobility should consider themselves 'properly' knighted unless they received their title from a crowned king. The order of proceedings through which this concept was emphasized was as follows: the king was first knighted, then crowned, and then he himself knighted the assembled nobles.[63]

The king was prepared to go to great lengths to honour 'the crown of his kingdoms' (*la corona de sus regnos*). He ordered the knighting ceremony to be prepared in Burgos and summoned the magnates, knights, and lesser nobles of Castile to that city, where he intended to receive his crown 'and the honour of knighthood' (*et tomar honra de caballería*). It was no coincidence that the ceremony was located in the town that was considered to be the capital of Castile (*caput Castelle*).[64] The 'Chronicle of Alfonso XI' also stresses that all those summoned attended the ceremony, with the notable exception of Don Juan Manuel and Don Juan Núñez de Lara. While preparations were getting underway, the king made his way to Santiago de Compostela. He entered the archiepiscopal city on foot, and when he reached the cathedral he took up his position for a night-long vigil during which he guarded the arms that lay on the altar of the church. At daybreak, mass was read by the Archbishop, Juan de Limia, who then blessed the king's arms. The king then took up the weapons himself, in order not to receive them from any other person, and approached the statue of St. James the Apostle that stood behind the altar, from which he 'received' the *pescozada* (slap) on the cheek that formed part of the symbolic ritual of the knighting ceremony. Alfonso XI was thus knighted by none other than St. James the Apostle.[65] 'As he had been knighted bearing arms, he ordered

---

[63] The ceremony is described in full in chs. XCIX, C, and CI of the 'Chronicle of Alfonso XI'. Parts of chs. XCIX and C are reproduced in Appendix II.

[64] The city received this title during the reign of Alfonso X, if not earlier (González Díez, 1984). By the fourteenth century it was more usually qualified as: 'head of Castile' and 'our chamber' (*cabeça de Castilla* and *nuestra camara*).

[65] The problem of how Alfonso XI could be knighted without receiving his title

that all those who were to be knighted in future should also bear arms when receiving their title'. The 'Chronicle' continues with a description of the king's journey from Santiago to Burgos, where he prepared for the coming ceremonies.

The Royal Coronation took place in August 1332.[66] Prelates, magnates, and other noblemen had all assembled there in order to be knighted by the king. Alfonso XI settled himself in his lodgings, which stood within the walls of the monastery of Las Huelgas, a Cistercian nunnery on the outskirts of the city that enjoyed particularly close ties to the Castilian royal family. It had been founded and established as a royal pantheon in 1187 by Alfonso VIII and his wife Eleanor of England, the daughter of Henry II and Eleanor of Aquitaine. Leadership of the foundation was divided between its abbess and another figurehead known as the 'Lady' (*Señora*), who was always recruited from the royal family and was often an *Infanta*.[67] Its symbolic importance and close association with the Castilian monarchy thus provided Las Huelgas with the ideal credentials for hosting a royal coronation.

On the day of his crowning, the king donned his regalia, which were decorated with silver and gold and the royal emblems of castles and lions, and mounted a very valuable horse. One of his spurs was fitted by Don Alfonso, the son of the *Infante* Don Fernando, who the chronicler says 'on some occasions called himself King of Castile' (*algunas veces se llamó rey de Castilla*), and the other by Pedro Fernández de Castro, who seems to have been the most important among the magnates present.[68] These and other magnates, and all the other people present, surrounded the king and proceeded on foot to the church. When they arrived, the king's spurs were removed by those who had fitted them. Alfonso XI's wife, Doña María, arrived

---

from any of his inferiors was solved through the use of a mechanical contraption that was built into the statue, which is today conserved in the monastery of Las Huelgas de Burgos. His supposed knighting by the statue also conferred on him the status of a Knight of the Order of Santiago. Herbers (1999) 90.

[66] In a charter dated August 13th, 1332, the king stated 'and because they begged our mercy now, when we received the crown in our aforesaid monastery' (*et porque nos pidieron merçet agora, quando reçibimos la corona en el dicho nuestro monesterio*). Peña Pérez (1990) 23.

[67] In 1332, for example, the *Infanta* Doña María, who was the daughter of Jaime II of Aragón and the widow of the *Infante* Don Pedro (Alfonso XI's uncle), held this post. (See Fig. I).

[68] He was a member of the third most important Castilian noble house, after those of Lara and Haro. Despite this, the bulk of his estates were situated in Galicia.

soon afterwards, accompanied by prelates and other people. The king and queen were seated on thrones next to the altar, he on the right, and she on the left. The Archbishop of Santiago read mass, whereafter the king and queen knelt before the altar in the offertory and received blessings from the Archbishop and the bishops.[69] The prelates unstitched the king's robes on the right shoulder, which the archbishop then anointed with holy oil.[70] The Archbishop and bishops blessed the crowns that had been placed on the altar. Once the bishops had been seated, the king approached the altar unaccompanied, took up the crown of gold and precious stones that awaited him there, and placed it on his head, then took up the other crown and placed it on the queen's head. Once again, the king and queen knelt before the altar, where they remained until the consecration took place. After that they returned to their sees, where they remained, crowns on their heads, until mass was over. On leaving the church, the king mounted his horse and his magnates followed him on foot. The queen left the church shortly afterwards.

The knighting of the nobility took place on the following day. The king summoned all those who were to be knighted, which the 'Chronicle' numbers at twenty-two magnates and ninety knights, to his palace. There he informed them that he intended to knight them on the following day; before that, he had ordered that they be provided with vestments of gold and silk and others, 'for each that which was appropriate' (*a cada uno lo que convenía*), as well as their swords.

---

[69] The most prominent ecclesiastical role on this occasion clearly fell to the Archbishop of Santiago. It is interesting to note, furthermore, that the Archbishop of Toledo, who was also Primate of all Iberia, was absent from the ceremony. The reasons for this are far from clear (see Linehan, 1987), but may have been linked to a general decline in the importance of Toledo's primacy (although the Archbishop of Toledo continued to be cited as Primate of Iberia in royal diplomas throughout Alfonso XI's reign) or it may have been due to the fact that Toledo's occupant at the time, Jimeno de Luna, was Aragonese and therefore not a 'natural' subject of Alfonso XI. On the other hand, it may simply have been a reflection of the importance of the role played by the Cult of Santiago in the king's knighting ceremony. It is also important to stress that Alfonso XI was not being crowned as an Iberian Emperor, but King of Castile. In this context, it is highly significant that the 'Chronicle' mentions the presence of Frenchmen, Englishmen, and Gascons at the king's coronation, all of whom would have entered Castile via the pilgrimage road that led to Santiago, but is totally silent regarding Aragonese, Portuguese, or Navarran subjects.

[70] Alfonso's anointing with oil was not typical of the medieval Castilian traditions. See Ruiz (1984).

In the afternoon they went to the church of Las Huelgas in a strictly ordered procession in which the king rode at the back, flanked by Don Alfonso *de la Cerda* and the Archbishop of Santiago and preceded by his magnates, who were in turn preceded by the lesser nobility:

> And in the afternoon of that day they went all together to the king's lodgings in some houses that belonged to the Bishop of Burgos, which were in a palace that the king had ordered to be decked in many cloths of gold and silk for the occasion. And the king ordered that the assembled company should proceed in front of him, two by two, each one preceded by a squire carrying his sword, and that the king should be followed by his bodyguard; and that those who were carrying the arms of these new knights should also proceed in an orderly manner and in twos, like their lords.[71]

Once they reached the monastery, each was assigned an altar where he must keep vigil over his arms overnight. The next morning, the king went to the church and knighted all of the noblemen, presenting each one with a sword and giving them the slap. They were all wearing armour when they were knighted, just as the king had decreed. Once they had received their titles, they took off their armour and put on the robes of gold and silk that the king had given them.

Afterwards, they went to eat in the royal palace in Las Huelgas. The king said that the feast had given him great pleasure, and that the two things that had pleased him the most were seeing the procession of knights on their way to watch over their arms in the church, and seeing them all sit down to eat with him in his palace. The last of the formalities took place on the following day, when four magnates who had been knighted the day before by the king in turn knighted their own vassals.[72]

---

[71] *Et ese dia en la tarde fueron todos ayuntados de la posada del Rey en las casas del Obispo de Burgos, en un palacio quel Rey avia mandado enderazar de muchos paños de oro et de seda para esto. Et el Rey mandó que fuesen todos delante dél de dos en dos, et que fuese ante cada uno dellos un escudero que le levase el espada, et á las espaldas del Rey que fuesen las sus guardas; et los que levasen las armas destos caballeros noveles que fuesen en pos los guardas de dos en dos ordenadamente, según que fuesen sus señores.* 'Chronicle of Alfonso XI': ch. CI.

[72] Pedro Fernández de Castro knighted thirteen vassals; Juan Alfonso de Alburquerque knighted nine; Ruy Pérez Ponce ten; and Pedro Ponce five. The Viscount of Tartás, a French nobleman who was a vassal of Alfonso XI and was also knighted by the king on this occasion, also 'knighted four noblemen from his country' (*armó quatro caballeros de su tierra*).

Clearly Fernán Sánchez de Valladolid, the author of the 'Chronicle', did not neglect any detail that might serve to glorify his royal patron. Many of the details he describes, such as the king's donations to the nobility, the order of the procession, and the communal feast, serve the purpose of emphasizing the union between the king and his noble vassals that was forged through these ceremonies. The whole sequence was thus designed to emphasize the king's position and power with respect to the nobility. They all revolved around the central idea that the nobility of Castile, without exception, should be bound to the king through personal service. The royal intention was that this concept should extend to all ranks within the kingdom's nobility, so that all Castilian nobles, be they magnates or merely *caballeros*, should do homage to the king as their 'natural Lord'. Moreover, these bonds of 'natural' vassalage were expected to be stronger than those that connected different ranks within the nobility itself.

In this context, Alfonso XI's must necessarily have regarded the re-incorporation of his opponents, Don Juan Manuel and Don Juan Núñez, into royal service as a priority. Indeed, he attempted to effect a reconciliation with the two magnates only a few months after his coronation.[73] At that time, the king's situation had worsened significantly due to the combination of a new alliance between the Muslim defenders of Granada and their Marinid north African neighbours, and some important noble defections from Alfonso XI's camp. The most damaging of the latter concerned Juan Alfonso de Haro, Lord of Cameros, who became Don Juan Manuel's ally,[74] and the king's favourite, Juan Martínez de Leyva, who became Juan Núñez de Lara's majordomo.[75]

---

[73] 'Chronicle of Alfonso XI': ch. CVI.

[74] He was third in the chronicler's list of magnates who were knighted by the king in 1332 but, unlike those who came first, second, fourth, and fifth on that list, was not among those who in turn knighted their own vassals on the third day of proceedings. A description of his defection follows the chapter on the coronation in the 'Chronicle'. Ibid.: ch. CII.

[75] Ibid.: ch. CIV.

Don Juan Manuel and Don Juan Núñez de Lara's Terms

In February 1333, the Marinids laid siege to Gibraltar[76] and prompted Alfonso XI into organizing the great military campaign to which he summoned Don Juan Manuel and Don Juan Núñez 'and all the other magnates of his kingdom, and his vassals the knights' (*et á todos los otros Ricos-omes del su regno, et caballeros sus vasallos que fuesen con él*).[77] The two aristocrats received royal summons despite their enmity to Alfonso XI because of their status as royal vassals who administered royal rents ('they held from him his moneys in certain territories').[78] This situation occasioned a specific type of royal-noble negotiation which is particularly relevant to our analysis of this period.

The ambitious conditions stipulated by Don Juan Manuel for his re-entry into royal service centred on increasing the substantial income he already received from the crown. He proposed that Alfonso increase the 400,000 maravedís that he received as an annual stipend and the 180,000 maravedís that he earned 'in certain lands of the king' (*en tierra cierta del Rey*—which is to say from the proceeds of royal taxation) to 600,000 and 300,000 maravedís respectively. He also demanded that his own holdings in the kingdom of Murcia be converted into an hereditary duchy that was to be exempt from all royal taxation and enjoy independent minting rights, when no such principality had ever existed in Murcia.[79]

Through these demands, Don Juan Manuel was evidently seeking to assume prerogatives that were of an unreservedly royal nature. Some of his earlier actions testify to the fact that this was his sustained ambition. When hostilities broke out between himself and the king in 1328, for example, he claimed to lay siege to the royal town of Huete in retaliation for the king's siege of Escalona in order that the king might understand that he was his equal (*andaua a ygualdad con el rey*).[80] It seems logical to identify this attitude with an attempt on the magnate's part to prolong the power he had wielded during Alfonso XI's regency. The fact that Juan Núñez de Lara demanded

---

[76] Gibraltar fell after a siege of three months, after which Alfonso XI's military energies were directed at its recovery. However, this campaign was abandoned in the very same year when a truce was signed with the Muslims.

[77] 'Chronicle of Alfonso XI': ch. CVII.

[78] *Tenian dél sus dineros en tierra cierta.*

[79] Ibid.: ch. CVII.

[80] 'Great Chronicle of Alfonso XI': ch. LXXXV.

similar sums of money from the king indicates that he also considered himself to be above the rest of the Castilian nobility. He also
demanded the Lordship of Biscay and all of the lands and settlements that had belonged to Don Juan, the son of the '*Infante*' Don
Juan, and his wife Doña Isabel:

> And that which Don Juan Núñez demanded from the king was that
> he should give him the Lordship of Biscay, and then he demanded
> that he hand over all the other settlements and places that had belonged
> to the *Infante* Don Juan and his wife Doña María Díaz, and all the
> other villages that had belonged to Don Juan the son of the *Infante*
> Don Juan, and to his wife, Doña Isabel: which it was said he should
> inherit because of his marriage to Doña María, the daughter of Don
> Juan and grand-daughter of the *Infante* Don Juan.[81]

In the event, these demands were not accepted by Alfonso XI, and
the two noblemen therefore neither took part in the campaign of
Gibraltar, nor did they return to royal service. Instead, their hostility towards the king was confirmed.[82]

Tension Over the Lordship of Biscay (1334)

The Lordship of Biscay played a pivotal role in Juan Núñez de
Lara's opposition to the king. Although Alfonso XI considered the
territory his by right, he did not attempt to impose that right in
practice before 1344. In that year, he entered Biscay by force and
was recognized as Lord in part of the region.[83] Juan Núñez, who
was faced with the possible loss of Biscay and various towns which
had been placed under siege through this royal campaign, was moved

---

[81] *Et lo que Don Joan Nuñez le enviaba demandar al Rey era, que le dexase el Rey desem-
bargadamiente el señorio de Vizcaya, et que le mandase luego entregar todas las villas et logares
que fueran del Infante Don Joan et de Doña Maria Diaz su muger, et todas las otras villas
que fueron de Don Joan fijo del Infante Don Joan, et de Doña Isabel su muger: ca decian que
lo debia él heredar por el su casamiento de Doña Maria su fija de Don Joan, et nieta del Infante
Don Joan, que él avia por muger.*

[82] The 'Chronicle' blames the king's withdrawal from the campaign for Gibraltar's
recovery and his signing of a truce with the Muslims at the end of 1333 on the
danger represented by the hostile actions of Don Juan Manuel, Juan Núñez de
Lara, and Juan Alfonso de Cameros back in Castile. ('Chronicle of Alfonso XI':
ch. CXXV). Hostilities between the king and Juan Núñez broke out again in 1334.
(Ibid.: ch. CXXXII).

[83] Ibid.: ch. CXXXIII.

to seek terms with the king. Intermediaries negotiated a treaty whereby the king agreed to restore the Lordship of Biscay to his disaffected magnate and to abandon his use of the title 'Lord of Biscay' in royal charters (*et que se non llamase Señor de Vizcaya en las sus cartas*).[84] A short while later, either at the end of 1334 or the beginning of 1335, an agreement was also reached between the king and Don Juan Manuel. At the same time, the marriage between Don Juan Manuel's daughter Constance and Pedro, heir to the Portuguese crown, was arranged.[85] Despite their ephemeral nature, these reconciliations emphasize the fact that the offer of a royal pardon was kept permanently open for the king's two most powerful adversaries, whom Alfonso XI urgently desired to re-integrate into his service.

The campaign we have been discussing produced one incident that is especially interesting in relation to what it can tell us about the imposition of royal power during this period. It took place at Rojas, which lies in the region of Bureba, where there was a fortress that belonged to a powerful nobleman, Lope Díaz de Rojas. The stronghold had been entrusted to a local knight called Diego Gil de Humada and a group of lesser nobles. Given Rojas was Don Juan Manuel's vassal, it is not surprising that entry to the fortress was denied the king when he approached it during the campaign for Biscay.[86] Its garrison then proceeded to add insult to injury by throwing stones and shooting arrows at the king's standard. After the bitter fighting that ensued, Diego Gil surrendered, entreating the king to be merciful and to allow his garrison to leave their tower safely. The king consulted with his nobles about what to do with these men who, despite being his 'natural subjects' (*naturales*), had attacked the royal coat of arms and standard. The nobles concluded that these men had committed treason, and the king therefore ordered the decapitation of Diego Gil and seventeen men under his command. Their deaths served to highlight the severity with which the king regarded the hostility of his 'natural' subjects, even when their actions were born of loyalty to other noblemen to whom they were linked

---

[84] Ibid.: ch. CXXXVI. Alfonso XI was titled Lord of Biscay in royal charters dated between January 6th, 1327 (Don Juan was executed in October 1326) and July 16th, 1334. In a charter dated November 18th, 1334 he did not use the title. González Crespo (1985).

[85] Ibid.: ch. CXL. The wedding did not take place until 1340, and was preceded by a war between Castile and Portugal.

[86] Ibid.: ch. CXXXVII.

by bonds of vassalage. Indeed, these executions represented Alfonso
XI's most forceful demonstration of the superiority he had claimed
through his coronation ceremony for the loyalty owed to himself as
the 'natural' lord of his subjects. It is absolutely clear that the enforcement of this superior type of loyalty was a fundamental landmark
in Alfonso XI's consolidation of royal power. The king's effectiveness
in reaching this milestone is celebrated by his biographer in the passage that concludes this sorry episode:

> . . . and from then on lesser nobles did homage to magnates, knights,
> and other lesser nobles, and received castles from them, only on con-
> dition that, should the king approach the castle or tower, whoever was
> defending it should allow him entry.[87]

The Siege of Lerma (1336)

The conflict between the king and Don Juan Manuel and Juan
Núñez de Lara reached its zenith in 1336, when the formulation of
an alliance of various magnates against the king, seemingly prompted
by Alfonso IV of Portugal, lent a new sense of urgency to this old
struggle.[88] The alliance included Pedro Fernández de Castro, Juan
Alfonso de Alburquerque, and Alfonso Téllez de Haro. The first two
were closely linked to the King of Portugal, the second even belonged
to the Portuguese royal family. The third was the brother of Juan
Alfonso de Haro, the last Lord of Cameros, who had been executed
by the king in 1334.

The most significant episode in this war was the Siege of Lerma,
during which Alfonso XI's forces confronted Juan Núñez de Lara
and his followers. Lerma, which lies some 30 km. to the South of
Burgos, represented the Lara family's seigneurial power-centre, and
had already been used in 1272 as the focus for the noble rebellion
against Alfonso X. Alfonso XI's biographer unequivocally links the
severity of the threat posed by Juan Núñez and his followers to the
importance of the 'see' (*solar*) of Lara, which had great historical and
political relevance, constituted a focus for the activity of 'evildoers',

---

[87] . . . *et desde entonces los Fijos-Dalgo pusieron condicion en los omenajes que fecieron á los
Ricos-omes et á los Cabaleros, et otros Fijos-Dalgo por los castiellos que dellos tovieren, que si
el Rey llegase al castiello et fortaleza, que qualquiera que lo toviese por otro, que lo acogiese en él.*

[88] Ibid.: ch. CLII.

and had no less than 800 armed men at its disposal, not including the inhabitants of the settlement:

> . . . because of the see of Lara, where this Don Joan Núñez came from, and because he was accommodating with evildoers, he had with him a very large company of lesser nobles, who numbered more than 800 without those from the village.[89]

The siege lasted from June to December 1336, during which time Don Juan Núñez was supported by Don Juan Manuel from his base at Peñafiel, and the King of Portugal, whose vassal he had become. He could not, however, count on the support of any of the Castilian nobles who had deserted the king just a few months previously. Indeed, two of those magnates, Juan Alfonso de Alburquerque and Pedro Fernández de Castro, had not only been reconciled with the king by this time, but even took part in the Siege of Lerma with their own troops—Pedro Fernández came with 800 mounted knights from as far away as León and Galicia.[90]

As Juan Núñez's impending defeat became ever more obvious, Don Juan Manuel escaped the kingdom and entered into the service of Pedro IV of Aragón.[91] The outcome of the Siege of Lerma is described by the 'Chronicle' in a passage whose eloquent testimony as to the Castilian monarchy's perception of royal power in relation to the high nobility deserves detailed analysis.[92]

Juan Núñez de Lara sent word to the king begging his forgiveness, and entreating him not to put himself and those who were

---

[89] . . . *ca por el solar de Lara, donde este Don Joan Nuñez venia, et porque consentia mucho los malfechores, tenia consugo muy gran compaña de omes fijos-dalgo, que eran mas de ochocientos, sin los de la villa.* Ibid.: ch. CLVI.

[90] Ibid.: chs. CVXIV & CLXVI. Pedro Fernández de Castro was reconciled with the king soon after his rebellion. Indeed, the 'Chronicle' mentions his reconciliation almost immediately after describing his rebellion (chs. CLIV & CLII, respectively). The speed of his re-integration into the king's service leads us to doubt the existence of a 'noble league' set up in opposition to the king at this time (in fact no more members of this supposed 'league' apart from those cited above are listed in the sources).

[91] There was friction between the kings of Castile and Aragón at the time due to a dispute between Pedro IV of Aragón and Leonor, Alfonso XI's sister, and her children. Don Juan Manuel's choice of Aragón over Portugal for his exile is explained by the defeat suffered by Portuguese troops at Villanueva de Barcarrota during the war, and the Portuguese king's subsequent lifting of the siege of Badajoz.

[92] 'Chronicle of Alfonso XI': ch. CLXXII; A significant interpolation of the passage is included in the 'Great Chronicle of Alfonso XI'.

with him to death, but to accept their entry into royal service.[93]
Alfonso XI could have allowed the besieged to starve to death, or
ordered their execution, but he considered it a shame to lose such
skilled warriors and preferred to have them in his service rather than
to let them die or execute them (*pero dolióse de tan buena compaña como
allí estaba, et quisolos ante para su servicio, que non dexarlos morir nin matar-
los*). Faced with the choice between the direct or indirect elimination of his adversaries and their pardon, the king opted for the latter.
The logic that underpinned his decision constitutes the key to understanding his attitude towards powerful rebels: he considered that the
integration of additional forces into his service could only serve to
enhance and extend his own royal power.

The Royal Pardon and Royal Service

Juan Núñez's defeat and return to royal service had implications for
both sides of this old quarrel. The 'Chronicle' does not mention
Biscay in this context, as that territory had already been restored to
the rebellious magnate during his brief reconciliation with the king
in 1334. It does, however, state that the king re-instated Juan Núñez
as his standard-bearer, and therefore also as his closest confidant.[94]
Despite the great rift that had separated the two sides, therefore, the
king's pardon was absolute and unequivocal in the generosity of its
terms. Juan Núñez also received the tenancy of some royal settlements on re-entry into Alfonso XI's service, but the issue of Juan
Núñez's claims on the tenancies that had previously been held by
Don Juan was not raised. In return for such an extravagant show

---

[93] The 'Great Chronicle' has Leonor de Guzmán acting as intermediary on behalf
of Don Juan Núñez and his followers. She was a member of the Andalucian branch
of the Guzmán family, who belonged to the upper echelons of the Castilian nobility (see Moxó (1969) 121), and was the lover of Alfonso XI and the mother of
many of his children. One of these children was the future Enrique II, who founded
the Trastámara dynasty after waging war on Pedro I (1350–1369). The motives
behind this addition in the 'Great Chronicle' are therefore clear, as it was compiled during the reign of Enrique II: by glorifying the figure of Leonor de Guzmán,
he enhanced the legitimacy of the new Castilian dynasty she gave rise to.

[94] The office of Royal Standard Bearer under Alfonso XI was held by figures
such as the '*Infante*' Don Juan, and his son Don Juan. Juan Núñez de Lara held
the post from 1328 to 1332, and then again from his re-entry into royal service
until his death in 1350. González Crespo (1985).

of regal mercy, the repentant nobleman was ordered to demolish the fortifications that surrounded his strongholds at Lerma and Villafranca de Montes de Oca and his castle at Abia, and promise not to raise any new fortifications without the king's permission. He was further required to hand over the castles of the Lordship of Biscay as security on the settlement. The chronicler's version of the meeting that took place between Alfonso XI and Juan Núñez lays particular emphasis on the idea that the king's pardon might be exchanged for future loyalty and service:

On the fourth of December, Don Juan Núñez ordered that the king's standard be brought into his fortress (at Lerma), and that a group of royal knights and squires be admitted along with it. And on that same day he came out of the castle riding a horse that the king had sent him, and the king also rode out to meet him. When Juan Núñez saw the king, he dismounted and approached the king on foot together with all of his followers, and started to kiss his hands. Don Juan Núñez wanted to remain standing while he addressed the king, but the king would not allow it. And despite the great dispute that ensued between the two on this subject, Don Juan Núñez was obliged to re-mount his horse, and he told the king that he knew that he had done him much disservice despite receiving the king's mercy on many occasions, and that he considered himself to be greatly at fault, and begged for mercy's sake that the king should not consider his errors or his guilt, nor that of his followers, and that he should desire to pardon them, for they would henceforth be prepared to serve him always and to die in his service. And the king said that it pleased him to pardon them, as he was sure that they would forever recognize the mercy he showed them now by serving him and dying in his service when necessary. And Don Juan Núñez and his followers kissed his hands and accompanied the king to his lodgings.[95]

---

[95] *Et quatro dias andados del mes de Deciembre Don Joan Nuñez mandó coger en el su alcázar (de Lerma) el pendón del Rey, con pieza de caballeros et escuderos que entraron con él. Et en este dia él salió al real en un caballo que le envió el Rey, et el Rey salióle á acoger: et Don Joan Nuñez desque le vió descendió del caballo: et él, et todos los suyos venieron de pie fasta do estaba el Rey, et besaronle las manos. Et estando de pie Don Joan Nuñez quisiera fablar con el Rey; mas el Rey non ge lo consintió. Et como quiera que la porfia fue entre ellos muy grande sobre esto, ovo á sobir Don Joan Nuñez en el caballo, et dixo al Rey, que conoscia que aviendole fechas muchas mercedes, qué el le feciera muchos deservicios, porque tenia que estaba en gran culpa; et que le pedia por merced, que non quisiese parar mientes á los sus yerros, nin á la su culpa dél, et de los que estaban allí con él, et que los quisiese perdonar, et que siempre serian tenidos de le servir et morir en su servicio. Et el Rey dixo que que le placia de los perdonar, et que los perdonaba, porque era cierto que esta merced que les agora facia siempre ge la conoscerian serviendole et moriendo en su servicio quando menester fuese. Et Don Joan Nuñez et todos los suyos fueron al Rey, et besaronle las manos, et llegaron con el Rey fasta su posada.*

As we can see, Juan Núñez's surrender was couched in ritual, such as the king's refusal to allow the repentant nobleman to address him from the ground and insistence that Don Juan Núñez re-mount his horse. The magnate's plea for mercy included an admission that he had rewarded previous royal pardons with further disservice, but this royal pardon was granted on the basis that Don Juan Núñez and his followers should in future serve the king loyally until their deaths.

For his part, Don Juan Manuel was eventually re-admitted into Alfonso XI's service in 1338, following the mediation of his mother-in-law Juana de Lara in 1337,[96] and his own meeting with the king in Cuenca, at which he received a royal pardon.[97] The 'Chronicle' identifies this event with the end of the conflicts between the king and his most powerful magnates, and concludes that: 'from then on great peace and much calm were introduced to the land' (*et desde allí adelante fincó la tierra en mucha paz et en mucho asosiego*). According to his biographer, Alfonso XI had fulfilled his primary task of maintaining peace, justice, and tranquillity in his kingdom, and was therefore thenceforth able to dedicate his energies to the war against the Muslims, the other main objective of his royal policy.[98]

The Monarchy's Authority Over the Nobility

The definitive re-integration of the great aristocratic rebels into Alfonso XI's service in either 1337 or 1338—depending on one's preferred

---

In a charter dated December 5, Alfonso XI refers to the war that he held against the King of Portugal 'and also against Don Juan Núñez hitherto' (*e aviamos fasta aquí con don Iohan Nuñez*). See González Crespo (1985) 242.

[96] '. . . and a letter arrived from Doña Juana, the mother of Don Juan Núñez, in which she said to the king that Don Juan, the son of the '*Infante*' Don Manuel who was in Aragón, and who desired to place himself at the king's mercy, and to serve him well and faithfully if he (the king) should so wish . . .' (*. . . llegó y una carta de Doña Joana madre de Don Joan Nuñez, en que envió decir al Rey, que Don Joan, fijo del Infante Don Manuel que estaba en Aragón, et que queria venire á la su merced del Rey, et que le serviria bien et lealmente dó él quisiese*), 'Chronicle of Alfonso XI': ch. CLXXV. In this letter, the strongholds and settlements of Escalona and Cartagena, and one of the castles of Peñafiel were pledged as security for any treaty between Don Juan Manuel and the king.

[97] Ibid.: ch. CLXXXVIII.

[98] Fernán Sánchez de Valladolid described the king's motives at the 1329 Parliament of Madrid thus: 'and it was his desire to maintain the kingdoms in peace and justice and tranquillity, and he wanted to dedicate his body to the service of God

interpretation—marked a watershed in the king's reign, and gave way to a second phase of his majority which is overwhelmingly identified with his military victories over the Moors in the narrative sources. However, the strengthening of his power with respect to the nobility also continued apace during this second phase of his majority, and culminated in the issuing of the Ordinance of Alcalá in 1348. The result was the establishment of a state of equilibrium between the high nobility and the authority of the Crown. This was in no way achieved through the subjection of a debilitated nobility to the power of a strong and authoritarian monarchy. In fact it reflected the development of a strong monarchy that was increasingly centralized and enjoyed an extension in its control over the administration of justice and taxation across the totality of crown possessions. Its fortification and centralization was compatible with the interests of the great feudal lords of the kingdom (both lay and ecclesiastical), whose developing powers were based on the ever more efficient and relevant administration of royally-delegated jurisdictional lordship.[99] Although Alfonso XI's nobility was subjected to his will, it was well compensated it in the process.

When Alfonso XI attained his majority, there was no royal authority to speak of in the Kingdom of Castile. The 'Chronicle of Alfonso XI' therefore emphasizes the steps taken by the young monarch to recover and strengthen his power as king. In Fernán Sánchez's version of events, Alfonso's regents, despite ostensibly functioning as substitute kings, in fact lacked legitimacy and undermined their authority through their continual disputes. Although Don Juan Manuel continued to display quasi-royal attitudes and ambitions after Alfonso XI's assumption of the throne, both he and Don Juan Núñez de Lara were eventually obliged to re-enter the royal entourage in order to legitimize their personal seigneurial power. Both remained faithful to the king until their deaths, Don Juan Manuel's in 1348, and Don Juan Núñez de Lara's in 1350, when Pedro I already occupied the Castilian throne.[100]

---

making war on the Moors' (*et que su voluntad era de mantener los regnos en paz et en justicia, et en sosiego, et por el su cuerpo que queria trabajar en servicio de Dios faciendo Guerra á los Moros*) (Ibid.: ch. LXXX).

[99] On jurisdictional lordship, see Moxó (1964), Estepa (1989), and Álvarez Borge (1993) 147–97.

[100] The 'Chronicle' only relates two events after 1344: the siege of Gibraltar, and the death of the king during the Black Plague of 1350. Those who served at the

It is important to stress that the king's power was ultimately expressed through the noblemen in his service: the greater the status and authority of the magnates he could attract to his household (and of course the vassals they brought with them) the greater the power of that household itself. An understanding of this fact provides the key to understanding relations between Alfonso XI and Don Juan Manuel and Don Juan Núñez de Lara. These relations were expressed through a combination of two conceptual frameworks that, although seemingly contradictory, in practice proved to be perfectly compatible. The first represented the classic structure of feudalism, while the second rested on the idea that the king, as the 'natural lord' of all his subjects, enjoyed a direct bond with all of them that superseded any other bonds of vassalage they might be subject to.

The position of the nobility in relation to the king was demonstrated through highly ritualized events such as the knighting ceremony that accompanied Alfonso XI's coronation. Indeed, it is not at all surprising that Juan Núñez de Lara, who absented himself from the original ceremony, was duly knighted by the king after their reconciliation.[101] With that, the re-integration of such an important figure into the king's household received its finishing touches.

Conclusion

The reign of Alfonso XI in general, and the first phase of his majority in particular, clearly witnessed a significant fortification of royal authority. However, the process whereby this was achieved was a far cry from the traditional stereotype that envisages a clear-cut conflict between crown and nobility. Instead, the Castilian king strengthened his position through the development of a system of relationships with his nobility which rewarded the participation of both sides. This socio-political framework was supported by an ideo-

---

siege of Gibraltar included Juan Núñez de Lara and Fernando Manuel, the Lord of Villena and Don Juan Manuel's son.

[101] 'And because Don Juan Núñez had not received the honour of knighthood until that time, the king knighted him with great pomp and ceremony: and Don Juan Núñez knighted another ten nobles on the same day that he himself had received that honour.' (*Et porque Don Joan Nuñez non avia rescebido honra de caballería fasta an aquel tiempo, el Rey armólo caballero, et fízole mucha honra en sus caballerías: et Don Joan Nuñez armó a otros diez caballeros en aquel dia que él fue caballero.*) Ibid.: ch. CXCIV.

logical structure expressed through the highly ritualized use of symbolism. Alfonso XI was succeeded by his son, Pedro I, whose reign soon degenerated into a state of near civil war in which he himself was killed, to be succeeded by his stepbrother Enrique II. It is not our intention to launch into a discussion of Pedro I's reign in this conclusion, but the brief glance that we shall cast in that direction provides us with a final and valuable insight into the reign of his father.[102] Indeed, the way in which the strength of the crown's authority was damaged under Pedro I implicitly emphasizes its consolidation under Alfonso XI. The two monarchs' contrasting styles of government also reveal how that power had been built up, and how it was possible to fail in its maintenance. Pedro governed without regard to the consensus of other sectors within the kingdom, and was therefore utterly unable to guarantee the order of feudal society, which was dependant on that consensus. While both kings were invested with the same royal authority, they differed in that Alfonso XI was inclined to pardon his most powerful enemies in order to incorporate them into his household, while Pedro I developed a marked tendency to favour the physical elimination of his adversaries.

---

[102] For a discussion of Pedro I's reign, see my forthcoming article 'Rebelión y rey legítimo en las luchas entre Pedro I y Enrique II'.

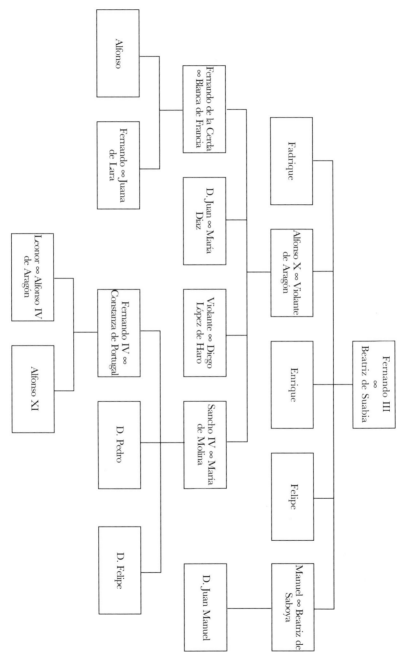

Fig. 9: The Castilian Royal Family

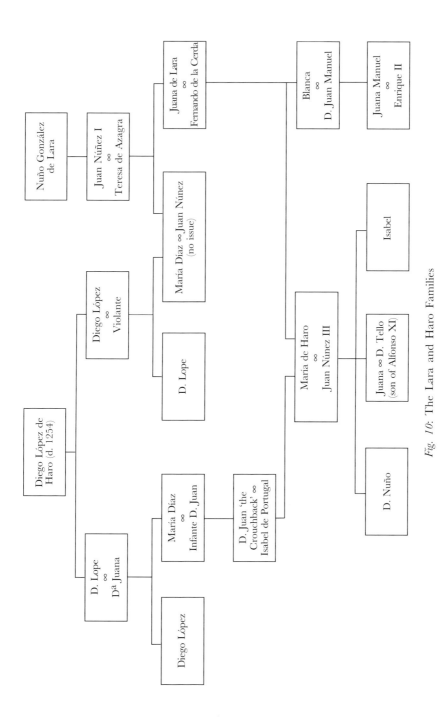

Fig. 10: The Lara and Haro Families

Appendix I

Asi como la estoria ha contado los fechos que pasaron en los regnos, debe contar el estado en que estaba la tierra en aquel tiempo. Et dice que avia muchas razones et muchas maneras en la tierra, porque las villas del Rey et todos los otros logares de su regno rescebian muy grand daño, et eran destroidos; ca todos los Ricos-omes, et los Caballeros vivian de robos et de tomas que facian en la tierra, et los tutores consentíangelo por los aver cada unos de ellos en su ayuda. Et quando algunos de los Ricos-omes et Caballeros se partian de la amistad de alguno de los tutores, aquel de quien se partian destroíale todos los logares et los vasallos que avia, diciendo que lo facia á voz de justicia por el mal que feciera en quanto con él estovo: lo qual nunca les estrañaban en quanto estaban en la su amistad. Otrosi todos los de las villas cada unos en sus logares eran partidos en vandos, tan bien los que avian tutores, como los que non avian tomado. Et en las villas que avian tutores, los que mas podian apremiaban á los otros, tanto porque avian á catar manera como saliesen de poder de aquel tutor, et tomasen otro, como porque fuesen desfechos e destroidos sus contrarios. Et algunas villas que non tomaron tutores, los que avian poder tomaban las rentas del Rey, et mantenian con ellas grandes gentes, et apremiaban los que poco podian, et echaban pechos desaforados. Et en algunas villas destas á tales levantábanse por esta razon algunas gentes de labradores á voz de comun, et mataron algunos de los que los apremiaban, et tomaron et destroyeron todos sus algos. Et en nenguna parte del regno non se facia justicia con derecho; et llegaron la tierra á tal estado, que non osaban andar los omes por los caminos sinon armados, et muchos en una compaña, porque se podiesen defender de los robadores. Et en los logares que non eran cercados non

Just as this history has recounted the events that took place in the kingdoms, so it should also describe the state of the land at that time. It is said that there were many different ways and reasons by which the king's towns and all the other parts of his kingdom were badly damaged, to the point of destruction; that all the magnates and knights lived on what they robbed or seized throughout the country, and that the regents consented to this because they depended on their support. And whenever one of those magnates or knights fell out with any of the regents, the regent whom they deserted would destroy all of his possessions and vassals, saying that he did so in the name of justice in retribution for the wrongs that had been done by him, but they never took anything from those who remained in the regent's favour. In all of the townships—those that had accepted a regent as well as those that had not—the people in every settlement were divided according to faction. In those that were controlled by a regent, those with most power oppressed the rest, not only because they desired to escape the control of one regent and adopt another, but also in order to destroy their rivals (within the town). In those towns that did not adopt a regent, powerful men took over the king's rents and used them to maintain large retinues while oppressing those who had little power, on whom they imposed unlawful taxes. In some of those towns the peasants rose up together for this reason and killed their oppressors and seized or destroyed all of their goods. Justice was not done in any part of

moraba nenguno; et en los logares que eran cercados manteníanse los más dellos de los robos et furtos que facian: et en esto tan bien avenian muchos de las villas, et de los que eran labradores, como los Fijos-dalgo: et tanto era el mal que se facia en la tierra, que aunque fallasen los omes muertos por los caminos, non lo avian por estraño. Nin otrosi avian por estraño los furtos, et robos, et daños, et males que se facian en las villas nin en los caminos. Et demas desto los tutores echaban muchos pechos desaforados, et servicios en la tierra de cada año: et por estas razones veno grand hermamiento en las villas del regno, et en muchos otros logares de los Ricos-omes et de los Caballeros. Et quando el Rey ovo á salir de la tutoria, falló el regno muy despoblado, et muchos logares yermos: ca con estas maneras muchas de las gentes del regno desamparaban heredades, et los logares en que vivian, et fueron á poblar á regnos de Aragón et de Portogal.'

the kingdom, and the land was in such a terrible state that men did not dare walk its roads without arms and plentiful company with which to defend themselves against robbers. Nobody lived in settlements that were not fortified, and those that were walled towns lived off the proceeds of robbery, peasants and noblemen alike. So bad was the state of the land that people were not even surprised to see dead men on the roads. Nor were they surprised by robbery, destruction, or any of the ill-deeds that were committed both in towns and on the roads. In addition, each year the regents imposed many unlawful taxes and duties on the land. Because of all this, many of the kingdom's towns and many other settlements belonging to magnates and knights fell into disuse. When the king emerged from the regency, he found the kingdom much depopulated, and many places barren, for many people, faced with such a bad situation, had abandoned their homes and possessions to go and live in Aragón or Portugal.

Appendix II

Et porque este Rey era muy noble en el su cuerpo, tovo por bien de rescebir la honra de la coronacion et otrosí honra de caballeria: ca avia voluntat de facer mucho por honrar la corona de sus regnos. Et otrosí desde luengos tiempos todos los ricos-omes et infanzones, et fijos-dalgo, et los de las villas todos se escusaban de rescebir caballería fasta en el su tiempo deste Rey Don Alfonso. Et por esto seyendo en la ciubdat de Burgos mandó tajar muchos paños de oro et de seda guarnidos con peñas armiñas, et con peñas veras: et otrosí

Because this king was very noble, he considered it right that he should receive the honours of coronation and knighthood, for he had a great desire to honour the crown of his kingdoms. It was also the case that all magnates, knights, lesser nobles, and townsmen until the time of this king Don Alfonso had declined to receive the knighthood. For this reason, when he was in the city of Burgos, the king ordered that many golden and silken cloths be woven,

mandó facer muchos pares de paños de
escarlata, et de otros paños de lana, los
mejores que pudieron ser avidos, con cen-
dales e con peñas: et mandó guarnescer
muchas espadas dellas con oro, et dellas
con plata las vaynas et las cintas: et mandó
enderezar todas las otras cosas que eran
menester para esto. Et desque lo tovo todo
guisado, envió decir á todos los ricos-omes,
et infanzones, et fijos-dalgo del su regno,
que se queria coronar et tomar honra de
caballería; et en aquel tiempo que queria
facer á los mas dellos caballeros, et darles
guisamiento de todo lo que oviesen menester
para sus caballerías: et que les mandaba
que viniesen todos a la ciubdat de Burgos
á dia cierto. Et todos venieron; mas Don
Joan fijo del Infante Don Manuel, nin Don
Joan Nuñez éstos non vinieron; mas todos
los otros ricos-omes, et infanzones, et omes
fijos-dalgo de las ciubdades et villas de los
regnos de Castiella et de León, et del regno
de Toledo, et de los regnos del Andalucía,
desque vieron las cartas quel Rey les envió,
guisaron sus cosas para se venir á la ciubdat de Burgos por el llamamiento que avian
del Rey. Et entretanto que ellos se ayunta-
ban para esto, el Rey salió de Burgos, et
fué por sus jornadas en romería á visitar
el cuerpo sancto del Apóstol Sanctiago. Et
ante que llegase á la ciubdat, fue de pie
desde un logar que dicen la Monjoya: et
entró asi de pie á la ciubdat, et en la
Iglesia de Sanctiago, et veló et toda esa
noche teniendo sus armas encima del altar.
Et en amaneciendo, el Arzobispo Don Joan
de Limia dixole una Misa, et bendixo las
armas. Et el Rey armóse de todas sus
armas, et de gambax, et de loriga, et de
quixotes, et de canilleras, et zapatos de
fierro: et ciñóse su espada, tomando él por
sí mesmo todas las armas del altar de
Sanctiago, que ge las non dió otro ninguno;
et la imagen de Sanctiago, que estaba encima
del altar, llegóse el Rey á ella, et fízole
que le diese la pescozada en el carriello.
Et desta guisa rescibió caballería este Rey

and that they be decorated with
ermine fur and mixed fur. He also
ordered that many cloths of scarlet,
and others of the finest wool, be
made, and that they should all have
fringes and furs. He also ordered that
the scabbards and belts of many
swords be decorated with gold and
with silver, and ordered all the other
necessary preparations. When these
had been made, he sent word to all
the magnates, knights, and lesser
nobles of his kingdom that he desired
to be crowned and knighted, and
also to knight most of them at the
same time, and to provide them with
all that they should need as knights,
so he summoned them to the city of
Burgos. They all came, apart from
Don Juan, the son of the 'Infante'
Don Manuel, and Don Juan Núñez,
who did not. All the other magnates,
knights, and the lesser nobles from
the towns and cities of the kingdoms
of Castile and León, Toledo, and the
kingdoms of Andalucia prepared
themselves for the journey to Burgos
to heed the king's summons as soon
as they read the letters that the king
had sent out. In the meantime, the
king left Burgos on a pilgrimage to
the holy remains of St. James the
Apostle. Before arriving in the city
(of Santiago) he dismounted and proceeded on foot from a place they call
Monjoya. He thus entered the city,
and then the church of St. James,
on foot. In the church he performed
a night-long vigil over his arms, which
lay on the altar. When dawn broke,
the Archbishop Don Juan de Limia
read mass and blessed the king's arms.
Then the king put on his armour:
his gambax, his coat, his thigh and
shin guards, and his shoes of iron,
and buckled his sword, taking all of
these items from the altar himself, in

Don Alfonso del Apóstol Sanctiago. Et porque él rescibió caballería desta guisa, estando armado, ordenó que todos los que oviesen á rescebir honra et caballería de allí adelante, que la rescibiesen estando armados de todas sus armas. Et el Rey partió de la ciudad de Sanctiago, et fue al Padron otrosí en romeria, porque en aquel logar aportó el cuerpo de Sanctiago. Et dende veno su camino para Burgos: et desque llegó á la ciubdat, falló que eran y venidos algunos de aquellos por quien avia enviado que rescibiesen dél caballería: et atendió fasta que todos fueron llegados . . .

Yuntados con el Rey en la ciubdat de Burgos los Perlados que vinieron á la honra de esta fiesta, et los Ricos-omes, et Infanzones, et omes Fijos dalgo de las ciubdades et villas, que avian á venir á la coronacion del Rey, et los que avian de rescibir caballeria dél, el Rey dexó la posada del Obispo de Burgos, en que él avia posado fasta allí, et fué posar en las sus casas que son en el compas de las Huelgas, que él avia mandado facer et enderezar para honra desta fiesta. Et el dia que se ovo de coronar vestió sus paños reales labrados de oro et de plata á señales de castiellos et de leones, en que avia adobo de mucho aljofar et muy grueso, et muchas piedras, rubíes, et zafies, et esmeraldas en los adobos. Et subió en un caballo de gran prescio, que él tenia para el su cuerpo, et la siella et el freno deste caballo, en que él cavalgó aquel dia, eran de grand valía: ca los arzones de esta siella eran cubiertos de oro et de plata en que avia muchas piedras; et las faldas et las cuerdas de la siella, et las cabezadas del freno eran de filo de oro et de plata, labrado tan sotilmente et tan bien, que ante de aquel tiempo nunca fué fecha en Castiella tan buena obra de siella, nin tan convenible para en aquel tiempo. Et desque el Rey fue encima del caballo, pusole una espuela Don Alfonso fijo del Infante Don Fernando, el cual algunas veces se llamó Rey de Castiella; et la otra espuela

order that he should not be given them by any other. He then approached the statue of St. James which stood above the altar and contrived that it should give him the slap on his cheek. In this way, Don Alfonso the king was knighted by St. James the Apostle. And because he had received the knighthood when fully armed, he decreed that all those who were to receive that honour in future should also do so bearing all their arms. The king then left the city of Santiago and continued in pilgrimage to Padrón, where the apostle's remains were discovered. After that, he made his way to Burgos. On arriving at the city, he saw that some of those he had summoned to be knighted had come, and waited until they should all be assembled. . . .

Once all the prelates, magnates, knights, and lesser nobles for the towns and villages who had come either to the coronation or to be knighted by the king had joined the king in the city of Burgos, he left the house of the Bishop of Burgos, where he had been lodging, and went to stay in his own houses which lay within the walls of Las Huelgas, which he had ordered to be prepared for the coming festivities. On the day of his coronation, he donned his royal vestments, which were decorated with emblems of castles and lions in silver and gold with thick ornaments full of pearls, and many precious stones, rubies, sapphires, and emeralds among them. He then mounted a fine horse whose saddle and bridle were very costly, as its stirrups were covered in gold and silver and embossed with precious stones. The saddle's cloths and girths and the bridle were all of gold and silver leaf that was so subtly and finely worked,

la puso Don Pero Fernandez de Castro. Et estos, et los otros Ricos-omes, et todos los otros que eran y fueron de pie derredor del caballo del Rey, fasta que el Rey entró dentro en la Iglesia de Sancta Maria la Real de las Huelgas cerca de Burgos. Et desque llegó á la Iglesia, los que avian puesto las espuelas, esos ge las quitaron. Et la Reyna Doña Maria su muger fué despues quel Rey un poco tiempo, et llevaba paños de grand prescio: et fueron con ella muchas buenas compañas de Perlados et de otras gentes. Et desque amos á dos fueron llegados á la Iglesia, tenian fechos dos asentamientos mucho altos cerca del altar, el uno á la mano derecha, el otro á la mano ezquierda: et subian á estos asentamientos por gradas: et estaban cubiertos de paños de paño de oro nobles. Et asentóse el Rey en el asentamiento de la mano derecha, et la Reyna á la mano ezquierda. Et eran allí el Arzobispo de Sanctiago Don Joan de Limia, et el Obispo de Burgos, et el Obispo de Palencia, et el Obispo de Calahorra, et el Obispo de Mondoñedo, et el Obispo de Jaen. Et aquel Arzobispo de Sanctiago, que llamaban don Joan de Limia de los de Batasella et de Pandecenteno, dixo la Misa, et oficiaronla las Monjas del monesterio. Et todos los Obispos estaban revestidos, et sus crozas en las manos, et sus mitras el las cabezas. Et estaban asentados en sus facistoles, los unos á la una parte del altar, et los otros á la otra. Et desque fue llegado el tiempo de ofrecer, el Rey et la Reyna venieron amos á dos de los estrados dó estaban, et fincaron los hinojos ante el altar, et ofrescieron: et el Arzobispo et los Obispos bendixieronlos con muchas oraciones et bendiciones. Et descosieron al Rey el pellote et la saya en el hombro derecho et ungió el Arzobispo al Rey en la espalda derecha con olio bendicho que el arzobispo tenia para esto. Et desque el Rey fué ungido, tornaron al altar: et el Arzobispo, et los Obispos bendixieron las coronas que estaban encima del altar. Et desque fueron

that such a fine saddle had never before been seen in the Kingdom of Castile, nor could another so fine have existed at that time. When the king mounted his horse, Don Alfonso, the son of the *Infante* Don Fernando, who on some occasions called himself King of Castile, fitted one of his spurs, and Don Pedro Fernández de Castro fitted the other. Then they, together with the other magnates and all the other people assembled there, followed the king's horse on foot until the king reached the church of Santa María la Real de las Huelgas, which lies close to Burgos. On reaching the church, the king's spurs were removed by the same two magnates who had fitted them. And the king's wife, Queen Doña María, who was dressed in fine clothes, followed closely behind him, in the good company of many prelates and other people. When both had arrived at the church, they were seated in two very tall thrones that had been placed on either side of the altar with steps leading up to them, which were covered in the finest gold cloth. The king sat in the right-hand throne, and the queen to his left. The Archbishop of Santiago Don Juan de Limia was there, as well as the Bishop of Burgos, the Bishop of Palencia, the Bishop of Calahorra, the Bishop of Mondoñedo, and the Bishop of Jaén. The Archbishop of Santiago, whom they call Don Luan de Limia, of the Batasella and Pandecenteno, read mass, aided by the nuns of the monastery. All of the bishops present were wearing their Episcopal robes and had their crosses in their hands and their miters on their heads, and were seated on either side of the altar. When the time came for the dedication, the king and queen knelt before the altar

bendicidas, el Azobispo redróse del altar, et fuése á sentar en un facistol; et los Obispos eso mesmo cada uno de fue á sentar en su logar. Et desque el altar fué desembargado dellos, el Rey subió al altar solo, et tomó la su corona, que era de oro con piedras de muy gran prescio, et pusola en la cabeza: et tomó la otra corona, et pusola á la Reyna, et tornó fincar los hinojos ante el altar, según que ante estaba: et estidieron asi fasta que fué alzado el cuerpo de Dios. Et el Rey et la Reyna fuése cada uno dellos á sentar en su logar: et estidieron asi las coronas puestas en las cabezas fasta la Misa acabada. Et dicha la Misa, el Rey salió de la Iglesia, et fue á su posada encima de su caballo, et todos los ricos omes de pie con él; et la Reyna fuése despues á poco tiempo. Et en este dia bofordaron, et lanzaron tablados, et jostaron muchas compañas. Et fecieron muchas alegrias por la fiesta de la coronacion.

Translated by Carolina Carl

and made their offer. The archbishop and the bishops then blessed them with many prayers, and unstitched the king's robes on his right shoulder. Then the archbishop anointed the king's right shoulder with holy oil that he had specifically for that purpose. When the king had been anointed, he returned to the altar, and the archbishop and the bishops blessed the crowns that had been placed there. Once they had done this, the archbishop and the bishops retreated from the altar and returned to their seats. Once they had left the altar, the king approached it alone and took up the crown, which was made of gold and precious stones, and placed it on his head. Then he took up the other crown and placed it on the queen's head. Then he knelt down in front of the altar as he had done before, and he and the queen remained thus until the Consecration. Then the king and queen returned to their seats where they remained with their crowns on their heads until mass was over. Then the king left the church and rode to his lodgings, accompanied by his magnates, who went on foot. The queen followed shortly afterwards. On that day there was much jousting, stages were erected and *bohordos* were thrown, and there was much rejoicing in celebration of the coronation.

Bibliography

Primary Sources

Catalán, D. (ed.) *Gran Crónica de Alfonso XI* (Madrid: 1977).
Cortes (1861) *Cortes de los antiguos reinos de León y de Castilla*, vol. I (Madrid: 1861).
García Martínez, A. (ed.) *Jofré de Loaysa, Crónica de los reyes de Castilla Fernando, Alfonso X, Sancho IV y Fernando IV (1248–1305)* (Murcia: 1982).
González Crespo, E., *Colección Documental de Alfonso XI. Diplomas reales conservados en el Archivo Histórico Nacional. Sección de Clero. Pergaminos* (Madrid: 1985).

González Díez, E., *Colección Diplomática del concejo de Burgos (884–1369)* (Burgos: 1984).
Martínez Diez, G. (ed.) *Libro Becerro de las Behetrías. Estudio y texto crítico*, 3 vols. (León: 1981).
Peña Pérez, F.J., *Documentación del Monasterio de Las Huelgas de Burgos (1329–1348)* (Burgos: 1990).
Rosell C. (ed.) *Crónica de Alfonso X*, ed., Biblioteca de Autores Españoles vol. LXVI (Madrid: 1953).
——— (ed.) *Crónica de Alfonso XI*, Biblioteca de Autores Españoles vol. LXVI (Madrid: 1953).
——— (ed.) *Crónica de Fernando IV*, Biblioteca de Autores Españoles vol. LXVI (Madrid: 1953).
——— (ed.) *Crónica de Sancho IV*, Biblioteca de Autores Españoles vol. LXVI (Madrid: 1953).

Secondary Sources

Álvarez Borge, I. (1993) *Monarquía feudal y organización territorial. Alfoces y merindades en Castilla (siglos X–XIV)* (Madrid: 1993).
Doubleday, S.R. (2001) *The Lara Family. Crown and Nobility in Medieval Spain*, Cambridge, Mass., 2001.
Escalona, J. (2002) "Los nobles contra su rey. Argumentos y motivaciones de la insubordinación nobiliaria de 1272–1273", in *Cahiers de Linguistique et de Civilisation Hispaniques Médiévales*, 25 (2002) 131–162.
Estepa Díez, C. (1989) "Formación y consolidación del feudalismo en Castilla y León", in *En torno al feudalismo hispánico* (Avila: 1989) 157–216.
———. (2003) *Las behetrías castellanas* (Valladolid: 2003).
Gómez Redondo, F. (1998–1999) *Historia de la prosa castellana medieval*, vols. I & II (Madrid 1998–1999).
González Minguez, C. (1976) *Fernando IV de Castilla (1295–1312). La guerra civil y el predominio de la nobleza* (Vitoria: 1976).
Herbers, K. (1999) *Política y veneración de los santos en la Península Ibérica. Desarrollo del Santiago político* (Poio: 1999).
Ladero Quesada, M.A. (1993) *Fiscalidad y poder real en Castilla (1252–1369)* (Madrid: 1993).
Linehan, P. (1987) "Ideología y liturgia en el reinado de Alfonso XI de Castilla", in *Génesis medieval del Estado Moderno. Castilla y Navarra (1250–1370)* (Valladolid: 1987) 229–243.
Moreta, S. (1978) *Malhechores-Feudales. Violencia, antagonismos y alianzas de clase en Castilla, siglos XIII–XIV* (Madrid: 1978).
Moxó, S. de (1964) "Los señoríos. En torno a una problemática para el estudio del régimen señorial", in *Hispania*, 94 (1964) 185–236.
———. (1969) "De la nobleza vieja a la nobleza nueva. La transformación nobiliaria castellana en la baja Edad Media", in *Cuadernos de Historia. Anexos de la revista Hispania*, 3 (1969) 1–210.
———. (1975) "La sociedad política castellana en la época de Alfonso XI", in *Cuadernos de Historia. Anexos de la revista Hispania*, 6 (1975) 187–326.
Ruiz, T.F. (1984) "Une royauté sans sacre: la monarchie castillane du Bas Moyen Age", in *Annales, Economies, Sociétés, Civilisations*, 39 (1984) 429–453.
Suárez Fernández, L. (1975) *Nobleza y Monarquía. Puntos de vista sobre la Historia política castellana del siglo XV*, 2nd ed. (Valladolid: 1975).

FAMILY MEMORIES:
INVENTING ALFONSO I OF ASTURIAS

JULIO ESCALONA
Instituto de Historia, CSIC

Most of what present day historians can say about the earlier phases in the development of the kingdom of Asturias derives from a handful of historical texts composed during the reign of Alfonso III (866–910): the two versions of the *Chronicle of Alfonso III* and the so-called *Prophetic Chronicle* and *Chronicle of Albelda*.[1] All earlier sources are very few and scattered, until these substantial works suddenly cast light on the period from the Arab invasion to the end of the ninth century. In the absence of comparable earlier evidence, historians have largely tended to take these chronicles at face value when approaching the otherwise intractable subject of the origins of the Asturian kingdom, despite their being almost two hundred years later than the 711 Arab invasion of Spain. This, though, is a great problem, since these texts are much less innocent than they look. For all their efforts in drawing a straight line connecting the Visigoths to the Asturians, the late ninth-century chronicles are—it is now recognised—the first coherent expression of a total u-turn in Asturian political identity, that took shape by the mid-ninth century, but did not make its way into historical writing until the 880s.

To analyse this thoroughly is well beyond my present concerns. I will instead, focus on one single element, namely, the way the ninth-century chronicles deal with the figure of King Alfonso I. Now, can this possibly be of any relevance? The answer, I think, must be affirmative, if only because the chroniclers at least seem to have attached great significance to him. Let us take, by way of introduction, a rough quantitative approach. Fig. 1 represents the number of words employed when describing the reigns of the Asturian eighth-century kings by two of the main texts to which I will refer later.

[1] *Chronicle of Alfonso III* and *Albeldensis*, ed. and Spanish trans. Gil (1985); *Prophetic Chronicle*, ed. Gómez-Moreno (1932) 622–627. An English translation of the *Rotensis* version of the *Chronicle of Alfonso III* in Wolf (1990) 159 ff.

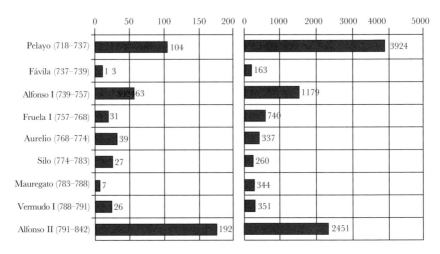

Fig. 1: Number of words used for describing the reigns of each of the eighth-century Asturian kings in the *Albeldensis* (left) and *Ovetensis* (right).

Rough as the method is, it is enough to reveal the basic facts: although the *Chronicle of Alfonso III* is much more detailed than the *Albeldensis*, the pattern is the same. Three kings clearly stand out. On the one hand, it is little wonder that Pelagius should have attracted so much attention, for he was considered the founder of the Asturian kingdom. On the other hand, Alfonso II's unusually long reign really needed a more detailed account, and also because important political developments took place then. But, what happened in between? Amidst six rather obscure figures, Alfonso I is the single outstanding landmark, an impression which is further reinforced by noticing that these three kings—Pelagius, Alfonso I and Alfonso II—are the only eighth-century rulers to whom any miracles are ascribed in the royal chronicle.

Clearly, for the late ninth-century chroniclers Alfonso I was a prominent character of their earlier history. My point, though, is that Alfonso I's function in the ninth-century chronicles was more than just that of a prestigious ancestor. Whichever his real deeds, he can be seen as a largely made-up, taylor-cut figure. This is certainly worth investigating. In the following pages, I shall first present the main primary sources and then briefly discuss the more relevant steps in the ninth-century development of an Asturian political identity moulded from visions of their eighth-century history. This will provide the background for analysing the role of Alfonso I in the late ninth-century chronicles, which I will discuss at length. In doing so, I hope that many of the intricacies in the chroniclers' discourse and procedures will become apparent.

I. Changing Political Identities in Early Medieval Asturias

The Source Material

The *Chronicle of Alfonso III* was written at the royal see of Oviedo with the main purpose of showing the Asturian kings as the natural heirs to the Visigoths. The work explicitly presents itself as a continuation to Isidore's Chronicle, running from Reccesvinth's accession (649) down to the death of Alfonso III's father, Ordoño I (866).[2] Two different versions of the chronicle are known: the so-called *Rotensis* and *Ovetensis* (or *Ad Sebastianum*). Against the long admitted view that *Ovetensis* was a later, more refined revision of *Rotensis*, it seems now well-established that they both derive from an earlier, lost archtype,[3] to which the *Rotensis* adheres to a great extent. The *Ovetensis*, on the other hand, carefully inspected and modified its source, by making a number of major changes and filtering the wording throughout the text. In doing so, its author or authors created a more strongly coherent text in support of what can be considered the late ninth-century Asturian 'official' truth about their history.

The so-called *Chronicle of Albelda* or *Albeldensis* was written in Oviedo around 882. It clearly belongs in the ideological milieu of Alfonso III's court, and it certainly dwells upon many issues which were also the focus of the royal chroniclers, but the *Albeldensis* is a peculiar work that mixes up, very un-systematically, different kinds of information: linguistic, geographic and historical, among others. Since it does not seem to have been 'monitored' as strictly as the royal chronicles were, there are many elements in it that differ from the more

---

[2] Gil (1985) 74 ff. convincingly argued that the original text could well run only to Ordoño I's early years, and have been continued later on, under Alfonso III.

[3] Prelog (1980) lxxx ff.; Gil (1985) 60 ff.

'official' texts. Therefore, it makes a good contrast to the *Rotensis* and *Ovetensis*.[4]

The Period of Carolingian Influence

Before proceeding with Alfonso I, it will be convenient to briefly review how a historical identity emerged in the early Asturian kingdom. The first decades in the history of the Asturian kingdom—the crucial phase in which the new polity came into being—are disappointingly obscure. Because most of our information derives from the ninth-century chronicles, modern visions of this period are often dominated by an image of great continuity with the Visigothic past, which is precisely what the chroniclers wanted to stress. Yet, for all that Alfonso III's courtiers would have us believe, such an inheritance would hardly satisfy the late eighth- and early ninth-century Asturian kings, who rather saw themselves as radically different from the Visigoths.

After the 711 Arab invasion of Spain, and the subsequent collapse of the Visigothic kingdom, there is hardly any contemporary trace of an Asturian monarchy before the 760s. If Pelagius's alleged victory at Covadonga ever occurred, it made no impact in sources of its time, such as the so-called *Mozarabic Chronicle of 754*; references to that episode in Arabic texts are themselves later than, and arguably dependent on the ninth-century Asturian chronicles. Instead, the impression is growing ever stronger that the first half of the eighth century was dominated by a multifocal pattern of power. Rather than a single expanding monarchy, several aristocratic kindreds competed for hegemony from a number of territorial centres which would eventually turn into royal sees inasmuch as the local ruler achieved kingship.[5] It was only from hindsight that such a complex magma was shaped into a single kingship and a linear—if somewhat erratic— dynastic succession.

We must wait until the reigns of kings Silo (774–783) and Mauregato (783–788), to find the first traces of substantial political developments

---

[4] See Gil, (1985) 81 ff.; Díaz y Díaz (1983) 228–232, conjectured it could have been written at San Salvador de Oviedo, as its library collection would account for the author's sources.

[5] Torrente (1997); Suárez (2002); Estepa (2002).

in the Asturian regions. It seems now ever clearer that this was not only due to internal transformations, but also to the increasing Carolingian influence. After the subjection of Septimania in 750, the Carolingians grew ever more active in northern Iberia in the second half of the eighth century, with even greater intensity in the period 770–800, following the establishing of the Ummayad dynasty, which put an end to serious internal struggles in al-Andalus.[6] The milestones of the uneven Carolingian progress on Iberia's eastern side are well known, from the ill-fated 778 expedition to Saragossa to the 801 conquest of Barcelona. Pamplona, the main stronghold in the Basque area, seems to have entered the Frankish sphere of influence, perhaps following a continued trend from the sixth century, as recent archaeological findings seem to indicate.[7] What happened further west, though, is not so well established. The available evidence suggests that the neighbouring polities, such as Álava, might have undergone some sort of informal domination, as satellites of the Franks. As for Asturias, the Carolingian factor has been long underestimated, partly because it was systematically denied by the ninth-century chroniclers. Yet, some independent bits of evidence from Frankish sources make rather clear that in the critical 790s King Alfonso II of Asturias was on more than good terms with Charlemagne, of whom he was no peer.[8] That was a crucial factor in the political growth of the Asturian monarchy under Alfonso II, as recent research reveals the great extent to which the Asturian contemporary political culture and ideology depended on Carolingian models.[9]

Although those Frankish references belong to the 790s, the whole process may well have started earlier. The evidence for this is much more difficult to deal with, but detailed analysis of the Asturian ecclesiastical sources has led A. Isla to suggest that as early as the reign of Mauregato (783–788), a growing proportion of the Asturian clergy were assuming the main themes of the Carolingian religious culture,

---

[6] By 776 Abd al-Rahman I had overcome rebels and resistants and was finally free to act against external powers; see Collins (1989), 170 ff.; Collins (1998), 66.

[7] Larrañaga (1993); Azkárate (1993).

[8] The *Royal Frankish Annals*, s. a. 798, and the *Annales Laurissenses*, s. a. 798 mention Asturian legates and presents being sent to Charlemagne. Einhard is somewhat more explicit in stating that Alfonso II had great pleasure in being called Charlemagne's own man (*Vita Karoli*, II, 16), ed. Holder-Egger (1907), English trans. Thorpe (1969). See Fernández Conde (1997).

[9] Fernández Conde (1997); Isla (1998a).

even if building on a basically Hispanic, post-Visigothic background.[10] Texts such as Beatus of Liébana's famous *Commentary on the Apocalipse*[11] or the Hymn—also often attributed to Beatus—*O Dei Verbum* in praise of St. James, but comprising an acrostic dedication to King Mauregato, are pieces in this renewed ideology that ultimately led the adoptionism controversy to burst out.[12] Adoptionism was instrumental in delivering a lethal blow to what little was left of a Spanish Church that had thitherto struggled to keep some notion of cross-Iberian unity and authority, even if under Muslim rule. I cannot deal here at length with the whole subject;[13] for my present interests, it will suffice to consider its wider implications in two different contexts: on the one hand, the global background of rising Carolingian hegemony within the Latin Christendom; on the other hand, the small scale process going on in Asturias, under the cover of the more general, large scale developments.

On the larger scale, the Carolingians took deep involvement in the adoptionism controversy. Hence the participation of relevant intellectual figures such as Alcuin or Benedict of Aniane, the sending of envoys such as Jonah of Orleans, the formal condemnation in Regensburg (792)[14] and in the council of Frankfurt (794),[15] as well as the prosecution of those adoptionists who where at the easiest reach, such as Felix of Urgel. The ultimate defeat of the Visigothic traditional doctrines defended by none other than Archbishop Elipandus of Toledo, the customary head of the Spanish Church, fuelled the claims of those who had decided to take a non-conformist stand towards their Muslim rulers, and who can be seen as the remote forerunners of the mid ninth-century martyrs of Córdoba.[16] More importantly, it broke into pieces whatever legitimacy the Spanish ecclesiastical establishment still enjoyed as leaders of all Iberian Christians and cast it on the Carolingian side, thus helping to enhance Charlemagne's desired image as the champion of Christendom.

---

[10] Isla (1998a).

[11] Ed. Romero-Pose (1985).

[12] Ed. Díaz y Díaz (1976) 239–242.

[13] On adoptionism, see d'Abadal (1949); Barbero and Vigil (1978) 311 ff.; Cavadini (1993); Isla (1998a) and Fernández Conde (2000) 101 ff.

[14] *Royal Frankish Annals*, Revised version, ed. Kurze (1895), s. a. 792.

[15] *Royal Frankish Annals*, ed. Kurze (1895), s. a. 794. See also *Concilia Francofordiensis Epistola synodica ad praesules Hispaniae Missa*, PL, 101, cols. 1331–1346, whose redaction is normally attributed to Alcuin.

[16] Wolf (1988) and Fernández Conde (2000) 105 ff.

On the smaller scale, the role played by some Asturian clerics in the overthrow of adoptionism is too great to go unnoticed.[17] In fact, the early date at which Beatus himself declared the debate to have gained notoriety not only in Spain, but in Francia too,[18] makes me wonder whether it was not this party's strategy to bring the whole affair as high as possible, in order to secure Frankish intervention. In doing so, they would arguably put themselves in a stronger position to force the Asturian élites—both secular and ecclesiastical—to allign with them.

A thorough analysis of those ecclesiastical texts points to major political changes taking place in Asturias in the 780s. This is consistent with the more explicit indications that can be gathered in the 790s from the earliest pieces of historiography. Again, the developments in the Carolingian milieu seem to have been determinant in shaping the Asturian ideology and practices.

In the context of the late eighth-century Carolingian build-up in northern Iberia, it is hardly surprising that a new, strongly consistent picture of the ending of Visigothic Spain was created. Texts such as the so-called *Chronologia regum gothorum*, *Moissac Chronicle* and *Aniane Chronicle*, probably composed in Caroligian-driven Septimania,[19] share a number of distinctive features; for instance, they blame the loss of Spain to the Arabs on King Witiza's sins and vices; they too misdate the Arab invasion to 714; more importantly, in their account the Visigothic period is rendered as definitely over, and a new period opens up under Frankish rule. Thus, the *Chronologia regum Gothorum* declares:

> Roderic reigned for 3 years. In this time, in the aera 752 [AD 714] the Sarracens were summoned because of the country's troubles, and they occupied the Spains, and seized the kingdom of the Goths, which hitherto they stubbornly possess in part. And they struggle with the Christians night and day, and they daily fight until God's predestination orders that they be cruelly expelled.

---

[17] Beatus was the first to attack Elipandus's teaching, according to the most renowned adoptionist polemist, bishop Felix of Urgell, in the few preserved fragments of a letter sent by him to Alcuin. See Levison (1946) 316–317.

[18] Beatus, *Adversus Elipandus*, ed. Löfstedt (1984), p. 9.

[19] PL, 83, cols. 1115–1118. For details on the manuscripts, see Martin (1997), p. 17, n. 18. For the date of composition, see Barbero and Vigil (1978) 240–244.

The kings of the Goths perished. In total they add up to 304 years
(. . .)
In the aera (x) reigned Charles, king of the Franks and patricius of
Rome.[20]

Here the Visigothic kingdom is, as it were, officially pronounced
dead (*Reges Gothorum defecerunt*) and, following a short computistic summary, the next entry implies that the fight against the Arabs is to
be led thereafter by the Franks.[21] The *Moissac Chronicle* is likewise
clear in stating that, after their defeat to the Arabs, the reign of the
Goths concluded: "The Goths were defeated by the Sarracens, and
thus ended the reign of the Goths in Spain and in less than two
years the Sarracens subjected almost all of Spain".[22] This interpretation fits nicely the aforesaid ecclesiastical developments and the
general mechanisms of political legitimation within the Carolingian
context:[23] power changed hands at God's will, and Charlemagne was
the present-day God-favoured leader, his unending victories being
the most obvious of all proofs. Both his commanding the elimination of all heretic thought from the Church and his leading the fight
against the Barbarians—Arabs included—were pivotal in this scheme.
And Spain was a field where both notions converged naturally: the
translation of power from the Goths to the Franks had already been
effected;[24] the condemnation of adoptionism came to legitimate a
similar shift in the ecclesiastical sphere.

Turning again to the Asturians, their close participation in the
780s Carolingian ecclesiastical policies—most evidently revealed by

---

[20] PL, 83, col. 1118: *Rudericus regnavit ann. III. Istius tempore era 752 farmalio terrae
Saraceni evocati Hispanias occupaverunt, regnumque Gothorum ceperunt; quo adhuc usque ex parte
pertinaciter possident; et cum Christianis die noctuque bella ineunt, et quotidie confligunt dum
praedestinatio usque divina de hinc eos expelli crudeliter jubeat. Reges Gothorum defecerunt. Sunt
sub uno ann. 314 (. . .) In era (x) regnavit Carolus Francorum rex et patricius Romae . . .* The
aera date for Charlemagne's accession is illegible in one manuscript, while the other
wrongly gives that of Charles Martel: 727; see Martin (1997), p. 19, n. 19.

[21] Martin (1997), p. 19.

[22] *Chronicon Moissacensis*, ed. Pertz (1826) 290: *Gothi debellati sunt a Sarracenis, sique
regnum Gothorum in Spania finitur et infra duos annos Sarraceni pene totam Spaniam subiciunt.*

[23] See the chapter by P. Fouracre in this same volume.

[24] In a similar fashion to that of the Septimanian texts, in northeast Spain the
traditional Visigothic *Laterculi*—running down to the 710s—were added notices from
the late eighth-century onwards, leaving most of the eighth century blank. See, by
way of example, the piece contained in ms. Escorial Z.II.2, fol. 6, ed. García Moreno
(1975), in which the notice of the extinction of the Visigoths is followed by
Charlemagne and Louis the Pious.

their joint strategy about adoptionism—also had a historiographical counterpart. By the very end of the eighth-century or the earlier years of the ninth, a brief historical piece was written in Asturias. Although lost in its original form, traces of it are to be found in a number of later manuscripts.[25] The part thereof which can be seen as derived from the original core, is a twofold text, comprising a brief summary of the reign of the Visigoths and a list of the Asturian kings down to Alfonso II's accession in 791. Although some northeastern features are here missing, such as the 714 date, or Witiza's liability for the defeat to the Arabs, the main argument remains the same: that the Visigoths were gone for good, and the Asturian kings belonged to a new period, even allowing for a five-year Arab interregnum that has the virtue of making even more obvious the breach between both. Thus, we read in the so-called *Annales Portucalenses Veteres* (long redaction = *Chronica Gothorum*):

> In the aera 349 [AD 311] the Goths left their country.
> In the aera 366 [AD 328] they entered Spain, and reigned there for 383 years.
> From their country they travelled to Spain for 17 years
> In the aera 749 [AD 711] the Goths were expelled from Spain.
> In the aera 750 [AD 712] the Sarracens obtained Spain.
> Before the lord Pelagius reigned, they reigned over Spain for 5 years. . . .[26]

Again, the idea that the Goths were dead and gone stands out, but in this case, the natural succession falls on the Asturians, but the gap between him and the Visigoths is not to be missed. Fortunately, another independent piece of evidence comes in support of this conclusion. A charter issued by King Alfonso II to the church of San Salvador de Oviedo in 812 included, by way of preamble, a prayer packed with historical references:

> Because you [God] are King of Kings, reigning over all things, heavenly and earthly, and granting worldly justice, in order to provide the peoples of the earth with worldly justice, you distribute kings, laws and judgements. By whose [God's] gift, among the kingdoms of several

---

[25] See Huete (1994) 12 ff.

[26] *Era CCC XL IX egressi sunt Gotti de terra sua. Era CCC LX VI ingressi sunt Hispaniam et regnaverunt ibi annis CCC LXXX III. De terra autem sua pervenerunt ad Hispaniam per XVII annos. Era septingesima quadragesima nona expulsi sunt de regno Hispanie. Era 749 Sarraceni Hispaniam adepti sunt. Antequam Dominus Pelagius regnaret Sarraceni regnaverunt in Hispania annis V.* (David (1947) 291–292).

other peoples, the Goth's victory shone nonetheless. But because You
[God] were offended by their prepotent proudness, in the era 749
[AD 711], the kingdom's glory, together with King Roderic, was
destroyed. He well deserved to suffer the Arab's sword. Of which
plague, by your right hand—Christ—was your servant Pelagius saved,
who, having been elevated to princely power, fought victoriously, hit
the enemy, and defended the Christian and Asturian people with sub-
lime victory.[27]

Links with the discourse of Carolingian legitimacy become here even
more apparent. There is a whole enunciation of the notion of *translatio imperii*. It is God who, in order to secure justice, distributes
power among kings. And then, victory—almost a metaphor for
God's judgement—is the proof of divine support for rulers, for victory indeed was the Goths' single claim to reign (*clara refulgit Gothorum
victoria*). Moreover, it was because of the latter's proudness that victory was denied to their king. Since the Arabs could not possibly be
presented as God-favoured, their victory is rather described as a
plague. Then—ignoring a substantial chronological gap—it was Pelagius, touched by God with victory, who rose to rulership.

The 812 charter is of great help in establishing the kind of political identity that had become official in the entourage of Alfonso II.
One which was strongly dependent on wider Carolingian developments, and was based upon rejection of, and distinction from the
Visigoths. The notion of an independent Asturian Church, with no
links to the southern post-Visigothic Christians, had its counterpart
in a God-devised rupture with Visigothic royalty and history.

The Ninth-Century Visigothic Revival

Thin as the evidence is, the aforementioned pieces of historical writing suffice to indicate which kind of vision of the Asturian origins

---

[27] Floriano (1949), doc. 24: "*Et quia tu es rex regum regens celestia simulque terrestria,
diligens in temporaliter iustitiam temporaliter vero terrarum populis pro optinenda iustitia distribuis
reges, leges atque iudicia. Cuius dono inter diversarum gentium regna non minus in terminis Spaniae
clara refulgit Gotorum victoria; sed quia te offendit eorum prepotens iactantia, in era dcc xl viiii
simul cum rege Roderico regni amisit gloria. Merito etenim arabicum sustinuit gladium. Ex qua
peste tua dexteera Christe famulum tuum eruisti Pelagium; qui in principis sublimatus potentia
victorialiter dimicans hostes percusit et christianorum asturumque gentem victor sublimando defendit.
Cuius ex filia filius clariori regni apice Froila extitit decoratus. Ab illo etenim in hoc loco qui
nuncupatur Ovetao fundata nitet aeclesia tuo omine sacra tuoque sacro nomine dedicata . . .*" On
this charter, see Fernández Conde (1971) 119–120 and Floriano (1975).

had been established in the royal entourage by the early ninth-century. Thereafter we do not have any trace of comparable writings until Alfonso III's historiographical cycle set out in the 880s. As I said before, the components of this group are so outstanding that they have tended to obscure all previous developments. This is even more important because the historical perspective they reveal is in striking contradiction with many features of what was 'official' history in the time of Alfonso II. Of paramount importance is that by the 880s the former rejection of a Visigothic identity had been replaced by the notion that the Asturian kings were the biological, dynastic and historical continuators of the Goths.

The rising neo-Gothic theory seems to respond to a combination of historical changes taking place from the mid-ninth century across the Iberian peninsula. During the later years of Alfonso II's long reign (791–842), Carolingian influence in northwestern Spain declined seriously, while the northeast remained under Frankish rule, albeit with ever increasing autonomy. Cultural contacts and exchange surely lived on, but the events taking place in the northwest ceased to be so dependent on the wider frame of Frankish policies. Nevertheless, the 'Carolingian factor' had already done its job. Having grown under its cover, Asturias was in the 840s a fairly developed polity by Iberian northern standards. It was even a valid reference for those opposing the Cordoban emirs, as witnessed by the repeated military expeditions against Asturias—increasingly seen as a major disturbing factor in the northern frontier—and the remarkable fact that in the later years of Alfonso II a notorious Muslim rebel could seek and obtain exile in Asturias.[28] All this seems to be pointing towards a rising new scene.

Ramiro I's short reign—under which a different branch of the Asturian royal families replaced that of Alfonso II—surely was of paramount importance, as C. Estepa has rightly pointed out.[29] A number of factors seem to indicate that some sort of consensus was then reached that made it possible to further the kingdom's political development, both in internal complexity and territorial expansion. This may well also relate to a greater degree of formalization

---

[28] Ibn Hayyan, *Muqtabis* II-1 ed. Makki and Corriente (2001) 298 ff.
[29] Estepa (1992).

of the relationship between kings and magnates, probably by means
of considering as royal officers those aristocrats who ruled *de facto*
over specific territories. Magnates begin by then to be termed *comites*—
a denomination implying both a high social status and a formal
denial of royalty—which is certainly relevant for a king who had to
face major aristocratic opposition in his early years.[30] It is utterly
plausible that a consensus of this kind among the Asturian ruling
elites—king and magnates—underlay the great territorial expansion
operated in the second half of the ninth-century, under kings Ordoño
I and Alfonso III. In a rather short time, the Asturian territory grew
to over twice its size, for the greater benefit of king, magnates and
clerics, who found in the newly gained plateau lands an inmense
source of revenue and power. This is the essential context within
which the royal chronicles must be considered.

At the same time, important changes were taking place in the south.
By the mid-ninth century conversions to Islam had increased to an
extent that the status of non-Arab population within the society of
al-Andalus became a relevant issue, nonetheless because among those
of Iberian provenance, whether Christians or Muslims, there was a
clear notion of descending from the Visigoths.[31] The second half of
the ninth century saw no shortage of tensions between the central
power and relevant groups, such as the Mozarab (Christian) communities—most famously Toledo—or the Berber clans, but also an
increasing number of indigenous converts trying to find a position
of their own within an Arab dominated society. A few from their
ranks (the so-called *Muwalladun*) eventually rebelled against their rulers,
gathered armed retinues and managed to hold control over small
territories where they were hard to fight.[32] This situation was not
definitively overcome until the reign of Abd al-Rahman III (912–961),
and more so by way of negotiation than military defeat.

It has been pointed out that Visigothic descent—frequently referring to king Witiza—seems to have become a sort of sign of iden-

---

[30] All the more interesting, considering that J. Fernández Conde may very well
be right in suggesting that young Ramiro I could have been a rebel against Alfonso
II, and even have ruled in parallel a part of the territory; Fernández Conde (1997).
[31] García Moreno (1999).
[32] Acién (1994); cf. Manzano (1991b); Fierro (1998); Wasserstein (2002). In this
brief summary I am much indebted to comments from Maribel Fierro.

tity for many non-Arab Andalusians, whether Christian or Muslim. That such an ancestry was invented in most cases makes no less a case for the relevance of the notion itself. Yet, for all the echoes of 'Visigothic feudalism' that can be spotted in the *muwalladun* rebels,[33] the greatest issue remained that of which position the converts should enjoy within the Andalusian society. In this debate, the reconsideration of the Arab invasion became a very sensitive issue, central to a change in the political identity that gradually set in, and remained so until the end of the Caliphate in the eleventh century. The modalities of subjection (whether pact or conquest), the status of the conquered lands and peoples, the position of converted Visigothic aristocrats, all became important matters in defining a legitimate vision of the complexities of ninth-century al-Andalus.[34] This would ultimately lead to a new historical consciousness that needed to account for more than the ethnic divisions among the invaders, and integrate the natives, the main representative of which would be the famous historian Ahmad al-Razi.

It is likewise relevant that those southern Christians who kept to their faith—the so-called Mozarabs—found themselves in a profoundly contradictory situation. On the one hand, the dominant Arabic language and culture permeated all social groups, even those who resisted conversion. Most Spanish Christians adapted themselves into the Islamic political framework, particularly in urban contexts, and most of all in Córdoba; some even made it into the administrative system, holding offices and taking part in the normal functioning of government.[35] Since the early days of Arab rule, the general trend for accomodation and even cooperation with the new rulers had greatly disappointed a minority who rather favoured resistence. Traces of this attitude were already present in the 780s, when adoptionism first burst out.[36] By the mid-ninth century a combination of factors led to another tide of active contestation from non-conformist Christians, the so-called 'martyrs of Córdoba'.[37]

In this turbulent context there was plenty of room for messianic and apocalyptic thought. From the mid-ninth century, several

---

[33] Acién (1994).
[34] Manzano (1997).
[35] See Wolf (1988) for examples and discussion.
[36] Cavadini (1993).
[37] Wolf (1988).

mutually influenced lines of such discourses spread among Christians, Jews and Muslims.[38] Premonitions of the advent of a new era were easily turned into predictions of an immediate ending for either the Ummayad or Arab rule in Spain at all.[39] As early as the 850s Alvarus of Córdoba already pointed out the existence of prophecies about the imminent end of Muslim rule. The 852 Toledo rebellion may have been fuelled by another wave of prophetic expectancy. This all, albeit collateral, may well have contributed to shaping the milieu from which the Cordoban martyrs emerged.[40] In the following years, prophecies and omens went on being adapted and reinterpreted as the consecutive dates for doom proved unreliable. By the 870s at least, one such branch of apocalyptic thought seems to have developed among those Andalusian groups who based their political identity upon the Visigothic inheritance, arguing that Muslim rule would be destroyed by nothing other than a Visigothic revival. A similar notion may well have been attached to the most relevant of all *muwallad* rebels, Umar ibn Hafsun, but this must be seen as another aspect of a growing trend among non-Arab groups in al-Andalus.

The most explicit formulation of these prophetic expectations was set up in al-Andalus sometime in the 870s. By adapting an oriental prophetic and computistic tradition to the Iberian context, the idea was construed that Arab rule over the Goths was to end when the latter should recover, and dated this to 884. The Goths were identified with the biblical people of Gog, and the Arabs with that of Magog. This was a means of reinforcing the notion of Visigothic revival by wrapping it up in Bible-based legitimacy. This construct, and other similar ones, surely became widespread in late ninth-century al-Andalus, but we know little about the effects they had. By contrast, a lot more is known about the impact in the north.[41]

By those years, the Asturian kingdom had grown big enough to be a major cause of concern for the emirs of al-Andalus, and it acted as a hegemonic power in the north, frequently intervening in the troubled Riojan frontier. It was only natural that non-conformist

---

[38] Gil (1978–1979); Fierro (1998).
[39] On the notorious case of ninth-century author Ibn Habib, see Aguadé (1991) 88–100.
[40] Gil (1978–1979).
[41] Torrente (2002).

southern Christians should turn to the Asturian kings. During Ordoño I and Alfonso III's reigns there was frequent communication between the Asturians and the southern Mozarabs, mainly those of rebellion-prone Toledo. Mozarab clerics seeking exile in Asturias were pivotal in the cultural development of Alfonso III's epoch. They were also major political collaborators, who helped adapt Asturias to many of the conceptions they brought from the south, most remarkably that of a Visigothic revival.

To turn into champions of Gothicism a king and dynasty whose own historiographical tradition largely consisted of rejecting such an inheritance was surely no little task. The finest formulations of the neo-Gothic ideal were developed at the royal see of Oviedo in the early years of Alfonso III. It was surely a Mozarab cleric working at Oviedo who combined the Gog and Magog prophecy—computations adapted—with several passages about the end of the Gothic kingdom, the survival of the Gothic people in al-Andalus, and some fairly accurate lists of Arab governors; then he added an interpretation of the whole piece predicting for AD 883 the immediate ending of Arab rule, which deed was to be effected by no one other than Alfonso III. This was the so-called *Prophetic Chronicle*, which greatly influenced the *Albeldensis*.[42]

Neo-Gothicism further developed into the main ideology presiding over the new Asturian historiographical cycle. Its main purpose was to present the Asturian kings as the legitimate cross-Iberian Christian leaders, ideologically entitled to recover the realm and glory that the Visigoths once held. Yet, its formulation was far from simple, and its ramifications were manifold. In the early years of Alfonso III, there were a number of recent political developments needing legitimation, of which Iberian hegemony was only the most general one. In order to accomplish this, the Chronicles of Alfonso III's cycle deployed a powerful, multifaced discourse in which the Asturian past was revisited, the pre-existent undesired historiographical elements deactivated, and new explanations provided to fill the legitimation voids of the time. Clearly, not all historical works were similarly consistent in doing so. The *Albeldensis Chronicle* is dominated by this hegemonic thought, but contains many elements from earlier or contemporary conflicting discourses. This is to some extent—but only

---

[42] Ed. Gómez Moreno (1932) 622–628.

to some extent—corrected by the *Rotensis,* but this work maintains much of the past, nonetheless because in many passages it is evidently contesting other opposing arguments. The *Ovetensis,* instead is a much more consistent, carefully filtered text, that even puts aside some of the issues that were of relevance for the *Rotensis* and goes ahead in establishing direct links, not with the last, declining Visigothic kings, but with the most glorious of that breed: Leovigild, Reccared, Reccesvinth and Chindasvinth.[43]

I have started by noting that the figure of Alfonso I stands out in the Chronicles of Alfonso III's time, among several other eighth-century rulers. The argument I will follow in the next pages is that the great importance attached to him was because he was the node crossed by a number of discourse lines which were essential in gaining legitimacy for issues of the utmost relevance in the 880s. He was indispensable for the internal consistency of a whole vision of the past, even if that meant that the inherited 'historical truth' should be greatly distorted.

II. Alfonso I in the Neo-Gothic Discourse

The *Albeldensis, Rotensis* and *Ovetensis* chronicles roughly agree about Alfonso I, although with differences of detail from one to the other.

> Adefonsus, Pelagius's son-in-law reigned for 18 years.
>   This was the son of Petrus, duke of Cantabria, and, as he came into Asturias, he took Pelagius's daughter, Bermesinda, by Pelagius's command.
>   And, on achieving power, he led many fights with God's help. He also invaded the towns of León and Astorga, long posessed by the enemy. The so-called Gothic Plains he depopulated to the river Duero and he extended the Christians' realm.
>   He was loved by God and men. He died due to natural causes.[44]

---

[43] Isla (1998b).
[44] Alb. XV, 3: *"Adefonsus Pelagi gener rg. an XVIII°. Iste Petri Cantabrie ducis filius fuit. Et dum Asturias uenit, Bermisindam Pelagi filiam Pelagio precipiente accepit. Et dum regnum accepit, prelia satis cum Dei iubamine gessit. Hurbes quoque Legionem atque Asturicam ab inimicis possessas uictor inuasit. Campos quem dicunt Goticos usque ad flumen Dorium eremauit et Xpianorum regnum extendit. Deo atque hominibus amauilis extitit. Morte propria decessit".*

This brief portrait in the *Albeldensis* regnal list—eloquently entitled *Ordo Gothorum Ovetensium Regum* ("List of the Gothic kings of Oviedo") will suffice to present the main facts about Alfonso I: a) his victorious military campaigns; b) his family liasons; c) his moral qualities.

Alfonso I's Military Activity

This is the aspect of Alfonso I's reign to which the three chronicles conceded the greatest length of text. In all three, the king's activity was twofold: he fought victoriously against his enemies; he extended the limits of his realm. Both aspects must be considered separately.

About Alfonso I's campaigns, the *Albeldensis Chronicle* simply stated: ". . . on achieving power, he led many fights with God's help. He also invaded the towns of León and Astorga, long possessed by the enemy. The so-called Gothic Plains he depopulated to the river Duero and he extended the Christians' realm".[45] The *Chronicle of Alfonso III* was much more explicit. Both recensions basically coincided, but the *Ovetensis* emphasized more the king's exemplary qualities. For clarity, I put in italics the main differences between them. The geographic implications of the *Albeldensis* and the *Chronicle of Alfonso III* are represented in Fig. 4.

> *Rotensis*:
> *After his [Favila's] death, Alfonso was elected king by the whole people, and he held the kingdom's sceptre with God's grace. The enemy's boldness was always oppressed by him.* Together with his brother Fruela, *he frequently moved his troops* and seized by combat many cities, that is: Lugo, Tuy, Oporto, Anegia, the metropolitan Braga, Viseu, Chaves, Ledesma, Salamanca, Numancia (now called Zamora), Ávila, Astorga, León, Simancas, Saldaña, Amaya, Segovia, Osma, Sepúlveda, Arganza, Clunia, Mave, Oca, Miranda, Revenga, *Carbonaria, Abeica,* Cenicero y Alesanco, and all the castles with their vills and hamlets. Killing all the Arabs *by the sword,* he took the Christians with him to the homeland.[46]

---

[45] Alb. XV, 3. See previous note.

[46] Rot. 13: "*Quo (Favila) mortuo ab uniuerso populo Adefonsus eligitur in regno, qui cum gratia diuina regni suscepit sceptra. Inimicorum ab eo semper fuit audatia conprensa. Qui cum fratre Froilane sepius exercitu mobens multas ciuitates bellando cepit, id est, Lucum, Tudem, Portugalem, Anegiam, Bracaram metropolitanam, Uiseo, Flauias, Letesma, Salamantica, Numantia qui nunc uocitatur Zamora, Abela, Astorica, Legionem, Septemmanca, Saldania, Amaia, Secobia, Oxoma, Septempuplica, Arganza, Clunia, Mabe, Auca, Miranda, Reuendeca, Carbonarica, Abeica, Cinasaria et Alesanzo seu castris cum uillis et uiculis suis, omnes quoque Arabes gladio interficiens, Xpianos autem secum ad patriam ducens*".

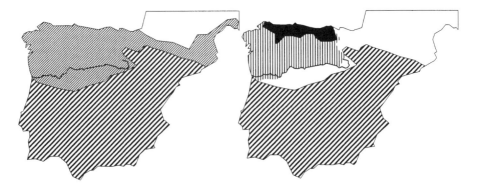

Fig. 2: The evolution of the Iberian northwest from the mid-eighth to the late ninth
century. The end of Arab control of the Duero plateau (left) and the Asturian
expansion under Ordoño I and Alfonso III (right).

Ovetensis:
The following facts prove how great his grace, virtue and authority were: together
with his brother Fruela, *he led many fights against the Sarracenes* and he
seized many cities *once oppressed by them*, that is, Lugo, Tuy, Oporto,
the metropolitan Braga, Viseu, Chaves, *Agata*, Ledesma, Salamanca,
Zamora, Ávila, Segovia, Astorga, León, Saldaña, Mave, Amaya,
Simancas, Oca, Veleia of Álava, Miranda, Revenga, *Carbonaria, Abeica,*
Brunes, Cenicero, Alesanco, Osma, Clunia, Arganza, Sepúlveda, and
all the castles with their vills and hamlets. Killing all the Arabs *who
occupied those cities*, he took the Christians with him to the homeland.[47]

These two must be among the most ever quoted passages in early
medieval Spanish historiography, since they lay at the foundations
of the whole 'Reconquista' ideology, as Barbero and Vigil eloquently
exposed.[48] Fig. 2 shows the situation in Iberia between the mid-
eighth and the late ninth century. After the first two decades of

---

[47] Ovet. 13: *"Post Faffilani interitum Adefonsus successit in regnum, uir magne uirtutis filius
Petri ducis, ex semine Leuuegildi et Reccaredi regum progenitus; tempore Egicani et Uittizani
princeps militie fuit. Qui cum gratia diuina regni suscepit sceptra. Arabum sepe ab eo fuit auda-
cia conpressa. Iste quante gratie uel uirtutis atque auctoritatis fuerit, subsequentia acta declarant:
simul cumfratre suo Froilane multa aduersus Sarracenos prelia gessit atque plurimas ciuitates ab
eis olim oppressas cepit, id est, Lucum, Tudem, Portucalem, Bracaram metropolitanam, Uiseo,
Flauias, Agata, Letesma, Salamantica, Zamora, Abela, Secobia, Astorica, Legione, Saldania,
Mabe, Amaia, Septemanca, Auca, Uelegia Alabense, Miranda, Reuendeca, Carbonaria, Abeica,
Brunes, Cinisaria, Alesanco, Oxoma, Clunia, Argantia, Septempublica et cunctis castris cum uillis et uiculis suis; omnes quoque Arabes occupatores supra dictarum ciuitatum interficiens Xpianos
secum ad patriam duxit".*
[48] Barbero and Vigil (1978) 216 ff.

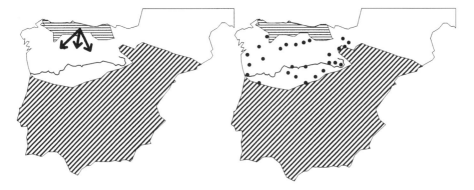

Fig. 3: Alfonso I's attacks on the plainlands, according to the *Albeldensis* (left) and the *Chronicle of Alfonso III* (right).

Muslim rule in Iberia, the territory controlled by them was significantly reduced. Between 730 and 750 Arab rule in southern Gaul was eliminated. More importantly, between 740 and 760, al-Andalus underwent great political unstability: a revolt of the numerous Berber troops, continued party struggles, and finally, the take over by the Ummayad refugee Abd al-Rahman I, who succesfully managed to claim power, but could not establish his rule firmly until the late 760s. Amidst those troubles, Arab rule in the Iberian northwestern quadrant faded out. The Central Mountains became the limit of their effective control (Fig. 2, left).[49] This reduction of Arab-ruled territory can hardly be credited to the Asturian kingdom, which was by then a tiny northern spot, plausibly ruled by a number of aristocratic lords, and which had no expectations of replacing the Arabs in ruling the plateau. Recent research suggests that in the Duero basin the population remained largely on its own, and, for over a century, it lacked any superior political articulation, until it was annexated by the Asturians in the second half of the ninth-century (Fig. 2, right).[50] I have indicated above that this was only possible after major political developments took place, some during Alfonso II's reign, others after the convergence of royal and aristocratic interests established under Ramiro I.

---

[49] For details, see Manzano (1991a).
[50] Escalona (1991); Escalona (2000a) Escalona (2002). For a detailed discussion in English, see Castellanos and Martín Viso (forthcoming).

But the story the chronicles told was quite a different one. They
had it that in the mid-eighth century, as al-Andalus agitated in troubles, Alfonso I seized the opportunity to lead a series of systematic
attacks on the plainlands, ultimately causing the complete depopulation of all cities in the Duero basin. The Arabs got killed, the
Christians were taken to the north. However, this view was not
shared by the three texts in the same terms. Whilst the *Albeldensis*
(Fig. 3, left) highlighted Alfonso I's campaigns, it only credited him
with having attacked León and Astorga, and having depopulated the
so-called Gothic Fields (modern Tierra de Campos, a region in
province Palencia). Instead, it was the royal chronicles that gave the
most exaggerated picture, one in which Alfonso I was supposed to
have raided an astounding number of cities and depopulated a really
huge territory (Fig. 3, right).

This was complemented by Alfonso I's other notable achievement.
The *Albeldensis* merely said that he 'extended his territory', but the
royal chronicles—the passage reads almost the same in both recensions—provided a list of the territories he allegedly controlled and
those which he did not. The Iberian northwestern quadrant was thus
divided in two parts, the lands under Asturian rule and those which
they emptied of all dwellers:

> By that time Primorias, Liébana, Trasmiera, Sopuerta, Carranza, Bardu-
> lias—now called Castile—and the coastal side of Galicia were popu-
> lated; *yet it is said that* Álava, Biscay, Alaón and Orduña were always
> possessed by their inhabitants, as Pamplona and Berrueza were.[51]

Unlikely as it seems that Alfonso I should have ever enjoyed the
means—or even had the aim—of depopulating a territory several
times the size of his kingdom, what we must now look at is the role
this notion played in the chronicle discourse.[52] The account of the

---

[51] Ovet, 14. *"Eo tempore populatur Asturias, Primorias, Liueria, Transmera, Subporta,
Carrantia, Bardulies qui nunc uocitatur Castella et pars maritimam Gallecie; Alaba namque,
Bizcai, Aizone et Urdunia a suis reperitur semper esse possessas, sicut Pampilonia [Degius est]
atque Berroza. Hic uir magnus fuit. Deo et ominibus amauilis extitit. Baselicas multas fecit.
Uixit in regno a. XVIII. Morte propria discessit".* On the meaning of *populare*, see Menéndez
Pidal (1960), Barbero and Vigil (1978) 225–228 and, more recently, Escalona (forth-
coming).

[52] For criticism of the role that the 'depopulation and repopulation of the Duero
basin' played in Spanish historiography see Barbero and Vigil (1978) 219 ff. I have
written—and spoken—at length trying to show that, by taking this construct at face
value, traditional historians have not only blurred this part of the Iberian early

reign of Alfonso III's father, Ordoño I (850–866), provides the first clue. The *Albeldensis* merely stated that "he extended the Christians' realm",[53] but the *Rotensis* elaborated more: ". . . the long abandoned cities, that is, León, Astorga, as well as Tuy and Amaya, he surrounded with walls and gave them high gates, and he populated them in part with his own people, in part with those coming from Spain".[54] Then, the *Ovetensis* made an even more explicit connection with Alfonso I: "he repopulated the long abandoned cities, of which Alfonso the Elder [Alfonso I] had expelled the Arabs, that is, Tuy, León, Astorga, and Amaya Patricia".[55] The combination of raiding the plateau and absorbing the northern lands is an image which probably has little to do with the eighth century, but is most relevant for the late ninth. Most cities allegedly attacked by Alfonso I one hundred years earlier where actually in the ninth century either seized by Ordoño I, or by his son, or were at least the latter's target for future expansion. The chroniclers' discourse becomes clear: Alfonso divided the northwest in two different spheres of status: a) the lands continually inhabited and ruled by the Asturians; b) the depopulated lands, which were open to be seized and exploited by the Asturian kings and elites. Then, the ninth-century Asturian kings began to recover and repopulate them with either their northern subjects or with Mozarabs from al-Andalus. In the kingdom of the new Goths there was only room for these two identities, while a complete denial was effected of the local population and of any power structures they might have developed during the hundred years in which they lacked higher rulers. This was obviously a very sensitive issue of Alfonso III's reign, that urgently needed to be legitimated.

Now, some elements in those accounts of Alfonso I's glorious deeds make me think they could have been largely made up to fill the needs of the chroniclers' discourse. Moreover, the way they were

---

medieval history, but also put a great obstacle to the development of modern settlement archaeology in the region, which is only recently emerging: Escalona (1991); Escalona (2000a); Escalona (2000b), Escalona (2001), Escalona (2002), Azkárate and Quirós (2001).

[53] Alb. XV, 11.

[54] Rot. 25: *Civitates ab antiquitus desertas, is est, Legionem, Astoricam, Tudem et Amagiam Patriciam muris circumdedit, portas in altitudinem posuit, populo partim ex suis, partim ex Spania advenientibus implevit.*

[55] Ovet. 25. *Civitates desertas ex quibus Adefonsus maior Caldeos ieecerat iste repopulavit, id est, Tudem, Astoricam, Legionem et Amagiam Patriciam.*

presented even seems to indicate that the version in the royal chronicles could be set up as an answer to alternative conceptions of the
Asturian past. To do so meant to develop a very complex line of
discourse, and the chroniclers—fortunately for us—could not keep
some inconsistencies from slipping into their narration.

First, the passage about the lands Alfonso I effectively ruled may
raise our suspicions at one specific point. The text declares that
Castile, among other territories, was absorbed into the Asturian kingdom in the time of Alfonso I, but Álava belonged to a group of
Basque territories which were said to have always been 'in the possession of their inhabitants'. This picture may well describe the historical situation of the region sometime between the mid-eighth and
mid-ninth centuries, but was clearly at odds with the rest of the
chronicle's discourse about Álava.

After having declared that in Alfonso I's time Álava was possessed
by its own inhabitants, we first hear about it in the *Rotensis* account
of the reign of Fruela I (Alfonso I's son).[56] He is said to have defeated
the "Basque rebels" (*Uascones rebellantes superavit*), a shocking word to
describe those who possessed their own country. Then we are told
that Fruela took with him a woman called Munina for his wife.
Munina bore Fruela a son, the future Alfonso II. The *Ovetensis* insists
in presenting Munina as a slave, by saying that "he defeated *and
tamed* the Basque rebels; from the Basque booty he ordered a certain adolescent called Munia to be reserved for him, and he bound
her in royal wedlock . . .".[57] Putting this all together, the episode
rather looks as standard hostage-taking; Munina surely 'belonged to
the local aristocracy, so marrying her would lay the foundations of
some—if volatile—alliance, which enabled young Alfonso II to seek
refuge by his mother's relatives when expelled from the throne by
Mauregato.[58] Thereafter we only find occasional mentions of *Vasconia*
and the *Vascones*, until the reign of Ordoño I, in which we are told
that the king had to defeat a coalition of Basques and Sarracens,
and he subjected the first to his rule.[59] Alfonso III himself had to
do likewise in 868.[60] García de Cortázar has rightly pointed out that

---

[56] Rot., 16.
[57] Ovet., 16.
[58] Rot.-Ovet., 19. Dacosta (1992); García de Cortázar (1997) 115–116.
[59] Rot., 25.
[60] García de Cortázar (1997) 116.

the ninth-century Asturian policies about Álava and Pamplona could account for the inclusion of several places from that area in the list of cities attacked by Alfonso I, according to the *Ovetensis*.[61] Again, we find that the eighth-century events point directly to contemporary sensitive political issues. The next image we see of Álava is one of full subjection and cooperation. The regional leader was a *comes*— implying a royal officer, whichever perception the locals could have of him—who acted at the kingdom's eastern frontier under the king's command. It is pretty evident that in the ninth century Álava represented a certain source of trouble, while Castile did not.[62] This is why very little is said about how Castile was incorporated into the kingdom, while the Alaban reputation as rebels was often repeated. A secondary line of discourse can be identified in the royal chronicle purporting to demonstrate that Álava was subjected—albeit reluctantly—to Asturias.

But *Rot.-Ovet.*, 14 tells it differently: Castile belonged to Asturias while Álava did not. The fact that the wording is so similar in both recensions makes me think that the chronicles could be dealing here with a piece of earlier material. The picture, though, does not seem to fit the mid-eighth century either. As I noted above, in this period all but the westernmost of the Iberian northern polities seem to have been in the sphere of the Carolingians. The earliest Arab attacks on them are better explained as a reaction to this growth of Frankish influence. In this context, it is most plausible that Castile and Álava were small independent territories heavily under Carolingian influence. A trace of this situation may have survived in the Arabic sources, in which Álava and Castile are referred to—often together—as separate, distinct units (*Alaba wal Qila*), whereas the Asturian kingdom is normally termed *Jilliqiyya* (Galicia). The fact that a separate name was in use for Álava and Castile may be reminiscent of their being formerly independent units. It is therefore, plausible that the paragraph in question originally referred to another king, but was intentionally ascribed to Alfonso I.

So it seems that the chroniclers' strategy in this passage was to move a great milestone in the kingdom's political development from its chronological context to that of Alfonso I. This argument would

---

[61] García de Cortázar (1997) 117.
[62] García de Cortázar (1997) 115–116.

surely be too feeble, should it be an isolated example. But a comparable procedure seems to have been followed by the chroniclers regarding Alfonso I's greatest deed, namely, the devastation of the Duero basin. This, though, must be pursued through the Arab historians.[63]

The greatest landmark in pre-eleventh century history writing in al-Andalus was the work of Ahmad al-Razi (888–955), the first to have articulated a coherent historiographical programme in which the Iberian Islamic history was considered as another element within the wider frame of Iberian history, rather than as a particular episode in the general history of Islam. Al-Razi is remarkable for having made use of a wide range of sources, including many of Christian provenance, either from Latin or from Arabic translations. His work, though, has not survived but in small fragments, as quotations within other authors' writings, most importantly the enormous *Muqtabis*, by eleventh-century historian Ibn Hayyan. Al-Razi's work was often quoted by Ibn Hayyan, but the first volume of the *Muqtabis*, dealing with most of the eighth century, is lost as well. Yet, a number of fragments from al-Razi also made their way—directly or indirectly via Ibn Hayyan—into the writings of Ibn al-Athir (1160–1234). Sánchez-Albornoz suggested that the Asturian stories in Mosul-based Ibn al-Athir derived from al-Razi, and reflected the latter's use of a lost Asturian chronicle from Alfonso II's reign.[64] Although Sánchez-Albornoz's conception of such a lost text can hardly be sustained now,[65] it seems obvious that al-Razi had access to historical material of Christian provenance whose discourse cannot be conciliated with that of the *Chronicle of Alfonso III*. The passage of al-Razi I am

[63] In dealing with the Arabic sources, I am particularly indebted to Maribel Fierro, Laura Bariani, Luis Molina and Eduardo Manzano. See a recent overview of Arabic texts dealing with the Asturian kingdom in Maíllo Salgado (2002).

[64] Sánchez-Albornoz rightly noted that, although al-Razi was contemporary to the Oviedo chroniclers, and thus, could have known the *Chronicle of Alfonso III*, his quotations do not belong to these texts, but to different material. Sánchez-Albornoz (1967a); Sánchez-Albornoz (1967b); Sánchez Albornoz (1967c).

[65] Sánchez-Albornoz was more than keen to take at face value the connections between the Asturian kings and the Visigoths, as the royal chronicles had them. Although he detected the Carolingian elements in Alfonso II's reign, he saw it as a period of Visigothic restoration. But this picture is the result of the chroniclers efforts to translate Alfonso II's achievements into a 'neo-Gothic language'. Sánchez-Albornoz described his hypothetical lost chronicle as full of Carolingian and neo-Gothic elements, which actually meant to mix up two different periods in Asturian historiography.

now concerned with is to be found in two versions: the one transmitted by Ibn al-Athir:

> In the same year 140 (757), after an eighteen year reign, Alfonso, king of Galicia died; he was succeeded by his son Fruela, who superseded his father in boldness, administrative abilites and firmness. He held absolute power and a glorious reign: he expelled the Muslims from the frontier strongholds and seized the city of Lugo, Portugal, Salamanca, Zamora, Ávila and Segovia.[66]

and the one transmited by Ibn Khaldun (1332–1406), then followed by al-Qalqashandi (1355–1418) and al-Maqqari (1590–1631):

> Alfonso, son of Peter, died in 142 (759–760) after an eighteen-year reign. His son Fruela succeeded him. This reigned for eleven years, in which his power increased, for that was the precise time in which Abd al-Rahman [I] was busy founding his new dynasty. Fruela was able to recover Lugo, Oporto, Zamora, Salamanca, Segovia and Castile, which had been occupied by the Muslims during the Conquest.[67]

The connections between these passages[68] and the aforecited fragments from Alb., XV, 3 and Rot.-Ovet., 15 are so evident that they must be related. Yet, it is outstanding that in the Arabic texts (as indeed in the *Albeldensis*), the Asturian attacks were much more limited, so totally unable to provoke the wholesale depopulation of the plateau; most importantly, in the Arabic versions it was not Alfonso I, but Fruela I who was said to have launched such attacks! Now, if al-Razi had access to historical material on early Asturias and if his ascribing those campaigns to Alfonso I is at odds with the Asturian chronicles, then this may add more to the suspicion that the royal chroniclers were not only shaping up their history at their greatest convenience, but also deactivating other existing, conflicting versions thereof.

---

[66] Ibn al-Athir, *Tarij fi-Kamil*, French partial translation in Fagnan (1898), p. 104.

[67] Ibn Khaldun, *Kitab al-Ibar*, French translation in Dozy, R. (1965), I, pp. 92–116. Al-Qalqashandi, *Subh al-Asa fi Kitab al-Insa*, Spanish translation Seco de Lucena (1975) 81. The text in al-Qalqashandi depends closely on Ibn Khaldun. It is typical of this branch to include the reference to Abd al-Rahman's early troubles and to add Castile (sic) to the list of seized cities. This seems to represent a later tradition, while Ibn al-Athir, whose quotations of Ibn Hayyan are very reliable, seems to be as close as we can get nowadays to the original passage by al-Razi. I am indebted to Luis Molina for his comments on this respect.

[68] The date for Alfonso's death is wrong in Ibn Khaldun, but sound in Ibn al-Athir. We cannot ascertain whether the sentence in Ibn Khaldun's version connecting the whole episode to Abd al-Rahman I's troubled early years belonged to al-Razi or was interpolated, but at any rate it fits much better Fruela's reign than Alfonso's.

To this we can add the evidence from the *Historia Silense*. This is
a twelfth-century Latin chronicle written—probably in León—in
praise of King Alfonso VI (1065–1109).[69] The author put together
a number of different, not necessarily compatible materials. As he
was trying to narrate history following a genealogical programme,
his discourse did not always keep to chronological order. Among
these inconsistencies, we find two relevant passages. In *HS*, 26, the
author followed the *Oventesis* in presenting the king as descended
from Reccared, but he did not fail to note Alfonso's marriage to
Pelagius's daughter. He also abbreviated and modified the passage
in the royal chronicles about the attacks to the plainlands:

> Together with his brother Fruela, he often led the army in campaign
> and took by force many of the cities oppressed by the barbarians; he
> removed from the churches the abominable name of Muhammad and
> had them consecrated in the name of Christ.[70]

Then, in *HS*, 32, when dealing with count Fruela, Alfonso's brother,
he turned back to speak of the same period, and assigned to him a
passage in which all the familiar ingredients are present:

> Fruela indeed, the generous offspring of Peter, the duke of the *Cantabri*,
> together with Alfonso the Catholic, his brother and his fellow in reign-
> ing, he often took arms against the barbarians, and from the coastal
> fringes of Asturias and Galicia down to the river Duero he seized and
> removed from their hands every existing city and castle and, after elim-
> inating the Ysmaelites by the sword, he returned them to the Christians'
> rightful possession.[71]

In this, as in so many other elements, the *Historia Silense*, by exag-
gerating the discourse line of the *Chronicle of Alfonso III*, seems to be
exposing the latter's methods. The crucial point here is the confusion between the two Fruelas: respectively, Alfonso I's brother and
his son King Fruela I. It seems plausible that the campaigns into
the plains were originally attributed to Fruela I. Then the royal

---

[69] See Gil (1995) 10–14.

[70] HS, 26: . . . *exercitum cum Froyla fratre sepius movens, quamplurimas a barbaris oppressas civitates bellando cepit, ecclesias nefando Mahometis nomine remoto in nomine Christi conse-
crari fecit . . .*

[71] HS, 32: *Igitur Froyla, Petri Cantabrorum patricii ducis generosa proles, cum germano fratre
Adefonso catholico atque regni socio arma contra barbaros crebro arripiens, ab ipsis maritimis
finbriis Asturie et Gallecie usque ad Dorium flumen, omnes civitates et castella que infra conti-
nentur ab eorum dominio eripuit, omnes quoque Ysmaelitas gladio extinguens eorumdem possessiones iuri christianorum mancipavit.*

chroniclers moved the whole episode one generation back, and assigned it to Alfonso *together with his brother Fruela*. Thanks to this resource—to shift from one Fruela to another—they managed to provide an acceptable transition from a long-established version to a new one. Not only this; they also poured military glory on a rather obscure character, but one who played a great role in the kingdom's dynastic evolution, as I will suggest in the next section.

But, before moving on to dynastic affairs, one more question needs to be asked. As we have seen, Alfonso I's image as a victorious warrior king has established itself firmly in Asturias in the 880s. Yet, only the two recensions of the *Chronicle of Alfonso III* engaged in the delicate task of putting together new and existing pieces of historical discourse, in order to create a narration that would support the notion that the whole Duero basin was emptied by Alfonso I of all its dwellers so that the ninth-century kings might justly recover it. Now, how was such a strange idea constructed?

True, the 'deserted place' was an appealing motif to clerical minds, to be found nearly everywhere in medieval hagiography.[72] It was not innocent at all, though. References to deserted spaces are frequently found in accounts of the activities of Carolingian missionaries in Germany when what was at issue was the right to seize the lands that were under no one's recognized possession. It was not really necessary that there be no inhabitants there. Sometimes, the argument could be used by way of denial of local communities. For example, when Frankish monks succeeded in removing the relics of St. Vincent from Valencia, they justified themselves with the most unbelievable argument that those relics were held in a church with no parishoners.[73] Exactly the same strategy was deployed in the eleventh-century when king Fernando I translated to Castile the relics of St. Vincent, St. Sabina and St. Cristeta from their martyrial shrine in Ávila, a city which lay beyond his kingdom's boundaries.[74] The situation in the Duero basin is strongly reminiscent of the process by which the Anglo-Saxon missionaries seized control of the West Midlands by denying the previous existence of any British Christian communities there, although recent research shows traces of churches, organized

---

[72] I am indebted to Julia Smith's stimulating comments on this point.
[73] See García Moreno (1999) p. 321, n. 91.
[74] *Historia Silense*, 94, ed. Pérez de Úrbel and González (1959) 197.

communities and bishops.[75] Likewise it seems increasingly plausible that the Duero dwellers had their own—albeit highly fragmented—ecclesiastical structure, one which was denied in the process of imposing northernborn bishops, together with Asturian rule on them.

This may provide a general context of how the 'lack of population' could be argued to deny the locals and claim the right to control the land. Yet, the formulation of such a process in the Chronicles of Alfonso III takes the argument to its very extreme limits. Now, it is very interesting to compare *Rot.-Ovet.*, 15 to the narration of Charles Martel's AD 737 campaign in Gothia (Septimania) in the *Continuations to Fredegar's Chronicle*:

> Rot.-Ovet., 15: "Together with his brother Fruela, he led many fights against the Sarracens and he seized *many cities* once oppressed by them, that is, Lugo, Tuy, Oporto, (. . .), *and all the castles with their vills and hamlets*. Killing all the Arabs who occupied those cities, *he took the Christians' with him to the homeland*."

> Fredegar's continuations: "And, having thus defeated their enemies, the Franks seized a great booty; after taking many captives, they *depopulated the Gothic region. The most famous cities, Nîmes, Agde, Biterre*, having their walls and defenses been torn down, they were set ablaze by him (Martel). *He devastated their suburbs, and the castles of the region.* Having dispersed the enemy's army, Christ reigning everywhere and with victory ornating his head, *he safely returned to his region, in the land of the Franks, the soil of his principatum*".[76]

Although clearly both passages are not verbally dependent, they are close enough in conception to suggest that the Frankish chronicle could have influenced the Asturians in building the whole notion of the depopulation of the Duero basin. Barbero and Vigil analysed very eloquently the many similarities that existed between the historical process of the eighth-century Duero basin, which was left void of all higher rule—either Christian or Muslim—and that of contemporary Septimania.[77] Here, Arab rule was only ephemerally established, and, until the region's eventual subjection to the Franks, its cities lived a separate existence, keeping to their Visigothic identity and legal traditions. But, as far as I know, no one hitherto has

---

[75] Bassett (1992).
[76] Ed. Krusch (1888) 177.
[77] Barbero and Vigil (1978) 213 ff.

noticed that the Asturian narration could be drawing on a previous Septimanian-related model. And we have seen above that historical conceptions developed under Carolingian rule in early ninth-century Septimania were quite influential in shaping the early Asturian historical consciousness. Stories of this kind about the Carolingian build-up in southern Gaul may have been known in late-ninth century Asturias to the extent that putting them to use about Alfonso I would make perfect sense.

Summing up, I think the chroniclers' strategy about Alfonso I's campaigns consisted of: a) taking a pre-existing account of the lands ruled by the Asturians—of uncertain origin and date—and ascribing it to Alfonso I's years; b) taking a pre-existing story about Fruela I's deeds and moving it back to Alfonso I; c) enhancing—after Carolingian models—the narration of the king's campaigns, in order to divide the Iberian northwest in a twofold territorial pattern: the northern mountainous lands populated with Christians and the Duero plainlands, totally void of all dwellers.

Complex and subtle as this scheme is, the need to argue for the plateau's depopulation would hardly account for the bother of making the whole discourse converge upon Alfonso I. In order to explain this, we need to move into the king's second set of attributes: kin relations.

Alfonso I's Kin Relations

The earlier generations of Asturian kingship were dominated by a number of regional powers of whom a dominating character could eventually claim superiority (Fig. 4). The absence of a formalized succession system, together with crossing marriage alliances between the main lineages would account for such a complex pattern, in which cognatic relations were equally important, if not more important than agnatic ones. Linear agnatic succession did not establish itself until the crucial period of Ramiro I's reign.

The reign of Alfonso II represents the first serious attempt to make sense of the earlier troubled period. History was narrated according to this anti-Visigothic, Carolingian-inspired scheme. Royal succession was also for the first time tightened up into a linear dynastic layout, even if one in which father-to-son succession was indeed rare. This is best illustrated by Alfonso II's 812 charter. Here, a vision of

a God-favoured royal dynasty is presented in which, strikingly, kingship flows from Pelagius down to Alfonso II, totally regardless of
other kings who actually ruled, such as Fávila or the whole of Alfonso
I's branch!:

> ... Of which plague, by Your right hand—Christ—was Your servant
> Pelagius saved, who, having been elevated to princely power, fought
> victoriously, hit the enemy, and defended the Christian and Asturian
> people with sublime victory. Fruela, his daughter's very conspicuous son,
> stood decorated with the culmen of kingship. By him was founded in
> the place called Oviedo the church dedicated in Your sacred name . . .[78]

If this is what could be considered as the early ninth-century 'official'
version, then by the end of the century a new conception had set
in, which largely contested it. The layout of royal succession and
blood relationships in all three texts can be narrowed down to two
alternating dynasties—those of Pelagius and Peter of Cantabria—
which interlinked precisely in the figure of Alfonso I, married to
Pelagius's daughter.

Historians have frequently tried to conflate the data in all three
chronicles into one single picture of Alfonso I's origin and relations,
but this largely obscures the fact that the three texts differ significantly
in crucial points. The main facts were established by the *Albeldensis*:
"Alfonso I was the son of Peter, duke of Cantabria, and, as he came
into Asturias, he took Pelagius's daughter, Bermesinda, by Pelagius's
command".[79] The *Rotensis*, instead, turned Alfonso's ancestry into
'royal', which in this context can only mean 'Visigothic': "Alfonso,
son of Peter, duke of the Cantabri, of royal ancestry, came to Asturias.
He married Pelagius's daughter, named Ermesind. With his father-in-
law he reached many victories . . .".[80] And perhaps showing a higher
'constitutional concern'—by contrast to the *Albeldensis*, which seems
to have assumed that his royal marriage gave Alfonso I the throne—
it explained his royal accession by election: "After whose [Favila's]
death, Alfonso was elected to the throne by the whole people".[81]

---

[78] Floriano (1949), doc. 24, 120–121. For the Latin text see above note 27. This
is also in accordance to some versions of the Asturian regnal lists in which Aurelius
is followed by Alfonso II, all other kings being written out; Gil (1985) 99.
[79] Alb. XV, 3. For the Latin text see above, note 43.
[80] Rot. 11: *"Adefonsus filius Petri Cantabrorum ducis ex regni prosapiem Asturias aduenit.
Filiam Pelagii nomen Ermesinda in coniungio accepit. Qui cum socero et postea uictorias multas
peregit . . ."*
[81] Rot. 13.

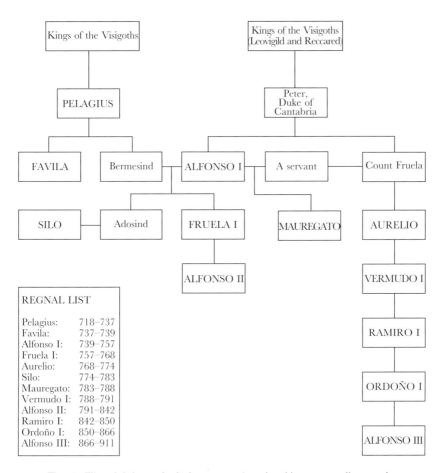

Fig. 4: The eighth- and ninth-century Asturian kings, according to the
Ovetensis Chronicle.

The *Ovetensis* recension pointed more directly to dynastic matters. It
not only condemned Pelagius's daughter to oblivion, but also sketched
a more prestigious ancestry for Alfonso I: "He was the son of Duke
Peter, born from the breed of kings Leovigild and Reccared. In the
time of Egica and Witiza, he (Peter) was the army's principal".[82]
Amancio Isla has rightly noticed that, while the *Rotensis* takes issue
in the debate on the ending of the Visigothic kingdom, by stressing
the sins of Witiza and his family and enhancing the virtues of

---

[82] Ovet. 13.

Roderic,[83] the *Ovetensis* seems to turn the page on that matter, in an attempt to 'deactivate' the inherited notion that the Visigoths perished due to their own sins.[84] In fact, *the Ovetensis* was more interested in stressing the continuity from the Gothic to the Asturian kingdom, which may well explain why in its account, the ancestry of Duke Peter of Cantabria is linked to the heyday of the Goths— Leovigild and Reccared, not to their sorrowful decline. Moreover, in this version, Petrus, and Alfonso I after him, would have as good a title to kingship as Pelagius himself, if not better!

The dynastic aspects help in understanding many of the chroniclers' concerns and methods. They not only invented the depopulation of the Duero basin, but also took great pains to move most positive elements from Fruela I's reign to his father, Alfonso I's. Thus, despite having been powerful and victorious, Fruela's image is rather dominated by his anger, which led him to kill his own brother and later for himself to be killed in retribution. So, what was the point in making a positive figure out of Alfonso I, by denigrating his son Fruela? Alfonso III's chroniclers were evidently interested in enhancing their king's line. This, though, was a hard thing to do, due to the intricacies of eighth-century succession. Alfonso I's direct agnatic line just would not do. His son Fruela fathered Alfonso II, who died without an heir, and was succeeded—perhaps after a period in which both kings coincided conflictingly[85]—by Ramiro I, the direct ascendent of Alfonso III. Moreover, Alfonso II was the archtype of Asturian pro-Carolingian policies, and the chroniclers had to make great efforts to write out all Frankish-scented elements and turn his more remarkable achievements into steps towards the restoration of the Visigothic kingdom. Besides, Alfonso II did not succeed Fruela I directly. King Aurelius (Fig. 4) represents a return to Alfonso I's family, but in his brother Count Fruela's collateral line. Then, Pelagius's kindred recovered the lead with Silo, but lost it to Mauregato—allegedly Alfonso I's son by a servant—and Vermudo, another son of Count Fruela's. Most importantly, despite Alfonso II's accession and long reign and despite Vermudo's being a cleric, this was the very point at which the late

---

[83] From the Carolingian period, this was the northern 'official' view, while Witiza's ascendancy had become a 'stamp of pride' among the southern Mozarabs by the mid-ninth century. See Menéndez Pidal (1956–1958).

[84] Isla (1998b) p. 309.

[85] Fernández Conde (1997).

ninth-century ruling dynasty connected to their earlier ancestors.

The whole plot becomes apparent. The chroniclers needed to emphasize the ruling kindred's claims to power. In order to do so, they had to minimize Alfonso II's branch. Their claims had to concentrate on the generation before Fruela I, but their most direct kin node was not a strong one, since count Fruela never achieved kingship. Their strategy was to focus the prestige of victory on Alfonso, and then make his brother participate in those campaigns by association (which would also account for crediting to this branch the achievements that seemingly belonged to Fruela I): *simul cumfratre suo Froilane multa aduersus Sarracenos prelia gessit atque plurimas ciuitates ab eis olim oppressas cepit.* The brother-to-brother scheme, though, was too feeble. It needed to be reinforced by means of a prestigious common ancestor: Duke Peter of Cantabria. It is really shocking to see how much discussion there has been among historians about such a character and his implications for the late Visigothic and early Asturian history. Too little emphasis has been put on the crude fact that Duke Peter is never mentioned in any source at all before the late ninth-century chronicles. Do we not have every reason to be suspicious about his entering the historical narration in the very last scene, to provide Alfonso I and count Fruela with a common ancestor of Visigothic provenance? It seems too obvious that Duke Peter was the missing indispensable link for making Alfonso III's dynasty the direct descendents of Kings Leovigild and Reccared, the most glorious references in their cherished Visigothic past. Therefore, concentrating the crucial eighth-century developments on Alfonso I can be seen as the central piece in a wider scheme aiming to devise a glorious past for Alfonso III, and legitimate his policies.

Alfonso I's Moral Qualities

Alfonso III's complex political agenda can explain the need to make a great historical landmark of Alfonso I. His reign was narrated as momentuous and he made his way with honours to the after life. Alfonso I's high moral quality is stressed by all three texts, even if with different components. For the *Albeldensis* his being "loved by God and men" went together with his peaceful death.[86] The *Rotensis*

---

[86] Alb. XV, 3.

went a lot further, by noting down his religious virtues, followed by
a death-bed miracle:

> He was a great man. He was loved by God and men. He built many
> churches. He reigned for eighteen years. He died due to natural causes.
> And I will not silence a miracle which I know for certain to have
> occurred. For when his soul departed in the silence of the night, and
> the palace guards were diligently watching over his body, suddenly the
> voices of angels were heard in the air by those present, singing: *'See
> how the just is taken and no one notices; and just men are taken and no heart
> realizes. From the face of iniquity the just is taken; he will be in peace in his
> grave.'* You must know that this is all true, do not think it fabulous: I
> would rather keep silent than speak falsities.[87]

This was reproduced by the *Ovetensis* recension almost verbatim. Only
the first lines were changed for the greater emphasis:

> So, the aforesaid Alfonso was indeed magnanimous. Without any offence
> to God or the Church, he led a life worthy of imitation. He built or
> restored many temples. He reigned for 18 years. He happily ended
> his life in peace. And I will not silence this wonderful miracle . . .[88]

By this means, Alfonso I became one among only three eighth-
century kings to have been marked by God with a miracle, and a
relevant one indeed, since the angelic choir on his death-bed clearly
implied his being summoned to heaven and sanctity.

---

[87] Rot. 14–15: *"Hic vir magnus fuit. Deo et ominibus amavilis extitit. Baselicas multas
fecit. Vixit in regno a. XVIII. Morte propria discessit. Nec hoc miraculum silebo, quod uerius
factum esse cognosco. Quumque spiritum emisisset in tempeste noctis silentia cum officiis palatinis
corpus custodissent, subito in aera auditur a cunctis uox angelorum psallentium: "Ecce quomodo
tollitur iustus et nemo considerat; et uiri iusti tolluntur et nemo percipit corde. A facie iniquitatis
sublatus est iustus; erit in pace sepultura eius". Hoc uerum esse cognoscite et nec fabulosum putetis:
alioquin tacere magis quam falsa promere maluissem.*

[88] Ovet. 14–15. *"Itaque supra dictus Adefonsus admodum magnanimis fuit. Sine offensione
erga Deum et eclesiam uitam merito imitabilem duxit. Baselicas plures construxit uel instaurabit.
Regnauit annos XVIII. Uitam feliciter in pace finiuit. Nec hoc stupendum miraculum pretermit-
tendum est, quod hora discessionis eius certissime actum est. Nam quum spiritum emisisset in tempeste noctis silentia et excubie palatine diligentissime corpus illius obseruassent, subito in aera
auditur a cunctis excubantibus uox angelorum psallentium: "Ecce quomodo tollitur iustus et nemo
considerat; et uiri iusti tolluntur et nemo precipit corde. A facie iniquitatis sublatus est iustus; erit
in pace sepultura eius". Hoc uerum esse prorsus cognoscite nec fabulosum dictum putetis: alio quin
tacere magis eligerem quam falsa promere maluissem.*

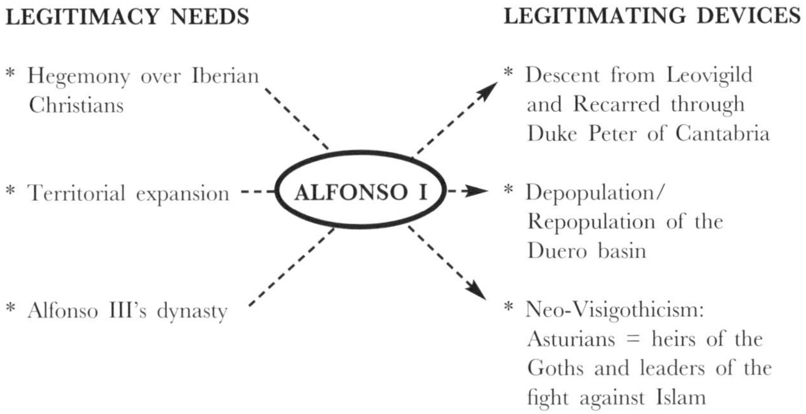

LEGITIMACY NEEDS   **LEGITIMATING DEVICES**

* Hegemony over Iberian
  Christians

* Territorial expansion ---(ALFONSO I)

* Alfonso III's dynasty

* Descent from Leovigild
  and Recarred through
  Duke Peter of Cantabria

* Depopulation/
  Repopulation of the
  Duero basin

* Neo-Visigothicism:
  Asturians = heirs of the
  Goths and leaders of the
  fight against Islam

Fig. 5: Alfonso I as a discourse node.

Conclusion: Alfonso I as a Discourse Node

I have tried to show that the image of Alfonso I in the late-ninth century chronicles largely resulted from a subtle, systematic manipulation of the historical and narrative material. This was aimed to 'deactivate' existing undesired visions of the eighth-century Asturian history, and replace them with a new one which fulfilled the legitimation needs of Alfonso III's time.

The result was that Alfonso I became the main figure in mid-eighth-century Asturian history. I have presented the many reasons why we can suspect that he did not actually play such a paramount role. The fact that he is said to have done so in the chronicles is largely due to his being what I would call a 'discourse node'. As shown in Fig. 5, Alfonso I was a point crossed by a number of discourse lines, all of which were of essential importance to Alfonso III's policies. In a dynastic dimension, he was the key element giving prestige to Alfonso III's dynastic branch, by means of his association to count Fruela, and his allegedly descending from Peter of Cantabria and the Visigothic kings. This helped to stress the whole notion of neo-gothicism, which ultimately was, as seen before, an ideology of Iberian-wide hegemony. In the meantime, most traces of a previous Carolingian-driven political growth were carefully erased. Moreover, the narration about the lands he populated and those which he devastated entailed a subtle discourse justifying the status of the kingdom's two main territorial components, and legitimating the Asturian take-over of the plateau.

All of those discourse lines cut across the figure of Alfonso I. Rather than a real king, he can be seen as an essential tool for discourse construction which went much further than just open statements. The multilayered nature of the chronicles' discourse needs to be emphasized. The texts can be read at several different levels, and some of their arguments can only work properly if they flow very unexplicitly. While some of the chroniclers' concerns—such as the Asturian 'gothicness'—were spoken out loud, others—such as their dynastic allegiance—remained largely hidden, and can only be exposed by carefully deconstructing the ways in which they manipulated, and added to their inherited historical material. The different degree of internal consistency in the three texts is essential in understanding the *Ovetensis'* most programmatic strategies.

Inevitably, another consequence of the kind of analysis I am proposing, and one I cannot deal properly with in this context, is that it casts considerabble doubt on how much we can learn about the Asturian eighth-century from those texts. The easy, short answer would perhaps be 'nothing', but I think this can be modified by a subtle consideration of the discourses the chroniclers were trying to deactivate. Certainly, more investigation about the Asturian elements in Arabic texts, and how close they can be to al-Razi's original work would also be of great help. Instead I think that it is no longer a valid approach to take the chronicles at face value, out of context, or to conflate the narrations in the three texts into a single discourse.

Surely, our most outstanding sources for the Asturian mid-eighth-century history say very little indeed about the eighth century while they tell a great deal about the late-ninth and their authors' political and cultural milieu. Also about the way in which their historical conceptions were a part of their political actions. When looking at the intricate web of meanings attached to him, we can see that Alfonso I probably never existed as we read in the texts, but whoever he was and whatever he did, his descendent Alfonso III had a taylor-cut ancestor made out of him, of whom to be very proud.

Acknowledgments

I started working on this paper while being on a post-doctoral research leave at University College London, funded by the Spanish Ministerio de Educación y Cultura. A preliminary version was delivered in a

Seminar at the University of St. Andrews within the St. Andrews-Madrid 2000–2001 Acción Integrada (see above Introduction). The final version was developed in the framework of a research project funded by the Spanish Ministerio de Ciencia y Tecnología, directed at the Departamento de Historia Medieval of the Instituto de Historia (Madrid, CSIC) by Dr. Isabel Alfonso in 2000–2002.

I am indebted to all those who have contributed with their comments to improve this paper, particularly the members of the St. Andrews-Madrid group, as well as Dr. Amancio Isla (Universidad Rovira i Virgili, Tarragona), Dr. Maribel Fierro (Instituto de Filología, CSIC, Madrid), Dr. Luis Molina (Instituto de Estudios Árabes, CSIC, Granada), Jorge Manzano, Teri Nava-Vaugh (Stanford University, California) and Hugh Kennedy (St. Andrews University). Needless to say I am the only one to blame for all possible shortcomings.

Bibliography

Acién Almansa, M. (1994) *Entre el feudalismo y el Islam. Umar Ibn Hafsun en los historiadores, en las fuentes y en la historia*, Jaén.

Aguadé, J. (1991) *Abd al-Malik b. Habib (m. 238/859). Kitab al-Tarij (La Historia)* (Madrid: 1991).

Azkárate Garai-Olaun, A. (1993) "Francos, Aquitanos y Vascones. Testimonios arqueológicos al sur de los Pirineos", *Archivo Español de Arqueología* 66 (1993) 149–176.

Azkárate Garai-Olaun, A.; Quirós Castillo, J.A. (2001) "Arquitectura doméstica altomedieval en la Península Ibérica", Archeologia Medievale, 28 (2001) 25–60.

Barbero, A.; Vigil, M. (1978) *La formación del feudalismo en la Península Ibérica* (Barcelona: 1978).

Bassett, S.R. (1992) "Church and diocese in the West Midlands: the transition from British to Anglo-Saxon control", in *Pastoral Care before the Parish*, ed. J. Blair and R. Sharpe (Leicester: 1992) 13–40.

Cavadini, J.C. (1993) *The Last Christology of the West: Adoptionism in Spain and Gaul, 785–820* (Philadelphia: 1993).

Castellanos, S.; Martín Viso, I. (forthcoming) "The local articulation of central power in the north of the Iberian peninsula, 500–1000", *Early Medieval Europe*.

Collins, R. (1989) *The Arab Conquest of Spain, 710–797* (Oxford: 1989).

—— (1998) *Charlemagne* (London: 1998).

D'Abadal i de Vinyals, R. (1949) *La batalla del adopcionismo y la desintegración de la Iglesia Visigoda*, (Barcelona: 1949).

Dacosta Martínez, A. (1992) "Notas sobre las crónicas ovetenses del siglo IX. Pelayo y el sistema sucesorio en el caudillaje asturiano", *Studia Historica. Historia Medieval*, 10, (1992) 9–46.

David, P. (1947) *Études historiques sur la Galice et le Portugal du VIe au XIe siècles*, (Lisbon: 1947).

Díaz y Díaz, M.C. (1970) "La historiografía hispana desde la invasión árabe hasta el año 1000", in *La storiografia altomedievale. XVII Settimane di Studio del Centro Italiano di Studi sull'Alto Medioevo*, (Spoleto: 1970) I, 313–343.

—— (1976) "Los himnos en honor de Santiago en la liturgia hispánica", in Díaz y Díaz, M.C. *De Isidoro al siglo XI. Ocho estudios sobre la vida literaria peninsular*, (Barcelona: 1976) 235–288.

—— (1983) *Códices visigóticos en la monarquía leonesa* (León: 1983).

Dozy, R (1965) *Recherches sur l'histoire et la literature de l'Espagne pendant le Moyen Âge* (Amsterdam: 1965).

Escalona, J. (1991) "Algunos problemas relativos a la génesis de las estructuras territoriales de la Castilla altomedieval", in *Burgos en la Alta Edad Media* (Burgos: 1991) 489–506.

—— (2000a) *Transformaciones sociales y organización del espacio en el alfoz de Lara en la Alta Edad Media*, PhD dissertation, CD-ROM ed. (Madrid: 2000).

—— (2000b) "Paisaje, asentamiento y Edad Media: reflexiones sobre dos estudios recientes", *Historia Agraria*, 20 (2000) 227–244.

—— (2001) "De 'señores y campesinos' a 'comunidades y poderes feudales'. Elementos para definir la articulación entre territorio y clases sociales en la Alta Edad Media castellana" in *Comunidades locales y poderes feudales en la Edad Media*, coord. I. Álvarez Borge (Logroño: 2001) 115–155.

—— (2002) *Sociedad y Territorio en la Alta Edad Media Castellana. La formacion del alfoz de Lara*, British Archaeological Reports. International Series 1079 (Oxford: 2002).

—— (forthcoming) "Comunidades, territorios y poder condal en la Castilla del Duero en el siglo X", *Studia Historica. Historia Medieval*.

Estepa, C. (1992) "Configuración y primera expansión del reino astur. Siglos VIII y IX", in *De Constantino a Carlomagno. Disidentes, heterodoxos y marginados*, ed. F.J. Lomas and F. Devís (Cádiz: 1992) 179–195.

—— (2002) "El poder regio y los territorios", in *La época de la Monarquía Asturiana. Actas del Simposio celebrado en Covadonga (8–10 de octubre de 2001)* (Oviedo: 2002) 451–467.

Fagnan, E. (1898) *Annales du Maghreb et de l'Espagne* (Argen: 1898).

Fernández Conde, F.J. (1971) *El Libro de los Testamentos de la Catedral de Oviedo* (Rome: 1971).

—— (2000) *La religiosidad medieval en España. I. Alta Edad Media (s. VII–X)*, Oviedo.

—— (1997) "Relaciones politicas y culturales de Alfonso II el Casto", in *Historia social, pensamiento historiográfico y Edad Media. Homenaje al Prof. Abilio Barbero de Aguilera*, ed. M.I. Loring García (Madrid: 1997) 597–611.

Fernández Conde, F.J.; Suárez, M.J.; Gutiérrez, J.A. (1997) "A transición en Asturias Aproximación historiográfica e percepción do territorio astur na Alta Idade Media", in *Galicia fai dous mil anos: o feito diferencial galego*, coord. G. Pereira Menaut (Santiago de Compostela: 1997) I, 391–412.

Fierro, M. (1998) "Four questions in connection with Ibn Hafsun", in *The Formation of Al-Andalus. I: History and Society*, ed. M. Marín (Aldershot: 1998) pp. 291–328.

Floriano Cumbreño, A.C. (1949) *Diplomática española del período astur (718–910)* (Oviedo: 1949).

Floriano Llorente, P. (1975) "El testamento de Alfonso II (Estudio paleográfico y diplomático)", *Boletín del Instituto de Estudios Asturianos*, 86 (1975) 593–617.

Fouracre, P. (2000) *The Age of Charles Martel* (Harlow: 2000).

García de Cortázar, J.A. (1997) "El espacio castellano y alavés en la época de Alfonso II el Casto", *Cuadernos de Historia de España* 74 (1997) 101–120.

García Moreno, L.A. (1975) "Sobre un nuevo ejemplar del Laterculus Regum Visigothorum", *Analecta Sacra Tarraconensia* 47 (1975) 8–19.

—— (1999) "Spanish Gothic consciousness among the Mozarabs in al-Andalus (VIII–Xth centuries)", in *The Visigoths. Studies in Culture and Society*, ed. A. Ferreiro (Leiden-Boston-Köln: 1999) 303–323.

Gil, J. (1978–1979) "Judíos y cristianos en España (S. VIII y IX)", *Hispania Sacra*, 31 (1978–1979) 9–88.

—— (1995) "La historiografía tradicional" in *La Cultura del Románico. Siglos XI al XIII. Letras. Religiosidad. Artes. Ciencia y Vida*, coord. F. López Estrada (vol. XI of *Historia de España Menéndez Pidal*, dir. J.M. Jover Zamora) (Madrid: 1995) 3–24.

Gil, J.; Moralejo, J.L.; Ruiz de la Peña, J.I. (1985) *Crónicas Asturianas* (Oviedo: 1985).

Gómez Moreno, M. (1932) "Las primeras crónicas de la Reconquista, el ciclo de Alfonso III", *Boletín de la Real Academia de la Historia*, 100 (1932) 562–623.

Holder-Egger, O. (1907) *MGH. Scriptores Rerum Germanicarum*, II (Hannover-Leipzig: 1911).

Huete Fudio, M. (1994) "Fuentes menores para el estudio de la historiografía latina de la Alta Edad Media hispánica (siglos VII–X)", *Medievalismo*, 4 (1994) 5–26.

Isla Frez, A. (1992) *La sociedad gallega en la Alta Edad Media* (Madrid: 1992).

—— (1998a) "El adopcionismo y las evoluciones religiosas y políticas en el Reino Astur", *Hispania* 200 (1998) 971–993.

—— (1998b) "Los dos Vitizas. Pasado y presente en las crónicas asturianas", in Hidalgo, M.J., Pérez, D and Gervás, M.J.R. (eds.), *"Romanización" y "Reconquista" en la Península Ibérica: nuevas perspectivas*, ed. M.J. Hidalgo, D. Pérez and M.J.R. Gervás (Salamanca: 1998) 303–316.

Kurze, F. (1895) *MGH. Scriptores rerum Germanicarum in usum scholarum* (Hannover: 1895, repr. 1950).

Krusch, B. (1888) *MGH. Scriptores Rerum Merowingicarum*, II (Hannover: 1888).

Larrañaga, K. (1993) "El pasaje del pseudo-Fredegario sobre el dux Francio de Cantabria y otros indicios de naturaleza textual y onomástica sobre presencia franca tardoantigua al sur de los Pirineos", *Archivo Español de Arqueología* 66 (1993) 177–206.

Levison, W. (1946) *England and the Continent in the eighth century* (Oxford: 1946).

Löfstedt, B. (1984) *Beati et Eterii adversus Elipandum*, Corpus Christianorum, Continuatio Medievalis, LIX (Turnhout: 1984).

Maíllo Salgado, F. (1990) *Zamora y los zamoranos en las fuentes arábigas medievales*, Studia Zamorensia. Anejos, 2 (Zamora: 1990).

—— (2002) "El Reino de Asturias desde la perspectiva de las fuentes árabes", in *La época de la Monarquía Asturiana. Actas del Simposio celebrado en Covadonga (8–10 de octubre de 2001)* (Oviedo: 2002) 229–249.

Makki, M.A.; Corriente, F. (2001) *Ibn Hayyan. Crónica de los emires Alhakam I y Abdarrahman II entre los años 796 y 847 [Almuqtabis II–1]* (Zaragoza: 2001).

Manzano Moreno, E. (1991) *La frontera de Al-Andalus en época de los Omeyas* (Madrid: 1991).

—— (1997) "El 'medio cordobés' y la elaboración cronística en Al-Andalus bajo la dinastía de los Omeyas", in *Historia social, pensamiento historiográfico y Edad Media. Homenaje al Prof. Abilio Barbero de Aguilera*, ed. M.I. Loring García (Madrid: 1997) 59–85.

—— (1991) "Señores y emires: familias aristocráticas y soberanía Omeya en Al-Andalus", *Cuadernos de Madinat al-Zahra*, 3 (1991) 97–110.

Martin, G. (1997) *Histoires de l'Espagne médiévale: Historiographie, geste, romancero*, París.

Menéndez Pidal, R. (1956–1958) *Floresta de leyendas heroicas españolas. Rodrigo el último Godo* (Madrid: 1956–1958).

—— (1960) "Repoblación y tradición en la Cuenca del Duero", *Enciclopedia Lingüística Hispánica*, 1 (Madrid: 1960) 29–57.

Pérez de Úrbel, J.; González Ruiz-Zorrilla, A. (1959) *Historia silense* (Madrid: 1959).

Pertz, G.H. (1826) *MGH. Scriptores*, I (Hannover: 1826).

Prelog, J. (1980) *Die Chronik Alfons III. Untersuchungen und kritische Edition der vier Redaktionen*, (Frankfurt-Bern-Cirencester: 1980).

Romero-Pose, C. (1985) *Beato de Liébana (Sancti beati a Liebana Comentarius in Apocalipsin)* (Rome: 1985).

Sánchez-Albornoz, C. (1966) *Despoblación y Repoblación en el Valle del Duero* (Buenos Aires: 1966).

—— (1967a) "¿Una crónica asturiana perdida?", in Sánchez-Albornoz, C., *Investigaciones sobre historiografía hispana medieval (siglos VIII al XII)* (Buenos Aires: 1967) 111–160.

—— (1967b) "El relato de las campañas de Alfonso I", in Sánchez-Albornoz, C., *Investigaciones sobre historiografía hispana medieval (siglos VIII al XII)* (Buenos Aires: 1967) 203–214.

—— (1967c) "La crónica del moro Rasis y la Continuatio Hispana", in Sánchez-Albornoz, C., *Investigaciones sobre historiografía hispana medieval (siglos VIII al XII)* (Buenos Aires: 1967) 267–302.

Seco de Lucena, L. (1975) *Al Qalqasandi. Subh al-Asa fi kitabat al-Insa* (Valencia: 1975).

Suárez Álvarez, M.J. (2002) "La Monarquía Asturiana. Nuevas perspectivas de interpretación", in *La época de la Monarquía Asturiana. Actas del Simposio celebrado en Covadonga (8–10 de octubre de 2001)* (Oviedo: 2002) 203–227.

Thorpe, L. (1969) *Einhard and Notker the Stammerer. Two lives of Charlemagne* (Harmondsworth: 1969).

Torrente Fernández, I. (1997) "Sedes regias de la monarquía asturiana", in *Historia social, pensamiento historiográfico y Edad Media. Homenaje al Prof. Abilio Barbero de Aguilera*, ed. M.I. Loring García (Madrid: 1997) 575–591.

—— (2002) "Goticismo astur e ideología política", in *La época de la Monarquía Asturiana. Actas del Simposio celebrado en Covadonga (8–10 de octubre de 2001)* (Oviedo: 2002) 295–315.

Wasserstein, D.J. (2002) "Inventing tradition and constructing identity: the genealogy of Umar ibn Hafsun between Christianity and Islam", *Al-Qantara*, 23/2 (2002).

Wolf, K.B. (1988) *Christian Martyrs in Muslim Spain*, (Cambridge: 1988)

—— (1990) *Conquerors and chroniclers of Early Medieval Spain* (Liverpool: 1990).

AN INTERPRETER OF LAW AND POWER
IN A REGION OF MEDIEVAL POLAND:
ABBOT PETER OF HENRYKÓW AND HIS *BOOK*

Piotr Górecki

University of California, Riverside

Law and Power, Past and Present

Sometime around the turn of the sixth and the seventh decades of the thirteenth century, Peter, a recently retired third abbot of the Cistercian monastery at Henryków, wrote a history of the localities incorporated into the estate of his monastery, and of the monastery itself, extending back about one full century into his past.[1] Conventionally known as the *Henryków Book*, Peter's history eclectically but skillfully combines several genres of document.[2] It is a 'book of conveyances' (*liber traditionum*),[3] that is, a record of the acquisitions of individual properties by the monastery—in this case richly supplemented by the early histories of those properties before the monastery received them. It incorporates elements of monastic necrology, biography, a treatise of advice in epistolary form, and Cistercian *exordium* literature.[4] Above all, it is a 'book of things to be remembered' (*liber memorandorum*),[5] a precautionary treatise whereby Peter expressly intended to give the monks of his community a level of knowledge about past events and relationships adequate to protect them from several kinds of conflict in the future.

---

[1] Grodecki (1949), reissued with a new preface by Matuszewski and Matuszewski (1991), hereafter abbreviated as *K.H.*, with page references to the 1991 edition.

[2] On the genres incorporated by the Book, see Matuszewski (1981), especially pp. 28–9, 77–9, 86–7, and Górecki (1997), pp. 263–5, 274–5.

[3] Guyotjeannin, Pycke, and Tock (1993), pp. 272–3; Geary (1994), pp. 84–7; Górecki (1997), p. 265.

[4] Matuszewski (1981), pp. 77–79; Górecki (1997), pp. 266–7, 274, 279–81, 288–91. I situate the work of Abbot Peter and his anonymous continuator in the genre extending back to the *Exordium Parvum* and the *Exordium Cistercii* in a chapter of a book in preparation.

[5] Clanchy (1993), pp. 133, 147, 171–2; Górecki (1997), p. 265, n. 21.

These anticipated conflicts concerned three closely interrelated subjects: property, human relationships, and power. Property is here
defined broadly to mean the physical holdings accumulated by the
monastery, the transactions whereby that accumulation took place,
and the long-term consequences of the property transfers to the
alienors, the recipients, and other persons. The human relationships
at issue entail a multilateral and negotiable network of long-term
contacts among those actors in the Henryków region who were in
a position, among other things, to affect those property interests. By
power, I mean access to several kinds of resources that the actors
brought to bear upon one another, and, after its foundation in the
1220s, upon the Henryków monastery, in order to maintain or
enhance their own position within the regional social and political
universe.[6] Peter developed these three subjects with reference to a
fourth, namely the passage of time. The histories of individual localities which make up the chapters of his *Book* span the social memories concerning their earliest possessors, their subsequent alienations,
ultimately in favor of the monastery, and later circumstances which
include, among other things, prevention or settlement of disputes
about the acquired properties.[7] Similarly, Peter's stories of interpersonal relationships span their formative phases, their subsequent development, and, very importantly, their social perception or understanding
over time and into his own present.

Peter described power with a rich and explicit vocabulary, and
he carefully situated power as a social phenomenon. He always
described it as a personal attribute. That is, although on the basis
of his work we may assess what he meant by power as an abstract
concept, he himself consistently attached it to particular actors as an
individual trait. He indentified particular persons as *potentes*,[8] or as
possessing *potestas* or *potentia*,[9] or as 'ruling' (*dominor, rego*),[10] or as enjoy-
ing *regimen* or *dicio*.[11] In other cases, he referred less directly to 'great
men' (*magni viri*),[12] or to actors attaining 'heights of honor' (*honoris*

---

[6] My working definition of that complicated and historiographically contested
construct in Górecki (1999), p. 100.

[7] Górecki (1998b); Górecki (1998a).

[8] *K.H.*, ch. 3, p. 111; ch. 45, p. 121.

[9] Ibid., ch. 32, p. 119; ch. 83, p. 134; ch. 200, p. 195.

[10] Ibid., ch. 2, p. 110; ch. 36, p. 120; ch. 47, p. 121; ch. 200, p. 195.

[11] Ibid., ch. 2, p. 110; ch. 8, p. 113.

[12] Ibid., ch. 105, p. 143.

culmen)[13] or 'abundance' (*opulentia*).[14] He deployed an equally explicit vocabulary to express an absence or a loss of power, likewise as a personal attribute. He referred to particular actors as 'small' (*exigui*),[15] as being 'oppressed' (*oppressi*)[16] or 'very much impeded' (*impediebantur valde*),[17] or as having 'diminished' (*decrevit*) from some prior social position.[18] Furthermore, he explicitly focused on illegitimate uses of power, by vignettes of particular actors who 'threaten[ed]' (*minor*),[19] 'inflict[ed] violence' (*exerceunt violentiam*),[20] 'molest[ed]' (*molestavit*),[21] and 'usurp[ed]' (*usurpavit*)[22] other people or places, including the space and resources of his own monastery—and he called one such a *tyrannus*.[23]

This attribute pertained to a wide variety of persons. Peter variously attached it to particular 'knights' (*milites*)[24] or 'lords' (*comites*),[25] ducal officials, individual canons of the Wrocław cathedral chapter, and specific 'ducal peasants' (*rustici ducis*).[26] Thus, he seemed to view power as a trait cutting across a fairly wide social spectrum, and his stories of the particular *rustici*, *milites*, *comites*, and others who possessed, enhanced, or lost that trait make up a fascinating glimpse of what we might call his sociology of power—a subject to which I cannot do justice here, apart from two quick observations. First, the resources that actually made up the *potestates* of, say, knights and peasants, were, in all kinds of ways, extremely unequal.[27] Second, overarching that inequality, was a common possibility that, whatever they were for a particular individual or status group, such resources could be enhanced or diminished. Therefore, one common, strongly dynamic, subject of Peter's histories of particular people and places, and thus of the *Henryków Book* in its entirety, was the acquisition,

---

[13] Ibid., ch. 6, p. 112.
[14] Ibid., ch. 3, p. 110; ch. 54, p. 123; ch. 82, pp. 133–4.
[15] Ibid., ch. 71, p. 128; ch. 74, p. 129.
[16] Ibid., ch. 82, p. 134; ch. 200, p. 195.
[17] Ibid., ch. 96, p. 139.
[18] Ibid., ch. 38, p. 120.
[19] Ibid., ch. 108, p. 144.
[20] Ibid., ch. 47, pp. 121–2; ch. 104, p. 142; ch. 108, pp. 144–5.
[21] Ibid., ch. 52, p. 123.
[22] Ibid., ch. 103, p. 142.
[23] Ibid., ch. 52, p. 123.
[24] Ibid., ch. 45, 47, p. 121; ch. 111, p. 146.
[25] Ibid., ch. 96, p. 139; ch. 109, p. 145.
[26] Ibid., ch. 32, p. 119; ch. 36, p. 120; ch. 83, p. 134.
[27] Perhaps Peter's best example of asymmetry of the *potestates* of knights and peasants is the outcome of the property litigation involving a group of ducal peasants, a knight, and the monastery, which I have described in Górecki (2000b), pp. 480–1.

maintenance, or loss of the resources that made up power in the society on which he reflected—or, more simply put, upward or downward social mobility.[28]

From Peter's perspective, the central determinant of mobility thus defined was the formation and maintentance of interpersonal relationships—which were one of the sources of power, because, in his view, power was strongly, even essentially, relational. That is, when Peter identified an actor as *potens*, or as possessing or wielding *potestas* or *potentia*, he consistently described that trait in terms of a connection with someone else: people enjoyed *potentia*, or were *potentes*, 'near' (*circa*) other,[29] especially important people, or 'within' (*inter*) particular groups.[30] Our author viewed this particular determinant of power as the initial, independent variable in the acquisition and retention of other resources that made up power, such as wealth, office, honor, ability to use force, and meaningful access to justice. To be sure, he portrayed those other resources as independently important in a logical sense, but he repeatedly stressed the primary function of significant interpersonal contacts in their attainment and in their retention over time.

Peter reconstructed the workings of power in the Henryków region in terms of a complicated chronological framework.[31] A central expository schema of his *Book* was a division of the preceding century into two periods: the deep past, which had no clear beginning but which included, as one undifferentiated chronological unit, the reigns of Dukes Bolesław the Tall (1163–1202), his son Henry I the Bearded (1202–38), and the latter's son, Henry II the Pious (1238–41); and, separated from that earlier past by the cataclysmic Mongol invasion of 1241, a more recent past, which blended into Peter's own present. Peter portrayed these two periods as globally different—the past as a time of benign and conflictless reign by the three 'old,' or 'glorious,' dukes who presided over a society infused by a generalized sense of interpersonal trust—a sense, and a collective ethic, which worked as a guarantor of security and permanence of all kinds of transactions, including property, in the nature of things as it were;[32]

---

[28] For Peter as an observer of social mobility, see Górecki (2000a), pp. 135–3.

[29] *K.H.*, ch. 3, pp. 110–11; ch. 111, p. 146; no. 205, p. 197.

[30] Ibid., ch. 32, p. 119; ch. 83, p. 134.

[31] Matuszewski (1981), pp. 29, 39; Górecki (1997), pp. 274–8.

[32] *K.H.*, ch. 74, p. 129; ch. 88–89, p. 137; compare Clanchy (1970).

and the post-1241 past and his own present as a systemically degenerate converse of all these qualities.[33]

Peter's image of power in the period of the 'old dukes' was something of a paradox. On the one hand, as he imagined it, power had been enormous and vested securely in the dukes; on the other, its actual use was unnecessary, because of that primeval state of harmony that had infused and defined the political and legal order, and in which the dukes were magnificently positioned at the center.[34] Furthermore, Peter situated in that same period the foundation and early endowment of his own monastery, and, very importantly, the initial formation of the network of relationships that affected that foundation and endowment—relationships which he imagined, by homology, as fully infused and defined by the original ethic of that bygone time.[35] Finally, he recalled the early past as a time of steady expansion, likewise under authority and protection of the 'old dukes,' of settlement and lordship throughout Silesia, specifically including that frontier region of that province where his monastery was established.[36]

In contrast, the post-Mongol past, and Peter's own present, were no longer characterized by that general sense of social trust and transcendent justice which had formerly been a source of security; or by dukes who presided over, guaranteed, and personally embodied those traits. Peter consistently described those later dukes with a range of epithets squarely opposed to their predecessors' dignity, age, and glory—consistently describing them as 'young' (*iuvenes*),[37] a feature he used to paint an especially severe portrait of Duke Bolesław II the Bald (1241–73).[38] Power dissipated: 'After the pagans came into this land, . . . the knights ruled in the land, and each of them seized as much out of the ducal inheritances as he wished.'[39] Most importantly from Peter's perspective, his monastery was no longer located within a secure network of relationships which in his view had characterized the past and the monastery's origins within it. The 'knights' seized portions of the monastery's estate,[40] and the youthful and

---

[33] *K.H.*, ch. 91, p. 138.

[34] See Peter's portrayal at ibid., ch. 8, p. 113, which I discuss at Górecki (1997), pp. 286–7, and Górecki (1984), pp. 35–8.

[35] *K.H.*, ch. 6–11, pp. 112–15.

[36] Ibid., ch. 36, p. 120; ch. 42, p. 120; ch. 91, p. 138.

[37] Ibid., ch. 74, p. 129; ch. 91, p. 138.

[38] Ibid., ch. 74, p. 129; ch. 104–5, pp. 142–3.

[39] Ibid., ch. 47, pp. 121–22.

[40] Ibid., ch. 103, p. 142; ch. 111, p. 146.

eccentric Duke Bolesław specifically—and, from Peter's perspective, spitefully—made himself unavailable as a source of relief against them.[41] Likewise, expansion of settlement continued, but now under knightly rather than ducal lordship, leading to further encroachments at the expense of the monastery and the dukes, and to a whole sequence of second-order complications.[42]

What Peter seems to have been describing, at least in the world centered on his monastery, was a wholesale transformation of the social and political order. On this occasion, let me avoid the difficult issue of correspondence between Peter's historical vision and the realities that that vision purported to describe. Instead, I would like to note that, by means of that vision, considered on its own terms, Peter was expressing concern with power and property. Prior to 1241, those two areas of social reality had worked in his monastery's favor—that is, property transactions had been secure, the actors involved in them intrinsically trustworthy, and the resulting relationships entirely non-conflictual.[43] Afterwards, just the opposite was the case: property transactions, even though licitly and carefully effected, had become uncertain, and, above all, relationships were no longer motivated or informed by trust and kindness. Peter wrote his story explicitly to invoke, and perhaps recapture, those desirable relations of power and property which he projected onto the past. To that end, he used several approaches, which, jointly and individually, position him as an astute observer and negotiator of relations of power and the law. I have explored several such approaches in previous work.[44] Here, I would like further to pursue one of them, namely Peter's his use of biography—specifically, his remembrance and interpretation of those actors whom he considered especially important for the position of his monastery, both in its foundational past and during his own present.

One such individual was Nicholas, a cleric of the chapter of the Wrocław cathedral, who had been active between the first years of the thirteenth century and 1227, the year of his death.[45] Toward the

---

[41] Ibid., ch. 105, p. 143.
[42] Ibid., ch. 47–8, pp. 121–2; ch. 80, p. 132; ch. 109–11, pp. 145–6.
[43] Ibid., ch. 74, p. 129; ch. 88–89, p. 137.
[44] Górecki (1996), (1997), (1998b), (2000b).
[45] *K.H.*, ch. 2–12, pp. 109–15; ch. 21–2, pp. 116–7; ch. 30, p. 118; ch. 33, 35, p. 119; ch. 43, p. 121; ch. 54–6, p. 123; ch. 65, p. 126; ch. 82, pp. 133–34; ch. 86–7, pp. 135–6; ch. 100, p. 140. I have used much of this biographical informa-

end of his life, in or shortly before 1222, Nicholas had initiated the foundation of the monastery at Henryków, and facilitated the egress into 'the territory of Henryków' of the first group of Cistercian monks, out of 'our mother house' at Lubiąż. The other individual was Albert, nicknamed the Bearded or Łyka, 'a rather powerful knight' ten to fifteen years Nicholas's junior, active between the second decade of the thirteenth century and sometime soon before Peter began to write.[46] Of the two, Peter viewed Nicholas as by far the more important. His life story was the only continuously biographical section of Peter's *Book*, placed at its outset as a political introduction, and, in the rest of the work, a chronological frame of reference for other events or transactions.[47] In contrast, Albert occurs relatively late in the text, and in fragments of the individual histories that make it up rather than as continuous biographical progression. Albert's biography was significant largely in terms of his relationship with Nicholas, and of the social perception and interpretation of that particular relationship over time. It is not an exaggeration to say that much of what Peter has to say about relations of power and law bearing upon his monastery, right up to his present, is an extended interpretation of the memories concerning those two men, and of the implications of those memories for the monastery's long-term political position.

Nicholas

Right from the outset of the *Book*, Peter placed Nicholas in several contexts which jointly establish his entrance status in Silesia, in the Henryków region, and of course in the narrative. The abbot noted that Nicholas had 'entered' Silesia soon after 1202, as an adult and 'a cleric,' and that his 'ancestors' had been 'neither very noble nor completely base, but . . . middling knights from the province of Kraków.'[48] In addition, Nicholas was a relative (*cognatus*) of the bishop

---

tion to explore Peter's approaches for invention, arrangement, and persuasion, Górecki (1997).

[46] *K.H.*, ch. 45–57, pp. 121–3; ch. 74–6, pp 129–30; ch. 106, p. 143; ch. 108, p. 144; ch. 111, pp. 146–7. For Albert, see: Bartlett (1993), p. 163; Jurek (1998), pp. 106, 109, 126, 149, 187, 194–96; Górecki (1984), pp. 39–43.

[47] *K.H.*, ch. 2, p. 109. On this and other chronological frames of reference, see Górecki (1997), pp. 274–5, and, much more broadly for Poland in general, Myśliwski (1999), pp. 339–49; Myśliwski (2000), especially pp. 11, 15–16, 18–21.

[48] *K.H.*, ch. 2–12, pp. 109–15.

of Poznań—the principal city of the northern Piast province of Great
Poland—named Paul, at that time 'an old and revered person' who
'had baptized the younger lord Duke Henry,' and who was for that
reason 'joined to the elder . . . [Duke] Henry . . . by a certain special
familiarity.'[49] The baptism took place in or shortly after 1196,[50] and
so Bishop Paul must have had known the older Henry of Silesia for
some time during the final years of the twelfth century. We may
further speculate that, around the same time, Nicholas's *cognatio* with
the old bishop had facilitated his entry into the ducal court in
Wrocław.

However, Peter's most emphatic classification of this important
immigrant was in terms of property. In that same introductory phrase,
Peter remarked that Nicholas had settled in Silesia 'in simplicity,
without a pace [of earth] in this land, whether in patrimony or in
any [other kind of] property.'[51] He did recall that, at the time of
his arrival in Wrocław, Nicholas had held two localities in 'patrimony' in his native Little Poland,[52] but none in the region of reset-
tlement; and he reiterated Nicholas's intial landlessness, specifically
in Silesia, throughout the *Book*.[53] What Nicholas possessed in Silesia
right from the outset, brought with him as it were, was a specialized skill, namely practical literacy—the key to his subsequent position. Promptly after his arrival, he impressed a certain Lawrence,
simultaneously canon of the cathedral chapter of Wrocław and 'chief
notary of . . . Duke Henry,' with his 'great rigor and discipline,' and
he 'adhered' to Lawrence as an assistant and scribe.[54]

At this juncture in his story, Peter moved abruptly from his somewhat atemporal opening recollection of Nicholas's entrance status,
to a dynamic and chronological narration about Nicholas's subsequent social climbing. Lawrence gradually 'began to accept him as
increasingly familiar . . ., and to introduce him to the duke's matters,' while Nicholas in turn 'served his lord with a faithful service.'[55]

---

[49] Ibid., ch. 21, p. 116.
[50] The estimated year of his birth—see Zientara (1980), pp. 165–77, and Rabiej
(1999), pp. 393–400.
[51] *K.H.*, ch. 2, p. 109: *intravit . . . Sleziensis terre provinciam simpliciter et non habuit tunc
temporis in hac terra sive in patrimonio sive in aliqua proprietate ad passum pedis.*
[52] Ibid., ch. 24, p. 117.
[53] Ibid., ch. 7–8, pp. 112–3; ch. 11, p. 115; ch. 18, p. 116; ch. 40, p. 120; ch.
43, p. 121.
[54] Ibid., ch. 2, pp. 109–10.
[55] Ibid., ch. 2, p. 110.

In 1209, Lawrence became bishop of another important western Polish city, Lubusz, and Nicholas 'received from the . . . duke the office of chief notary'—a position which, Peter added just here, gave him, 'rule over the whole land of Silesia, if I may so put it.'[56] Peter underscored this outcome a bit later in the narrative, when he closed his vignette of Nicholas on a moral note, and recalled that, 'in all his great fortune,' the notary had 'prudently kept himself in a posture of great humility, even though no cleric before or after him ever rose to such power near the dukes in this land.'[57] These are the first passages in the *Book* were Peter referred to power, expressed his vision of its constituent elements (that is, characterized power as a personal attribute, a dimension of a particular relationship 'near' someone else, and an object of deliberate social climbing), and related power to property.

Thereafter, Nicholas systematically capitalized on that power. He used it to acquire the particular group of villages in the lowland region of the Oława river system which subsequently became the 'territory of Henryków'—and with whose histories Abbot Peter was specifically concerned in several subsequent chapters of the *Book*.[58] All of the holdings he acquired had had belonged to a substantial population of earlier possessors, peasants and small knights, for at least one full generation before 1209[59]—whom Nicholas systematically expropriated, one by one, always, Peter was careful to add, 'with the permission of,' 'by the grace of,' or 'having requested' Duke Henry to do so.[60] In the process of receiving these holdings, Nicholas consolidated them into what Peter variously called one 'proper inheritance,' 'his own wealth,' or one enlarged, substantial estate, 'the territory of Henryków.'[61] In addition, Nicholas altered a central element in the ecology of that 'territory,' and reinterpreted its place-name, *Henryków*, in what appears to have been a strategy to change the

---

[56] Ibid., ch. 2, p. 110: *summe notarie offitium et ut verum dicam regimen tocius terre Sleziensis . . . committeretur.*

[57] Ibid., ch. 3, pp. 110–1: *licet ante eum vel post eum in hac terra circa dominos duces tam potens clericus nunquam surrexit.*

[58] Ibid., ch. 26–7, pp. 117–8; ch. 29–44, pp. 118–21.

[59] Two sketches of that population include Grüger (1977), and Górecki (1983), pp. 19–25.

[60] *K.H.*, ch. 7, p. 112; ch. 29, p. 118; ch. 32, p. 119; ch. 38, p. 120.

[61] Ibid., ch. 7, p. 112 (*bona*); 27, p. 117 (*conpetens hereditas*); ch. 34, p. 119 (*totum territorium istud*); ch. 39, p. 120 (*hoc territorium Heinrichow*).

proprietary association with that estate away from its former possessors, and in favor of himself and Duke Henry the Bearded.[62]

Sometime in the course of this process, while he was rising in his
'opulence,' Nicholas decided to use the estate he had accumulated
at Henryków to endow some group of the religious. In a long and
complicated section, Abbot Peter reconstructed Nicholas's steps that
led to the selection of the Cistercians as beneficiaries, the foundation itself, and recruitment of the first group of monks in or shortly
before 1227.[63] Peter used that passage, very explicitly, to reconstruct
(or invent), first, a very particular balance of initiatives behind the
resulting monastic foundation, and, second, a very particular interpretation of Nicholas's role in the alienation of his estate during that
foundation. In other words, Peter presented Nicholas's foundation
initiative and its consequences as a complicated relationship, centered
on the possession and alienation of property; and he used this story
to sort out (or, again, to invent) the elements of that relationship.

According to Peter's image, the central partners in that relationship were Nicholas and Henry the Bearded. Right from the outset
of his plans, Nicholas required the duke's permission to dispose of
the 'territory of Henryków' in favor of the new monastery. Immediately
after deciding to endow the Cistercians, he ruminated on 'how he
might gain the duke's consent' to the gift.[64] He elicited that consent
in 1222, by inviting to his estate at Henryków a substantial assembly, including 'all the greatly born of this land,' Duke Henry the
Bearded, the duke's son the younger Henry, and, very importantly,
three mediators whom he asked to present his request to the elder
Henry—the bishops of Wrocław, Poznań, and Lubusz, with all whom
(as Peter reminded his audience just at this point of his narrative)
he had long enjoyed connections.[65] The assembly of 1222 is an excellent example of an exercise, by Nicholas, of power in the sense
meant here. For a specific, strategic purpose, Nicholas orchestrated
three resources he had systematically accumulated since about 1209:
an estate, within which he hosted the assembly, and which was itself
the intended object of his conveyance; a history of contacts with the
three bishops; and a history of contact with Duke Henry.

---

[62] Ibid., ch. 35, p. 119; on Nicholas's activities here, see Górecki (1998b), pp.
143–4.
[63] Ibid., ch. 4–11, pp. 111–4.
[64] Ibid., ch. 4, p. 111.
[65] Ibid., ch. 6, p. 112.

Peter's vignette of Duke Henry in the ensuing process is really quite odd. The duke began by resisting Nicholas's initiative. Here and elsewhere in the *Book*, Peter reiterated several times that Nicholas's plan had preempted Henry's expectations with regard to the estate Nicholas had accumulated: 'The duke thought that after the end of Nicholas's days, he and his descendants would possess all these inheritances,' but 'whilst the duke thought one thing, Almighty God illuminated his servant's breast' to dispose of his holdings otherwise.[66] The subject of the rest of Peter's narration of the Henryków assembly was the difficult but ultimately successful elimination of Henry's resistance—when at last the duke agreed to the foundation Nicholas had initiated, subject, however, to carefully specified terms. Peter reconstructed the intervening negotiations between the three bishops and the duke, concerning Nicholas's initiative, in painstaking detail, by means of a passage which contains the most substantial segment of Nicholas's biography, and which indeed comprises the longest continuous narrative on any subject in the *Henryków Book*.[67]

These negotiations concerned the conditions of Henry's consent to the foundation of the monastery. Throughout the relevant passage, Peter couched that consent in a majestic image expressing a mixture of reluctance and great power: even though, he had Henry say, every transaction taking place under my 'rule' was conditional on the whim of his will—on 'our "it shall be" or "it shall not be"'— nevertheless, in order not to frustrate 'so pious a proposal,' the duke now gave his consent, subject, however, to his own appropriation of Nicholas's founding initiative.[68] Several times, and with great emphasis, Peter had Henry insist that (and these are the exact two words) the *auctoritas fundationis* of the monastery should be 'attributed' not to Nicholas, but to himself and his branch of the Piast dynasty, especially his son Henry.[69] In those same passages, Henry reminded the three bishops and all assembled that, in every sense and all along, Nicholas had been his political creature, and that therefore the estates he had acquired in 'the territory of Henryków' from 1209 onward were in fact not his own, but the duke's.[70] In other words, Peter

---

[66] Ibid., ch. 3, p. 110.
[67] Ibid., ch. 6–9, pp. 112–4.
[68] Ibid., ch. 8, p. 113.
[69] Ibid., ch. 7–8, p. 113; ch. 10, p. 114.
[70] Ibid., ch. 7–8, pp. 112–3; ch. 10, p. 114.

used his image of the events of 1222 to classify the proprietary status of Nicholas's estate. He reiterated that classification throughout his work, as he noted that all the acquisitions of the monastery, including Henryków, had formerly belonged to Duke Henry and his dynasty.

Peter devoted the rest of the story about the events at Henryków to a description of what, fully aware of the current dangers of that word, I will call a ritual.[71] Toward the end of the assembly, Duke Henry commanded the performance, before all assembled, of a sequence of acts which he—and of course Abbot Peter himself—intended to define the web of legal relationships between the duke, his son, his other descendants, Nicholas, and the future monastery. Nicholas 'knelt before the dukes, resigned all his possessions to them,' and epitomized the transfer by giving the dukes his cowl. In response, the two Henrys formally re-conferred the *auctoritas fundationis* back upon Nicholas. After these transfers, the older Henry spelled out the formal content of the *auctoritas fundationis* which he had been so strongly asserting, and he further divided that *auctoritas* among his son and Nicholas[72]—thus, as Peter portrayed it, formally enabling Nicholas to proceed with the recruitment of the first group of monks.[73]

By means of this complicated scene, Peter presented the most important single event of his work as a collective negotiation with—indeed, against—ducal power. That event reflected, and further defined, a complicated set of relationships affecting, on the one hand, several actors, and, on the other, the position of all of them with respect to his monastery—or, to put that the other way around, the monastery's position within a local political universe. To Peter, the central question affecting all these issues was the exact nature of the connection between Nicholas and the older Henry. That connection can be without anachronism described as both personal and real, in the technical legal sense of those words: the former established through service, office, and favor, the latter through the duke's

---

[71] I am alluding, of course, to Philippe Buc's recent critique of this construct, in Buc (2001), which requires a much fuller response than can be sustained in reference to Peter's retrogressive image of this one act of submission. Wherever one now stands, after Buc's work, on what might be called the epistemology of ritual, Abbot Peter surely thought he was describing one, and implied that his audience would have found the description, and the event itself, meaningful and authoritative.

[72] *K.H.*, ch. 10, p. 114.

[73] Ibid., ch. 11, p. 114.

grants of an estate to Nicholas. The meaning of that relationship which Peter clearly wished to convey to his monks in his story of 1222, and in repeated reminders throughout the *Book*, was a degree of dependence of Nicholas on the duke so extreme as to enable Henry to negate the importance, indeed the reality, of Nicholas's initiative altogether—and thus, first, substitute himself for Nicholas as the real founder, and, second, re-allot to Nicholas a role in the foundation which was entirely derivative of his own. That, as Peter saw it, had been the most important aim, and the successful function, of the ritual between Nicholas and the two Henrys.

Now, here again I am relatively unconcerned about the degree of correspondence between Peter's complicated construction of this scene in the later 1260s, and the realities that were its purported historical subject almost half a century earlier. What seems more important is that, at the time Peter was writing, he was confronting several alternative traditions, or sets of memories, concerning, on the face of the record, those same past realities. Those alternative traditions are reflected in several charters, issued by Piast dukes and ecclesiastics associated with Silesia, Great Poland, and Little Poland, in 1225, 1228, 1236 and 1268,[74] that is, spanning the entire period upon which Peter reflected in the *Book*. The existence of these divergent traditions regarding the issues he himself repeatedly identified as central strongly suggests that, by means of the *Book* itself, he was actively negotiating that divergence, in favor of one particular interpretation.

The first three charters take us back to the period that makes up the beginning of Peter's own story. In 1225, Duke Władysław Odonic, ruler of Great Poland, gave the monastery of Lubiąż a substantial estate in the far north of his duchy, and added a modest gift for, as he put it, 'the new shoot' and 'daughter of that monastery' which was 'to be built in the patrimony of lord Nicholas, notary of the duke of Silesia'—that is, the Henryków monastery.[75] Three years later, Duchess Grzymisława of Kraków, widow of Leszek the White

---

[74] *Schlesisches Urkundenbuch*, vol. 1, ed. Heinrich Appelt (Vienna, Cologne, and Graz, 1963–71), vol. 2–4, ed. Winfried Irgang (Vienna, Cologne, and Graz, 1978–88), vol. 5, ed. Winfried Irgang (Cologne, Weimar, and Vienna, 1993), vol. 6, ed. Winfried Irgang and Daphne Schadewalt (Cologne, Weimar, and Vienna, 1998) [hereafter *S.U.*], 1:no. 252 (1225), pp. 184–5; no. 286 (1228), p. 210; no. 290 (1228), pp. 213–4; 2:no. 124 (1236), pp. 81–2; 4:no. 78 (1268), pp. 65–6.

[75] *S.U.*, 1:no. 252 (1225), p. 184: *territorium contuli beate Marie in Lubens . . . et filie eiusdem cenobii que construenda est in patrimonio domini Nicholai notarii ducis Zlesie.*

who had died in 1227, noted a gift of a holding in Little Poland by
Nicholas to 'his' monastery.[76] Also in 1228, Duke Henry the Bearded
himself referred to the estate of the new monastery as 'all the inheritances which [Nicholas] has possessed in our duchy by our grace
while he was alive, whether by reason of purchase, or through some
kind of gift.'[77] In the same charter, Henry used this particular interpretation of Nicholas's tenure, and of his own relationship with
Nicholas, as the rationale for appropriating the founding initiative
from the notary.[78] Less than a decade later, Paul, bishop of Poznań,
likewise in Great Poland, confirmed his own gift to the Henryków
monastery, and in passing revisited the subject of Nicholas and his
estate. '[F]or remission of our sins and the remedy of the soul
of . . . Duke Władysław [Odonic],' Paul was donating an estate to
'the house . . . at Henryków, . . . in the diocese of Wrocław, founded
by . . . Nicholas, notary of Duke Henry of Silesia.'[79]

Quite consistently with one another, and with Abbot Peter's narration much later, the two dukes and the bishop all identified Nicholas
as Duke Henry's notary. This relationship, linking the two men
through office, was the common core of the remembered knowledge
about Nicholas. That, however, is where the similarity ends. Władysław,
Grzymisława, and Henry differed in their formal proprietary classification of Nicholas's estate, while Henry and Bishop Paul differed in
their emphasis on Nicholas's role in the foundation. In 1225, Władysław
referred to Nicholas's estate as a *patrimonium*—a term somewhat
unusual in thirteenth-century Polish sources, but, when used, referring to a fully inheritable, ancestral estate, and most specifically contrasted with an acquisition,[80] which is indeed how Duke Henry
classified Nicholas's estate three years later, when he described it as

---

[76] Ibid., no. 286 (1228), p. 210. This is a register only, summarized by the editor, Heinrich Appelt; the archival original is not available to me at the moment.

[77] Ibid., no. 290 (1228), p. 214: *omnes hereditates quas in ducatu nostro sive racione emp-
cionis sive donacionis quocumque modo nostra gracia vivens possedit.*

[78] Ibid.: *dominus Nycolaus beate memorie quondam notarius noster possessiones suas quas in
terra nostra habuit in manus nostras et filii nostri Henrici olim resignavit ea . . . racione ut . . . flos
ordinis Cysterciensis nostra et filii nostri auctoritate in Henrichow insereretur et ibidem famulis
Christi . . . claustrum construeretur.*

[79] Ibid., 2:no. 124 (1236), p. 81, lines 36–9: *domus . . . de Henrichow ordinis Cysterciensis
que est sita in dyocesi Wratislauiensi quam fundavit frater noster felicis recordacionis Nycolaus
notarius Henrici ducis Slesie, in remissionem peccatorum nostrorum et pro remedio anime predicti
Wlodizlai ducis Polonie contulimus* an estate.

[80] On this distinction in medieval Poland, see Górecki (2000b), pp. 485–9, 497–511.

a complex of holdings received by the duke's 'grace,' by 'purchase,' or by 'some kind of gift.' Also in 1228, Duke Henry repeatedly minimized Nicholas's role in the actual endowment to a 'proposal,' and portrayed himself as the real donor, whereas in 1236 Bishop Paul specifically mentioned Nicholas as 'founder,' and, in the context of his own additional gift, associated the Henryków monastery with another duke, Władysław, the ruler of Great Poland, the province of which he was bishop—perhaps deliberately eclipsing Henry. These discrepancies suggest a strong political logic in the memories surrounding the transactions Abbot Peter situated in 1222.

These discrepancies were presumably related to political conflicts between Dukes Henry and Władysław that lasted until their deaths in the late 1230s, and so to broader issues of Piast dynastic politics, which I am unable to explore at present. In the present context, they are interesting as a marker of a continuous and competing set of traditions lasting fully into Peter's own present—when, in 1268, Pope Clement IV issued for the monastery of Henryków a letter concerning exactly those same subjects. The letter is addressed directly to the monks and the abbot of Henryków—that is, to Peter—in answer to an earlier 'request by you.' The purpose of that request had been papal confirmation of a brief history of the monastery's foundation. Clement's letter noted that Peter's request had 'contained' this history, and thus Peter and the monks had sent the papal curia some kind of memorandum,[81] which was then transcribed into, or summarized as, the *narratio* of the papal letter, and further validated by its *dispositio*. Not surprisingly, the subjects of that memorandum were Nicholas and Duke Henry the Bearded, their relative roles in the alienation of Nicholas's estate to the monastery, and the proprietary classification of that estate—exactly the topics on which the traditions concerning the foundation diverged, and with which Peter was most clearly concerned throughout his *Book*.

In a complicated passage, Peter had informed the papal curia that, 'in accordance with Nicholas's pious disposition'—and 'on the condition' stipulated by Nicholas, that Duke Henry 'cause a monastery of [the Cistercian] Order to be ... founded with ... possessions of this kind [*possessiones huiusmodi*]'—Henry 'founded and endowed [the]

---

[81] *S.U.*, 4:no. 78 (1268), p. 66, lines 1–2: *Exhibita ... nobis vestra petitio continebat* the material summarized in Clement's *narratio*.

monastery' with the estate Nicholas had accumulated.[82] This way of putting things attributes much of the initiative to Nicholas, while clearly identifying the duke as the essential founder and donor. The classification of Nicholas's estate as 'possessions of this kind' is a bit enigmatic. Of what kind? The papal letter further narrates that Nicholas had initiated the foundation by 'relinquish[ing] into the duke's hand certain possessions that had belonged to him, and which he had held of the duke in fief.'[83] In other words, this particular document presented, and perhaps resolved, the ambiguities of this relationship in the language of feudal lordship: the interpersonal connection between Duke Henry and Nicholas, and the property enmeshed in it, were both classified as a fief.

Who did the classifying? Was the language of feudal lordship devised and supplied by Abbot Peter himself, along with his initial 'request' and whatever supporting record he submitted to the papal chancery before 1268? Or, was it applied by learned clerks at some subsequent phase of formulation and refinement of that 'request,' for example, in the cathedral chapter of Wrocław, or indeed at the papal chancery itself? Whoever, and at whichever stage, actually cast the old and ambiguous relationship between duke and notary in feudal language, the effect, in the context of 1268, seems quite clear. The formula represented yet another attempt at expressing and coherently ordering, and thus perhaps eliminating, the discrepancy among the accumulated memories about the events to which it pertained—an outcome futher validated by its incorporation in the papal letter, just as Peter wished. Within a year after the issuance of Clement's letter, Peter retired as abbot, and devoted the remaining years of his life to writing the *Book*—of which the central subject was the one relationship, deep in the past, about which he had solicited help from the Roman curia, and to which we now, as it were, come with him full circle.

In the late 1260s, Abbot Peter composed, and used, one short written record, and undertook the writing of another, explicitly in order to negotiate within a range of divergent traditions that cen-

---

[82] Ibid., lines 4–6.

[83] Ibid., lines 3–4; the core relevant phrase, spanning lines 3–6, is: *quasdam possessiones ad eum spectantes quasque ab eodem duce tenebat in feudum in manibus ipsius ducis sub ea conditione dimisit ut de parte possessionum huiusmodi monasterium vestri ordinis in . . . Henrichow . . . de novo fundari faceret.*

tered on a particular past actor, and that affected relationships fundamental for the legal and political position of his monastery. Which of these traditions was, relatively speaking, accurate—whether in the deep past on which Peter was reflecting, or in his own present around 1268—is empirically inaccessible, and perhaps meaningless. Whatever those past realities may in fact have been, Peter's own emphatic and repetitive reiteration of one, particular version of them was a sustained act of selection and interpretation within the resulting heritage of tradition and memory, which concerned two subjects: power, that is, the balance of volition and agency between Henry and Nicholas; and the law, that is, the formal proprietary classification of Nicholas's estate, and the implications of that classification for the identity of the donor in its conveyance. This is the sense in which Abbot Peter acted both as a witness, and as an interpreter, of law and power in the Henryków region.

Albert

Peter's recollection of Albert was, in a sense, a part of his remembrance of Nicholas. The earliest action Peter attributed to Albert was explicable in terms of Nicholas's biography. Around 1209, at the time 'when [Nicholas] shone with the opulence in things, and . . . was a newcomer,' Albert 'attached himself' to him 'with a certain special familiarity,' and 'said that he was his relative.' Albert continued to assert this particular tie until Nicholas's death in 1227, and, after Nicholas died, 'for that reason,' he 'often said that he was advocate of this cloister by reason of kinship . . . with Nicholas.'[84] In other words, Albert joined in, or, as it were, adopted for his own use, Nicholas's upward mobility, exactly at the time when Nicholas had reached an initial phase of success on that trajectory. Albert did this in two phases: first, by deliberately shaping the social reputation concerning his connection with Nicholas; second, with Nicholas gone, by capitalizing on the implications of that connection, and asserting a formal relationship with the monastery.

Albert continued to express that latter claim over the subsequent years, and reiterated it, apparently with special emphasis, 'when Duke

---

[84] *K.H.*, ch. 54, p. 123.

Henry [II], our founder, was also dead after the pagans,' that is, after 1241.[85] Thus, Abbot Peter presented the disappearances of two crucial actors in his story, Nicholas in 1227, and the younger Henry in 1241, as the specific occasions for Albert's escalation of his claims based on his earlier association with Nicholas. Furthermore, at this point in his narration, Peter recalled that other persons had long nursed similar claims, on a similar basis: 'The sons of a certain Siegród said and say the same thing . . . Siegród likewise reputed himself to be Nicholas's relative, because he had formerly been a neighbor of Henryków.'[86] Albert, Siegród's sons, and perhaps Siegród himself, had all created a particular set of social memories, focused on Nicholas, either, in Albert's case, by careful maintenance of a relationship and its their subsequent manipulation, or, as with Siegród and sons, by a partisan interpretation a fact suggesting that a relationship had existed—the fact of nearby residence, or 'neighborhood.' Peter's description of both claims, and his attention to their implications, in the present tense shows that these interpretations remained highly plausible into his own present. Here then we have another area of permanent ambiguity, based on a divergent set of memories concerning Nicholas and the relationships that had surrounded him.

Meanwhile, in the period spanning the 1220s, the Mongol invasion, and the mid-1240s, Albert actively reinforced that relationship and its carefully manufactured implications. Sometime before 1229, he married into the local nobility—he 'took as wife a daughter of a certain noble [*cuiusdam nobilis*] named Dzierżko, by whom he begat a daughter.'[87] That year, his wife 'suddenly died,' perhaps in childbirth, but Albert's connection with Dzierżko remained important well beyond 1241.[88] Right after her death, he used his interlude as a widower to establish a direct connection with the newly established monastery. He gave the monks a small portion of his estate, Ciepłowoda, then set off to the eastern Baltic on one of the early crusades then underway in that region.[89] On the eve of the departure, he

---

[85] Ibid.: *Albertus iunxit se ei* [i.e., Nicholas] *quadam familiaritate speciali dicens se esse eius cognatum unde defuncto . . . Nycolao et post paganos domino duce Heinrico nostro fundatore etiam defuncto sepe dixit Albertus se esse ratione cognationis domini Nycolai advocatum huius claustri.*

[86] Ibid.: *Id ipsum dixerunt et dicunt filii cuiusdam Segrodonis. Qui . . . Segrodo quia olim vicinus erat Heinrichow etiam reputavit se esse domini Nycolai cognatum.*

[87] Ibid., ch. 46, p. 121.

[88] Ibid., ch. 46, p. 121; ch. 111, p. 146; see text at note 100 below.

[89] Górski (1971), pp. 34–41; Christiansen (1980), pp. 79–88, 100–1; Biskup and Labuda (1986), pp. 110–26.

made a further post-obit gift for the monks, in the event he perished, promising 'that if he did not return, the cloister . . . was to
possess the entire territory of Cieplowoda, but that if he did return,
[it] was to receive [only] the portion he had given it earlier.' In the
event, he came back 'from Prussia, healthy and whole,' remarried—
this time to a German wife, 'by whom he begat sons and daughters'—and ushered in a long period when '[t]he cloister possessed'
the initial modest gift 'from him and his sons, peacefully and for
many years.'[90]

Peter carefully crafted this early part of Albert's story by blend-
ing a stretch of biography with a happy ending, and portraying the
knight in terms of a sequence of laudable actions and their consequences: pious gifts, enactment of a knightly journey, crusading,
remarriage, and a substantial period of peaceful coexistence with the
saints and their earthly custodians. In these respects, the early Albert
served Peter as an embodiment of the moral and political qualities
of the time of the 'old dukes.' On the other hand, the context within
which Peter located Albert after 1241 could not be more different.
That context was the global disorder resulting from the Mongol invasion. Significantly, this was the sole terrain on which Peter cast the
remainder of Albert's biography. In other words, after 1241 Albert
mattered as an actor specifically insofar as he related to that passage from the blissful past toward the difficult present with which
Peter was concerned throughout his *Book*.

Within this setting, Albert cuts an ambiguous figure. On the one
hand, Peter portrayed him as an example of all that went wrong
with the exercise of power in Silesia after 1241. That is, Albert
promptly took advantage of the post-Mongol disarray to expand,
consolidate, and reorganize his estate—actions which Peter explicitly portrayed as part of the broad systemic degeneration: 'The knights
dominated the land, and each seized whatever pleased him from the
ducal inheritances. And so . . ., for a modest sum of money, Albert
acquired from the boyish Duke Bolesław two ducal inheritances' just
to the east of Cieplowoda.[91] He consolidated the three localities into
one large estate and one single unit of property: '[H]aving ousted
the heirs of those two villages, he joined [the arable] to his village

[90] Ibid., ch. 46, p. 121.
[91] Ibid., ch. 47, p. 122.

of Ciepłowoda. For this reason the names of those [two] villages were completely obliterated, and changed to the name of . . . Albert's village, *Ciepłowoda*.'[92] He culminated this proprietary transformation[93] by recruiting new settlers, a step Peter likewise placed in the same moral and political context: 'While this and many other similar evils, very harmful to the dukes, were occuring in the land, Albert began to settle . . . Ciepłowoda, including the said [two annexed] villages, with Germans.'[94] Finally, 'in those days' he emerged as 'very powerful near the duke and throughout the land.'[95] What we have here is an individual vignette of vigorous social climbing and aggressive seizure of property, which Peter presented as, at least in substantial degree, morally homologous with the period during which it occurred.

Yet, on the other hand, during exactly the same period, Albert served the monks as a source of protection against other 'knights' who, quite like him, embodied the post-1241 realities. In particular, he successfully mediated conflicts between the monastery and two difficult neighboring knights, one named Peter Stoszowic, the other Przybek. As Albert had done, Peter and Przybek expanded their estates eastward—but, unlike Albert, by outright seizure, not purchase at a bargain, and at the expense of the monastery, not the duke. As with Albert, Peter explained these seizures in terms of the surrounding context. '[T]he foul pagans,' he remarked, 'entered this province, and did many things worthy of lament and tears, . . . and so Peter son of . . . Stosz saw that the cloister was nearly destroyed and usurped for himself' two areas of forest belonging to the monastery, 'because they adjoined his village of Piotrowice.'[96] Likewise, recalling that 'after the pagans each knight plundered whatever and in whatever amount he wanted,' he added that '[a]mong other [seizures], a certain knight Przybek son of . . . Dzierżko placed by his presumption [a village or a boundary] within the boundaries of the cloister.'[97]

Albert helped the monks against Peter Stoszowic at two phases in the ensuing conflicts. First, after about two agonizing years when his

---

[92] Ibid., ch. 48, p. 122.

[93] For the significance of changes in place-names for property transfer (much of it documented by Peter himself elsewhere in the *Book*), see Górecki (1998b), pp. 143–4; Górecki (1998a), pp. 545–7.

[94] *K.H.*, ch. 49, p. 122.

[95] Ibid., ch. 111, p. 146.

[96] Ibid., ch. 103, p. 142.

[97] Ibid., ch. 103, p. 142; ch. 111, p. 146.

predecessor as abbot, Bodo, sought justice before the ineffectual Duke Bolesław II, that duke finally allowed a trial in the matter, at which Albert 'spoke the word of the cloister'[98]—that is, formally represented the monastery. Second, after Bolesław's verdict at that trial in favor of the monastery remained ineffective—and, despite the verdict, 'Stoszowic menaced [the contested area] so severely that no one dared to live there under the cloister's authority'—Albert 'advised' the abbot to agree to a compromise by surrendering a part of the holding Peter had transgressed. Bodo did so, and as a result 'Peter was reconciled with the cloister, and allowed the establishment of a village [in the contested region] under the cloister's authority.'[99] Meanwhile, Albert also arranged a similar territorial compromise with Przybek—who, as Abbot Peter reminded his monks at just this point, had been his brother-in-law by the long deceased Polish first wife[100]—this time by assembling the knight and a large group at a nearby hilltop, and ordering 'four peasants' to trace a new linear boundary through the contested area below. Again, as a result, 'the cloister remained in this place in tranquillity and peace for a long time.'[101]

Abbot Peter's presentations of those outcomes echo his earlier image of the happy significance of Albert's presence near the monastery after his return from the Prussian crusade. In this sense, Albert, as imagined by Peter, facilitated the restoration of those desirable real-ities from the pre-Mongol past with whose recovery Peter was so concerned. On the other hand, his help was manifestly self-interested, since it coincided with his own open and explicit assertions of advo-cacy over the monastery—indeed, was a practical performance of precisely that role. In this regard, Albert's actions were a continuation of his purposeful manipulation of the political realities that had ini-tially been focused on Nicholas and spanned the decades before 1241. Thus, as deployed in Peter's narrative, the figure of Albert the Bearded emerges as a personalized focal point, a locus as it were, of the agenda, fears, and hopes that recur throughout the *Book*. In this sense, Albert fully resembles Nicholas—and so the two narratives are as related to one another as were the actual men to whom they

---

[98] Ibid., ch. 106, p. 143.
[99] Ibid., ch. 108, p. 144.
[100] Ibid., ch. 111, p. 146: *Hic idem Albertus fuerat sororius dicti militis Pribiconis.*
[101] Ibid., pp. 146–7; see more fully, Górecki (1984), pp. 41–2.

refer. The remainder of what Peter has to say about Albert clearly
and explicitly pursues that agenda, to allay the fears and strengthen
the hopes, once again through careful retroactive presentation.

Albert was long dead by the time Peter began to write the *Book*
in the late 1260s. Nevertheless, the abbot thought it important to
reflect on Albert, and especially to reinterpret the memories concerning him, and to draw out the implications of those memories,
and of their reinterpretation, for his monks. He remembered Albert
above all as a relentless social climber, a 'keen' character. He opened
his longest continuous biographical passage about Albert with an
explanation of that trait, in words suggesting special attention or
care: 'We have spoken at length about Albert . . ., yet it is appropriate and . . . necessary for our successors that we say something
more . . . about . . . [his] person and his keenness.'[102] He closed the
same passage with an expression of moral ambivalence about this
knight which does not recur in any other context or passage in the
Book; and he tempered that ambivalence with a note that appears
oddly coy: 'Although, for the future use of the cloister, we have
said . . . some contrary things about him, he should not be separated
from . . . the brothers' prayers, but should very much be included in
them, because thanks to him the cloister possesses two inheritances,'
including the modest initial gift of 1229.[103]

Given Albert's involvement on behalf the monastery, especially as
a peacemaker, this seems, on the face of it, a rather restrained,
indeed stingy, attribution of posthumous credit—suggesting that, from
Peter's perspective, that entire involvement had been, and remained,
shrouded in moral ambivalence. Significantly, Peter resolved the
quandary by focusing specifically on the discrepancy of memories
concerning Albert's connection to Nicholas. In his posthumous
reflection on the knight, the abbot specifically addressed the subject
of Albert's ancestry, for the express purpose of refuting Albert's puta-
tive kinship with Nicholas. He framed the refutation, and its implications for the monastery, as a formal proof, which he directed to
his monks didactically. He began with the promise to demonstrate

---

[102] *K.H.*, ch. 53, p. 123: *Licet in longum de sepedicto Alberto et suo facto extendimus trac-
tatum tamen est congruum et nostris successoribus valde necessarium adhuc de persona dicti Alberti
et eius subtilitate scribendo aliquid loqui.*

[103] Ibid., ch. 57, p. 123: *Licet pro utilitate claustri futura simus de persona . . . Alberti
quedam contraria scribendo locuti, tamen non est ab oratione fratrum communi segregandus sed
valde adiungendus quia per eum claustrum possidet duas hereditates.*

'[t]hat Albert should not be associated with Nicholas by any tie of kinship,' carried out that demonstration by recalling the very different ancestry of the two men—Albert's through his father 'from Germany,' and through his mother from the 'Walloon street' of Wrocław, Nicholas's from a middling knightly family in 'the province of Kraków'— and he clinched the demonstration by an exclamatory assertion of successful proof—*Ecce cognatio.*[104]

Immediately afterwards, he presented his monks with one of his emphatic and belabored political lessons: 'Thus we again and again persuade our successors, that, after viewing these writings and statements, they shall place no man over themselves by reason of any kinship, except only those who issue, or may [in the future] issue from the stock of the glorious duke of revered memory, Henry the Bearded.'[105] The result was a deliberate refutation of the basic premise on which Albert had systematically built his network of political associations, since perhaps as early as 1209. By his careful interpretations of the biographies of Nicholas and of Albert, of their intersection, and of the implications of that intersection over time, Peter sought to refute a pattern of relationships that, if widely accepted, threatened to complicate the one connection he thought most important: between the monastery and the dukes of Silesia. His need to do so in the 1260s indicates that Albert had in fact succeeded in passing as Nicholas's relative—that is, that the kinship tie he had asserted had become a part of that same tradition, or set of social memories, concerning an early network of important relationships and resulting patterns of power, with which Peter was otherwise concerned, and which he sought to renegotiate in his monastery's favor.

Law and Power Reinterpreted

In his reflections on the history of his monastery and estate, Abbot Peter of Henryków was centrally concerned with law and with power. His expression of those concerns provides a case study of the meaning of these two categories in the historical past, to him as a participant and observer, and to the population he observed, as well as

---

[104] Ibid., ch. 55, p. 123: *Ut Albertus nulla cognatione esset coniunctus Nycolao.... Ecce cognatio.*

[105] Ibid., ch. 56, p. 123.

to us as medievalists. Considered as a discreet dimension of social reality, the law is reflected in his work somewhat obliquely. Like other medieval authors, Peter operated within a clear but tacit framework of right and wrong, and he brought the law to bear as part of that framework in several ways.

First, quite simply, he was concerned with legal matters. In the case of Nicholas, those matters concerned property: its classification, and its implications for the identity of his monastery's original benefactors. In the case of Albert the Bearded, those matters concerned advocacy over the monastery, and the ties of kinship, friendship, neighborhood, and other association that affected advocacy. In his negotiations among several competing interpretations of these subjects, in favor of one particular preference, Peter positioned himself as a legal advisor to his community. This is the sense in which his work is about the law, although—with one major exception—he himself did not cast his argument in technical legal language. Instead, he framed his *Book* above all as an exhortatory, highly rhetorical, intellectually eclectic treatise of advice.

Perhaps as a result, it is a bit difficult to pin down the specific formal legal system or systems of the European Middle Ages—Canon Law, for example—on which Peter drew in his argument.[106] He had a very strong sense of legal right and wrong, and the whole thrust of his work implies the existence and authoritative force of some such system or systems; his interpretations make no sense against a presumed background of normative vacuum, a kind of political negotiation at large, so to speak.[107] The trouble, from our perspective, is the great complexity of normative frames of reference to which he turned, ranging from biblical material, open-ended exhortation, images of ducal justice or injustice, ethically-significant periodization, to (possibly) formal systems of law. This seamless quality of his ethical framework greatly complicates the indentification of that last compontent—with, however, that one major exception.

---

[106] I would like to thank John Hudson for prompting me to think through this issue in a fascinating discussion at St Andrews in April, 2001.

[107] We are, I think, in the midst of a new appreciation of what might be called the intrinsic, or autonomous, force of norms and normative systems, and a slight retrenchment from models of open-ended process; current examples of taking norms seriously include White (1987), Hudson (1994), Brown (1999); Hudson (2000), Górecki (2000b), Brown (2001).

In a section of the *Book* unrelated to Nicholas, the abbot explicitly invoked for his monks, in the form of an explicit rule, a norm of the 'Polish law' of property. This is his most direct reference to one major legal system operating in medieval Europe, namely, the customary law of a people or a region. I have explored elsewhere the logic of Peter's invocation of this norm within the situational context where it occurs. At present, the norm is important because in a substantive sense it converges with Peter's preoccupations with the legal classification of the personal and real relationships centering on Nicholas. The norm Peter invoked distinguished, under 'Polish law,' between ancestral estates ('patrimonies') and acquisitions.[108] Its invocation was a classification of different kinds of property, which, as we have seen, was also his central aim in remembering and interpreting Nicholas. Now, for whatever reason, Peter did not employ this distinction specifically in connection with Nicholas, but Nicholas's own contemporaries did—Duke Władysław in 1225, in referring to Nicholas's estate as a *patrimonium*, and Duke Henry in 1228, by characterizing it as a series of acquisitions.[109] Between them, these references all converge upon a common set of legal concepts and categories, and this is the sense in which Peter was clearly drawing on a differentiated system of contemporary law.

In contrast to law, Peter said much and clearly about power. How did he respond to it? Occasionally, he drew explicit attention to its importance—as when he related the 'power' of Nicholas or Albert the Bearded 'near the dukes' and 'in the land' to their actions, or concluded one story of political success by reminding his monks 'how good it is to know great men'[110]—but his most important approach went beyond this kind of association, exhortation, or moralizing. Throughout the *Book*, he interpreted particular interpersonal relationships—the specific ingredient in terms of which he conceptualized power—explicitly in order to safeguard his monastery from danger. In particular, he focused on the implications of the lives of two persons, Nicholas and Albert, as mediated by social memory and reputation, for the relationship between his community and the Piast dukes, which he viewed as fundamental.

---

[108] Górecki (2000b), pp. 482–4.
[109] *S.U.*, 1:no. 252 (1225), p. 184; no. 290 (1228), p. 213.
[110] *K.H.*, ch. 3, pp. 110–1; ch. 105, p. 143; ch. 111, p. 146.

Ironically, by means of his *Book*, he did exactly what he most disliked about Albert the Bearded: he actively sought to shape collective memory as a resource of power. He did so by confronting competing interpretations of particular relationships, and, with great emphasis and considerable repetition, worked to present one interpretation as right—that is, both truthful and politically beneficial—and the others as wrong—that is, false, in Albert's case actively fabricated, and politically dangerous. This is the specific sense in which his *Book* is an exercise in legitimation, and indeed of its converse, de-legitimation—a partisan presentation of a particular, preferred set of understandings of the deep past and its implications for the present and future, and an equally partisan subversion of the alternatives.

Bibliography

Bartlett (1993): Robert Bartlett, *The Making of Europe: Conquest, Colonization and Cultural Change 950–1350* (Princeton: 1993).

Biskup and Labuda (1986): Marian Biskup and Gerard Labuda, *Dzieje Zakonu Krzyżackiego w Prusach: gospodarka—społeczeństwo—państwo—ideologia* [The history of the Teutonic Order in Prussia: economy, society, state, ideology] (Gdańsk: 1986).

Brown (1999): Warren Brown, "The Use of Norms in Disputes in Early Bavaria," *Viator*, 30 (1999), 15–40.

—— (2001): *Unjust Seizure: Conflict, Interest, and Authority in an Early Medieval Society* (Ithaca: 2001).

Buc (2001): Philippe Buc, *The Dangers of Ritual: Between Early Medieval Texts and Social Scientific Theory* (Princeton: 2001).

Christiansen (1980): Eric Christiansen, *The Northern Crusades: The Baltic and the Catholic Frontier, 1100–1525* (Minneapolis: 1980).

Clanchy (1970): Michael Clanchy, "Remembering the Past and the Good Old Law," *History*, 55 (1970): 165–76.

—— (1993): *From Memory to Written Record: England 1066–1307*, 2nd ed. (Oxford: 1993).

Geary (1994): Patrick Geary, *Phantoms of Remembrance: Memory and Oblivion at the End of the First Millennium* (Princeton: 1994).

Górecki (1983): Piotr Górecki, "*Viator* to *ascriptitius*: Rural Economy, Lordship, and the Origins of Serfdom in Medieval Poland," *Slavic Review*, 42 (1983), 14–35.

—— (1984): "Politics of the Legal Process in Early Medieval Poland", *Oxford Slavonic Papers, n.s.*, 17 (1984), 23–44.

—— (1996): "*Ad Controversiam Reprimendam*: Family Groups and Dispute Prevention in Medieval Poland, c. 1200," *Law and History Review*, 14 (1996), 213–43.

—— (1997): "Rhetoric, Memory, and Use of the Past: Abbot Peter of Henryków as Historian and Advocate," *Cîteaux*, 48 (1997), 261–93.

—— (1998a): "Local Society and Legal Knowledge: A Case Study from the Henryków Region," in Henryk Gapski, ed., *Christianitas et cultura Europae: Księga Jubileuszowa Profesora Jerzego Kłoczowskiego—Cześć 1* [*Christianitas et cultura Europae*: A Jubilee Book for Professor Jerzy Kłoczowski—Part 1] (Lublin: 1998), pp. 544–50.

—— (1998b): "Communities of Legal Memory in Medieval Poland, c. 1200–1240," *Journal of Medieval History*, 24 (1998), 127–54.

—— (1999): "Violence and the Social Order in a Medieval Society: The Evidence from the Henryków Region, ca. 1150–ca. 1300," in Balázs Nagy and Marcell Sebők, eds., *The Man of Many Devices, Who Wandered Full Many Ways: Festschrift in Honor of János M. Bak* (Budapest: 1999), pp. 91–104.

—— (2000a): "Words, Concepts, and Phenomena: Knighthood, Lordship, and the Early Polish Nobility, c. 1100–c. 1350," in Anne Duggan, ed., *Nobles and Nobility in Medieval Europe: Concepts, Origins, Transformations* (Woodbridge: 2000), pp. 115–55.

—— (2000b): "A Historian as a Source of Law: Abbot Peter of Henryków and the Invocation of Norms in Medieval Poland, c. 1200–1270," *Law and History Review*, 18 (2000), 479–523.

Górski (1971): Karol Górski, *L'Ordine teutonico alle origini dello stato prussiano* (Turin: 1971).

Grodecki (1949): Roman Grodecki, ed. and tr., *Księga henrykowska. Liber Fundationis claustri sancte Marie Virginis in Heinrichow* (Poznań and Wrocław: 1949).

Grüger (1977): Heinrich Grüger, "Das Volkstum der Bevölkerung in den Dörfern des Zisterzienserklosters Heinrichau im mittelschlesischen Vorgebirgslande vom 13.–15. Jahrhundert," *Zeitschrift für Ostforschung*, 27 (1977), 241–61.

Guyotjeannin, Pycke, and Tock (1993): Olivier Guyotjeannin, Jacques Pycke, and Benoît-Michel Tock, *Diplomatique médiévale* (Turnhout: 1993).

Hudson (1994): John Hudson, *Land, Law and Lordship in Anglo-Norman England* (Oxford: 1994).

—— (2000): "Court Cases and Legal Arguments in England, c. 1066–1166," *Transactions of the Royal Historical Society*, 6th ser., 10 (2000), 91–115.

Jurek (1998): Tomasz Jurek, *Obce rycerstwo na Śląsku do połowy XIV wieku* [Foreign knighthood in Silesia until the mid-fourteenth century], 2nd ed. (Poznań: 1998).

Matuszewski (1981): Józef Matuszewski, *Najstarsze polskie zdanie prozaiczne: zdanie henrykowskie i jego tło historyczne* [The oldest Polish sentence in prose: the sentence of Henryków and its historical background] (Wrocław: 1981).

Matuszewski and Matuszewski (1991): Józef and Jacek Matuszewski, ed., *Liber Fundationis claustri sancte Marie Virginis in Heinrichow, czyli Księga henrykowska* (Wrocław: 1991).

Myśliwski (1999): Grzegorz Myśliwski, *Człowiek średniowiecza wobec czasu i przestrzeni (Mazowsze od XII do pol. XVI wieku)* [Medieval man with regard to time and space: Masovia from the twelfth to the mid-sixteenth century] (Warsaw: 1999).

—— (2000): "Between Memory and Anticipation: Temporal Consciousness of Mazovian Society, the 12th—the mid-16th Century," *Acta Poloniae Historica*, 82 (2000), 5–36.

Rabiej (1999): Piotr Rabiej, "Henryk II Pobożny" [Henry II the Pious], in Stanisław Szczur and Krzysztof Ożóg, eds., *Piastowie: Leksykon biograficzny* [The Piasts: a biographical lexicon] (Kraków: 1999), pp. 393–400.

White (1987): Stephen D. White, "Inheritances and Legal Arguments in Western France, 1050–1150," *Traditio*, 43 (1987), 55–103.

Zientara (1980): Benedykt Zientara, "Henryk II Pobożny" [Henry II the Pious], in Andrzej Garlicki, ed., *Poczet królów i książąt polskich* [A roll of Polish kings and dukes] (Warsaw: 1980), pp. 165–77.

POLITICAL STRUGGLE AND THE LEGITIMATION OF THE TOLEDAN PRIMACY: THE *PARS LATERANII CONCILII*

PATRICK HENRIET

Université de Paris IV-Sorbonne—SIREM

The subject of my research might seem more suitable for a collection of religious history—devoted, for example, to problems of ecclesiastical history and geography, to use the title of a most famous and useful dictionary—than in a book on political legitimation. Therefore, before proceeding further, it seems to me useful to note in what spirit this subject has been proposed: it is a matter of suggesting, or simply of recalling, through the analysis of one specific case, that during the Middle Ages, political and religious matters were indissoluble and a conflict involving solely clerics was not necessarily devoid of political elements. If the desire to dominate, on a symbolic as well as a 'real' level, land and men can be qualified as political, then the following pages, although not referring to kings or lay aristocrats, have their place here.

The angle of observation thus chosen is that of the Episcopal battles fought in Spain and Portugal, from the eleventh century, the reorganization of the ecclesiastical map and more particularly the primacy demanded by the see of Toledo. One of the initial stakes, political in every sense of the word, appears immediately. Could the map of the dioceses and the ecclesiastical provinces be independent from those of the kingdom? More explicitly, could a bishop be dependent on a metropolitan situated in another kingdom than his own? This question acquired a capital importance in the twelfth century, that is to say, during the great advancements of the Reconquest and at the same time, of the reconstruction of the ecclesiastical map, which is in many respects, a construction.[1] This was vital for the two first kings of Portugal, Afonso Enriquez (1128–1185) and Sancho I (1185–1211) who clashed with the Bishops of Compostela's pretensions

---

[1] Mansilla Reoyo (1994).

to exercise their dominance over the Portuguese dioceses formerly dependent on Mérida. The eminently political character of these conflicts is clearly confirmed in various texts, both royal and ecclesiastical, dating from this period.[2] Already in 1096, Urban II had accepted the exemption of the diocese of Burgos by remarking that Alfonso VI, king of *Hispania Citerior*, "would not accept, under any condition that the bishop of Burgos be submitted to the metropolitan of Tarragona, as Burgos was situated inside the limits of his kingdom while Tarragona depended on the Count of Barcelona".[3] A century later, in the 1180s, King Fernando II of Léon—if we are to believe the partisans of the see of Santiago de Compostela—convinced the bishop of Zamora to obey the Church of Santiago instead of Braga as "it must have pleased him to adorn his kingdom rather than another's."[4] Then in 1239, during the proceedings of the dispute between the bishops of Toledo and Tarragona for the control of the Church of Valencia, we find clearly stated the formula by which "kings are the lords of the bishops".[5]

When seen in this context, Toledo's claims to primacy posed the question of the possibility of a permanent, law-founded, pan-hispanic domination. During the Middle Ages, such an ideal could only be compared in Iberia to the notion of *Imperium*, but this claim, made essentially by Alfonso VI, then by his grand-son Alfonso VII, did not rest on any legal construction and, in the long term, it was never pursued as insistently as the question of primacy.[6] Had it been formulated on a level other than symbolic, it would have made for difficult relations between the different kingdoms. Those engaged directly in the conflict could hardly have been unconscious of this. Thus in 1217, the procurator of the Church of Braga made it clear to Pope Honorius III that the acceptance of primacy would most defiantly signify the domination of Toledo *super provinciam Narbonensem, super comitatum Barchinonensem, super regnum Aragonie, super regnum Navarre,*

---

[2] For the following examples, cf Feige (1978) 319–321.

[3] *Ceterum, Ildefonsus, hispaniae citerioris rex, Burgensem episcopum Tarraconensi metropolitano nequaquam patiebatur esse subiectum, ea de causa, quod infra regni sui terminos Burgus sit, Tarracon* (sic) *autem in Barchinonensis comitis potestate,* ed. Mansilla (1953) n° 37, 56.

[4] *Ut pocius obediret Compostellano quam Bracarensi archiepiscopo, quia magis sibi debebat placere suum regnum decorare quam alterius,* in a document dating from 1198/1199, ed. Feige (1978) 300.

[5] *Quod reges episcoporum domini erant,* Feige (1978) 319–320.

[6] Recent clarification on the question of the imperial title: Gambra (1997) 671–714.

super regnum Castelle, super regnum Legionense, super regnum Portugallie, super totam terram quam adhuc habent sarraceni in Hispania, que ultra terciam partem Hispanie est.[7] This text is eloquent, for if the conflict is 'ecclesiastical' the representative of the prelate gives, after the province of Narbonne, a list of political entities. And to clarify things even further he later on adds: "It would be a scandal in all the kingdoms of Spain if, by this reason, each king of Spain should be subjected to the king of Castile."[8]

I will not deal here with the question of the origins of the right of primacy and its Visigothic roots. Suffice it to recall that if the word and the concept existed, they were not though equipped with any institutional consistency.[9] In reality, the question of primacy does not arise until 1086, from the moment the Frenchman Bernard de Sédirac takes possession of the recently recovered see of Toledo. In 1088, putting forward a dignity obtained *ex antiquo*, Urban II granted to the new see a rather vague right of primacy.[10] In the following years, as the bishops of Braga (1100?), then of Compostela (1120) reached the archepiscopal rank, the oppositions to the domination of Toledo could only grow. There were several episodes, of which Peter Feige has retraced the history all throughout the twelfth century.[11] In a more or less diplomatic fashion, the papacy generally supported the Toledan claims and went as far as deposing archbishops who refused to obey the prelate, as it happened two consecutive times for the incumbent of Braga, John Peculiar (1145 and 1150).[12]

In the history of the battle for primacy, the text studied here is both late and exceptional. Late, as it refers to the Fourth Lateran Council (1215), during which the archbishop of Toledo, Rodrigo Jiménez de Rada is supposed to have vigorously attacked his Hispanic adversaries. Exceptional, as the source reporting the events, behind the appearance of an objective report, is in reality a rather detailed narrative, which offers list of the different arguments for legitimating— or even, if to a lesser extent, rejecting—primacy. The question of these legitimations can therefore be studied here by way of a case

---

[7] Feige (1978) 405–406. Commentary ibid., 281–285.
[8] *Preterea cum scandalum esset per omnia regna Hispanie, cum per hoc quilibet rex Hispanie submitteretur regno Castelle*, Feige (1978) 423.
[9] Rivera Recio J.F. (1955).
[10] Mansilla Reoyo (1953) n° 24, 40 and n° 26, 42.
[11] Feige (1978) (1988) (1991).
[12] Feige (1978) 284–300.

as concrete as it is privileged. The concept of 'legitimacy' is here understood in its most 'weberian' sense, that which permits a power— and in the Middle Ages the power held by an archbishop is evidently one of the most enviable and respected within the Christian society—the ability to auto-justify itself in order to exist and to develop.[13]

The *Pars concilii Lateranii* recounts the intervention during the Fourth Lateran Council of the archbishop of Toledo, Rodrigo Jiménez de Rada in the presence of Pope Innocent III as well as an assembly of prelates, clerics and laymen. In the extended version—which the Church of Toledo decided to keep for posterity's sake by including it in a codex entirely devoted to the question of primacy—it seems to be composed of two different parts.[14] An originally independent part begins with the words *Et quoniam velut umbra*. Its structure was, at least initially, that of a charter, with its preamble, its notification, a *promulgatio* and a *narratio*. The story ended with a datation.[15] A shorter version of this part, together with a list of the Hispanic bishops present at Lateran IV, was written in a 1200×1250 script on the end-leaf of codex containig a collection of the privileges granted to the Church of Toledo, produced in the first half of the thirteenth century.[16] However, in the 'complete' version, the *Pars concilii Lateranii* (hereafter PCL) is preceded by another much shorter and entirely narrative text. The *quoniam velut umbra* part is here notably much longer.

After having recalled the progress of the council at Lateran, qualified as *sancta et universalis sinodus*, in the presence of various Eastern patriarchs, the author of the story reviews a sermon by Jiménez de Rada, delivered in front of both clerics as well as laymen in at least a half-

---

[13] Weber (1947).

[14] This long version has been edited by Loaysa (1595), by Fita (1902) 182–195 and García y García (1987) 204–208. Loaysa's edition (1595), revised with some adjustments by Mansi, is quite inaccurate and sometimes strays notably from the manuscripts. García y García's version is full of mistakes and does not use that of Fita, which he seems not to have known but which is by far the best. This last one gives a paralell retranscription of the Madrid manuscripts, Biblioteca Nacional, Vitr. 15.5, fol. 22–23v, and ms. 10.040, fol. 20–22.

[15] García y García (1987), 208 indicates a list of fourteen Hispanic bishops present at the council, just after the text. Examination of the manuscript shows that this list does not follow the dating, but in fact is to be found in folio 22, beneath the image of the sermon of Jiménez de Rada which will be commented further on.

[16] The short version of the *Quoniam velut umbra* has been edited two times: Fita (1902) I/2, 40–43, and Rivera Recio (1951) 336–337.

dozen languages.[17] It is also said that during the council, the arch-bishop of Toledo obtained the status of pontifical legate as well as the forthcoming submission of Seville, which had not yet been recon-quered.[18] The piece *velut umbra* then relates another scene, now sit-uated *in pleno consitorio*. This time Jiménez de Rada claims the Toledan rights to primacy in the presence of the Pope and the archbishops of Compostela and Braga.[19] He involves himself in the controversy with these two last ones, the author of the PCL handing over the right to speak to Rada and his adversaries, even if their arguments are briefly alluded to. After having noted the absence of the arch-bishops from Narbonne and Tarragona, he concludes giving the date.

Rada's participation in Lateran IV and his heated exchange with his two main adversaries have been known since the publication of the PCL in 1595 by García de Loaisa.[20] It immediately aroused the wrath of all the partisans of St. James' Hispanic preaching, which saw itself challenged when, in fact, during the early modern age it was practically state policy.[21] It was principally for this reason that in 1748, in the third volume of his famous *España Sagrada*, Enrique Flórez imprudently as well as vigorously contested the authenticity of this text, without even undertaking an exploration of the archives of the Toledan cathedral.[22] The writing of the PCL was for him a "shameful process" that offended not only the "Spanish nation", but "all nations" as well.[23] However during the same period, the Jesuit Andrés Marcos Burriel, who was by then the most knowledgeable concerning the archives of Toledo, had consulted the principal PCL manuscript and had vouched for its authenticity, bringing with him

---

[17] *Auctoritates et rationes propositas in latino exposuit laycis et illiteratis in lingagiis maternis*, ed. Fita (1902) 183.

[18] *Obtinuit per decennium, iuxta petitionem suam, legationis officium in Yspaniam exercere* (. . .) *Obtinuit etiam quod quam cito civitas Yspalensis redderetur cultui christiano, sine strepitu iudicii et de plano iure primatus subesset ecclesie Toletane*, ed. Fita (1902) 184.

[19] *Et impetrata audiencia ab eodem papa, proposuit in pleno consistorio coram ipso et cardi-nalibus et pluribus archiepiscopis et episcopis et abbatibus et canonicis et aliis clericis querimo-niam de Bracharensi et Compostellano et Tarraconensi et Narbonensi archiepiscopis, quod nolebant ei tanquam primati suo obedire*, ed. Fita (1902) 186.

[20] García de Loaysa (1595) 287–292.

[21] Kendrick (1960).

[22] Henriet (2001) 300–302.

[23] *Ofensivo no solo a la Nación española, sino a todas la Naciones, por el interés de sus Escritos, y honor de la verdad que vulneró. Y siendo tales sus vicios, con todo esso le han tribu-tado cultos los Estrangeros, que se precian de ser críticos*, Flórez (1748) 47.

a scholar as important as Gregorio Mayans y Siscar.[24] It was however Flórez's position that long since prevailed, especially in nineteenth-century Spanish scholarship. We know today with certainty that it was erroneous.[25] The allusion to the Toledan disputes in a letter from Pope Innocent III, as well as an early twentieth-century discovery of a non-Hispanic list of bishops present at Fourth Lateran Council, confirms both the presence of Jiménez de Rada at the council and the authenticity of the dispute on the question of primacy.[26] Moreover, diverse manuscripts exist to confirm that the PCL is definitely a text from the thirteenth century, most certainly written by a Toledan cleric sometime between 1215 and the 1250s.

As said above, the shorter version—*Velut umbra*—of PCL was transmitted by a folio from the thirteenth century, which today features as the end-leaf of a collection of privileges, *De primatu*, composed soon after Lateran IV.[27] In its longer version, the text occurs in two other collections devoted to the question of primacy by Toledan clerics. The second, which dates from the fourteenth century, is an unfinished copy of the first.[28] This one, today preserved at Madrid (Biblioteca Nacional), was completed in 1253. It comprises, first, illuminations of the different Visigothic councils, accompanied by short texts, and then the different pontifical privileges which could support the arguments of the partisans of the Toledan primacy. The PCL, which comes after, is without a doubt, out of place today, as the quires became disorganized during a binding operation. However this manuscript is not just the oldest transmitting the 'long' version

---

[24] Mestre (1970) 90–217.

[25] Fita (1902) I/3, 61, thought that Madrid, Biblioteca nacional, ms. Vitr. 15.5, fol. 22–23v, was a forgery from 1320. The direct rejection of the PCL still appears at a recent date in works of reference. See the article "Santiago" of the *Dicionario de Historia Eclesiastica de España*: "Después del siglo XI la creencia en la predicación de Santiago en España posee la universalidad en la Iglesia occidental (la supuesta negación de un arzobispo toledano en el concilio de Letrán, siglo XIII, se contiene en un texto espúreo)"; Guerra Campos (1975).

[26] Luchaire (1905); Rivera Recio (1951).

[27] Biblioteca capitular de Toledo, ms. 42–21. Rivera Recio (1951) 335–338. Recent description of the manuscript: Hernández (1996²) XVII. Copy: Biblioteca Nacional de Madrid, ms. 13042, fol. 39–40 (XVIIIᵉ s.). The pages transmitting *Velut umbra* could originate, according to Fita (1902) I/3, 53–54, from the manuscript 42/22 of Toledo (middle of the 13th century).

[28] Biblioteca Nacional de Madrid, ms. Vitr. 15/5, fol. 22–23v (dated from 1253); ms. 10040, fol. 20–22 (XIVᵉ s.). Cf. also ms 13028 (XVIIIᵉ s.), fol. 35–38. Feige (1978) 347–348.

of the PCL, but also the only one to display illustrations—I hesitate in speaking of illuminations—which support the text, or even, in at least one case, go beyond it. It is important therefore to comment on these few folios as a coherent whole, within which words and images rely on each other to support the legitimacy of the Toledan claims to primacy over all of Spain.[29]

The sermon given by Jiménez de Rada is in itself the first factor of this legitimacy. The objective here is to show how the archbishop of Toledo occupied a pre-eminent position not only in a Hispanic context but also in the heart of Christendom. The beginning of the text therefore takes care to mention the four Eastern patriarchs: those from Constantinople and Jerusalem were present, while Antioch and Alexandria, absent, had sent a representative.[30] The universal character of the council was furthermore made explicit from the first sentence.[31] Finally, the reference to the Eastern prelates is followed by a list of the archbishops and bishops—these last ones numbering four hundred and twelve. As for other clerics and laymen "we have no way of counting them".[32] This desire to place the struggle for primacy in a universal context can be found in other contemporary Toledan texts. Notably, the collection of documents in support of primacy which now contains the shorter version of the *Velut umbra*, includes a privilege which, on the banks of the Tagus, must have appeared quite exotic: in a bull dated February 25th, 1204, Innocent III granted the archbishop of Tirnovo a right of primacy over Bulgaria.[33] Without a doubt, we have here one of the very first Hispanic manuscripts, perhaps the first even, to mention this kingdom. But the stakes were clear: Bulgaria, Valachia and *Hispania*, *même combat . . .*

---

[29] Feige (1978) 345–369; Feige (1988); Linehan (1993) 328–332 and 359–368.

[30] *Fuerunt patriarche II, Constantinopolitanum et Iherosolimitanus. Antiochenus autem patriarcha gravi langore detentus venire non potuit, sed misit pro se vicarium Antarodensem episcopum. Alexandrinus vero patriarcha sub dominio sarracenorum constitutus, similiter venire non potuit, sed misit vicarium suum Petrum diachonum germanum suum,* ed. Fita (1902) 183.

[31] *Celebrata est sancta et universalis sinodus Rome,* ed. Fita (1902) 182.

[32] *De abbatibus* [I suppress here an *autem,* added by Fita] *et aliis religiosis personis, et decanis et prioribus, prepositis archidiaconis et aliis clericis secularibus et procuratoribus principum, conciliorum et communitatum de diversis mundi partibus congregatis, non fuit numerus,* ed. Fita (1902) 182.

[33] Conserved in the ms BCT, 42–21, fol. 68v. Hernández (1996²), n° 643, 529. The copy is partial and concentrates on the passages giving effective power to the

The privileged position of the archbishop of Toledo within a cos-
mopolitan Christian community is afterwards marked by the sermon
given in front of the council. The author makes clear that "since
both clerics and laymen from different parts of the world had gathered together",[34] and because he desired to be understood by the
learned men as well as the *illiterati*, Jiménez de Rada spoke in all
languages, whether that be Italian, German, French, English, Basque
("Navarran") and "Spanish".[35] The beginning and end of the sermon are however in Latin.[36] The anonymous laudator of Jiménez
de Rada compares this intervention with the age of the apostles, and
undoubtedly, more implicitly with a Pentecostal scene. Indeed since
the time of the apostles, nobody had preached the divine word in
so many languages, *in uno et eodem sermone*.[37] This reference is unsur-
prising and is frequently found when interpreting, during the Middle
Ages, an astonishing or miraculous linguistic achievement. Yet in a
Hispanic context and within this textual entourage, it could very well
hide an ulterior motive, which can easily be detected. In Spain and
Portugal, the see of the apostles *par excellence*, or in any case presented as such, was evidently that of Santiago de Compostela, which
Jiménez de Rada devoted himself to belittling in the second part of
the PCL. His polyglot sermon is also a way to show that at Lateran
IV, the apostolic legitimacy was more Toledan than Compostelan.

The role of Jiménez de Rada's intervention in the battle for primacy is highlighted, in a particularly striking fashion, thanks to an
illustration, one of the oldest representations of Lateran IV that we
possess.[38] The lower half of the folio describing Rodrigo's multilin-
gual intervention is indeed occupied with a group of seated characters who form a circle around a figure holding an episcopal crosier
and speaking to the assembly.[39] Curiously, interpretation of this scene

primate/patriarch of Tirnovo (anointing and crowning the king, consecrating bishops, etc.).

[34] *Sed quia de diversis mundi partibus tam clerici quam layci ibidem convenerant* (. . .), ed.
Fita (1902) 182.

[35] *In lingagiis maternis videlicet Romanorum, Teutonicorum, Francorum, Anglorum, Navarrorum
et Yspanorum*, ed. Fita (1902) 183–184.

[36] *Proposuit verbum Dei, incipiens et finiens in latino sermone*, ed. Fita (1902) 183.

[37] *Cum a tempore apostolorum vix crederetur seu ab aliquo audiretur vel scriptum repertum
fuisset aliquem alicubi sub tot modis ydiomatum seu linguarum in uno et eodem sermone verbum
Domini predicando taliter exposuisse*, ed. Fita (1902) 184.

[38] Foreville (1966).

[39] Plate I.

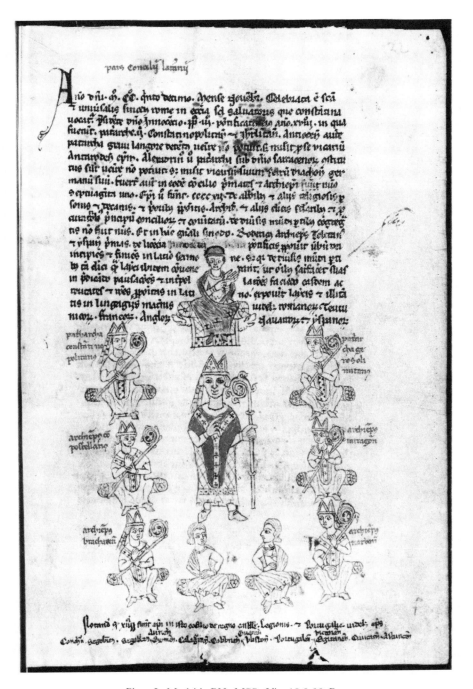

Plate I: Madrid, BN. MSS. Vit. 15.5,22 R.

has previously posed a few problems. Antonio García y García, went so far as to affirm that the central character was not Jiménez de Rada, but instead and most likely, Innocent III, while the character at the top, seated on a throne and wearing a flat hat, was perhaps the emperor—actually absent from Lateran IV.[40] A close examination of this miniature compared with those that precede and follow it, leave, nevertheless, no room for doubt: we most certainly have a representation of Rada's intervention. The other characters are identified thanks to a legend, with the exception of two figures situated in the lower part of the scene. Therefore we have from left to right and from top to bottom, the patriarchs of Constantinople and Jerusalem, then the archbishops of Compostela, Tarragona, Braga and Narbonne. The character at the top is the Pope. The two anonymous figures at the bottom do not have any distinctive signs, but the absence of a hat allows us to see that they are not tonsured. They probably represent that public of laymen for which the archbishop from Toledo would have used half a dozen languages. Identification of the scene, therefore does not pose any problems.[41] However, there is a possibility that the meaning of this picture goes beyond that of a simple illustration. Indeed, let us take another look at the archbishops gathered around the speaker. We have here the four Hispanic metropolitans of the moment, including, according to the Visigothic tradition, Narbonne. Unlike the Pope, the patriarchs and the laymen, these four prelates played no role in the first part of the PCL and appear only in the section inaugurated with *velut umbra*. They would therefore have nothing to do in this drawing if it only illustrated, as claims Raymonde Foreville, Rada's polyglot sermon.[42] Their presence rather constitutes a sort of link between the two sections of the PCL, between the "universal" sermon and the Hispanic controversy. The image could not be any clearer in indicating the role of this first part: to set down beforehand the legitimacy and the centrality of Jiménez de Rada, who is larger in this drawing than the Pope and all his adversaries, before going into detail about the quarrels and discrediting the arguments presented by the archbishops of Braga and Compostela. If the archbishop from

[40] García y García (1987) 203–204.
[41] Arguments in Henriet (2002).
[42] Foreville (1966) 1126.

Toledo is one of the foremost personalities of Christendom, if he is listened to with admiration by the entire universe, how then could he not be right in his strictly Hispanic claims?

The first adversary of the primacy to challenge Jiménez de Rada was the archbishop of Braga, Esteban Soares de Sylva, whose name, like that of the archbishop of Compostela, is not mentioned. The attack, in a first time, is situated on legal rather than symbolic ground. The archbishop of Toledo exhibits and reads diverse privileges granted by the popes Honorius, Gelasius, Lucius, Adrian and Innocent, which conform to the primacy.[43] Moreover he claims to possess many other pontifical documents all favorable to his interests, that he will produce when the moment comes.[44] He then shows a privilege granted by the cardinal Hyacinth, pontifical legate in Spain between 1154–1155, and 1172–1174, who commands the archbishop of Braga to obey that of Toledo *tanquam primatem vestrum*.[45] Another bull from Hyacinth recommends the suffragans of Braga to do the same.[46] These documents are known, perfectly datable, and are furthermore recorded in the Madrid codex consecrated to the primacy.[47] The Toledan arguments are therefore founded on a documentary base, theoretically incontestable, susceptible to being produced and read publicly. Many of these items, at least the most explicit and yet the most useful, are recent, very recent even. Indeed the text cites a bull from

---

[43] In the order of the text but not of the chronology, Honorius II (1125), Gelasius II (1118), Lucius II (1144), Adrian IV (1156) and Innocent III (1211).

[44] *Addidit etiam idem archiepiscopus Toletanus se habere alia plura privilegia et munimenta et scripta que ostenderet tempore suo*, ed. Fita (1902) 186.

[45] Bull originating in fact from Alexander III, but most certainly brought by Hyacinth: Ms Vitr. 15–5, fol. 28v (but attributed to Adrian IV). Cf. Mansilla (1953), n° 116, 136. Other copies: Hernández (1996²) n° 619, 519.

[46] It is in fact a *sententia* (1172) concerning the suffragans of Compostela and not of Braga: Mansilla (1953), n° 97, 115–116 (with wrong datation); Texts concerning Braga: *Ibidem*, n° 116 and 118, 136–138; Hernández (1996²) n° 618, 518.

[47] Gelasius II: Ms Vitr. 15–5, fol. 15 (07/11/1118), ed. Mansilla (1953) n° 55, 73–74. Cf. also n° 52 (25/03/1118), 71–72, and 53 (25/03/1118, 72 (ms Vitr. 15–5, fol. 28v). Honorius II: Ms Vitr. 15–5, fol. 15v–16 (30/11/1125), ed. Mansilla (1953) n° 64, 81–82; Lucius II: Ms Vitr; 15–5 (13/05/1144), fol. 16r, ed. Mansilla (1953) n° 72, 88–90. Cf. also Mansilla (1953), n° 73, 90. Adrian IV: Ms Vitr 15–5 (09/02/1156, fol. 24–24v) and Ms vitr. 15–5 (16/02/1156), fol. 16–16v, ed. Mansilla (1953) n° 100 et 101, 118–121. Innocent III: Ms Vitr. 15–5 (04/03/1210), fol. 17v–18, ed. Mansilla (1953) n° 422, 439–441. For a complete list of the manuscripts that reproduce these different pontifical privileges, Hernández (1996²) n° 561 et 559 (Gelasius II), n° 569 (Honorius II), n° 576 (Lucius II), n° 599–600 (Adrian IV), n° 647 (Innocent III).

Innocent III, dating from the 4th of March 1210, that is to say only five years before the dispute at Lateran IV.[48] In the PCL, the archbishop of Braga's response is not detailed. Esteban Soares de Sylva would then have been contented to reply that this discussion had no reason to take place and that he was completely unaware of Legate Hyacinth's *sententia*.[49] We can nevertheless learn more about the arguments of the archbishops of Braga in their fight against Toledan and Compostelan encroachments. Indeed, right after the Lateran council, the controversy between the two sees continued. The resulting events are known to us thanks to the statements made during a confrontation between the representatives of both archbishops. So in a very significant way, while the Toledans were busy producing dated papers and privileges, the Portuguese willingly put themselves on another level, that of the 'immemorial'. Faced with Toledan pretensions, the point is made that since an 'immemorial' era, the prelates of Braga had been directly submitted to the Church of Rome.[50] And Jiménez de Rada responds, conversely, that nothing in this affair could be termed immemorial and that Braga had been justly submitted to Toledo for sixty years[51]—in other terms, and in all probability, ever since a pontifical bull dating from the 19th of January 1156, in which Pope Adrian IV reminded the archbishop of Braga, John Peculiar, of his duty of obedience towards the Toledan prelate.[52] Rada knew his archives well. He therefore concentrated on facts and dates when facing a badly defined claim of timelessness.

In front of the papacy Braga's opponents still possessed yet another strategy to produce a different effect from the recalling of bulls which it was always possible to claim as false or unknown. According to the PCL, Rodrigo might have indeed chosen, in the second phase of the dispute, to recall the history of the see of Braga at the beginning of the 12th century. In other words, he might have opportunely made reference to the ambitious and misguided action taken by the

---

[48] Ed. Mansilla (1953) n° 422, 439–441. Hernández (1996²) n° 647.

[49] *Et quod sententiam predicti Iacinti penitus ignorabat*, ed. Fita (1902) 187.

[50] *Ponit procurator Bracarensis archiepiscopi, quod a tempore, cuius non extat memoria, ecclesia [Bracarensis im]mediate suffuit [Romane] ecclesie*, Feige (1978) 396.

[51] *[Respondet] archiepiscopus, quod non est verum, sed a tempore, cuius extat memoria [et etiam a LX anni]s suffuit Toletane ecclesie*, Feige (1978) 396.

[52] Ms Vitr. 15–5, fol. 28v. Mansilla (1953) n° 99, 117–118. Other copies: Hernández (1996²) n° 598.

archbishop Maurice Bourdin. French in origin, Bishop Maurice of Coimbra had became archbishop of Braga near the end of the year 1108 or early in 1109.[53] Initially, much like his predecessors and successors, he found himself engaged without much originality in conflicts with the archbishops of Compostela and especially of Toledo for the domination of different dioceses, among them those of León and Oviedo.[54] His initial relations with the papacy had been excellent, since in 1114 he obtained from Pascal II, during a voyage to Rome, a pontifical arbitration particularly favorable to his see and rather anti-Toledan.[55] But after the election of Gelasius II, in 1118, Maurice found himself on the side of the opponents of the new pope and in particular with the emperor Henry V, to whom he had already been sent on a mission in 1116 or 1117. The continuation of his career, as brilliant as it was ephemeral, is known thanks to diverse sources, both imperial and pontifical. Maurice was made pope at St. Peter's in Rome by the emperor and took the name of Gregory VIII. His position quickly deteriorated, even more so with the arrival on Peter's throne of Callixtus II, who confined him to the fortified place of Sutri. It was there that he was captured in 1121 before being imprisoned in southern Italy in the abbey of Cava, then in various other places.[56]

According to the PCL, the story of Maurice Bourdin was probably the center of the controversy between Toledo and Braga. Failing to making his adversary acknowledge Hyacinth's judgment, Jiménez de Rada did indeed choose to recount this episode of Braga's less than glorious past. The version of the PCL is full of errors, but it is no less effective in terms of legitimation. Among the mistakes we find the affirmation that Maurice had before been the bishop of Osma, when it was in fact Coimbra,[57] as well as the legend by which he was supposed to have tried to oust Bernard de Sédirac from the Toledan see.[58] The emperor Henry V is mistaken for an 'Otton' and

---

[53] David (1947) 454. Erdmann (1940).

[54] David (1947) 454–465.

[55] Feige (1978) 154.

[56] Resume of the career of Maurice: Schwaiger (1994).

[57] *Deinde ipso procurante* [= Bernard of Toledo] *electus est in episcopum Oxomensem*, ed. Fita (1902) 187–188.

[58] *Videns autem quod dominus Bernardus senuerat* [tenuerat Fita], *immemor eiusdem beneficiis, exuens pellem ovinam, non erubuit pellem lupinam induere, et accedens ad curiam supplicavit domino Pascali pape II ut dominum Bernardum senem et inutilem amoveret, et eum sibi substitueret in ecclesia Toletana*, ed. Fita (1902) 188.

even more surprising, Pope Callixtus II becomes Alexander II.[59]
However these variations do not affect the text's overall coherence.
The confusion between Coimbra and Osma, voluntary or not, helps
make clear the necessary obedience of the Hispanic prelates to Toledo.
Indeed according to Rada, a large part of the Toledan clergy had
been chosen after the conquest of the city by Bernard de Sédirac,
while he traveled through Southern France and stayed in Limoges,
upon returning from a voyage to Rome.[60] Among his recruits, Maurice
Bourdin, *de quo fit sermo*. Jiménez de Rada goes back on Bernard de
Sédirac's role in his *De rebus Hispaniae*, in which he quotes, besides
Maurice, eight clerics who had later secured the sees of Braga, Osma,
Sigüenza, Segovia, Palencia, Toledo, Valencia and Zamora. This list
is interesting for various reasons. Firstly because it allows for an
understanding of the confusion between Coimbra and Osma, this
last city appearing twice in the list along with the bishops Peter and
Raymond de la Sauvetat, the latter becoming afterwards the archbishop of Toledo. But is this misunderstanding as innocent as it
seems? Whatever the case may be we will note that without question Osma found itself in the ecclesiastical province of Toledo, which
enabled the author of the PCL to suggest that being the bishop of
this see, Maurice had been directly subjected to Bernard of Toledo,
towards whom, much like his colleagues, he owed his career. Let us
also reveal in this list, the presence of Compostela—thanks to Bernard
d'Agen, bishop of Sigüenza, then of the Galician see—and of Valencia
in the time of the Cid—thanks to Jerome of Périgueux.[61] If we add
to these two careers, not only that of Maurice but also that of his
predecessor, Gerard, monk of Moissac, we realize that in Rada's
sketch, since its restoration, the see of Toledo had provided prelates
for the dioceses of Castile, but also for all the other ecclesiastical
provinces of the Peninsula: namely Braga, but also Tarragona—with
Valencia—and Compostela. This lovely story of the first Toledan
prelate recruiting clerics to assure the management of the Hispanic
church, must not be accepted as historical fact: it is above all a construction, based on facts more than a century old, that gave Toledo

---

[59] *Gelasius papa II qui et mortuus est durante discordia, cui successit Alexander papa II cui reconciliatus est Oto imperator*, ed. Fita (1902) 188.

[60] *Cum dominus Bernardus quondam archiepiscopus Toletanus romanam curiam visitasset et ad propria rediens per Lemovicensem civitatem transitum fecisset, traxit inde clericos et pueros in Toletana ecclesia collocandos et nutriendos*, ed. Fita (1902) 187.

[61] About this last one, Lacombe (1999).

a central spot on the ecclesiastical map, over which it claimed to dominate in the name of its primal authority. The story of the PCL is less detailed on this point than that in the *De rebus Hispaniae*, but it moves in an identical direction: recent history proves Toledan centrality. And if the PCL was, in its supplemented version—the only one to report Maurice Bourdin's story—written before the *De rebus Hispaniae*, it would then be the first to witness the 'recruiting' of Bernard of Toledo.[62]

By insisting on the career and the character of Maurice Bourdin, whom no one had been able to openly support, Jiménez de Rada played it very carefully. Maurice's memory was as alive in as well as outside of the Peninsula. In Coimbra and Braga, he was remembered, it is true, as a kind and pious prelate, to confirm this description is the *Vita* of the founder of Santa Cruz de Coimbra, Tello, as well as those of the priest Martin of Soure or Gerard of Braga.[63] Nevertheless, these texts usually only circulated on a local level,[64] and we are consequently tempted to accredit the PCL when it describes the archbishop of Braga, speechless and reddening under the words of his adversary.[65] Outside of Portugal Maurice's reputation was most definitely atrocious. If Braga partisans called him Maurice his adversaries did not hesitate nicknaming him "Burdinus", the mule, or even "the bastard".[66] Above all, they referred to him at length as the puppet of a schismatic emperor and an enemy of Rome. It is therefore not surprising that we find, early on, a very negative portrait of Maurice in the *Historia Compostellana*, composed soon after the events. In this laudatory chronicle of Compostela and therefore of an archiepiscopal see which as such found itself involved in various disputes with Braga, Maurice was described, according to Callixtus II, as a creature of the "king of the Teutons".[67] Outside

---

[62] Linehan (1993) 359–368, who proposes a revision of the relations of dependence between the Ms Vitr. 15.5 and Rada's *De rebus Hispaniae* as they have been presented by Feige (1988).

[63] Erdmann (1940) 51–55; David (1947) 445.

[64] Only real exception: the *Vita* of Gerard of Braga, former monk of Moissac, which has been preserved by a manuscript from this monastery (ms Paris, BNF, lat. 5296 C, fol. 133v–142r).

[65] *Murmurare ceperunt inspicientes, erubescentem faciem archiepiscopi Bracharensis*, ed. Fita (1902) 190.

[66] David (1947) 445–449.

[67] *Historia Compostellana*, ed. Falque (1988) II, 3, just before the letter from the Pope. II, 14, end.

of the peninsula Maurice was a celebrity: he was negatively mentioned by authors such as Suger or Otto of Freising, as well as the *Liber Pontificalis* and diverse Italian chroniclers. Last but not least, Jiménez de Rada could count on a providential aid in Rome since there existed a fresco representing the defeat and captivity of Maurice 'Bourdin'.

Desiring to reinforce the credibility of his discourse, Rada is supposed to have made reference first to an *authentica scriptura*—that it would be adventurous to pretend to identify—and secondly to a *pictura laycorum* (meaning "for laymen"). Better yet, it is said he invited spectators of the controversy to raise their eyes and contemplate a mural depicting his words.[68] Upon viewing the images, a general murmur is supposed to have passed through the room, in support of the Toledan prelate while at the same time confounding the archbishop of Braga. The author of the PCL was certainly well informed. Indeed we know that Callixtus II had exhibited a series of frescoes representing the pontiffs engaged in the Investiture Controversy and victories over anti-popes in a room of the Lateran palace, near to the chapel of Saint Nicolas.[69] Maurice Bourdin held a prime place in this iconographic program, mentioned by many visitors.[70] The frescoes no longer exist, but modern drawings have been preserved which allow a general appreciation.[71] That representing Maurice Bourdin occupied a special place in the program for it showed the pope and the emperor unfolding the text of the Concordat of Worms (1122), which was most likely reproduced on the fresco. The emperor

---

[68] *Si quis astancium dubitat, erigat oculos ad presentes loci parietes, et ad oculum videbit igitur istoriam picturatam,* ed. Fita (1902) 190.

[69] Ladner (1935) 269–280, and Walter (1970) 162–166. The *Liber pontificalis* mentions the enterprise in the *Vita* of Callixtus II: ed. Duchesne (1892) 378–379.

[70] Cf. Arnulf of Lisieux, Ep. 21, ed. J.A. Giles, *Epistolae*, Oxford, 1844, p. 109 (PL 201, col. 34–36); John of Salisbury, ep. 59, PL 199, col. 39D; Suger, *Life of Louis le Gros*, ed. H. Waquet (Paris: 1964) 205 (with the mention at p. 200 of *cujusdam Burdini, depositi Bracarensis archiepiscopi, imperatoris Henrici violentia in sedem apostolicam intrusi*).

[71] Two very different pictures: that from the codex of Onophrius Panvinius (but perhaps not by him), from the end of the sixteenth century (Biblioteca Vaticana, Cod. Barb. Lat. 2738, fol. 104, under the famous copy of the mosaic of the Triclinium, featuring St. Peter, Charlemagne and Leon III), and that ordered by cardinal Rasponi under Alexander VII (Biblioteca Vaticana, Cod. Barb. Lat. 4423, fol. 25). Ladner (1935) 271–272, shows that the Panvinis' drawing is close to the original while that of Rasponi differs greatly. It is therefore the first that we will comment on. Reproductions in Ladner (1935) 273 (Panvinius) and 279 (Rasponi).

was standing up, without being humiliated, but the pope, sitting on his throne trampled the miserable Maurice Bourdin underfoot. A legend accompanying these frescoes makes a point to note, on the one hand Callixtus II, "honor to the homeland and adornment of the Empire", and on the other the bad Bourdin.[72] This short text was otherwise well known in thirteenth-century Spain, since Jiménez de Rada re-transcribed it in his *De rebus Hispaniae*.[73] All this was evidently too favorable to Toledan interest for it not to be picked out. Furthermore, the PCL does not content itself with making allusion to the frescos, but it gives its own version in the margin of the manuscript, under the shape of two very expressive drawings. The artist proved his inventiveness as neither of the two images directly follows the fresco in the Lateran.[74] In the middle of the page, the emperor 'Otto' lies under the feet of Pope 'Alexander'.[75] A bit more to the bottom, he points to the unfortunate Bourdin, chained in his prison, the Episcopal cross turned upside down as a sign of his deposition.[76] The message is clear, but its meaning is more in-depth. Whereas both the text and the Lateran fresco pinpoint the idea of *reconciliatio* of the emperor and the pope that allows for Maurice's capture and imprisonment,[77] these illustrations rather emphasize that the agreement gave way to the victory of Rome and the abasement of the Empire. The allusion to Worms (*pax reformata inter imperium et ecclesiam romanam*) has disappeared, leaving room for this image of the pope pointing to a vanquished imperial figure. The fight for Toledan primacy is therefore likened to that of Rome against the Empire, during an era when the question still stirred up controversy.

After having confounded Braga, Jiménez de Rada still had the problem of Compostela to resolve. The author of the PCL, repeats, later

---

[72] *Ecce Kalixtus honor patrie, decus imperiale . . . Burdinum nequam damnat pacemque reformat.* The inscription is known by the chronicles of Otto of Freising, MGH, SS 20, 256, and by the drawing of the cardinal Rasponi (cited in the previous note).

[73] *De rebus Hispaniae*, ed. Fernández Valverde (1987), VI, 27, 212. Jiménez de Rada complacently transcribes the text from a letter of Gelasius II to Bernard of Toledo, which brings to mind the excommunication and the deposition of Maurice: ibid. 211, and Mansilla (1953) n° 53, 72.

[74] It is also the opinion of Walter (1970) 163.

[75] Legends: *Alexander papa* and *Oto imperator*. See plate II.

[76] Legends: *Alexander papa* and *Burdinus*. See plate II.

[77] *Cui successit Alexander papa II cui reconciliatus est Oto imperator et pax reformata est inter imperium et ecclesiam romanam*, ed. Fita (1902) 188.

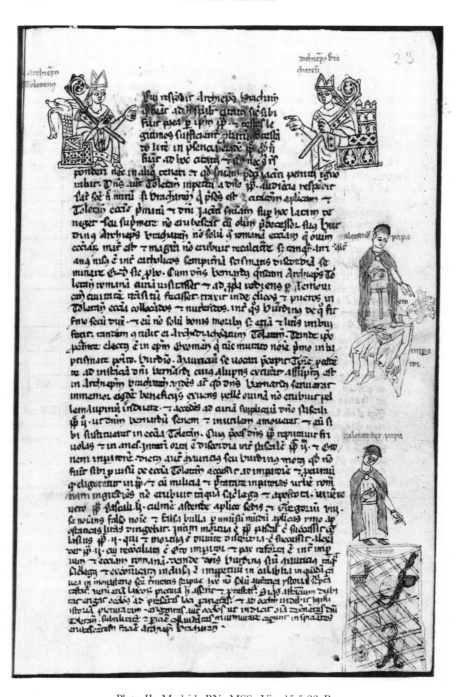

Plate II: Madrid, BN. MSS. Vit. 15.5,23 R.

to demolish, the principal argument of the supporters of St. James: the see of Compostela was founded in the honor of an apostle, a kinsman of Christ and the one who converted Spain to Christianity, whose relics can be found in the cathedral. How could such a church submit to Toledo?[78] Rada's response once again is composed of two distinct parts. Just as when faced with Braga, he pretended to be an expert on pontifical diplomas, which permits him, for example, to refer back to the text founding the Galician see as a metropolis. "If the archbishop of Compostela insists on the antiquity of his church, this antiquity can be said to be of a duration of 109 years," claims Rodrigo.[79] Situated in 1106, this year has hardly any importance as the Compostelan church did not then benefit from any pontifical privileges. Yet referring back to the manuscript of Madrid, we realize that the copyist had initially written *centum*, before adding a 'IX' between the lines.

He probably did not understand the model he had in front of him, or he simply miscalculated. The privilege to which he makes allusion and by virtue of which Calixtus granted to Santiago the rights of the ancient city of Mérida, then occupied by Muslims, is in fact well known, but it dates from 1120.[80] This error of date was not corrected in a later copy of the manuscript of Madrid, Vitr. 15/5.[81] However it is true that, unlike a number of other pontifical bulls, already cited, which accorded the right of primacy to the Toledan see, this one had no particular reason to address Toledo. It was therefore not copied: if two cartularies from the Toledan church have re-transcribed a letter written in 1120 from Calixtus II to Diego Gelmírez, it is only because it mentions Bernard of Toledo.[82] The privilege at the source of a centuries' worth of Compostelan pretensions and dating from the same year, is however, carefully ignored. This would explain Rodrigo's wavering chronological order, or at least that of the author of the PCL. This error changes nothing

---

[78] *Ita nobilis fundata in honore apostoli Jacobi Domini consanguinei, qui primo in Yspania verbum Domini seminavit et infinitos ad fidem Christi convertit, cuius corpus in eadem ecclesia requiescit, nunc, quod absit, impetat obedire ecclesie Toletane*, ed. Fita (1902) 190.

[79] *Si antiquitatem Compostellane ecclesie allegat, antiquitas ista in centum et IX annorum spacio continetur*, ed. Fita (1902) 191.

[80] *Historia Compostellana*, ed. Falque (1988) II, 16, 254–255.

[81] Madrid, Biblioteca Nacional, ms. 10040, fol. 21v (XIVᵉ s.).

[82] Biblioteca Capitular de Toledo, ms 42–21 (XIIIᵉ s.), fol. 66v, and 42–22 (XIIIᵉ s.), fol. 48–48v. Hernández (1996²), nº 562, 492. This bull seems unpublished.

in regards to Toledan arguments: just as the archbishop of Braga, who demanded an immemorial tradition, was met with very precise privileges, likewise that of Compostela was reminded of the circumstantial and recent nature of its archiepiscopal dignity.

In the sentences that follow this passage, every word counts. The privilege was granted in order to promote the pilgrimage to the Apostle's relics, whose body, "it is thought", lies in Galicia.[83] Before this period, up until a recent date, the church was *parvissima*.[84] Finally the Toledan see is much older than that of Compostela, as it had been founded by Saint Eugenius.[85] For the historian this reference to Eugenius is not without interest. The worship and even the knowledge of this supposed disciple of Saint Paul was in fact, in this case, extremely recent on the banks of the Tagus. It was not established until the archbishop Raymond of La Sauvetat made the discovery in 1148, during a visit to Saint-Denis, of a saint who would be considered later on as the first archbishop of Toledo.[86] Moreover Jiménez de Rada presented Eugenius as a direct disciple of Paul, despite the fact that a story of the translation, written in Toledo during the middle of the 12th century, characterized him according to the old *Passio* as a disciple of Saint-Denis sent to Spain from Arles.[87] The relics— nothing but an arm—were not definitely acquired until 1156, that is barely half a century before the IV Lateran Council.[88] However these recent events have little importance if it was possible, as a consequence, to claim filiation with a foundation dating from the earliest years of Christianity. Nevertheless Saint James was an apostle, unlike Eugenius. So Rada did well to underline the special link that united Toledo to the Virgin, who had before appeared to Ildefonso, one of his remote predecessors.[89] This story in which the mother of Christ had given her tunic to the saint, was famous throughout the

---

[83] *Ob reverentiam beati Jacobi cuius corpus ibidem creditur esse sepultum*, ed. Fita (1902) 191.

[84] *Nam usque ad hec tempora oratorium quoddam parvissimum erat locus ille in quo nunc sita est ecclesia Compostellana*, ed. Fita (1902) 191.

[85] *Antiquior est ergo ecclesia Toletana que fundata est a tempore Eugenii, Pauli apostoli discipuli*, ed. Fita (1902) 191.

[86] Rivera Recio (1963); Linehan (1993) 272–278.

[87] *Translatio brachii sancti Eugenii Toletum*, ed. Rivera Recio (1963) 179 (does not even mention Saint Paul). *Passio*: Rivera Recio (1963) 144–145

[88] Rivera Recio (1963) 176–183. Cf. note 87 as well as Henriet (2000) 70–75.

[89] *Precipue Toletana ecclesia quam ipsa beata Virgo corporaliter dignata est visitare, cum quondam beato Ildefonso archiepiscopo Toletano sacrificium Domino offerenti (. . .)*, ed. Fita (1902) 192.

West and the Pope too was most likely acquainted with it. Moreover Innocent III must have had his opinion about Toledo's version of the Marian cult, which had three years prior, played a role in the great victory of Las Navas de Tolosa, precisely organized by Rodrigo.[90]

Where notoriety is concerned, Eugenius was no match for Saint James. Hence the famous passage from Rada attacking the weakest link of the Jacobean cult—a passage which was later considered as apocryphal and scandalous, even anti-patriotic by the apostle's most fervent supporters.[91] After having admitted the effective presence of Saint James' relics in Compostela—which the Toledans did unenthusiastically—the question still remained as to whether or not the son of Zebedee really did convert Spain to Christianity. We know that the answer to this question was not always evident. In the early modern age, fierce battles were fought in order for the papacy to conciliate the legend of the seven 'varones apostólicos' and that of Saint James, while carefully managing the supporters of the co-patronage of Saint Teresa over Spain and definitely accepting the apostle's Hispanic preaching.[92] In the Western Middle Ages, we can consider the acceptance of the *Golden Legend* as a giant step in favor of this 'official' version, even if Jacopo da Voragine echoed the traditions that recognized this preaching but deemed it ineffective. This progressive success was not an easy one, if we remember the reserves and silences of Gregory VII in the eleventh century.[93] Even on the peninsula, critics of the Apostle, whether they be more or less explicit, abounded. Let us cite only the several alternative stories about the conversion of the peninsula, among which the seven 'varones apostolicos' was the most famous, or the controversy which, during the tenth century, opposed Abbot Cesarius of Montserrat against the bishops of the province of Tarragona.[94] Nevertheless Jiménez de Rada—or perhaps simply, the anonymous author of the PCL—goes very far in his opposition to the Compostelan see, his questioning of the Jacobean preaching being expressed publicly, in very brusque terms, which, in addition, ridicules the supporters of the apostle: how

---

[90] *De rebus Hispaniae*, ed. Fernández Valverde (1987), VIII, 10, 273; González (1960), I, 1031 ff.

[91] Henriet (2001) 300–302.

[92] Kendrick (1960).

[93] Gregory VII's reserves: Mansilla (1953) n° 8, 15.

[94] Díaz y Díaz (1967). Cesarius of Montserrat: Mansilla (1994) II, 219–222.

could Saint James, decapitated in Jerusalem, have come to Spain?
How could he have converted the masses without preaching?[95] Even
if it means having to peddle legends, Rada does not fear to give an
account of a story he claims to have heard as a young child, from
certain saintly women: having made it to Spain, Saint James was
supposed to have converted by his preaching only a single 'elderly
woman'. Aware of his failure, he then returned Eastward and could
have died during the journey (*in repatriando*) . . .[96] The Toledans evidently could not present this version as authentic or even orthodox,
since it opposed the passage in the Acts of the Apostles (Act. 12,2)
which mentions Saint James as a martyr. To at the same time deny
the apostolic preaching, the condition of martyr and to question a
passage of Scripture was decidedly too much . . . But what the author
of the PCL subtly tells us—in Jiménez de Rada's lips—is that traditional legends concerning to the Galician apostle were many, unreliable and when all was said and done, these tales peddled by holy
nuns were not more absurd than the affirmation of an Hispanic
preaching.

With the controversy between Toledo and Compostela, we observe
a confrontation between two very different forms of logic, each one
representing a particular strategy of legitimation linked to the conditions and to the specific history of each see. One thing they could
not agree on was surely the role held by the relics as a legitimating resource. Let us turn back to the PCL: if, once the question of
the Jacobean mission had been put aside, the archbishop of Compostela
wanted to continue the dispute, what could he bring forward?, asks
Rodrigo in almost these terms. The relics of the apostle obviously.[97]
The ground here is rocky, as questioning Saint James' presence in
Galicia would have been more audacious than to reject his Hispanic
preaching. To accomplish this would have ridiculed the most famous
cult in Christendom and condemned a pilgrimage protected by both
popes and kings for over a century. Rodrigo therefore plainly asserts
his faith: *cum credentibus credo*.[98] But he quickly puts into context the

---

[95] *Quomodo ergo ibi predicavit si nondum intravit? Quo ergo aliquos sine predicatione convertit?*, ed. Fita (1902) 192.

[96] *Ita quod unam tantum mulierem vetulam sua predicatione convertit, et sic, diffisus quod nihil
profisceret in predicando, mortuus est in repatriando*, ed. Fita (1902) 194.

[97] *Et si nobilitatem sepulture corporis eiusdem ibidem allegat* (. . .), ed. Fita (1902) 194.

[98] Jiménez de Rada knows how to recuperate the prestige of the Jacobean cult
whenever it comes in handy, for example to contradict the Hispanic legend of

importance of this fact. On the one side, there is no unanimity as
"some say that the body lies in Jerusalem."[99] But on the other side,
of what value is a good reputation that rests on the possession of
relics trampled upon daily by the feet of pilgrims? If the body of
the Virgin had not already been abducted in Heaven, as Jiménez
de Rada claims firmly to believe—*firmiter*, an adverb that he did not
use when, a few lines higher, he scoffed half-heatedly at the general
opinion concerning the presence of the Jacobean relics in Galicia—
would it have then been desirable that the remains of the mother
of Christ receive the same treatment as those of the son of Zebedee?[100]
Evidently not! Rada declares that he would rather be cut into pieces
and die.[101] While using prudence as to the authenticity of the relics,
the Toledan speech goes quite far in its criticism of both the relics
and the pilgrimages. These few rarely quoted lines, deserve a good
place next to the other medieval texts, more numerous than we
would believe, which criticize any given aspect of the cult of saints
without, however, condemning it. We must also admit that this judgment supports particularly well what we know of Rodrigo's interest—or more likely his lack of interest—in the relics. The PCL can
therefore list Eugenius as the first archbishop of Toledo without ever
making allusion to the presence of his arm in the Cathedral. We
detect the same silence in the *De rebus Hispaniae*. Compared to his
contemporary and rival, Lucas of Tuy, it seems that Rada had never
attempted seriously to promote any cult in his church other than
that of the Virgin, by definition more disembodied than that of any
of the other saints.[102]

Two lines of logic therefore exist. On the one side, that of the
legitimacy founded on the possession of prestigious, efficient and well-
known relics. This is Compostela. On the other side, that of the
domination resting on History—the history of an *urbs regia* illustrated
for centuries by its archbishops, its councils and its kings—, on a
universal patronage, that of the Virgin, as well as on a privileged

---

Charlemagne: *De rebus Hispaniae*, ed. Fernández Valverde (1987) IV, 11, 130. Cf.
also the use of the *Privilegio de los Votos: ibidem*, IV, 13, 133.

[99] *Licet quidam dicant quod Iherosolimis requiescat corpus*, ed. Fita (1902) 194.

[100] *Sed absit quod propter huiusmodi gloriam primacie, vellem quod corpus beate Virginis, quod
firmiter credimus in celestibus cum Domino glorificatum, in ecclesia Toletana fuisset aliquatenus
tumulatum, pedibus humanis cotidie conculcandum*, ed. Fita (1902) 194.

[101] *Sed utinam pocius dilaniarer et sic membratim vitam finirem*, ed. Fita (1902) 194.

[102] Toledo and the Virgin: Herbers (1994).

relationship with a center, that is to say Rome. This is Toledo. The
personality of Rodrigo Jiménez de Rada counts for a lot in this construction, but we must absolutely not underestimate what it owes to
very ancient traditions. Already in the seventh century the *Lives of
the fathers of Mérida* very significantly opposed the metropolis of
Lusitania, which built its prestige on the life of its saintly archbishops, the possession of the body of Saint Eulalia and the existence
of a reputed pilgrimage, to the city of Toledo, presented above all
as a center of power.[103] On the one hand, the materialization of
the sacred thanks to the relics and the legitimation of a power by
the presence and protection of efficient saints. On the other hand, the
prestige of a city full of history, in itself a justification to which can
be added other kinds of legitimacy. In the last case, the absence—
for the Virgin—or simply the non-mention—for Eugenius—of relics
clearly indicates that the roots of the legitimation lay elsewhere.

To conclude, we would like to stress a few elements important to a
study of conflicts—political or religious—as well as strategies of legitimation. A reading of the PCL, allows us to identify three quite
different strategies. The guiding thread of the text being woven by
an ardent defendant of Toledo, the remarks of his adversaries are
therefore only vaguely perceptible, but they can be all the more successfully reconstituted as they are not otherwise unknown. In Braga,
in the absence of favorable pontifical diplomas and of incontestable
or very prestigious relics, independence is justified by an appeal to
an ancient past, chronologically ill-defined, an 'immemoriality', which
seems all the more necessary that there be no need to recall the
recent history of the see in the battle against Toledo (action of
Maurice 'Bourdin', bull from 1156). In Compostela, it is the presence of a universally celebrated apostle, Saint James, which has
founded the prestige and liberty of this city. The legitimation of those
claims functions here on a double level that recalls the action of the
saint *in vivo* and *post mortem*. *In vivo* is the direct conversion of Spain
to Christianity and consequently the exclusion of all submission to
a see other than Rome. *Post mortem* are the everyday miracles and
the existence of one of the three great pilgrimages of the Christian
world. There is no equivalent to such a pilgrimage in the Iberian

---

[103] Collins (1980).

peninsula, even less so in Toledo. Finally in this last city, the defendants of the primacy founded their pretensions on a knowledge both partial and erudite of the different pontifical privileges accorded to the see since the conquest of the city in 1085.

These three discourses of legitimation reveal, if not three conceptions, at least three different modes of usage, or even three modes of instrumentation of the temporal framework. In Braga we have a time without reference only characterized by its length. The absence of events and ruptures—"it has always been that way"—is the principal argument. In Compostela, time has a beginning: it is the preaching of Saint James. This will forever mark Hispanic history. But to this past preaching corresponds in the present the action of apostolic relics, which perpetuate, at least on a symbolic level, Compostela's paramount position within the Iberian religious landscape. Finally, in Toledo time is historical, datable and indeed marked by precise events. Toledo's glory is ancient but not immemorial, as it is a fact of the Visigothic era, a time during which a special alliance was effected between the Virgin and the saintly bishops. Above all, the primacy can be legally founded through time by different pontifical privileges, which can be consulted in the archives and which accord a priority and a hierarchic superiority to the Toledan see. Three kinds of time therefore: the unreferenced, very long term (Braga); the Christian long term inaugurated by a foundational apostolic predication (Compostela); the medium to short term, marked by the memory of the Visigothic era and the remembrance of privileges dating back, for the most part, to the preceding century.

This brings us to the end of our analysis of the PCL, a text as astounding as it is revealing, above all, of the role of ecclesiastical conflicts in the creation of discourses of legitimation perfectly conscious, well constructed and filled with ferocious arguments. The confrontations, more or less soft, that took place in 1215 and in the following years between the sees of Toledo, Braga and Compostela are but a sample, indeed served by an exceptional text, of what characterized the peninsula since the end of the eleventh century, that is to say, since the start of the reconstruction of the ecclesiastical map, broken into pieces after 711. In many instances, we have come to know these conflicts through thick files that are also circumstantial, teeming with details, arguments and counter arguments. Therefore those concerning the conflicts between Braga and Compostela at the end of the twelfth century, or between Toledo and

Tarragona in the 1240s.[104] These files have been known for a long time, today they are mostly edited, but they have been largely studied in a fairly traditional way, that of a history of ecclesiastical institutions and jurisdictional divisions. However there are other possible approaches, among them a history of legitimations and ideologies. Some will argue that, despite everything, this is a topic of strictly ecclesiastical history devoid of social and political elements. We believe, however that these conflicts which continually mix religious discourses and territorial disputes, or the search for dominance and the affirmation of a particular sacredness, show to what point the categories 'religious' and 'political'—as we use them today—are meaningless in this contex. The 'political' does not depend on the 'religious' any more than the 'religious' depends on the 'political', but these two quite anachronic notions are in fact interdependent to the point of forming a reality that historians are hardly able to name.[105] This situation will undoubtedly live on as long as it remains impossible to construct a legitimation that is not, at least in part, 'religious'. The study of these phenomena can only be a collective one, and it would lead us much too far for the moment.

Translated from the French original by Chantell Arcand.
I thank Julio Escalona and Hugh Kennedy for their revision of the text.

Bibliography

Castell Maiques, V. (1996) *Proceso sobre la ordenación de la Iglesia valentina. 1238–1246*, 2 vols. (Valencia: 1996).
Collins, R. (1980) "Mérida and Toledo: 550–585", in E. James ed., Visigothic Spain: New Approaches (Oxford: 1980) 189–219.
David, P. (1947) *Études historiques sur la Galice et le Portugal du VIe au XIIe siècle* (Lisbonne-Paris: 1947).
Díaz y Díaz, M.C. (1967) "En torno a los orígenes del cristianismo hispánico", in J.M. Gómez-Tabanera ed., *Las raíces de España* (Madrid: 1967) 423–443.
Duchesne, L. (1892) ed., *Le* Liber pontificalis. *Texte, introduction et commentaire*, II (Paris: 1892).

---

[104] Braga/Compostela: Erdmann (1927) 266–282, 303–324; Feige (1978) 377–395. Toledo/Tarragona: Castell Maiques (1996).
[105] Cf. the concepts of 'politische Religiosität', or of 'political theology', frequent in Germanic historiography: about this last one see the introductory remarks by Suntrup (2001) 1–11.

Erdmann, C. (1927) *Papsturkunden in Portugal* (Berlin: 1927).
—— (1940) *Mauritio Burdino (Gregorio VIII)* (Coimbra: 1940).
Falque, E. (1988) ed., *Historia Compostellana* (CCCM 70) (Turnhout: 1988).
Feige, P. (1978) "Die Anfänge des portugiesischen Königtums und seiner Landeskirche", *Gesammelte Aufsätze zur Kulturgeschichte Spaniens* 29 (1978) 85–436.
—— (1988) "Zum Primat der Erzbischöfe von Toledo über Spanien. Das Argument seines westgotischen Ursprungs im toledaner Primatsbuch von 1253", in *Fälschungen im Mittelalter. Internationaler Kongreß der Monumenta Germaniae Historica. München, 16.–19. September 1986*, (Monumenta Germaniae Historica Schriften, 33/1), I, (Hanover: 1988) 675–714.
—— (1991) "La primacía de Toledo y la libertad de las demás metrópolis de España. El ejemplo de Braga", in *La introducción del Cister en España y Portugal* (Burgos: 1991) 61–132.
Fernández Valverde, J. (1987), *Roderici Ximenii de Rada Historia de rebus Hispaniae sive Historia gothica* (CCCM 72) (Turnhout: 1987).
Fita, F. (1902) "Santiago de Galicia. Nuevas impugnaciones y nuevas defensas", *Razón y Fé* (1902), I/2, 35–45 and 178–195; I/3, 49–61.
Flórez, É. (1748) *España Sagrada*, 3 (Madrid: 1748).
Foreville, R. (1966) "L'iconographie du XIIᵉ concile œcuménique. Latran IV (1215)", in *Mélanges offerts à René Crozet*, II, eds. P. Gallais et Y.R. Riou (Poitiers: 1966), 1121–1130.
Gambra Gutiérrez, A. (1997) *Alfonso VI: cancillería e imperio*, I (Fuentes y Estudios de Historia leonesa 62) (León: 1997).
García y García, A. (1987) "El concilio 4 Lateranense y la península ibérica", in *Iglesia y derecho* 2, (Bibliotheca Salmanticensis. Estudios, 89) (Salamanca: 1987) 187–208.
García de Loaysa (1595) *Collectio conciliorum Hispaniae* (Madrid: 1595).
González, J. (1960) *El reino de Castilla en la época de Alfonso VIII*, 3 vols. (Madrid: 1960).
Guerra Campos, J. (1975) "Santiago", in *Dicionario de Historia Eclesiastica de España*, IV (Madrid: 1975).
Henriet, P. (2000) "Hagiographie et historiographie en péninsule ibérique (XIᵉ–XIIIᵉ s.). Quelques remarques", *Cahiers de linguistique hispanique médiévale* 23 (2000) 53–85.
—— (2001) "La dignité de la religion chrétienne et de la nation hispanique, ou Enrique Flórez et l'*España sagrada*. A propos d'une réédition", *Revue Mabillon* n. s. 12 (= t. 73) (2001) 296–306.
—— (forthcoming) "Du cosmos à la Chrétienté. Images d'évêques dans quelques manuscrits hispaniques des Xᵉ–XIIIᵉ siècles", in *La imagen del obispo en la Edad Media*, eds. M. Aurell/A. García de la Borbolla (Pamplona: forthcoming).
Herbers, K. (1994) "Politik und Heiligenverehrung auf der iberischen Halbinsel", in *Politik und Heiligenverehrung im Hochmittelalter*, ed. J. Petersohn (Sigmaringen: 1994) 177–275.
Hernández, F.J. (1996²) *Los cartularios de Toledo. Catálogo documental* (Madrid: 1996²).
Kendrick, T.D. (1960) *Saint James in Spain* (London: 1960).
Lacombe, C. (1999) *Jérôme de Périgueux (1060?–1120), chapelain du Cid* (Périgueux: 1999).
Ladner, G. (1935) "I mosaici e gli affreschi ecclesiastico-politici nell'antico palazzo lateranense", *Rivista di Archeologia Cristiana* 12 (1935) 265–292.
Linehan, P. (1993) *History and Historians of Medieval Spain* (Oxford: 1993).
Luchaire, A. (1905) "Un document retrouvé", *Journal des savants* (1905) 557–568.
Mansi, J.D. (1759–1798) *Sacrorum conciliorum nova et amplissima collectio*, 22, 1071–1075.
Mansilla Reoyo, D. (1953) *La documentación pontificia hasta Innocencio III, 965–1216* (Rome: 1953).
—— (1994) *Geografía eclesiástica de España. Estudio historico-geográfico de las diocesis*, 2 vols. (Rome: 1994) (Publicaciones del Instituto español de Historia eclesiastica, 35).

Mestre, A. (1970) *Historia, fueros y actitudes políticas. Mayáns y la historiografía del XVIII* (Valencia: 1970).

Nascimento, A.A. (1998) *Hagiografia de Santa Cruz de Coimbra* (Lisbonne: 1998).

Rivera Recio, J.F. (1951) "Personajes hispanos asistentes en 1215 al IV concilio de Letrán (Revisión y aportación nueva de documentos. Datos biográficos)", *Hispania Sacra* 4 (1951) 335–355.

—— (1955) "Encumbramiento de la sede toledana durante la dominación visigótica", *Hispania Sacra* 8 (1955) 3–34.

—— (1963) *San Eugenio de Toledo y su culto* (Toledo: 1963).

Schwaiger, G. (1994) "[Grégoire VIII]", in *Dictionnaire historique de la papauté*, ed. Ph. Levillain (Paris: 1994) 750–751.

Suntrup, A. (2001) *Studien zur politischen Theologie im frühmittelalterlichen Okzident. Die Aussage konziliarer Texte des gallischen und iberischen Raumes* (Münster: 2001) (Spanische Forschungen der Görresgesellschaft 56).

Walter, Ch. (1970) "Papal political Imagery in Lateran Palace", *Cahiers archéologiques* 20 (1970) 155–176.

Weber, M. (1922) *Wirtschaft und Gesellschaft* (Tübingen: 1947. First edition: 1922).

ALBERTANO OF BRESCIA, ROLANDINO OF PADUA AND THE RHETORIC OF LEGITIMATION

FRANCES ANDREWS

University of St. Andrews

Conflict was endemic in early and mid-thirteenth century northern Italy. In an area of vast written culture it stimulated the development of the language of politics, generating ideal material for exploration of the development of political thinking and experimentation with ideas of legitimacy. The techniques deployed by those with *de facto* 'potestas', be they lords or communes, to acquire the legitimacy to maintain or enhance that power are exposed and sometimes debated in a variety of written sources. This creativity has of course long been recognized by historians of political ideas, from Hans Baron or Helene Wieruszowski to James Banker, Quentin Skinner and, more recently, Cary Nederman, to name only some of the most prominent non-Italian scholars.[1] The usual corpus of literature deployed in modern discussions of communal political thinking of this period focuses either on the so-called 'pre-humanist' rhetorical writings of masters such as Guido Faba who taught *ars dictaminis* at the University of Bologna from the early 1220s to the 1240s,[2] or on the 'podestà literature'. The latter encompasses specialized treatises on city-government such as the anonymous *Oculus pastoralis* (c. 1222), with its series of model speeches for a podestà or Orfino da Lodi's poem *De sapientia potestatis* (1245/6).[3] It also traditionally takes in Giovanni da Viterbo's *Liber de regimine civitatum* (completed by 1253), and Brunetto

---

[1] See for example: Baron (1988) 94–133; Wieruszowski (1971) 589–629; Banker (1974) 3–20; Skinner (1978), esp. I, 28–35; Nederman (1997).

[2] On Guido Faba or Fava, see now Bausi (1995).

[3] "Oculus pastoralis pascens officia et continens radium dulcibus pomis suis", ed. D. Franceschi, *Memorie dell'Accademia delle scienze di Torino. Classe di scienze morali, storiche e filologiche*, fourth series 11 (1966). Also edited as "Oculus pastoralis sive libellus erudiens futurum rectorem populorum" by Ludovico Muratori in *Antiquitates Italicae medii aevi sive dissertationes* IV (Milan: 1741) cols. 92–128; Orfino da Lodi, "De regimine et sapientia potestatis", *Archivio storico lodigiano*, 2nd series 16 (1968) 3–115 (with Italian translation, originally edited by A. Ceruti, *Miscellanea di storia italiana* VII (Turin: 1869) 29–94.

Latini's *Livres dou tresor*, compiled in exile in Paris in the early 1260s, circulated very widely thereafter, and influential for example at the court of Alfonso *el sabio*, king of León and Castile 1252–84.[4] These texts have been explored particularly in terms of their use and adaptation of Ciceronian ideas about politics and human society. Thus they demonstrate the role of reason and persuasion in stimulating man's propensity to unite into communities, a natural inclination which is invigorated by the speech of a wise and eloquent man, allowing others to realize their social sentiments and live harmoniously together, united by consensus, not coercion.[5]

What I propose to do in this paper is to explore the construction of legitimacy and who and what was being legitimised by interposing two writers less 'canonical' in this historiographical context, though certainly not in others: Rolandino of Padua and Albertano of Brescia. This will I hope provide an alternative approach to the dynamic controversies over legitimacy in this region and a broader context for the 'canonical' texts identified above.

Rolandino of Padua is the author of a well-known chronicle of the March of Treviso, written in 1260–62.[6] It is an account of the crowded events of his lifetime in the Trevisan March, in the northeast corner of mainland Italy, encompassing the cities of Padua, Verona, Vicenza, Treviso and the surrounding countryside. His story begins in the late twelfth century, but half the text is focused on the 1250s, the very recent past. The central theme is the attempt by Ezzelino III da Romano to establish—and to legitimate—a regional lordship or *signoria*, at first aided and later opposed by his brother Alberic.

Rolandino was writing after the denouement of his story. Following nearly twenty years of rule, Ezzelino had been forced out of Padua in 1256 by an army of crusaders led by a papal legate. After being wounded and taken in battle, he had died in September 1259. In

---

[4] Giovanni da Viterbo (Johannis Viterbiensis), "Liber de regimine civitatum", ed. G. Salvemini, *Bibliotheca iuridica medii aevi* III (Bologna: 1901); Brunetto Latini, Li *Livres dou Tresor*, ed. Francis J. Carmody (Los Angeles: 1949). The literature on Alfonso is vast, but see Estepa Díez et al. (1998) and O'Callaghan (1998).

[5] See for example, Nederman (1992).

[6] Rolandini patavini, "Cronica in factis et circa facta marchie Trivixane", ed. A. Bonardi, *Rerum Italicarum Scriptores*, 2nd series VIII/1 (Città di Castello: 1905) 169–360. *Cronica* is more correctly translated as 'chronicles' (a hangover from a previous genre) but Rolandino's work was conceived of as an organic whole and for clarity and ease of reference I will use 'chronicle' when referring to it.

August 1260 Alberic too was captured and put to the sword along with all his sons, while his wife and daughters were burnt. Rolandino's text occupies a prominent position in the corpus of writings on Ezzelino and was central to the seminal work of Girolamo Arnaldi on chronicle writing in the March.[7] It has also been ransacked by historians for all manner of reasons, from a search for evidence of Ezzelino's military techniques to demonstrating or disproving the continuity of university life during the nineteen years when Ezzelino da Romano dominated Padua.[8]

The account is first and most obviously a *damnatio memoriae*. The blackening of Ezzelino's name had already begun during his lifetime and can be traced in particular to the letters produced by the papal chancery when the crusade against Ezzelino was launched.[9] But Rolandino's account played an important role in the development of this negative myth of Ezzelino as a tyrant and wicked lord, a tradition which was to survive in oral culture down to the mid-20th century. His work is addressed to his fellow-citizens in Padua and, unusually for the genre of urban chronicles from which it develops (but hardly surprising in view of the scope of the subject-matter), it is not limited to the events of one city. As we will see, it was intended to be 'useful', both to the commune and people of Padua and to other peoples everywhere. As a *damnatio memoriae* of the previous regime, it constructs legitimacy for the commune which replaced it, contributing to the redefinition of the political community in Padua and the March, providing 'a secure orientation of memories', as Arnaldi puts it.[10] It promoted the aggregation of shared interests in a community devastated by two decades of war; a community which had also included whole-hearted supporters of Ezzelino, as Rolandino himself makes clear.[11]

---

[7] See Arnaldi (1963).

[8] See for example, the various papers in Cracco ed. (1992).

[9] See Ortalli (1992) 613 and Fasoli (1985).

[10] Arnaldi (1963) 101. See also Dean (1997) 36 on republics as 'lands of competing memories.'

[11] This is further confirmed by a single earlier chronicle from one of Ezzelino's circle: Gerardus Maurisius, "Cronica Dominorum Eccelini et Alberici fratrum de Romano", ed. G. Soranzo, *Rerum Italicarum Scriptores*, 2nd series VIII/4 (Città di Castello: 1914). Although Soranzo's title matches the subject matter well, in the preface to his Italian translation Flavio Fiorese notes that the earliest manuscript (14th-century), is simply "Cronica domini Ecelini de Romano", *Gerardo Maurisio, Cronaca ezzeliniana (anni 1183–1237)*, ed. F. Fiorese, Testi inediti o rari IV (Vicenza: 1986).

The author states that as a young man of twenty-two, his father had handed him a sheaf of notes about events in the March of Treviso and asked him to continue and improve them.[12] This followed his return from study at the university of Bologna. The reference to his father probably understates the influence of his teacher in Bologna, Boncompagno da Signa, whom Kenneth Hyde portrays as seeking to broaden rhetorical studies in the direction of historiography, even creating a 'first school of academic historians'. Apart from Boncompagno's own *Liber de obsidione Anconae*, this school inspired only one direct response, that of Rolandino, whose chronicle was completed some forty years later.[13]

Beyond this familial and university context, Arnaldi argues convincingly that the status of the author and his father as notaries, depositaries of *publica fides*, renders the chronicle a 'public' discourse even in its gestation. On completion in 1262 it certainly became a public, official document. A postill records the solemn reading of the chronicle in the monastery of Sant'Urbano in Padua in April 1262:

> De tempore, quando approbatum est hoc opus et a quibus personis et ubi: Perlectus est hic liber et recitatus coram infra scriptis doctoribus et magistris, presente eciam societate laudabili bazallariorum et scollarium liberalium arcium de Studio paduano. Erant quoque tunc temporis regentes in Padua viri venerabiles: magister Agnus, magister Iohannes, magister Zamboninus, profundi et periti doctores in phisica et sciencia naturali; magister Tredecinus, in loica [sic] providus indagator et doctor; magister Rolandinus, magister Morandus, magister Zunta, magister Dominicus, magister Paduanus, magister Luchisius in gramatica et rethorica vigiles et utiles professores. Qui ad hoc specialiter congregati predictum librum et opus sive cronicam sua magistrali auctoritate laudaverunt, approbaverunt et autenticaverunt solempniter in claustro sancti Urbani in Padua, currente anno Domini millesimo ducentesimo sexagesimo secundo, indictione quinta, die tercia decima intrante mense aprilis.[14]

This passage and possible sources and parallels for the actions it describes were studied at length by Arnaldi in the 1960s and later.[15]

---

[12] Rolandini patavini, "Cronica", ed. Bonardi, prologus, p. 7: *Pie namque memorie pater meus, notarie artem excercens in Padua, animum suum applicuit, ut non solum conctractus* [sic] *scriberet, set et facta quedam de Marchia tarvisina more bonorum simplicium antiquorum notaret, notata quoque michi dedit in scriptis, quibus me aliqua superaddere iussit....*

[13] See Hyde (1985).

[14] Rolandini patavini, "Cronica", ed. Bonardi, book 12 para. 19, 173–4.

[15] See Arnaldi (1963) 79–110 and (1973).

All that we need note here is that it identifies the author of the chronicle, master Rolandino, as a teacher of grammar and rhetoric in the fledgling university of Padua and that it contains all the elements of a standard authentication of a legal document: the place, year, indiction, day, and the witnesses. The simple inclusion of the name of Rolandino in the list of masters indicates that this paragraph was appended to the chronicle probably by a different writer after the public acknowledgement which it records. The reading, which amounted to a 'publication *ante litteram*', turned the text into a manifesto for the intellectual elite of Padua. The audience of masters and students was the first interpreter of the work of Rolandino: both legitimating his text as a public, official, authenticated 'document', and strengthening its status as history in the service of politics. This may have been confirmed by its inclusion among the books of the commune thereafter.[16]

So, in Padua in April 1262 condemnation of the 'tyrant' Ezzelino was a matter of gossip and concern, at least among this group. The 'promulgation' of the chronicle served to legitimate the changes brought about by victory and the rule of the commune which replaced the Ezzelinian regime, a commune which shared personnel with the masters of the university here named. Rolandino himself, for example, had worked as a communal notary and had been holding the important office of notary of the seal when Ezzelino took the city in 1237.

Rolandino's text is elegant and the latin reflects his Bolognese training. He constructs complex prose, not a bald sequence of annalistic 'facts'. The narrative is full of persuasively memorable images: an account of one of the innumerable campaigns of the Paduan army in the area of Treviso records that they came so close to the walls and towers of the city that they could hear the bells and even voices within.[17] His approach clearly develops out of the urban annals tradition, but it is a regional account of recent rather than universal history, listing city officials instead of emperors. It is a new kind of history devised perhaps because the traditional framework was insufficient to his purpose. He was writing a 'chronicle' not a 'how-to' treatise on government in the tradition of podestà literature

---

[16] As posited by Arnaldi (1963).
[17] Rolandini patavini, "Cronica", ed. Bonardi, book 2 para. 17, p. 40.

described above, but his purpose parallels such literature. Just as treatises on rule describe how a podestà should behave and were intended to be used by them, Rolandino begins his preface by stating a pragmatic concern to provide a record for the honour and use of the commune and people of Padua and other peoples everywhere: *Intencio est huius libri breviter et summatim colligere omnia, que hic notantur ad honorem et utilitatem et documentum tocius comunancie et populi paduani et aliorum populorum ubique.* This will be achieved first by reference to the model of *antiqui nostri predecessores* and their honourable and wise actions against those who presumed anything contrary to the honour of Padua in either peace or war (*werra*). In second place the text is to contain health warnings against tyrants and their rule:

> Item . . . dantur multe moniciones et castigamenta salubria, quibus paduana gens, que semper libertatem dilexit et diligit, pro salute sua potest manifeste videre, quia horribilis est crudelitas tyrannorum in civitatibus, quibus presunt . . . quid pessima operentur dominia, quia manus impias extendunt non solum ad seculares, set et loca ecclesiastica dissipant, carcerant religiosos, turres et pallacia dirruunt, devorant divicias, pauperes orphanant et pupillos, viduant mulieres, res omnes destruunt et personas.[18]

This list of crimes against churches and religious, the poor and women is familiar to any reader of high medieval chronicles, though the destruction of towers and palaces perhaps resonated uniquely in urban north Italy. In the text itself, Rolandino uses a range of similarly familiar techniques to condemn and to explain Ezzelino's misguided actions and their consequences. He implies, for example, unnatural brutality or poor use of astrology, but ultimately ascribes the turn of events against him to the intervention of divine justice. In conformity with its chronicle form however, the text lacks a complete explanatory framework for what replaces the rule of the 'tyrant'. Beyond a general celebration of *libertas*, and invocation of divine providence as the basis of communal rule, his articulation of how this rule is to be maintained is implicit rather than overt.[19]

---

[18] Rolandini patavini, 'Cronica', ed. Bonardi, preface p. 5.

[19] He attributes to a speech given by Gerardo de' Rangone of Modena, podestà of the Veronese *fuorusciti* before the *consilium* of Paduans in 1230, the idea that the rule of cities (and thus the restraint of wrong-doing) proceeds from divine providence: *De summa Dei providencia creditur processisse quod sunt in civitatibus regimina constituta, ut scilicet violencie refrenentur, prohibeantur rapine, iura conserventur illesa, maleficia et superbie retundantur.* . . . Rolandini patavini, "Cronica", ed. Bonardi, book 3, para. 2, p. 42.

Rolandino shared expectations with his immediate audience, the masters of the *Studium* and the ruling elite in Padua and these can, perhaps be articulated. I am thinking here of what Wolfgang Iser has called 'literary indeterminacy': that what is stated does not exhaust the intention of the text. The gaps which an author leaves in his narrative, of [explanatory] details which are not supplied, play a vital role in evoking the reader's response and links readers—or in April 1262, listeners—and the author in a conspiracy of common understanding.[20] What Rolandino expected his audience's understanding to be is not easily determined, but as a step towards excavating these expectations it is revealing to draw parallels with the second of my authors, Albertano of Brescia.

Albertano is best known to later medievalists as the author of a treatise adapted by Geoffrey Chaucer, on the basis of an intermediary French translation, in his *Tale of Melibee*. He was recently somewhat extravagantly described by Enrico Artifoni as 'il maggiore intellettuale italiano della prima metà del Duecento'.[21] Certainly he was a very widely disseminated author in the late middle ages. As James Powell, who has written an important monograph on Albertano, observes, 'he ranks among the most popular of all medieval writers, not only in the number of manuscripts of his writings that have survived but also in the number of authors who [drew] on his work in significant ways.'[22] Moreover, his works were translated into several Italian *volgari*, French, German, Dutch, Czech and Catalan.

We know more about Albertano than about many other mid-thirteenth-century writers, but much remains obscure.[23] He perhaps studied at Bologna like Rolandino, but if he did he left no trace and he may simply have attended a smaller *Studium* or even a local school and acquired a professional qualification, not a qualification to teach—he does not call himself *magister* or *doctor legum*.[24] At home in Brescia,

---

[20] See for example Iser (1989).

[21] Artifoni in a review of *I peccati della lingua*, in *L'Indice*, 2 Feb. 1989, p. 27, as cited by Navone in her Introduction to *Albertano da Brescia, Liber de doctrina dicendi et tacendi. La parola del cittadino nell'Italia del duecento*, ed. Paola Navone (Florence: 1998) xi.

[22] Powell (1992) 121.

[23] This summary of his career is closely based on the discussions in Powell (1992) 1–3 and *Albertano da Brescia*, ed. Navone, introduction.

[24] *Albertano da Brescia*, ed. Navone, xxiv and xxii, where she understands Powell to argue that Albertano might have studied at either Bologna or Padua (he argues, Powell (1992) 61, that Albertano may not have been a product of either institution). This prompts Navone to point out that Padua was only founded in 1222,

as Claudia Villa has shown, he read and made marginal notes in
two tenth-century manuscripts from the Cathedral Chapter library.[25]
One of these includes a copy of Augustine's *De civitate Dei* (only partially annotated by Albertano), the other is the Queriniana library
Seneca *Epistolae morales ad Lucilium*, and indeed Seneca's letters are a
major source for his writings. As a *causidicus* he took full part in the
public life of his time. His activities can be documented with certainty from April 1226,[26] when he appears as '*Albertanus iudex*' in a
renewal of the Lombard league (a league of cities united against the
intervention of imperial authority). It is therefore no surprise to learn
that 12 years later (1238) he spent a short time imprisoned in Cremona
following the surrender to imperial troops of a fortress of which he
had been captain. During the intervening years he had developed a
career as an official of the Brescia commune, carrying out the delicate business of enquiries (*inquisitiones*) into the rights and properties
of the commune in the city and contado.[27] In the 1240s he moved
further afield, accompanying his fellow Brescian Emmanuele de Maggi
when he went to be podestà of Genoa in 1243. Although no auto-
graph judicial or administrative acts survive, he was a prominent
figure in Maggi's entourage, since he gave a sermon to a confraternity of Genoese judges and notaries.[28] He does not however appear
to have followed Maggi in his later career (which took him to Parma
and Rome). In the late 1240s Albertano seems to have been in
Brescia and the last document to record his presence is a peace
treaty with Bergamo dated 11 May 1251. We may assume that he
died sometime not long thereafter.

Albertano is described by others as a *iudex* but describes himself
as a *causidicus*. Scholars are not altogether agreed about what this

---

whereas the first record of Albertano is 1226, by when he ought to have completed
his education. She therefore concludes that he either shortened his training or was
at Bologna—or perhaps moved to Padua with the migration of students and masters which was the beginning of the university in Padua. Her discussion reflects the
general view of Italian scholarship which insists on a link with the university world.

[25] Villa (1969).

[26] Navone draws attention to a reference to an 18th century record of an 'Albertus
de Brixia' notarius among the witnesses of a truce between Mantova and Reggio
in 1225, which she suggests may refer to our author, *Albertano da Brescia*, ed. Navone,
p. xxii n. 1.

[27] Powell (1992) 2.

[28] *Sermone inedito di Albertano giudice di Brescia*, ed. Luigi Francesco Fé d'Ostiani
(Brescia: 1874). I have not been able to consult the new edition, *Albertano sermo
Januensis con introduzione, traduzione ed annotazioni* by Oscar Nuccio (Brescia: 1994).

meant in practice: was he an expert in the law who had a strong basis in rhetoric and grammar or an orator accustomed to scholastic exercises and excursions into juridical terrain?[29] Powell adopts a Roman definition, arguing that 'with some allowance for a greater role . . . as legal advisors', medieval *causidici* such as Albertano can be compared with the professional pleaders at Rome, not scholarly lawyers, but orators knowing only enough law to understand the advice they got from the jurisconsults.[30] The recent editor of one of his works, Paola Navone, objects that a modern local historian (Paolo Guerrini) records Albertano as enrolled in the college of judges in Brescia, which must have required some juridical instruction, though perhaps not necessarily a long training.[31] What matters to us here is that his career reflects the typical combination of arms and administration of a city professional. He was well-read, certainly had some understanding of civil law and was a good public speaker—both as a *causidicus* and as a preacher—and indeed must have been an expert in the art of persuasion.

As well as the sermon given in Genoa in 1243, four further sermons and three treatises by Albertano survive. His first treatise, written or at least started while he was a prisoner in Cremona in 1238, is addressed to his son Vincenzo and entitled *De amore et dilectione Dei et proximi et aliarum rerum et de forma vitae* (On love and affection for God and neighbours and other things and on the form [or rule] of life).[32] A second treatise, the *Liber de doctrina dicendi et tacendi* (On the doctrine of speaking and remaining silent), dated 1245, was dedicated to his son Stefano,[33] while his third treatise followed soon after, being written in 1246 for his son Giovanni, a surgeon. Finally, four sermons were delivered to the confraternity of *causidici* in Brescia in about 1250.[34] Although it has rightly been argued that Albertano's

---

[29] *Albertano da Brescia*, ed. Navone, p. xxiii n. 3

[30] Once again, Navone appears to misunderstand Powell. See Powell (1992) 11 n. 1; *Albertano da Brescia*, ed. Navone, p. xxiii n. 3.

[31] *Albertano da Brescia*, ed. Navone, pp. xxiii–iv, n. 3.

[32] 'De amore et dilectione Dei et proximi et aliarum rerum et de forma vitae: an edition'. Edited by Sharon Hiltz as her PhD dissertation, University of Pennsylvania, 1980, on the basis of a manuscript in the Pennsylvania university library.

[33] Ed. Paola Navone, initially as a dissertation undertaken at the University of Florence 1988.

[34] *Sermones quattuor, edizione curata sui codici bresciani*, ed. M. Ferrari (Lonato: 1955). Several of Albertano's works are now accessible on the web, put there by Angus Graham on http://freespace.virgin.net/angus.graham/albertano

works must be taken as a whole, forming interlocking elements of a coherent philosophy, I will concentrate here on the third of the treatises, the *Liber consolationis et consilii*, written for his surgeon son Giovanni and on the sermon delivered in Genoa,[35] since these will provide a sufficient basis for discussion.

Two factors might be thought to exclude Albertano's works from a discussion of legitimacy as framed for example by Spiegel.[36] Albertano was in no sense a historian and his work is not usually analyzed within the 'pre-humanist' and 'political' context discussed by historians of ideas.[37] Powell, for example, identifies him as a moral and social thinker, seeking solutions to basic problems in the communal society with which he identifies. Yet, as Cary Nederman has shown with reference to Cicero's moral and rhetorical works, such texts contained a great deal that was pertinent to political speculation by their medieval readers.[38] By the same token, later translators of Albertano's writings reworked them for a different social and political climate. Thus, most notably, Chaucer's adaptation of the *Liber consolationis* in his *Tale of Melibee* replaces urban references with a framework of sovereignty more appropriate to his 14th-century English audience,[39] while the Catalan translation turns the wealthy urban Melibeus into 'Cant' Melibeu.[40] This is not just a literary adaptation to a recognizable local context. It suggests that the adaptors had identified a political context in Albertano's work—that of the Italian city—which was not appropriate to their own purposes. It seems to me justifiable therefore to seek the potential political context in Albertano's plot.

The shorter and earlier text, a sermon given to Genoese *causidici* and notaries in 1243, is styled *super confirmatione vitae illorum* (on the confirmation of their way of life) and follows the sermon structure we might expect.[41] After an invocation, "let our meeting be in the

---

[35] *Liber consolationis et consilii ex quo hausta est fabula de Melibeo et Prudentia*, ed. T. Sundby (Copenhagen, Paris and London: 1873). There is also an edition of the Catalan translation, which I have not been able to consult: *Llibre de consolacio i consell*, ed. G.E. Sansone (Barcelona, 1965).

[36] Spiegel (1997).

[37] An exception is Stillwell (1944) who is however only indirectly concerned with Albertano's own work.

[38] Nederman (1997).

[39] See Stillwell (1944).

[40] *Llibre de consolacio i consell*, cited Powell, *Albertanus of Brescia*, 127 n. 19.

[41] This summary owes much to Powell (1992) 57–61.

name of the Lord", it opens with an apologetical topos, "that in daring to speak before the wise he will rely not on his own wisdom but on Christ's mercy". The sermon proper then begins with a passage from the Sermon on the Mount (Matthew 5:3) in which Christ describes the apostles as the salt of the earth. Albertano elaborates, suggesting that his audience too are the salt of the earth for, just as by the apostles Christians were brought to faith and the sweetness of eternal life, so by their wisdom his audience should bring the acts of men coming to them for advice or assistance to the flavour of reason, the salt of justice and the sweetness of the precepts of the law—as throughout, he applies these words to himself and his audience, as one of the confraternity, not set apart. The image of the salt of the earth is then expanded by comparison to baptism: just as when priests make us Christian they place salt in our mouths saying "Receive the salt of wisdom that it may profit you in eternal life" so we must have the salt of wisdom in the mouth. Here he quotes Paul's letter to the Colossians 4:6: "let your speech always be seasoned with a grain of salt so that you may know how to respond to anyone" (*sermo vester semper in grano sale sit conditus, ut sciatis quomodo oporteat vos unicuique respondere*).

This short paragraph sums up the essentials of Albertano's solution to the evils of society: it highlights the crucial role of *causidici* as purveyors of reason, justice and wisdom, and the absolute importance of speech adapted to suit the audience as the means by which this wisdom is communicated—not surprising from an orator. It also places Christian teaching at the centre of his idea of professional life—not surprising in a confraternal sermon.[42]

Having established his audience as the wise, Albertano goes on to analyse the nature of wisdom: what it is, how it begins and what is necessary to it (*commoda*). The answers are traditional: the beginning of wisdom is fear of the Lord; wisdom is the knowledge of the perfect good of the human mind and of divine and human things and so on. Most significantly, knowledge must be made public and debated, so that it may grow; if not it will quickly fade and disappear. This, of course, is achieved through speech. He then runs through the seven ways in which speech must be shaped. First he emphasises the need to ascertain the truthfulness of those who ask for counsel or

---

[42] On such lay confraternal sermons, see Meersseman (1977).

aid and for good speech: since speaking well is the beginning of friendship—*amicitia*, a word with both moral and political value—whereas speaking evil is the beginning of enmity (this echoes a theme prominent in his earlier treatise on love and friendship). They must speak sweetly and with sweet words, so as to multiply their friendship. They must speak softly and with soft replies, since this will calm anger, whereas harsh speech excites fury. They must speak prettily and honestly, avoiding crudity (*turpia*), which corrupts morals. They should use ornate and composite words but must speak with knowledge (*scienter*), avoiding ambiguity or sophistry. Finally, they must speak wisely and with good intent, without fraud, malice or damage to others. The moral force of the knowledgeable speech of *causidici* is thus established and, as Powell observes, this is done entirely without reference to Roman law.

The sermon then turns to the practical virtues of their profession: they should check whether matters brought to them are true and sincere, and whether they consent to reason and what the consequences will be. Here he is completely pragmatic: they should find out who would approve and who would oppose the matter so as to establish whether the case can be brought to effect or not, and he warns that something which may seem good at the beginning may in its outcome lead to evil. They must seek to calm turbulent souls and appetites, making them obedient to reason, and—taking a different tack—they must use the goods they acquire moderately and knowledgeably. In the final section of the sermon he explicitly re-applies the salt of the earth analogy to both the *causidici* and to the notaries (*tabelliones*) in his audience: notaries, through whom all men's acts are seasoned and acquire the flavour of decisiveness (*firmitas*) (so that the laity may truly say *sine vobis litteratis nihil possumus facere*).

As Powell has pointed out, this sermon gives *causidici* and notaries—and therefore the main body of urban officialdom—an 'almost priestly status,' separated from the main body of the non-professional laity. It is a clear example of the way that Albertano blurs 'secular and sacred'[43] and I would argue that this is a framework, almost a manifesto, for the legitimating power of professional speech in society. Good speech is here portrayed as both a moral force for the individual and the confraternity and a moral force in society, a means

---

[43] Powell (1992) 60.

of guiding that society towards wisdom through reason. It is the first step towards a legitimation of a system of rule based not just on speech but on the speech of professionals.

This analysis of the Genoa sermon allows us some idea of the moral nature of Albertano's writings, and the fusion of secular and sacred in his world view. It does not resolve all the issues which might concern us here. He identifies his audience as the *causidici* and notaries of Genoa, but as so often with sermons, the relationship between the text we have and the sermon he gave is problematic. In this case the opening lines tell us that he wrote and edited it himself, so it is perhaps more reliable as an indication of the author's thinking than the many sermons which survive only as notes by a member of the audience.[44] It is not however a direct record of his words as spoken in Genoa in 1243.

The *Liber consolationis et consilii*, composed three years later, is a much longer text and presents different problems of transmission.[45] Ostensibly written for one of his sons, no attempt can be made to establish the means of dissemination, since the earliest manuscripts await detailed study. However, it was quickly distributed far enough for a Tuscan translation to be undertaken in Paris in 1268–9. It takes the form of a dialogue dealing with one of the acute problems of urban society: vendetta. Albertano employs the example of a wealthy young man, Melibeus, who goes out one day, leaving his much-loved wife and daughter at home. He closes the door, but three of his neighbours and enemies, seeing that he is away, bring a ladder, get in through a window and beat up his wife Prudence and their daughter, wounding the daughter in five symbolic places, her eyes, ears, mouth, nose and hands and leaving her half dead. On his return Melibeus takes to weeping and tearing his clothes in fury. To calm him down, his wife at once starts to reprove him (*coepit illum instanter ammonere*) and from this point onwards, most of the text is shaped through a dialogue between husband and wife. Prudence advises Melibeus to call his friends and relatives and to act on their counsel. Melibeus duly calls together a 'great multitude' (though no relatives are mentioned) and the conclusion of this counsel is predictable: that they should undertake vendetta. Prudence, in

---

[44] On the latter, see Bériou (1998).
[45] *Liber consolationis et consilii*, ed. Sundby.

keeping with her name, cannot accept this conclusion, but she bides her time and intervenes only when the friends have left. The discussion between husband and wife takes the form of a scholastic exchange and continues for some one hundred pages in the printed text. Melibeus objects to each step of Prudence's advice, forcing her to explain the grounds for her arguments and allowing Albertano to explore a wide range of moral issues and to demonstrate the importance of reason and of course, prudence. Eventually his wife convinces Melibeus that vendetta is inappropriate and, in the closing section of the treatise, peace is made with the former enemy by a ritual reconciliation which bears many sacramental elements.

The whole work is an unusually explicit discussion of the virtues of female advice and it is also very obviously a condemnation of the violence of vendetta.[46] Once again however, a prominent theme is the speech of professionals. In the initial 'counsel of war', Melibeus sets out the situation, and responses are then given by men speaking as the corporate voice of all those of the same status present. Thus the first response is given by a surgeon—the profession of the initial addressee, Giovanni. Since it is the office of a surgeon to heal not to harm, he refuses to advise on the subject of vendetta. He is followed by a physician who makes an analogy with medicine: just as in medicine opposites provide relief, so the same applies in vendetta and war: peace cures war. The advice which follows, from *vicini* and former enemies (who should never be trusted), is condemned by Albertano as that of flatterers and yes men. Then one of the 'wise *causidici*' present rises to speak on behalf of them all. What he says is an illustration of some of the points made in the sermon to the Genoese—and echoes its pragmatism: this is a difficult business because of the injury and evil recently committed and because much more serious things may follow on account of it. It is also difficult because of the wealth, power and large number of neighbours on the two sides. The *causidicus* therefore advises Melibeus to fortify his house, but expresses serious doubts about carrying out a vendetta. He begs for time to consider the issue with his fellow *causidici*, cit-

---

[46] The idea of vendetta as a legally tolerated form of violence in the Italian middle ages has been queried in a debate neatly summarised by Dean (1997). See Kuehn (1991). But see also Wickham (1997) for an example of twelfth-century acceptance of violent defense of property as proof of right of ownership.

ing a number of authorities to justify the delay, and promising to counsel him usefully once they have deliberated. The words of the *causidici* are followed by the speech of the young who, fortified by their strength and numbers, praise Melibeus, his wealth, power and kin, criticize the wise for their delays and proposed deliberations and recommend immediate vendetta. Swayed by youthful enthusiasm, almost everyone then leaps up shouting *sic, sic, fiat, fiat*. When an old man tries to object on behalf of the other elders present, pointing out that those who want war do not know what it is like, he is drowned out and forced to yield. Melibeus then concludes the meeting by taking a vote and the decision to proceed with the vendetta is upheld. It is already apparent to a modern reader that this account is designed to open the way to an explanation of the virtues of the considered speech of *causidici*, as well as other professionals such as surgeons and physicians and of the old and experienced. This was presumably equally apparent to a thirteenth-century audience, as was the coincidence of the professions of the author and his son and that of two of the groups singled out for prominence in this account.

There is no need to give a detailed analysis of the debate between Melibeus and Prudence which follows this account. The main thrust is the need for good counsel, how that is achieved (for example by study), from whom (God, self, good and proven friends, the old, the wise and experts, starting with a few and only later asking the many) what is to be avoided (haste, indiscretion, the counsel of idiots, flatterers, former enemies, the fearful, drunk, wicked and hypocritical, the young), what the obstacles to good counsel are (for example that it is difficult for the rich and powerful to obtain good counsel), what to do with counsel once obtained (examine the truth and sincerity of the matter, the causes and consequences, whether it consents to reason) and when counsel should be accepted (when diligently prepared and found to be good and useful). Crucially in this case, where Melibeus needs to change his mind, they also discuss the circumstances when counsel can be changed.

Prudence enumerates her criticisms of the way that Melibeus takes counsel: he asked for the counsel of too many, he showed anger and haste, told them what he wanted to hear, was content with just one body of opinion and did not examine the advice presented. He also followed the opinion of the mass rather than that of the wise and his friends, a point illustrated with a direct example from communal life:

Si enim ad multitudinem, et non ad sensum respexeris, nunquam bonum consilium habere valebis; nam stultos semper invenies in centuplum, quam sapientes; et stulti stulta diligunt, et animum suum semper ad stultitiam inclinant; sapientes vero pauci paucos inveniunt sapientes; quare in partitis, quae in consiliis fieri consueverunt, semper succumbunt. Inde est, quod in partitis, quae in consiliis civitatum fieri consueverunt, consilia semper malum sortiuntur effectum, si voluntatem multitudinis, et non paucorum sapientiam, sectantur.[47]

The treatise then goes on to analyse the specific counsel given in the example at the opening, identifying the advice of the *causidici*, the old and the wise as *planum et rectum*, in particular with regard to self-protection. This provides an opportunity both to discuss how to behave in war, an aspect of Albertano's own experience and to condemn another evil of Italian urban society, the building of towers. These are dismissed as the product of pride, generating fear and hatred, and being anyway worth nothing unless defended at great cost and with the help of prudent and wise friends. Instead, self-defence should be built from the love of citizens (*amor civium*) and virtue, as well as the usual ditches, and walls of city defences. The advice of the young is simply dismissed out of hand while, again in a purely pragmatic passage, Prudence points out that whereas his enemies have lots of sons and relatives, Melibeus is alone because he has no male children or brothers or cousins or the others necessary to frighten his enemies into withdrawing. To this pragmatism is added, finally, the role of judges and the law: only judges have jurisdiction over vendetta, *ut leges dicunt*. When Melibeus rejects the intervention of earthly, secular judges on the grounds that few care about infamy or monetary loss, Prudence replies that if he is not satisfied with secular judicial solutions he must turn to God. This leads to a consideration of the religious symbolism of the attack: the three enemies symbolise the flesh, the world and the devil; the daughter's five wounds recall Christ's wounds but also mark the five senses, the windows through which the three enemies enter the body and the soul. Thus ultimately, the punishment is divinely inspired. Melibeus insists that if he appears to do nothing others will not be deterred and may repeat the injuries. Prudence repeats that the authority to take revenge belongs to judges, and here again the reference to urban life is explicit. Magistrates and Podestà should be elected who will

---

[47] *Liber consolationis*, ed. Sundby, cap 30.

investigate, solicitously pursue and punish wrong and wrong-doers, rather than suffer their contempt and invective, by which they will lose dignity and office.[48]

After a further section discussing the need for patience, the idea that by attacking his enemies he commits aggression, not defence,[49] the role of money, poverty and wealth and the evils of war, Prudence at length gives her advice. The solution must be reconciliation and concord. Melibeus's enemies are found to be very sad and keen to be forgiven. Prudence meets them secretly, exhorts them to regret their actions and to seek indulgence and reassures them that Melibeus is benign. Melibeus agrees to reconciliation, calls his faithful friends and relatives—now included—who approve the plan. The enemies attend with just a few jurors as guarantors and acknowledge their guilt in a form close to that of the confessional prayer. Melibeus raises them with his hand and tells them he will take advice and then sends them away. He then consults the doctors who tell him his daughter is convalescing and so decides that he will take his enemies goods and send them overseas. Once again, Prudence intervenes, warning him that his action would be iniquitous because he is already enormously wealthy. He does not need their money and would rightly be accused of greed. This leads to a discussion of the importance of honour and a good reputation. Sending them away would be an abuse of power, converting his authority over them into eternal disgrace and anyway—Albertano as ever, reasons with his feet on the ground—even if Melibeus could do this *de jure*, he could never get away with it *de facto*: it would simply provoke a new vendetta. Finally Prudence discusses divine justice, the need for mercy and clemency and at last, Melibeus submits entirely, accepting reconciliation. A ritualised encounter then follows: his former enemies

---

[48] *Liber consolationis*, ed. Sundby, cap 40: *Tales itaque judices et potestates potius eligant, maleficia et malefactores investigare, sollicite insequi atque punire quam patiantur ab eis contempni et deici atque cum suo vituperio a dignitate et officio removeri* . . . It is interesting that Chaucer changes the reference here from judges and podestà to judges and sovereigns: 'Also a wys man seith that "the judge that correcteth nat the synnere commandeth and biddeth hym do synne." And the juges and sovereyns myghten in hir land so muchel suffre of the shrewes and mysdoeres that they sholden, by swich suffrance, by proces of tyme wexen of swich power and myght that they sholden putte out the juges and the sovereyns from hir places, and atte laste maken hem lesen hire lordshipes.' *Riverside Chaucer*, ed. L. Benson et al., 3rd edn. (Oxford, 1987) 230.

[49] Here the reference is at last to the Codex: the right to use force to repel force is only acknowledged if undertaken immediately and without delay and not for revenge but for defence.

kneel and weep at Melibeus and Prudence's feet, the adversary makes a speech telling Melibeus he will thereby be more powerful and then Melibeus replies, with the consent of Prudence. He first evokes the role of sweet words and good speech in the creation of friendship which we saw in the Genoese sermon. The contrition, penitence and devotion of his enemies leads him to clemency and he receives them with a kiss of peace. Raising them with his hand, he sends them away with the words of the Gospel: *'ite in pace et amplius nolite peccare'* (John 8,2).

The fusion of secular and sacred in this idealised peace is complete. Albertano's argument is not hermetic, but it places divine judgement at the centre of human affairs. And alongside divine judgement stands the role of professional advice based on reason, the experience of the old and the rule of law as the solution to the problem of vendetta. As James Powell has argued, the whole body of his works can be seen as an adaptation to the life of professional men and lay city dwellers of the *forma vitae*, the rule or proposal of life usually adopted by regular religious. It is concerned with the moral authority of the individual. But there is also an evident political thrust: the legitimation as a political class of the *causidici*, the professional 'experts' of urban, communal government and their counsel, expressed through speech.

Of course Albertano owes a great deal to other twelfth and thirteenth-century thinkers including some of those I listed at the beginning, though as Powell and others have shown, his main sources were classical and late antique writers. I am here however concerned with him as an explicitly pragmatic, moralising lay writer, rooted in the same professional context as Rolandino. There are substantial parallels in the two men's careers. Both men were 'urban professionals'; both experienced first hand the struggles for legitimate authority in northern Italy; both write with explicit moral purpose; both were concerned with vendetta. Rolandino traces the origins of the wars in the March to a vendetta. Albertano shows how a vendetta could and should be pacified.[50]

Although I have no reason to suppose that Rolandino knew or used Albertano's work, familiarity with his text allows us, as twenty-

---

[50] For a real vendetta between non-nobles which ended peacefully see Waley (1990).

first-century observers, to come closer to unravelling the 'conspiracy of common understanding'—the shared expectations—of Rolandino and his audience in 1262. This allows us to extract one of the possible plots from his narrative and to isolate one way in which authority, *potestas*, could be legitimised.

As Quentin Skinner has observed, Rolandino's text is punctuated at every significant point with speeches: short bursts of direct speech, brief dialogues, references to speeches made and, most importantly, the 'texts of speeches given, as Rolandino states, verbatim *vel similia*.[51] This is of course a standard literary technique. It allows expression of the supposed viewpoint of different parties, without their being owned by the writer. It also reflects a growing genre in thirteenth-century Italy and one arguably initiated by Rolandino's teacher in Bologna, Boncompagno da Signa in his *Liber de obsidione Anconae*: the 'ars concionandi' and the use of model speeches as carriers of political messages—here we return to the 'podestà literature' typified by the *Oculus pastoralis* with its model speeches.

Rolandino gives the texts of thirteen formal 'public' speeches, four of which were delivered before a council.[52] The whole work includes twelve books but it is significant that the speeches are not distributed throughout the text. Rather, they are grouped in the first three books which deal with the period down to 1237 when Padua fell to Ezzelino and in books eight and nine which deal with the events of 1256 when the city was taken by the Crusaders. No formal speech texts are given in the account of the nineteen years when Ezzelino was lord in Padua. If nothing else, this is a neat illustration of a point recently reiterated by Trevor Dean: "Whereas the art of public speaking was the quality most prized in communal podestà, the advent of the *signoria* was marked by silence."[53] It is also, I would argue, an indication that Rolandino, like Albertano and like the authors of the so-called 'podestà literature,' acknowledged the role of speech as a legitimating force.

That this might be the case is strengthened by a second point evident in Rolandino's account of the taking of Alberic da Romano. At this point in his narrative he inserts a passage not found in any other account of the episode. A piece of wood is placed in Alberic's

[51] Skinner (1978) vol. 1, 32.
[52] Listed in Arnaldi (1963) 155 and note 1.
[53] Dean (1999) 471.

mouth like a bridle, to prevent him speaking, except when the wise
and discrete podestà of Treviso has it removed to allow him to con-
fess to a Franciscan:

> . . . inimicis tamen gaudentibus et voluntarie occurrentibus, impositum
> est ei statim ligneum quoddam frenum, ne scilicet aliquibus loquere-
> tur aut aliquid loqui possit, preter quod predictus vir sapiens et dis-
> cretus Marchus Badoarius Tarvisinorum potestas fecit Albricum ipsum
> tanto tempore sine freno manere, quanto cum fratre Minore quodam
> confessus est.[54]

The parallels with the tongue-cutting of other cultures (Byzantium
for example) and the desire to humiliate the enemy are self-evident.
Yet whether or not it happened, Rolandino's decision to insert this
episode here suggests that he may have wished to underline the persuasive power of speech and the need to control it. As well as legitimating the new regime by enumerating the evils of the 'tyranny' of
Ezzelino and 'documenting' a version of the past to direct future
thinking, Rolandino shared with his audience an understanding of,
and a professional interest in, the link between political authority
and persuasive, legitimising speech.

Like Albertano, as professionals of speech, Rolandino (and his
audience) placed this at the centre of their view of political life.
Albertano made explicit the need for 'professional' speech. Rolandino
made no such narrow definition and neither author isolated speech
in the way that I have done here. Both also, for example, acknowledged the power of written discourse and ultimately invoked Christian
ideas of sin and punishment as the cause of political failure. Yet by
isolating the issue of speech, I hope to have drawn attention to the
way that the reading of 'moral texts' such as Albertano's may contribute to our understanding of political life and thought in a text
such as Rolandino's chronicle. Both serve as a context for the discussion of discourse in podestà literature and to the increasing importance of speech itself as a legitimating technique in thirteenth-century
communal thinking—something that was associated with the new
and developing *ars concionandi*. I will leave questions about whether
or not this reflected an exclusively 'guelf' view of the nature of political legitimation to experts in political thought.

---

[54] Rolandini Patavini, "Cronica", ed. Bonardi, Book 12, cap. 16, 172.

Acknowledgments

I am very grateful to the Leverhulme Trust and to the Alexander von Humboldt Stiftung for funding which enabled me to work on the sources which prompted this article.

Bibliography

Arnaldi, G. (1963) *Studi sui cronisti della Marca trevigiana nell'età di Ezzelino da Romano*, Studi storici 48–50 (Rome: 1963).
—— (1973), "Cronache con documenti, cronache 'autentiche' e pubblica storiografia", in *Fonti medioevali e problematica storiografica. Atti del congresso internazionale Roma 1973*, 2 vols. (Rome: 1976) vol. 1, 351–74 (reprinted in *Storici e storiografia del medioevo italiano*, ed. G. Zanella (Bologna: 1984) 111–37.
Banker, J.R. (1974) "Giovanni di Bonandrea and civic values in the context of the Italian rhetorical tradition", *Manuscripta* 18 (1974) 3–20.
Baron, H. (1988) "The Memory of Cicero's Roman Civic Spirit in the Medieval Centuries and in the Florentine Renaissance", in *In Search of Florentine Civic Humanism. Essays on the Transition from Medieval to Modern Thought* (Princeton: 1988), pp. 94–133 (originally published 1938).
Bausi, F. (1995) "Guido Fava", *Dizionario Biografico degli Italiani* 45 (Rome: 1995) 413–419.
Bériou, N. (1998) *L'avènement des maîtres de la parole: La prèdication à Paris au XIII⁰ siècle*, 2 vols. (Paris: 1998).
Cracco, G. ed. (1992) *Nuovi studi ezzeliniani*, Nuovi studi storici 21, 2 vols. (Rome: 1992).
Dean, T. (1997), "Marriage and mutilation: vendetta in late medieval Italy", *Past and Present* 157 (1997) 3–36.
—— (1999) "The Rise of the Signori", in *The New Cambridge Medieval History*, vol. 5, ed. D. Abulafia (Cambridge: 1999) 458–78.
Estepa Díez, C. et al. (1998), *El legado de Alfonso X*, Colección Alfonso X el Sabio 3 (Murcia: 1998).
Fasoli, G. (1985) "Ezzelino da Romano, fra tradizione cronachistiche e revisione storiografica", in *Storia e cultura a Padova nell'età di Sant'Antonio*, Fonti e ricerche di storia ecclesiastica padovana 16 (Padua: 1985) 85–101.
Hyde, J.K. (1985) "La prima scuola di storici accademici da Buoncompagno da Signa a Rolandino da Padova", in *Storia e cultura a Padova nell'età di Sant'Antonio*, Fonti e ricerche di storia ecclesiastica padovana 16 (Padua: 1985) 305–322.
Iser, W. (1989) *Prospecting: From Reader Response to Literary Anthropology* (Baltimore: 1989).
Kuehn, T. (1991) *Law, Family and Women: toward a legal anthropology of Renaissance Italy* (Chicago: 1991).
Meersseman, G.G. (1977) *Ordo Fraternitatis. Confraternite e pietà dei laici nel medioevo*, 3 vols. (Rome: 1977).
Nederman, C.J. (1992) "The union of wisdom and eloquence before the Renaissance: the Ciceronian orator in Medieval Thought", *Journal of Medieval History* 18 (1992) 75–95 (reprinted in Nederman, 1997).
—— (1997) *Medieval Aristotelianism and its Limits. Classical Traditions in Moral and Political Philosophy, 12th–15th Centuries*, Variorum Collected Studies, 565 (Aldershot: 1997).
O'Callaghan, J.F. (1998) *Alfonso X, the Cortes and Government in Medieval Spain*, Variorum Collected Studies 604 (Aldershot: 1998).

Ortalli, G. (1992) "Ezzelino : generi e sviluppi di un mito", in Cracco ed. (1992) 609–625.

Powell, J.M. (1992) *Albertanus of Brescia: the Pursuit of Happiness in the Early Thirteenth Century* (Philadelphia, 1992).

Skinner, Q. (1978) *The Foundations of Modern Political Thought*, 2 vols. (Cambridge: 1978). Also published in Italian as *Le origini del pensiero politico moderno* (Bologna: 1989).

Spiegel, G.M. (1997) *The Past as Text* (London: 1997).

Stillwell, G. (1944) "The political meaning of Chaucer's 'Tale of Melibee'", *Speculum* 19 (1944) 433–44.

Villa, C. (1969) "La tradizione delle 'ad Lucilium' e la cultura di Brescia dall'età carolingia ad Albertano", *Italia medioevale e umanistica* 12 (1969) 9–51.

Waley, D. (1990) "A blood-feud with a happy ending: Siena 1285–1304", in *City and Countryside in late medieval and renaissance Italy. Essays presented to Philip Jones*, ed. T. Dean and C. Wickham (London: 1990) 45–53.

Wickham, C. (1997) "Derecho romano y práctica legal en las comunas urbanas italianas del siglo xii", *Hispania* 197 (1997) 981–1007.

Wieruszowski, H. (1967) "Rhetoric and the classics in Italian education of the thirteenth century", in *Politics and culture in Medieval Spain and Italy* (Rome: 1971), pp. 589–629, originally published in *Studia Gratiana* XI (1967) 169–208.

INDEX